AREA 10

VERTIGO CRIME

WRITER
CHRISTOS N. GAGE
ART
CHRIS SAMNEE
LETTERS
CLEM ROBINS

AREA 10

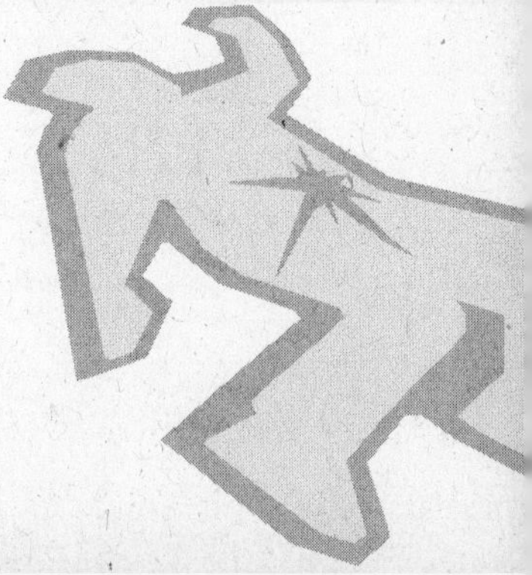

Karen Berger SVP – Executive Editor
Jonathan Vankin Editor
Mark Doyle Asst. Editor
Robbin Brosterman Design Director – Books
Louis Prandi Art Director

DC COMICS
Paul Levitz President & Publisher
Richard Bruning SVP – Creative Director
Patrick Caldon EVP – Finance & Operations
Amy Genkins SVP – Business & Legal Affairs
Jim Lee Editorial Director – WildStorm
Gregory Noveck SVP – Creative Affairs
Steve Rotterdam SVP – Sales & Marketing
Cheryl Rubin SVP – Brand Management

AREA 10
VERTIGO CRIME

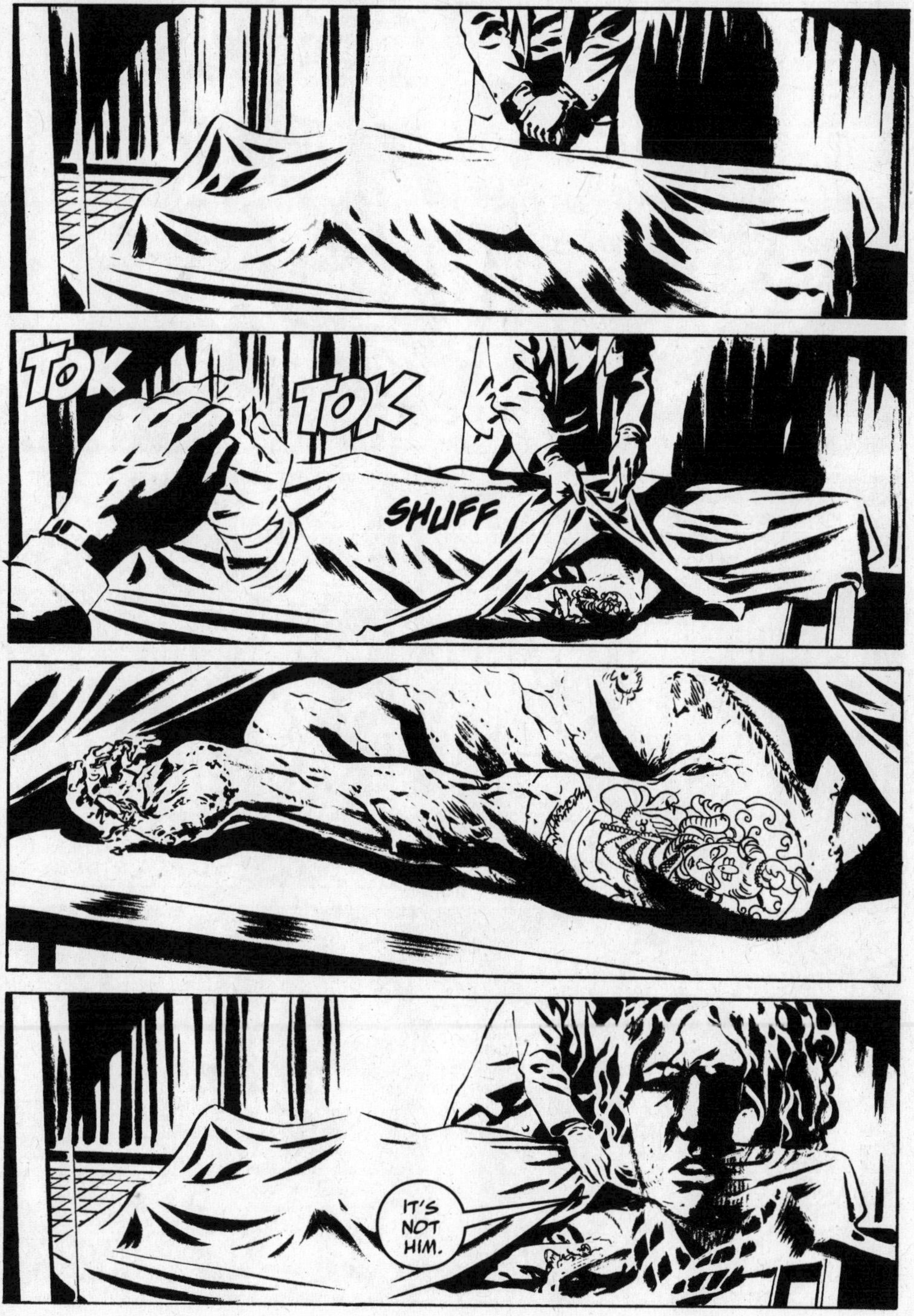
TOK
TOK
SHUFF
IT'S NOT HIM.

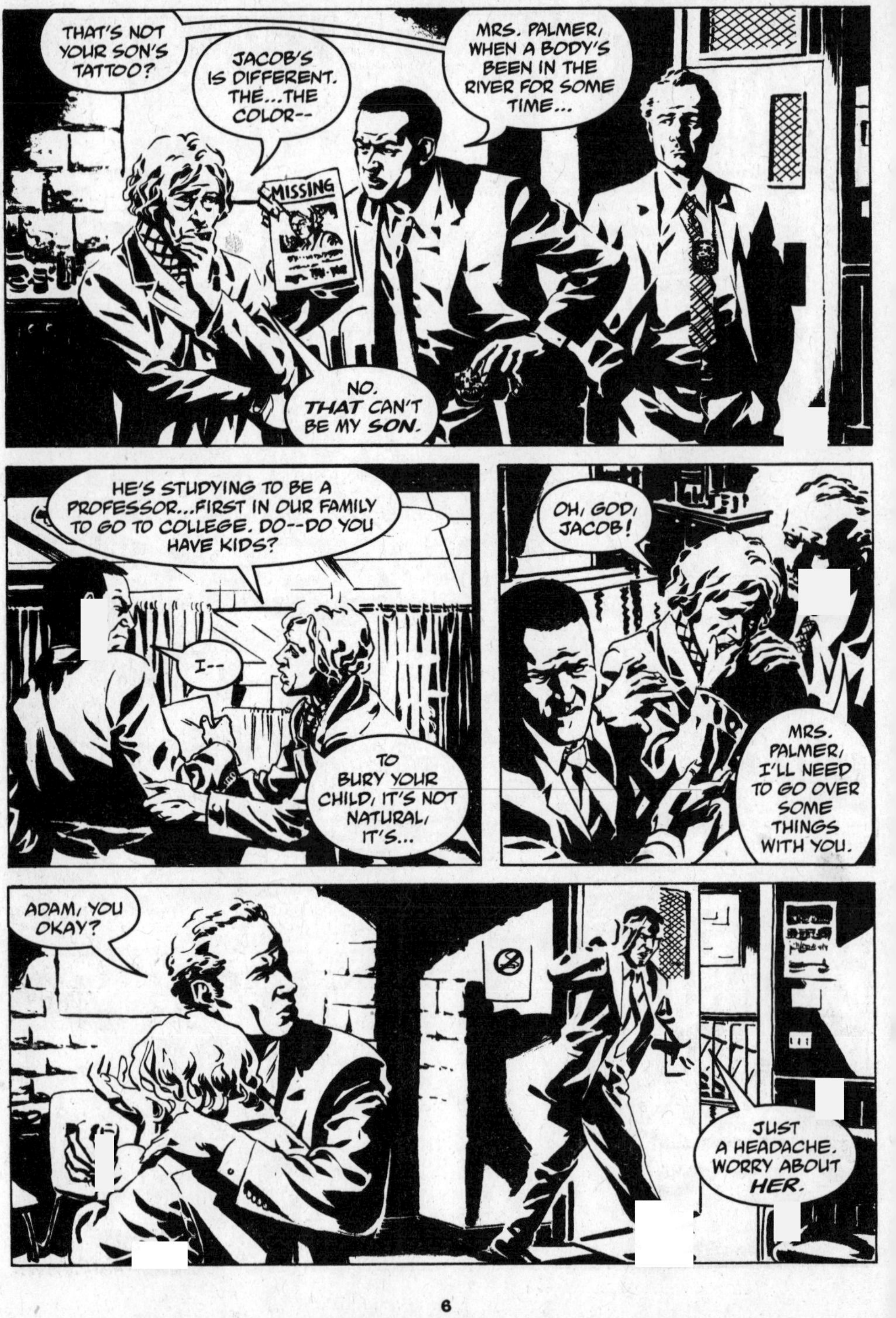
THAT'S NOT YOUR SON'S TATTOO?
JACOB'S IS DIFFERENT. THE...THE COLOR--
MISSING
MRS. PALMER, WHEN A BODY'S BEEN IN THE RIVER FOR SOME TIME...
NO. *THAT* CAN'T BE MY *SON*.
HE'S STUDYING TO BE A PROFESSOR...FIRST IN OUR FAMILY TO GO TO COLLEGE. DO--DO YOU HAVE KIDS?
I--
TO BURY YOUR CHILD, IT'S NOT NATURAL, IT'S...
OH, GOD, JACOB!
MRS. PALMER, I'LL NEED TO GO OVER SOME THINGS WITH YOU.
ADAM, YOU OKAY?
JUST A HEADACHE. WORRY ABOUT *HER*.

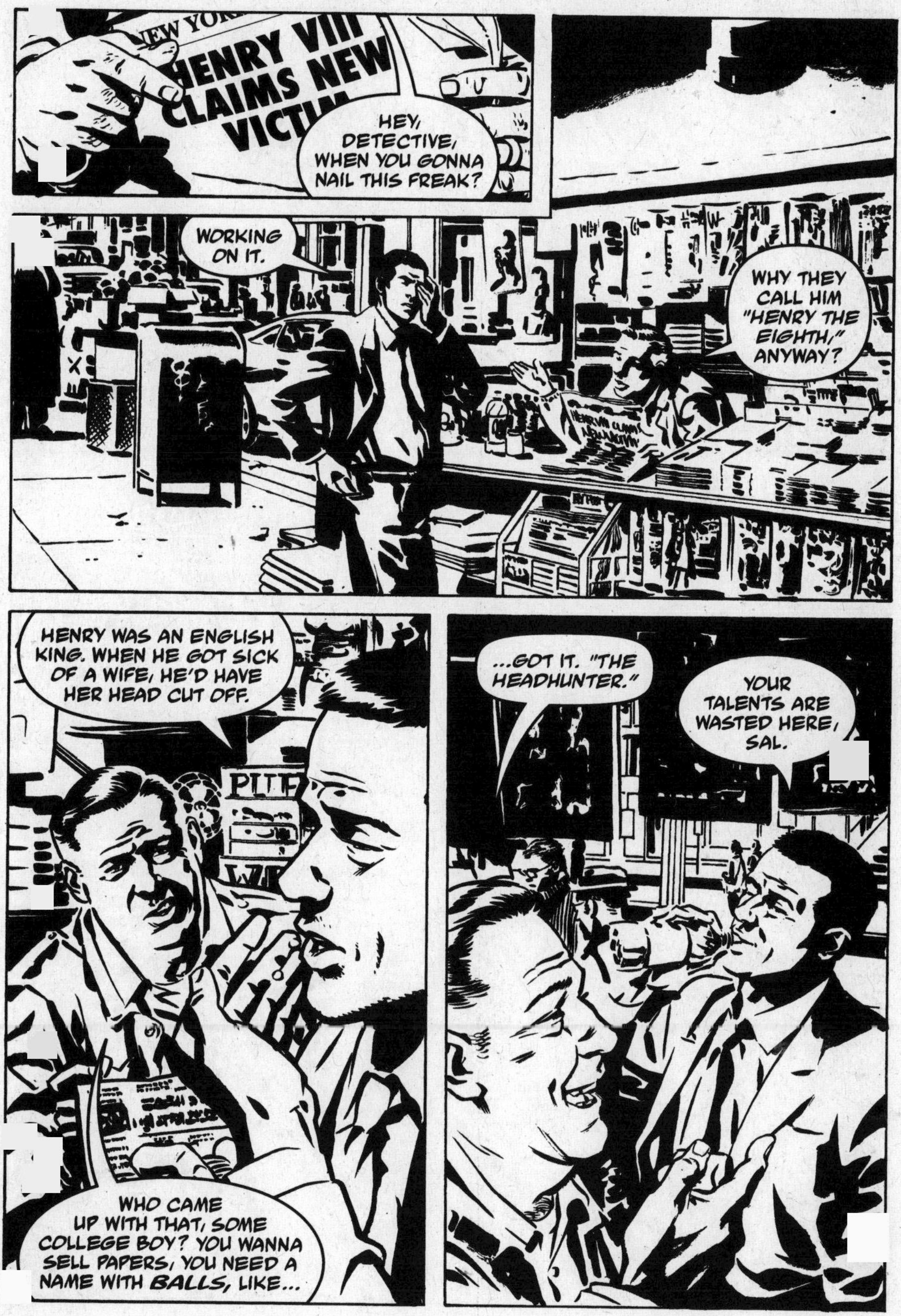
NEW YORK
HENRY VIII CLAIMS NEW VICTIM
HEY, DETECTIVE, WHEN YOU GONNA NAIL THIS FREAK?
WORKING ON IT.
WHY THEY CALL HIM "HENRY THE EIGHTH," ANYWAY?
HENRY WAS AN ENGLISH KING. WHEN HE GOT SICK OF A WIFE, HE'D HAVE HER HEAD CUT OFF.
WHO CAME UP WITH THAT, SOME COLLEGE BOY? YOU WANNA SELL PAPERS, YOU NEED A NAME WITH *BALLS*, LIKE...
...GOT IT. "THE HEADHUNTER."
YOUR TALENTS ARE WASTED HERE, SAL.

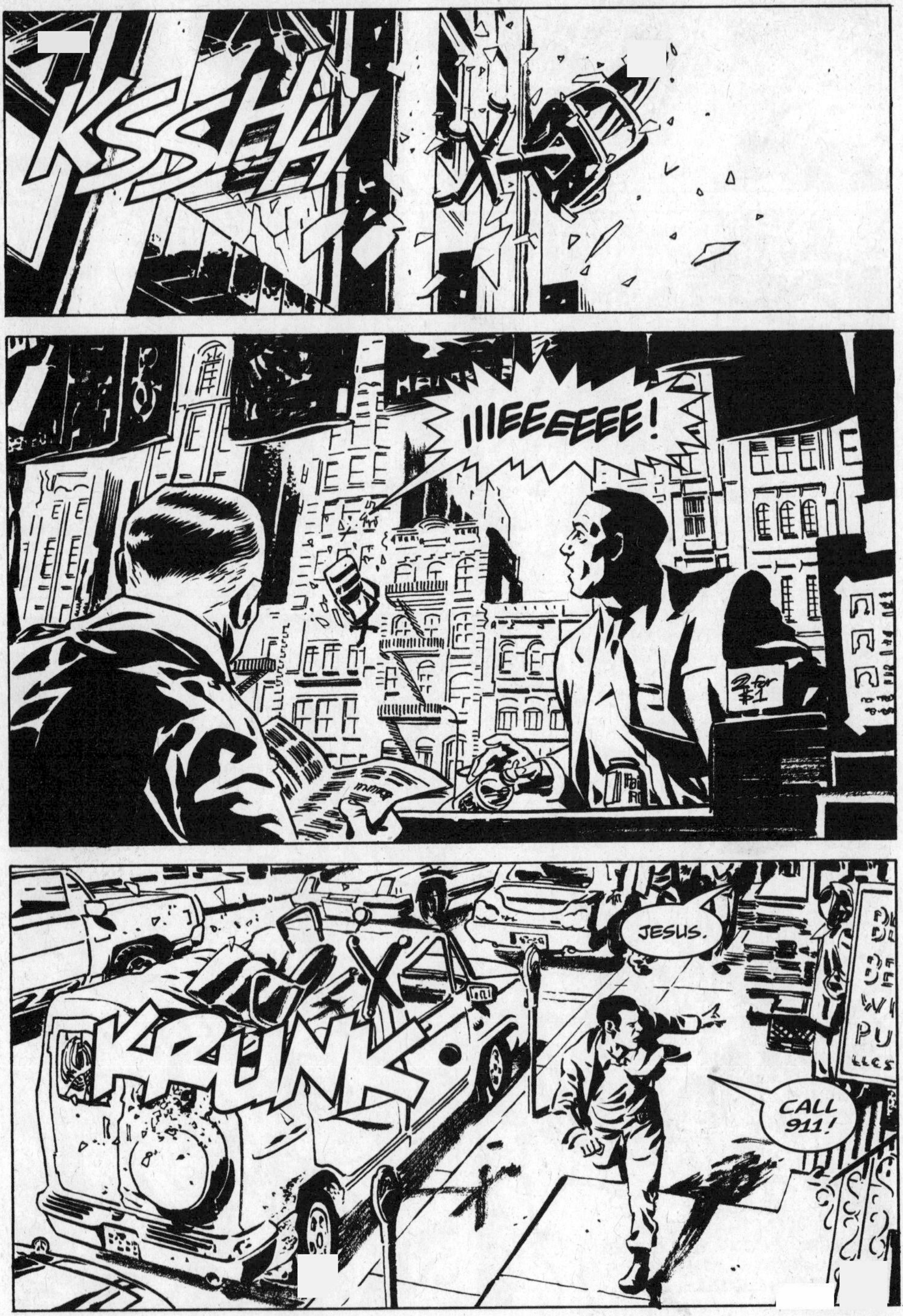
KSSH
IIIEEEEEEE!
2 for $1
JESUS.
CALL 911!
KRUNK

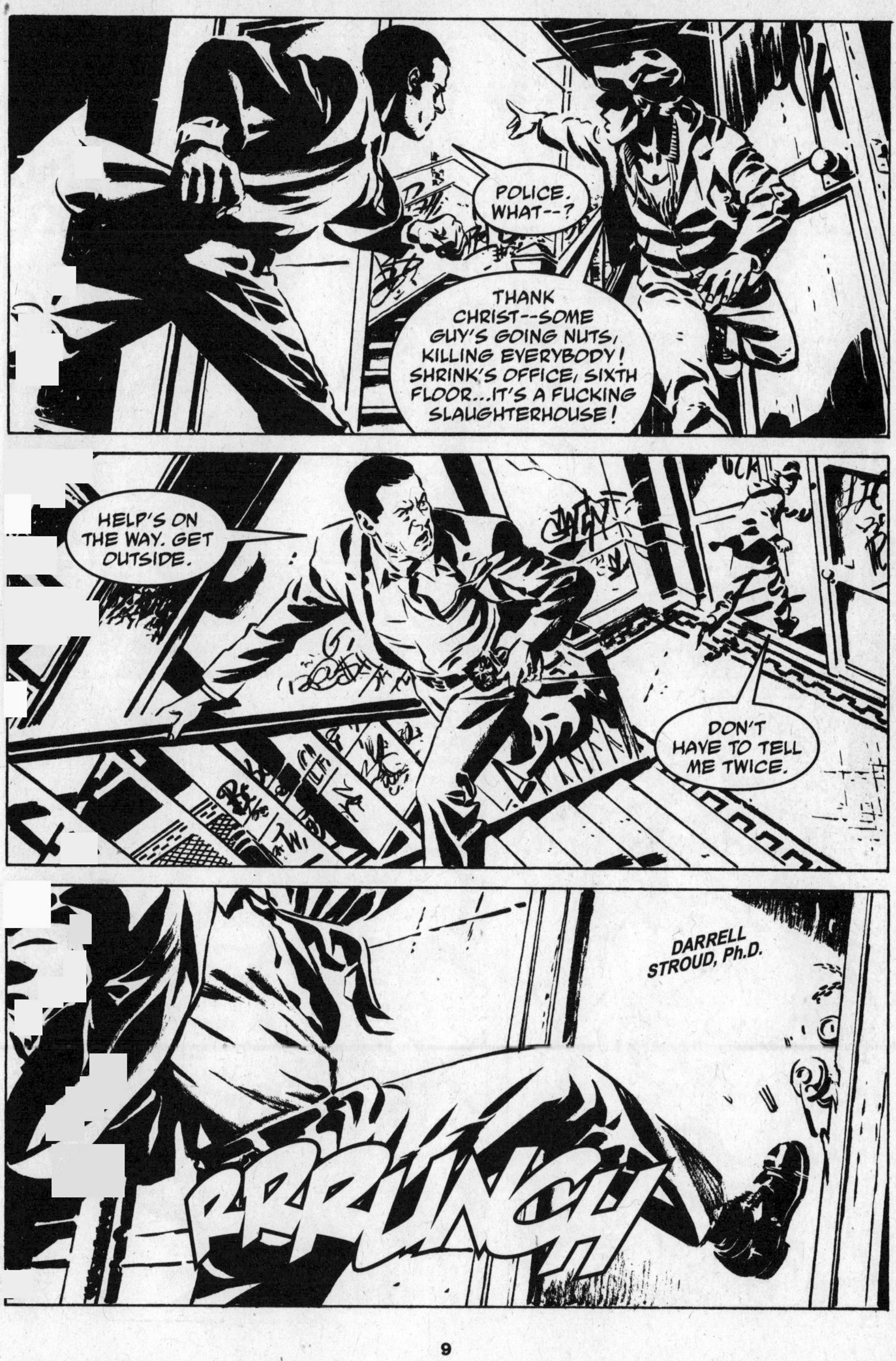
POLICE. WHAT--?
THANK CHRIST--SOME GUY'S GOING NUTS, KILLING EVERYBODY! SHRINK'S OFFICE, SIXTH FLOOR...IT'S A FUCKING SLAUGHTERHOUSE!
HELP'S ON THE WAY. GET OUTSIDE.
DON'T HAVE TO TELL ME TWICE.
DARRELL STROUD, Ph.D.
KRRUNCH

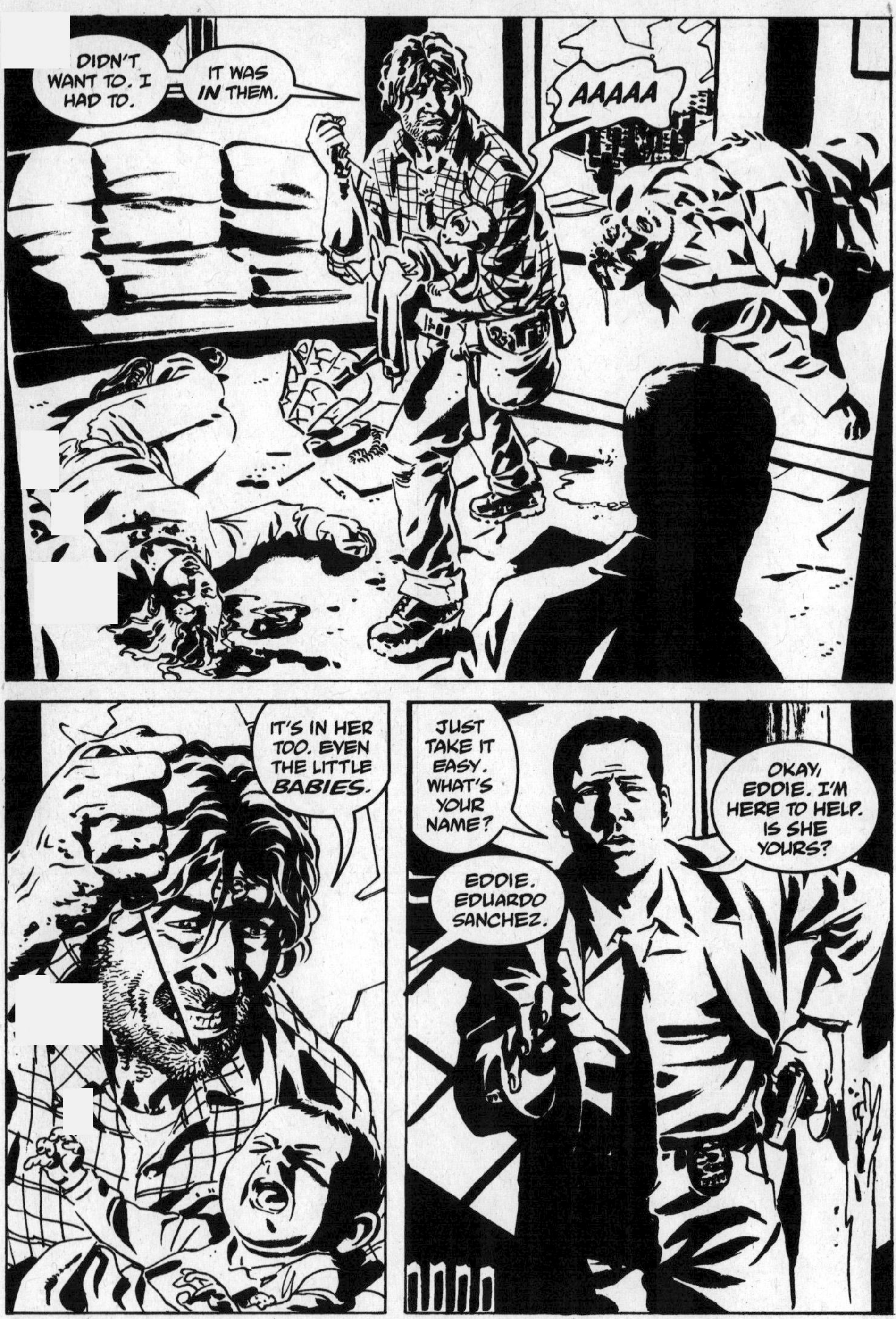
DIDN'T WANT TO. I HAD TO.
IT WAS *IN* THEM.
AAAAA
IT'S IN HER TOO. EVEN THE LITTLE *BABIES*.
JUST TAKE IT EASY. WHAT'S YOUR NAME?
EDDIE. EDUARDO SANCHEZ.
OKAY, EDDIE. I'M HERE TO HELP. IS SHE YOURS?

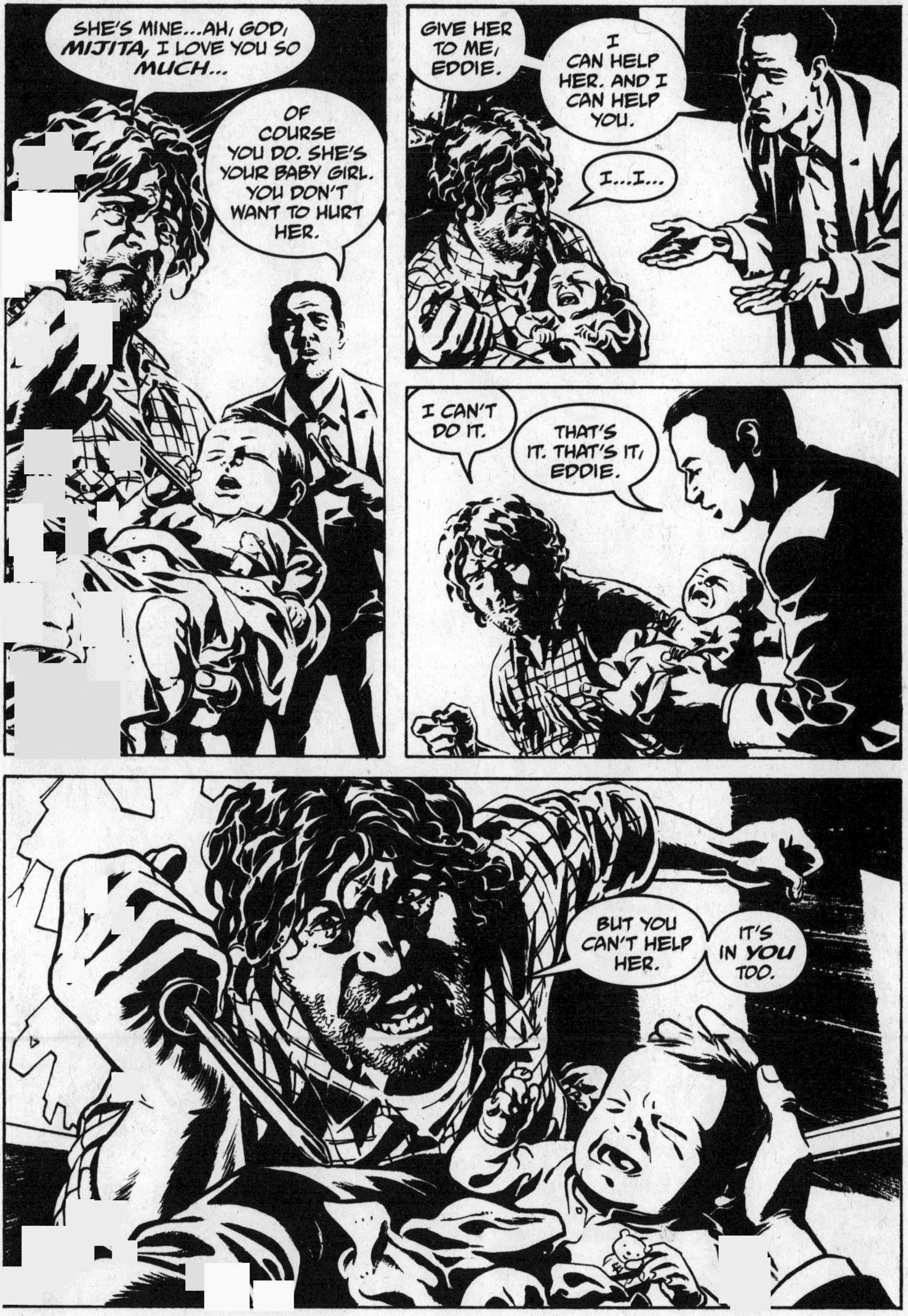
SHE'S MINE...AH, GOD, MIJITA, I LOVE YOU SO MUCH...
OF COURSE YOU DO. SHE'S YOUR BABY GIRL. YOU DON'T WANT TO HURT HER.
GIVE HER TO ME, EDDIE.
I CAN HELP HER. AND I CAN HELP YOU.
I...I...
I CAN'T DO IT.
THAT'S IT. THAT'S IT, EDDIE.
BUT YOU CAN'T HELP HER.
IT'S IN YOU TOO.

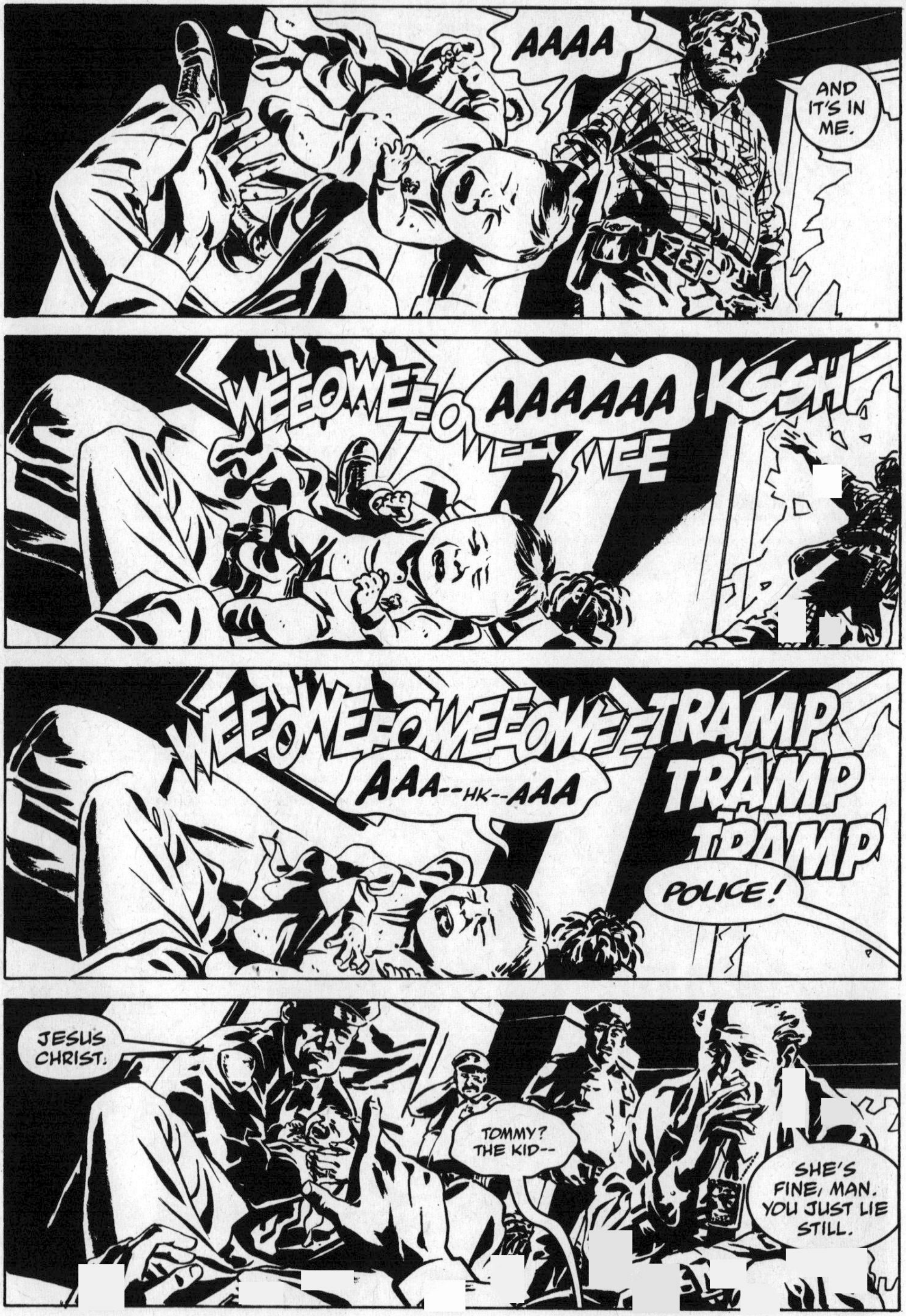
AAAA
AND IT'S IN ME.
WEEOWEEOWEEOWEE
AAAAAA
KSSH
WEEOWEEOWEEOWEE
TRAMP
TRAMP
TRAMP
AAA--HK--AAA
POLICE!
JESUS CHRIST.
TOMMY? THE KID--
SHE'S FINE, MAN. YOU JUST LIE STILL.

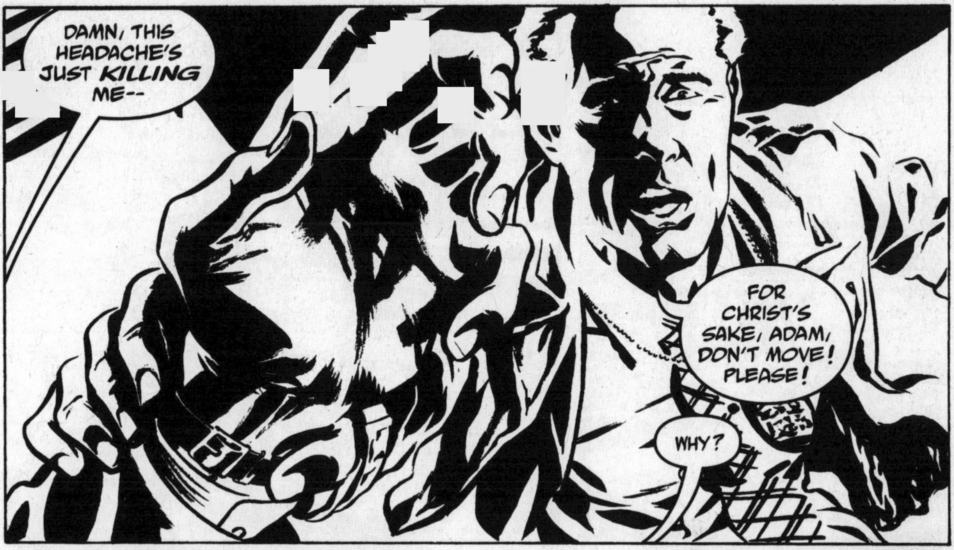
DAMN, THIS HEADACHE'S JUST KILLING ME--
FOR CHRIST'S SAKE, ADAM, DON'T MOVE! PLEASE!
WHY?

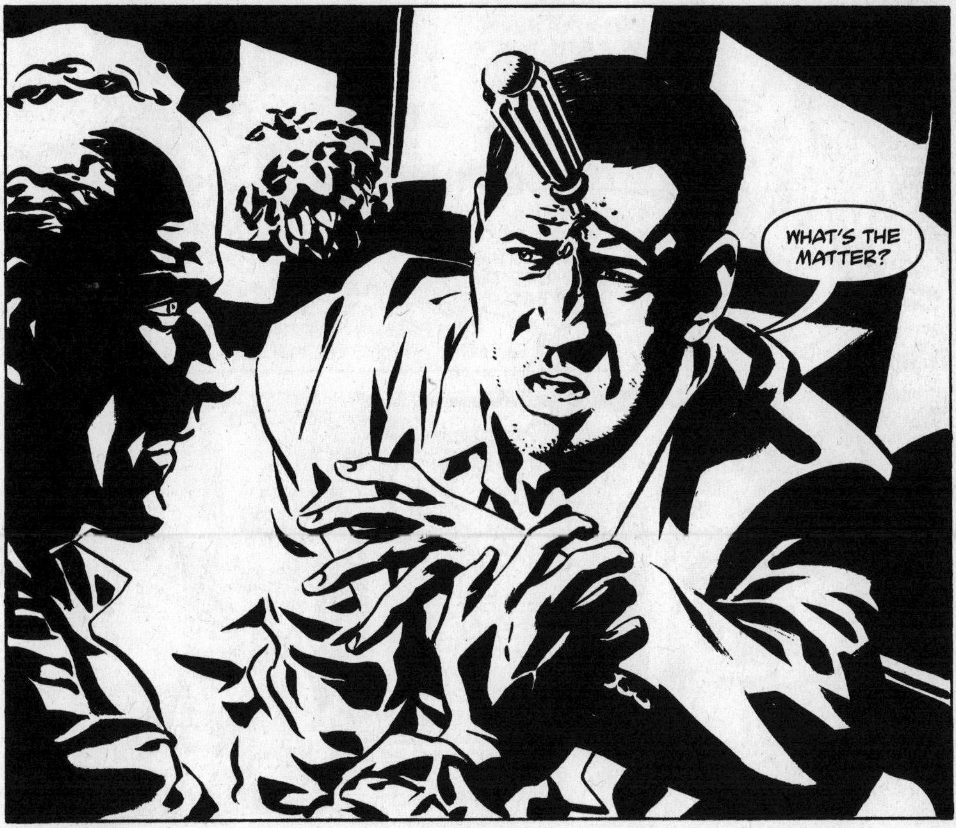
WHAT'S THE MATTER?

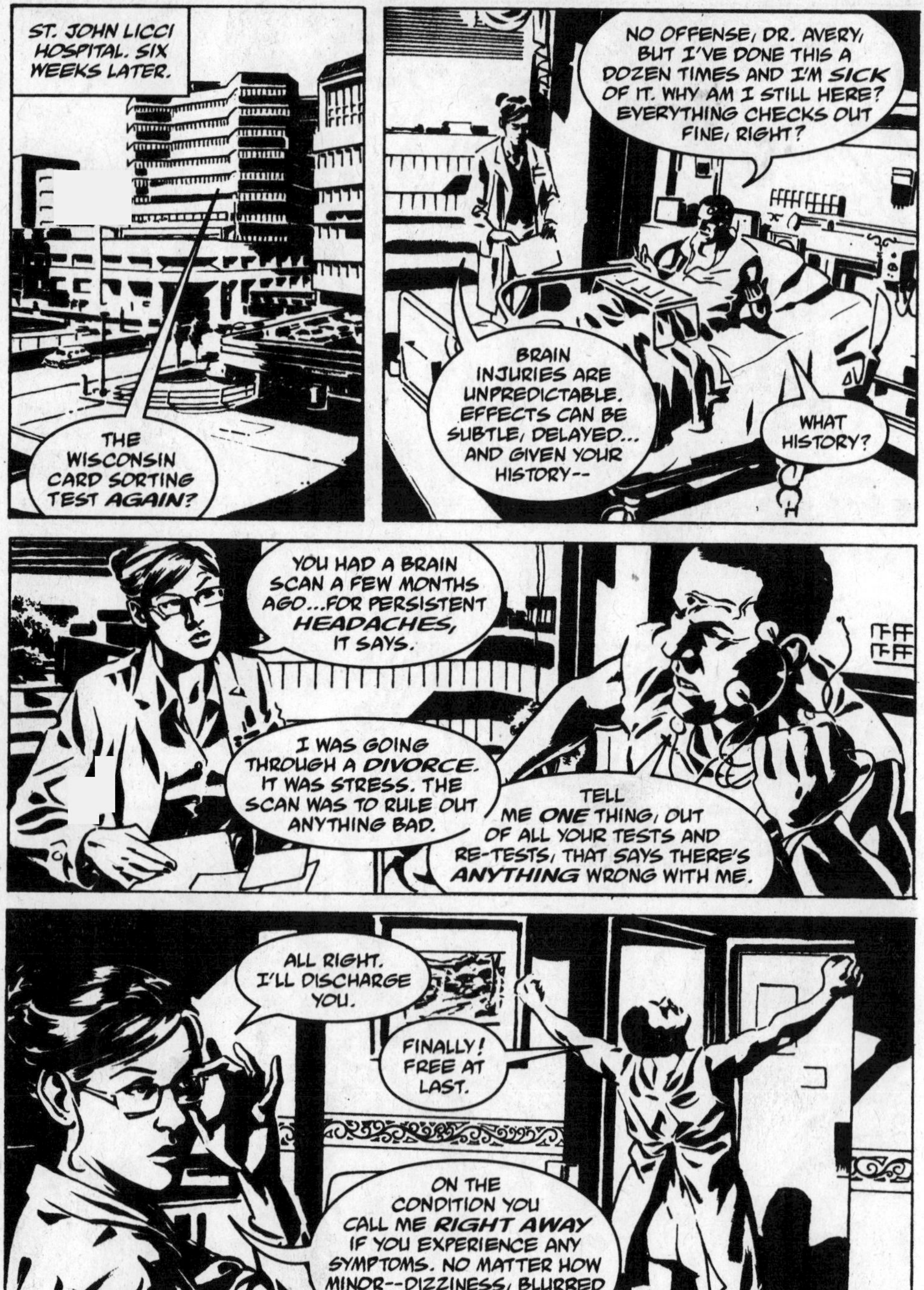
ST. JOHN LICCI HOSPITAL. SIX WEEKS LATER.
THE WISCONSIN CARD SORTING TEST AGAIN?
NO OFFENSE, DR. AVERY, BUT I'VE DONE THIS A DOZEN TIMES AND I'M SICK OF IT. WHY AM I STILL HERE? EVERYTHING CHECKS OUT FINE, RIGHT?
BRAIN INJURIES ARE UNPREDICTABLE. EFFECTS CAN BE SUBTLE, DELAYED... AND GIVEN YOUR HISTORY--
WHAT HISTORY?
YOU HAD A BRAIN SCAN A FEW MONTHS AGO...FOR PERSISTENT HEADACHES, IT SAYS.
I WAS GOING THROUGH A DIVORCE. IT WAS STRESS. THE SCAN WAS TO RULE OUT ANYTHING BAD.
TELL ME ONE THING, OUT OF ALL YOUR TESTS AND RE-TESTS, THAT SAYS THERE'S ANYTHING WRONG WITH ME.
ALL RIGHT. I'LL DISCHARGE YOU.
FINALLY! FREE AT LAST.
ON THE CONDITION YOU CALL ME RIGHT AWAY IF YOU EXPERIENCE ANY SYMPTOMS. NO MATTER HOW MINOR--DIZZINESS, BLURRED VISION, DEPRESSION...

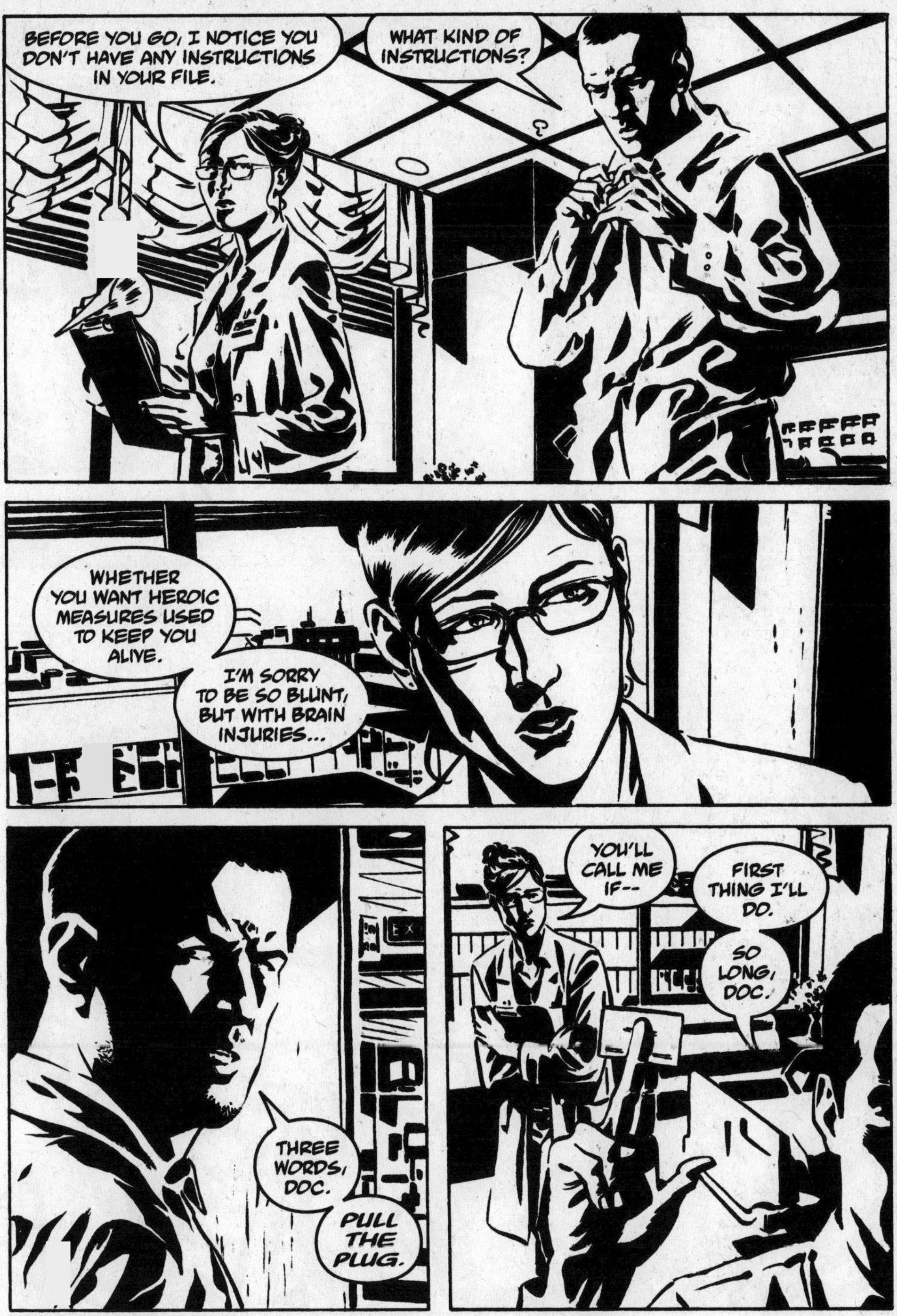
BEFORE YOU GO, I NOTICE YOU DON'T HAVE ANY INSTRUCTIONS IN YOUR FILE.
WHAT KIND OF INSTRUCTIONS?
WHETHER YOU WANT HEROIC MEASURES USED TO KEEP YOU ALIVE.
I'M SORRY TO BE SO BLUNT, BUT WITH BRAIN INJURIES...
THREE WORDS, DOC.
PULL THE PLUG.
YOU'LL CALL ME IF--
FIRST THING I'LL DO.
SO LONG, DOC.

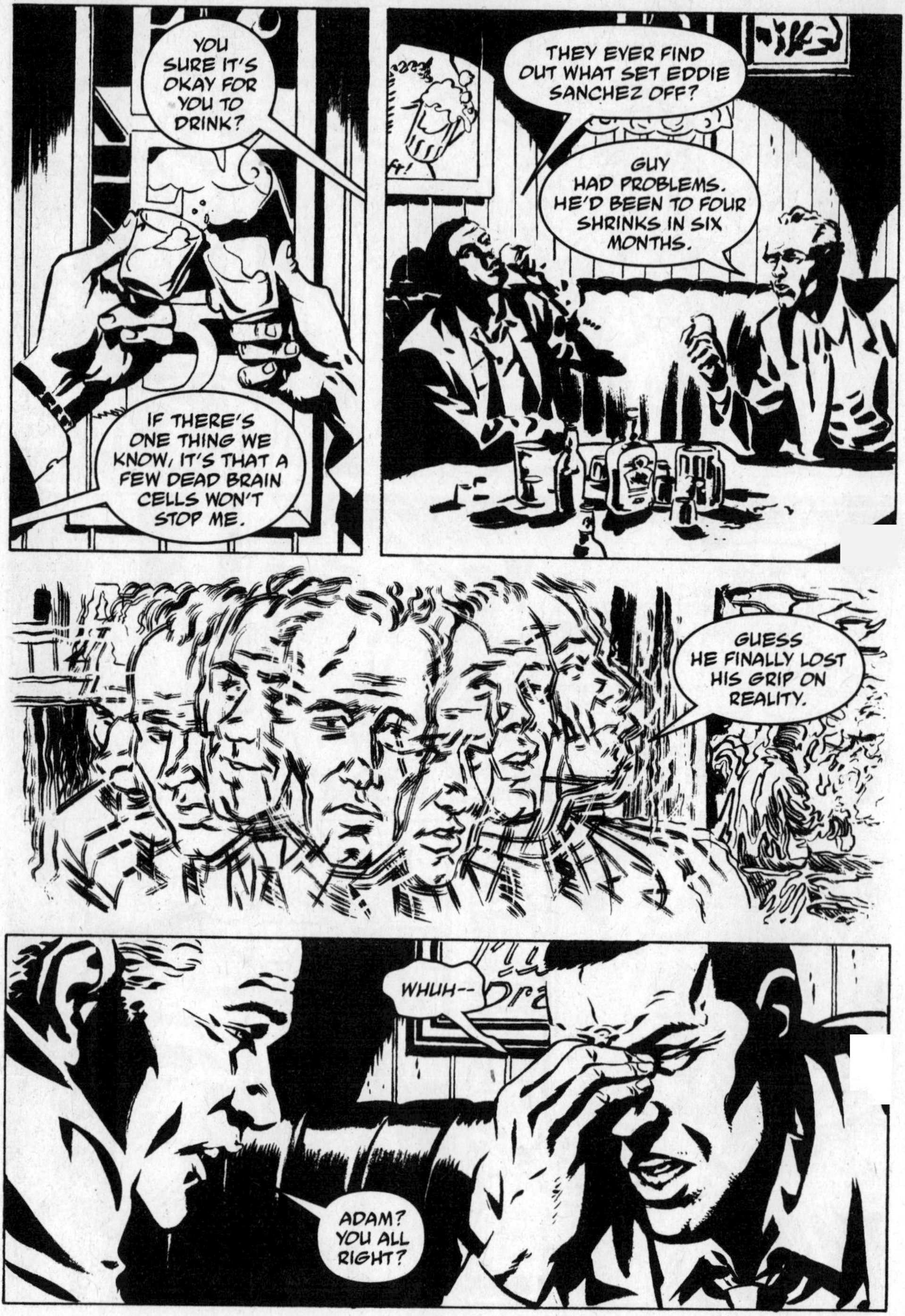
YOU SURE IT'S OKAY FOR YOU TO DRINK?
IF THERE'S ONE THING WE KNOW, IT'S THAT A FEW DEAD BRAIN CELLS WON'T STOP ME.
THEY EVER FIND OUT WHAT SET EDDIE SANCHEZ OFF?
GUY HAD PROBLEMS. HE'D BEEN TO FOUR SHRINKS IN SIX MONTHS.
GUESS HE FINALLY LOST HIS GRIP ON REALITY.
WHUH--
ADAM? YOU ALL RIGHT?

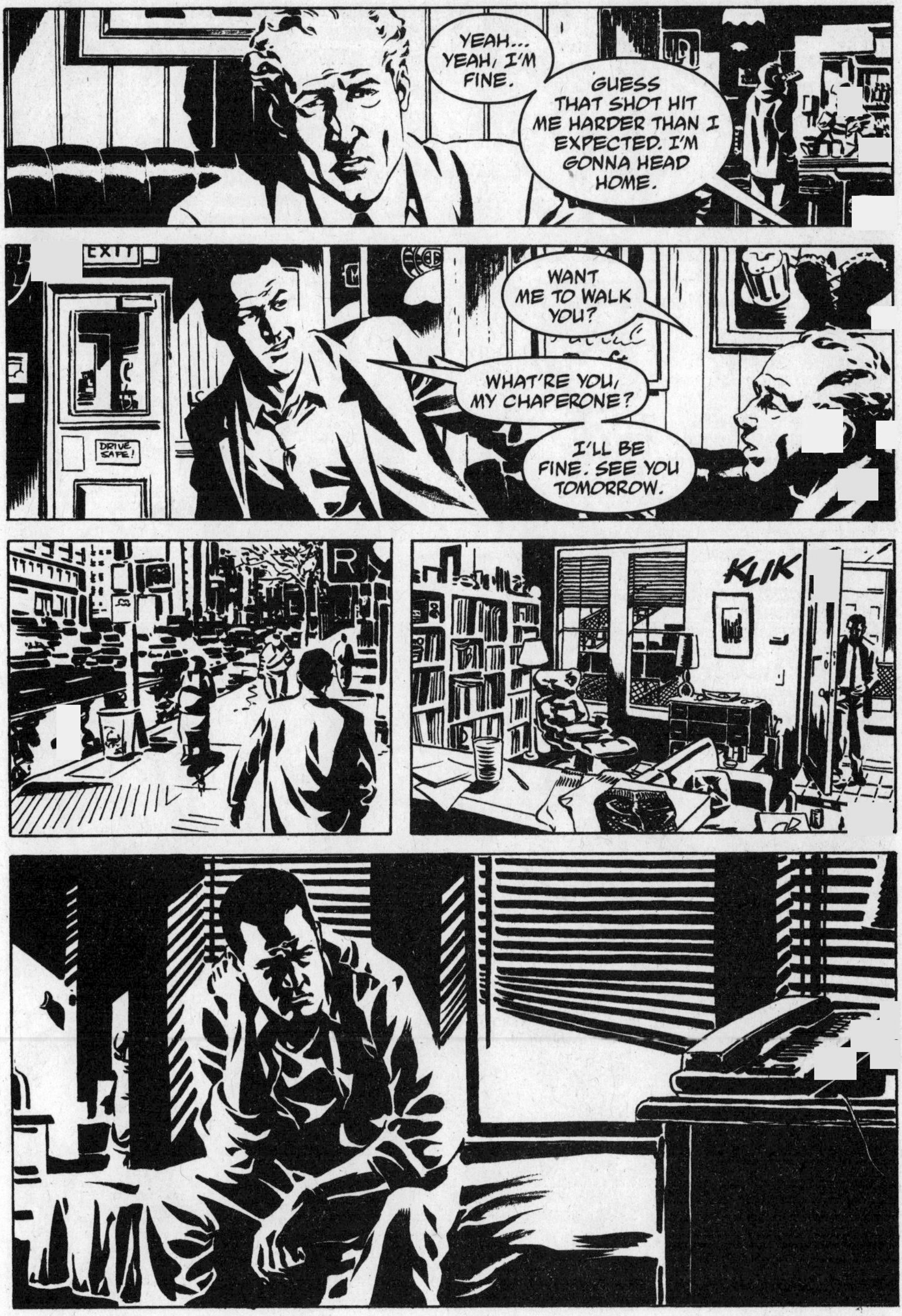
YEAH... YEAH, I'M FINE.
GUESS THAT SHOT HIT ME HARDER THAN I EXPECTED. I'M GONNA HEAD HOME.
EXIT
WANT ME TO WALK YOU?
WHAT'RE YOU, MY CHAPERONE?
I'LL BE FINE. SEE YOU TOMORROW.
DRIVE SAFE!
KLIK

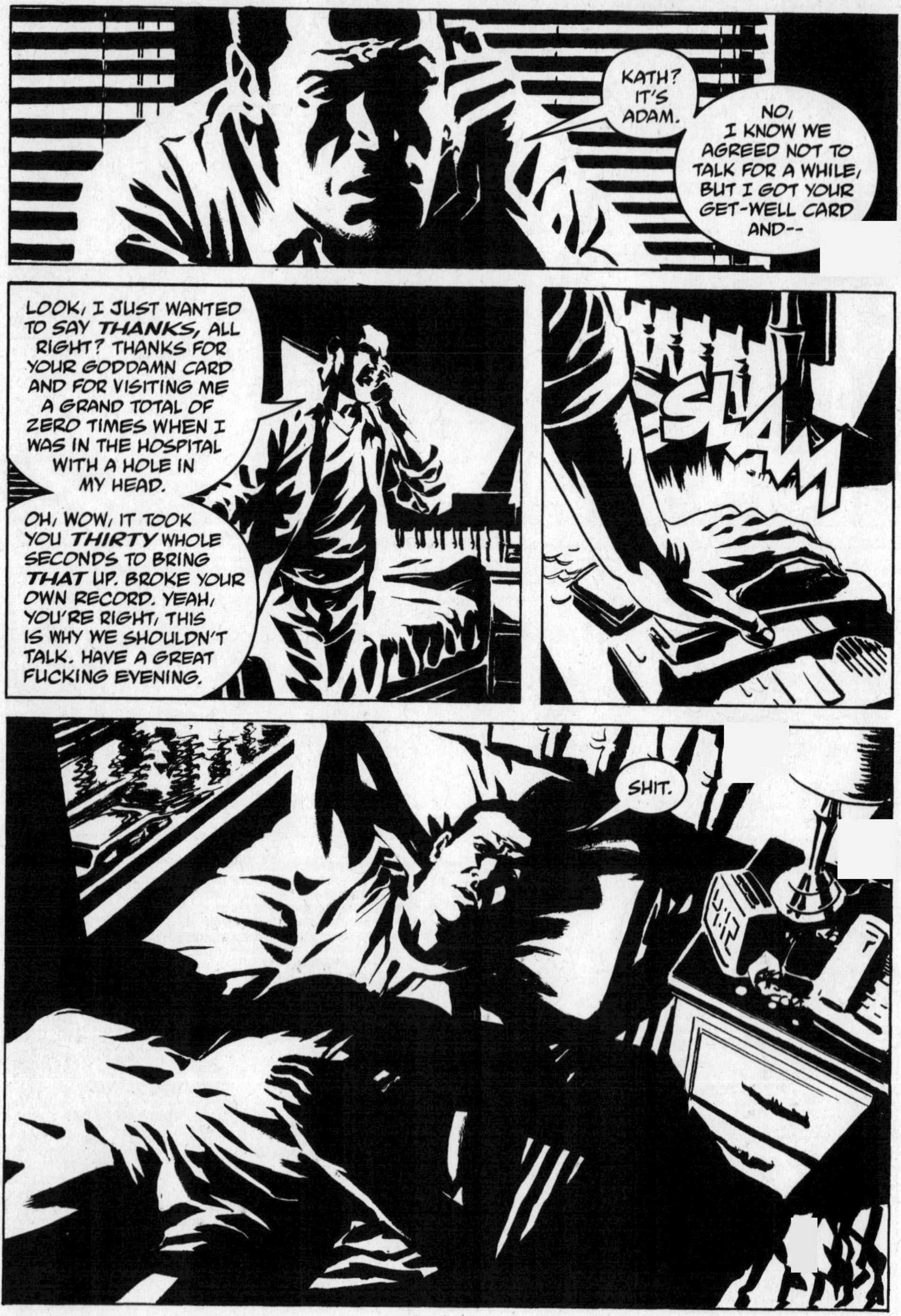
KATH? IT'S ADAM.
NO, I KNOW WE AGREED NOT TO TALK FOR A WHILE, BUT I GOT YOUR GET-WELL CARD AND--
LOOK, I JUST WANTED TO SAY THANKS, ALL RIGHT? THANKS FOR YOUR GODDAMN CARD AND FOR VISITING ME A GRAND TOTAL OF ZERO TIMES WHEN I WAS IN THE HOSPITAL WITH A HOLE IN MY HEAD.
OH, WOW, IT TOOK YOU THIRTY WHOLE SECONDS TO BRING THAT UP. BROKE YOUR OWN RECORD. YEAH, YOU'RE RIGHT, THIS IS WHY WE SHOULDN'T TALK. HAVE A GREAT FUCKING EVENING.
SLAM
SHIT.

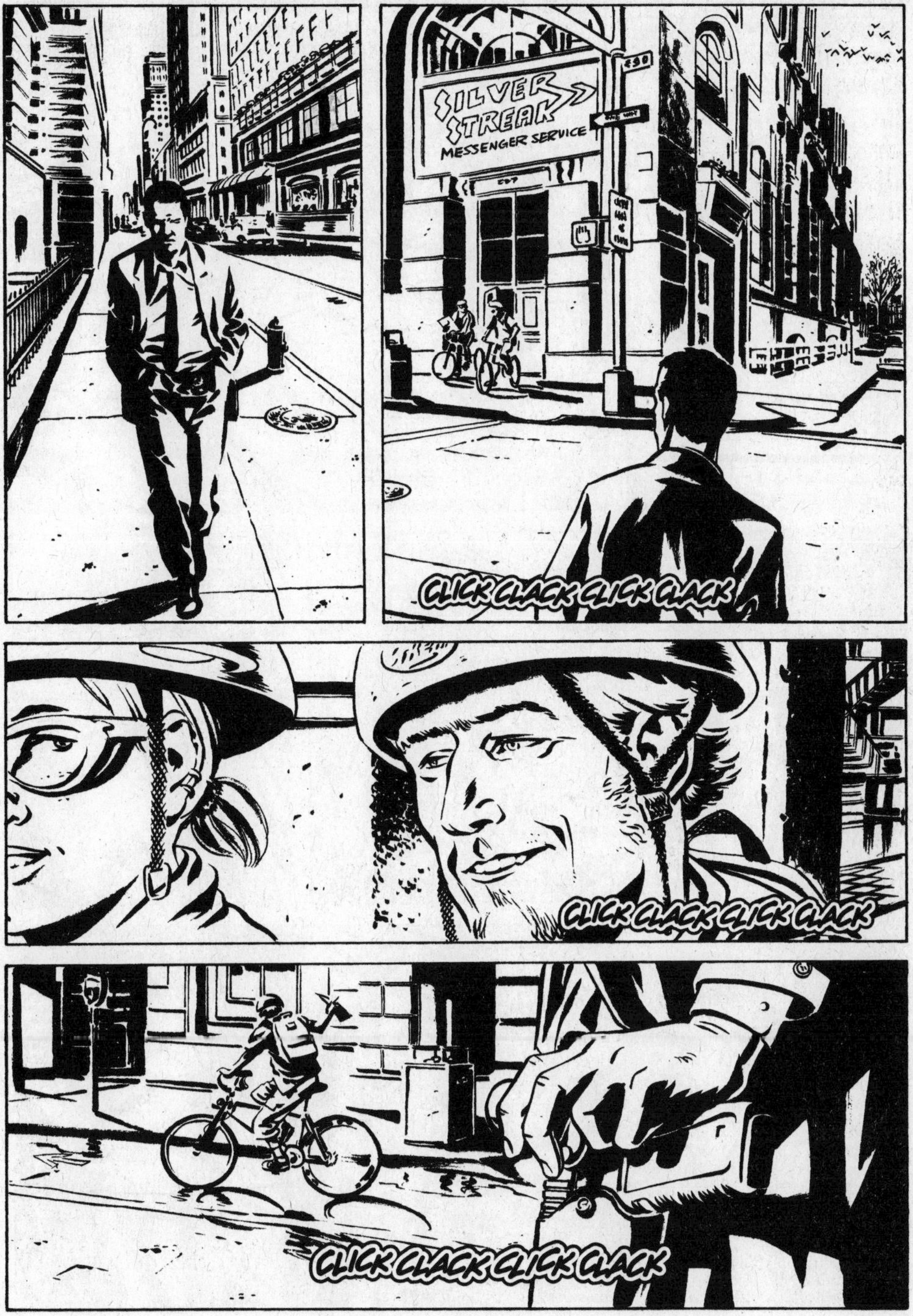
SILVER STREAK
MESSENGER SERVICE
CLICK CLACK CLICK CLACK
CLICK CLACK CLICK CLACK
CLICK CLACK CLICK CLACK

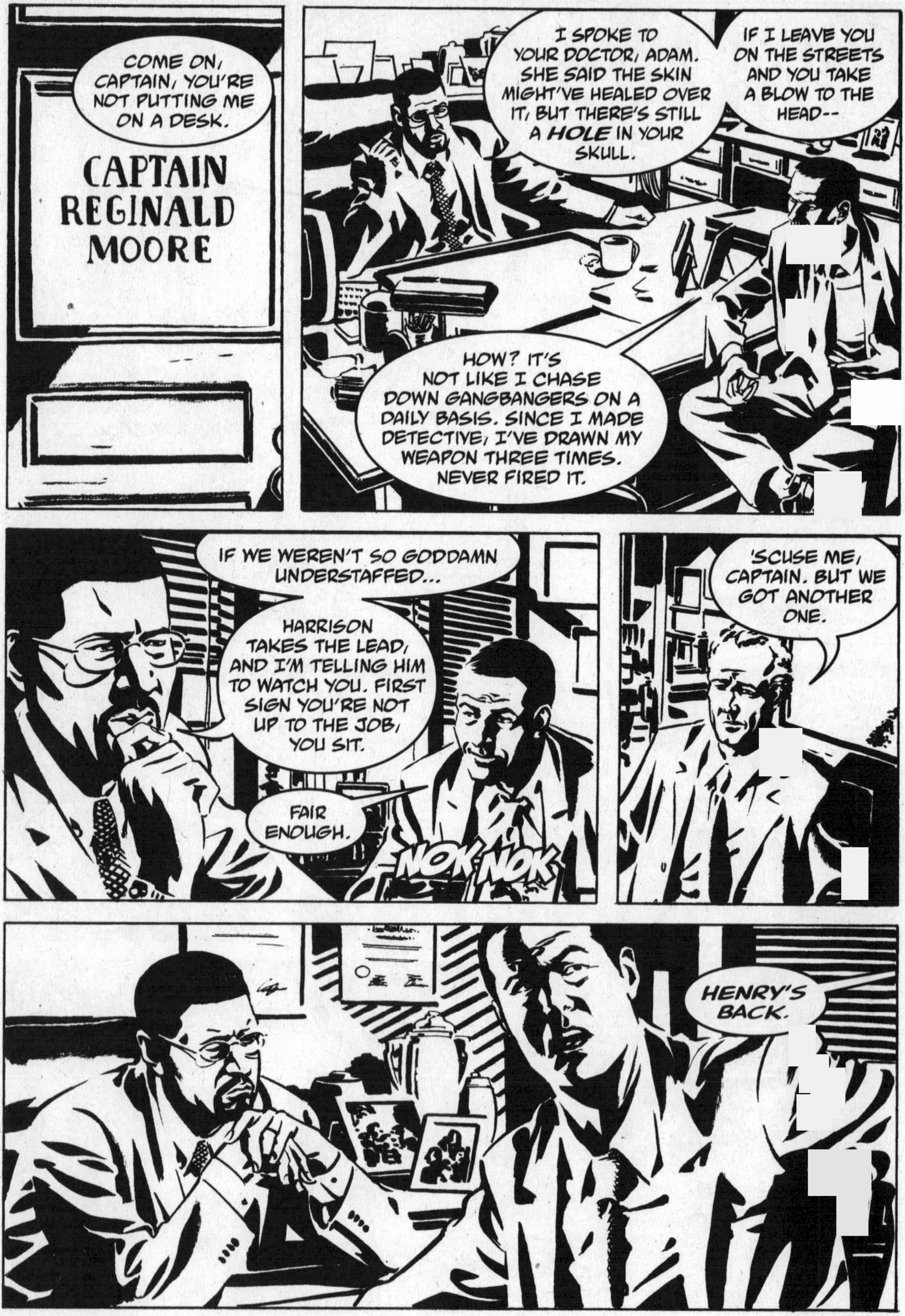
COME ON, CAPTAIN, YOU'RE NOT PUTTING ME ON A DESK.
CAPTAIN REGINALD MOORE
I SPOKE TO YOUR DOCTOR, ADAM. SHE SAID THE SKIN MIGHT'VE HEALED OVER IT, BUT THERE'S STILL A *HOLE* IN YOUR SKULL.
IF I LEAVE YOU ON THE STREETS AND YOU TAKE A BLOW TO THE HEAD--
HOW? IT'S NOT LIKE I CHASE DOWN GANGBANGERS ON A DAILY BASIS. SINCE I MADE DETECTIVE, I'VE DRAWN MY WEAPON THREE TIMES. NEVER FIRED IT.
IF WE WEREN'T SO GODDAMN UNDERSTAFFED...
HARRISON TAKES THE LEAD, AND I'M TELLING HIM TO WATCH YOU. FIRST SIGN YOU'RE NOT UP TO THE JOB, YOU SIT.
FAIR ENOUGH.
NOK NOK
'SCUSE ME, CAPTAIN. BUT WE GOT ANOTHER ONE.
HENRY'S BACK.

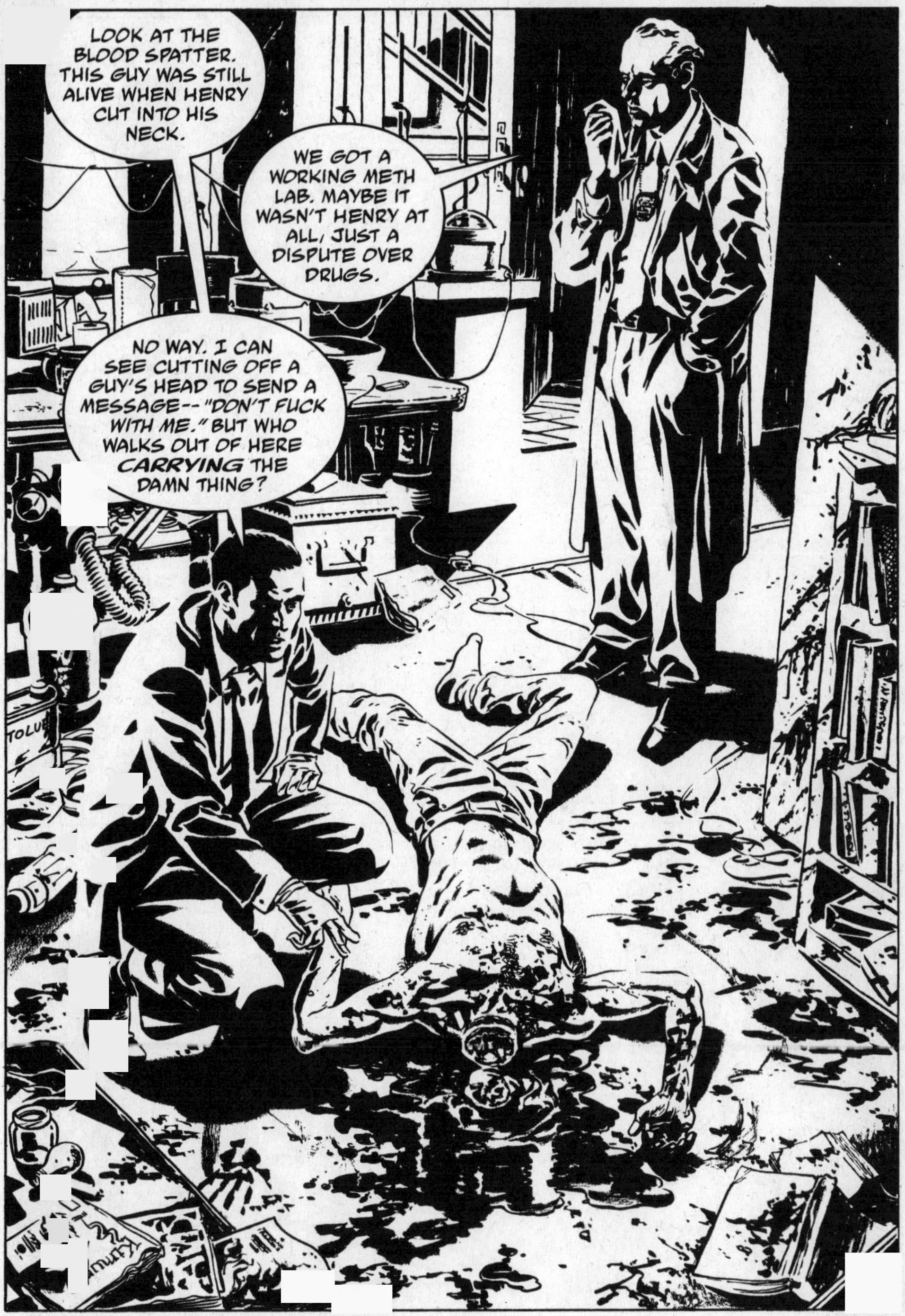
LOOK AT THE BLOOD SPATTER. THIS GUY WAS STILL ALIVE WHEN HENRY CUT INTO HIS NECK.
WE GOT A WORKING METH LAB. MAYBE IT WASN'T HENRY AT ALL, JUST A DISPUTE OVER DRUGS.
NO WAY. I CAN SEE CUTTING OFF A GUY'S HEAD TO SEND A MESSAGE-- "DON'T FUCK WITH ME." BUT WHO WALKS OUT OF HERE *CARRYING* THE DAMN THING?
TOLU

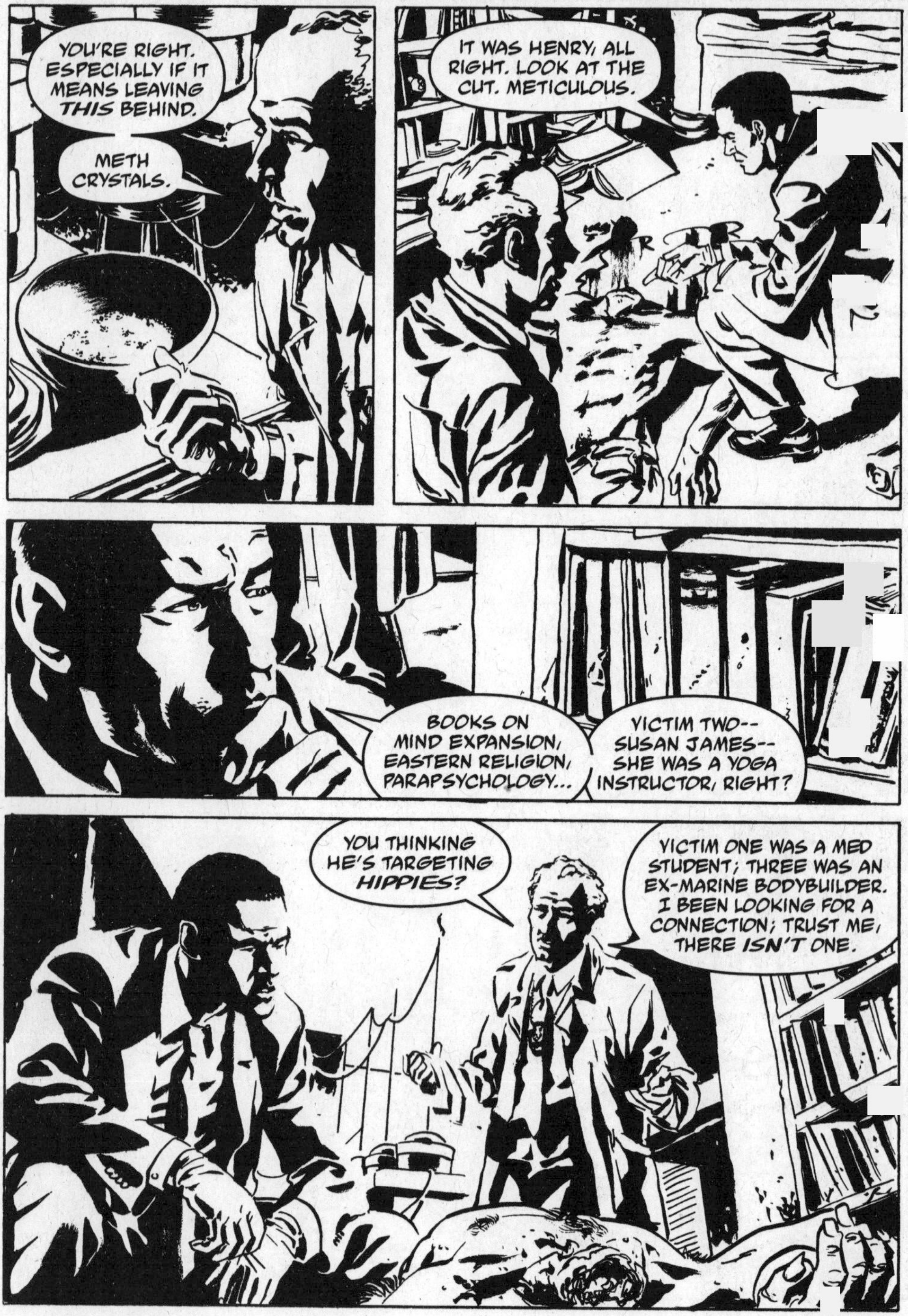
YOU'RE RIGHT. ESPECIALLY IF IT MEANS LEAVING *THIS* BEHIND.
METH CRYSTALS.
IT WAS HENRY, ALL RIGHT. LOOK AT THE CUT. METICULOUS.
BOOKS ON MIND EXPANSION, EASTERN RELIGION, PARAPSYCHOLOGY...
VICTIM TWO-- SUSAN JAMES-- SHE WAS A YOGA INSTRUCTOR, RIGHT?
YOU THINKING HE'S TARGETING *HIPPIES*?
VICTIM ONE WAS A MED STUDENT; THREE WAS AN EX-MARINE BODYBUILDER. I BEEN LOOKING FOR A CONNECTION; TRUST ME, THERE *ISN'T* ONE.

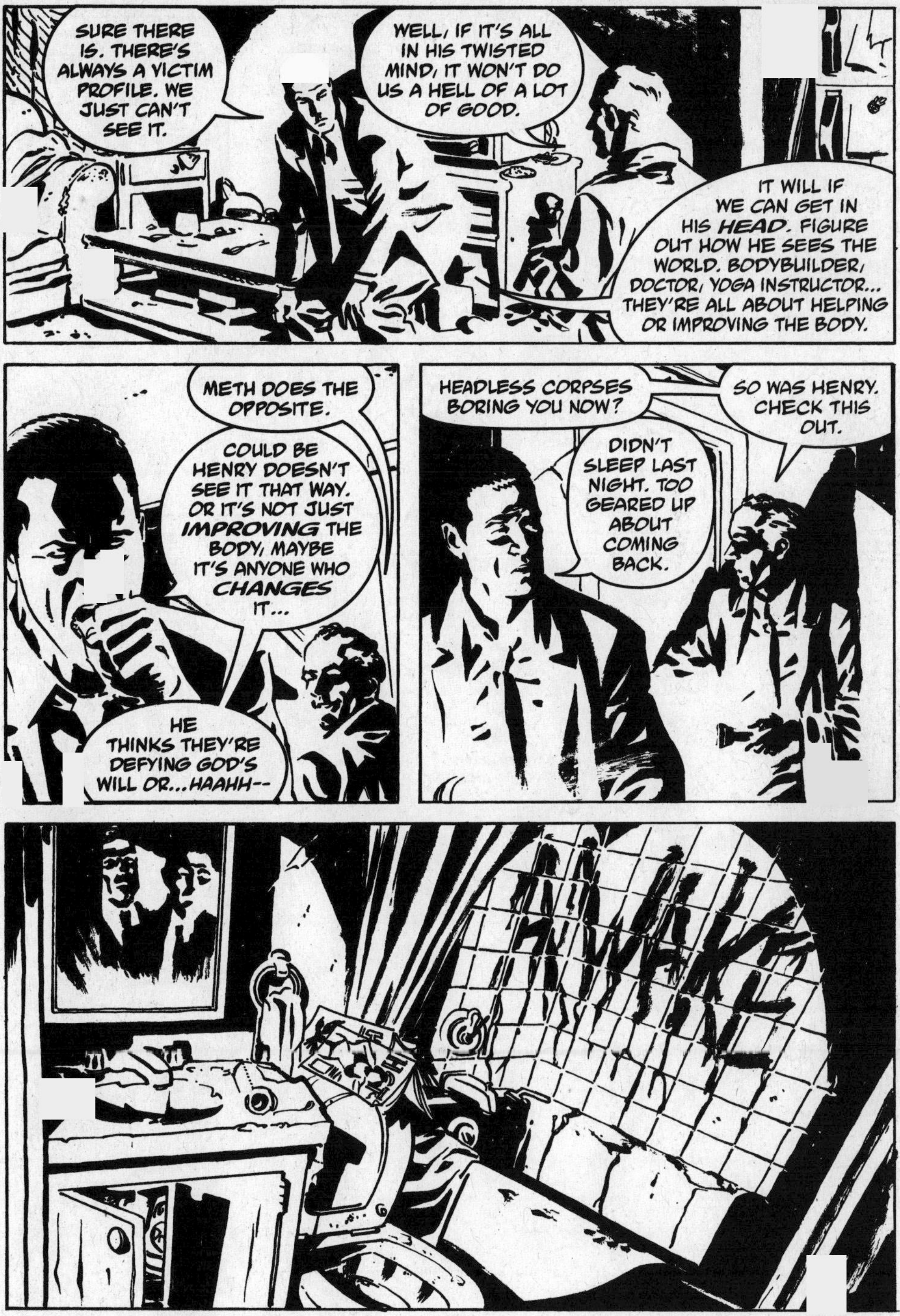
SURE THERE IS. THERE'S ALWAYS A VICTIM PROFILE. WE JUST CAN'T SEE IT.
WELL, IF IT'S ALL IN HIS TWISTED MIND, IT WON'T DO US A HELL OF A LOT OF GOOD.
IT WILL IF WE CAN GET IN HIS HEAD. FIGURE OUT HOW HE SEES THE WORLD. BODYBUILDER, DOCTOR, YOGA INSTRUCTOR... THEY'RE ALL ABOUT HELPING OR IMPROVING THE BODY.
METH DOES THE OPPOSITE.
COULD BE HENRY DOESN'T SEE IT THAT WAY. OR IT'S NOT JUST IMPROVING THE BODY, MAYBE IT'S ANYONE WHO CHANGES IT...
HE THINKS THEY'RE DEFYING GOD'S WILL OR...HAAHH--
HEADLESS CORPSES BORING YOU NOW?
DIDN'T SLEEP LAST NIGHT. TOO GEARED UP ABOUT COMING BACK.
SO WAS HENRY. CHECK THIS OUT.

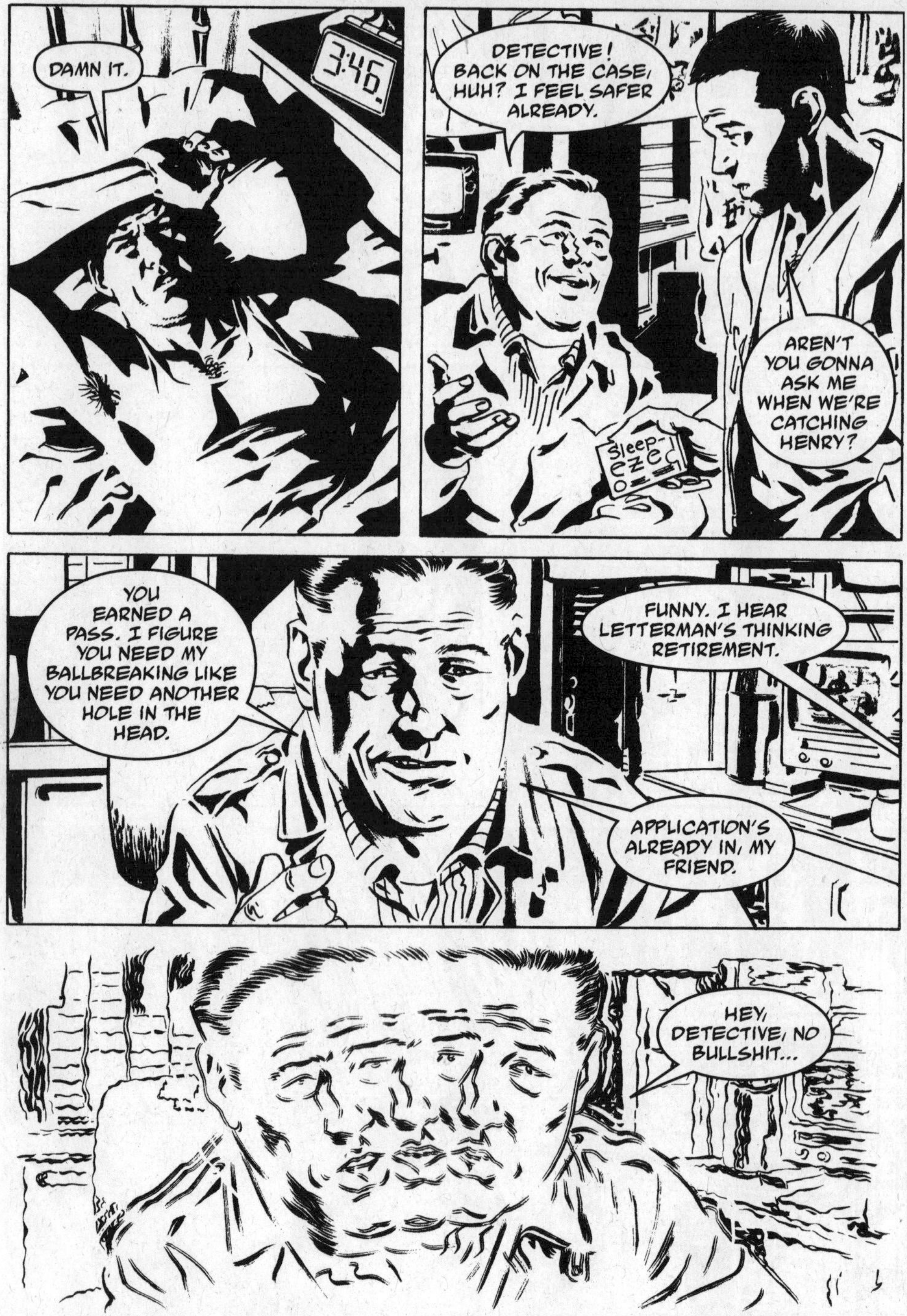
DAMN IT.
3:46
DETECTIVE! BACK ON THE CASE, HUH? I FEEL SAFER ALREADY.
sleep-eze
AREN'T YOU GONNA ASK ME WHEN WE'RE CATCHING HENRY?
YOU EARNED A PASS. I FIGURE YOU NEED MY BALLBREAKING LIKE YOU NEED ANOTHER HOLE IN THE HEAD.
FUNNY. I HEAR LETTERMAN'S THINKING RETIREMENT.
APPLICATION'S ALREADY IN, MY FRIEND.
HEY, DETECTIVE, NO BULLSHIT...

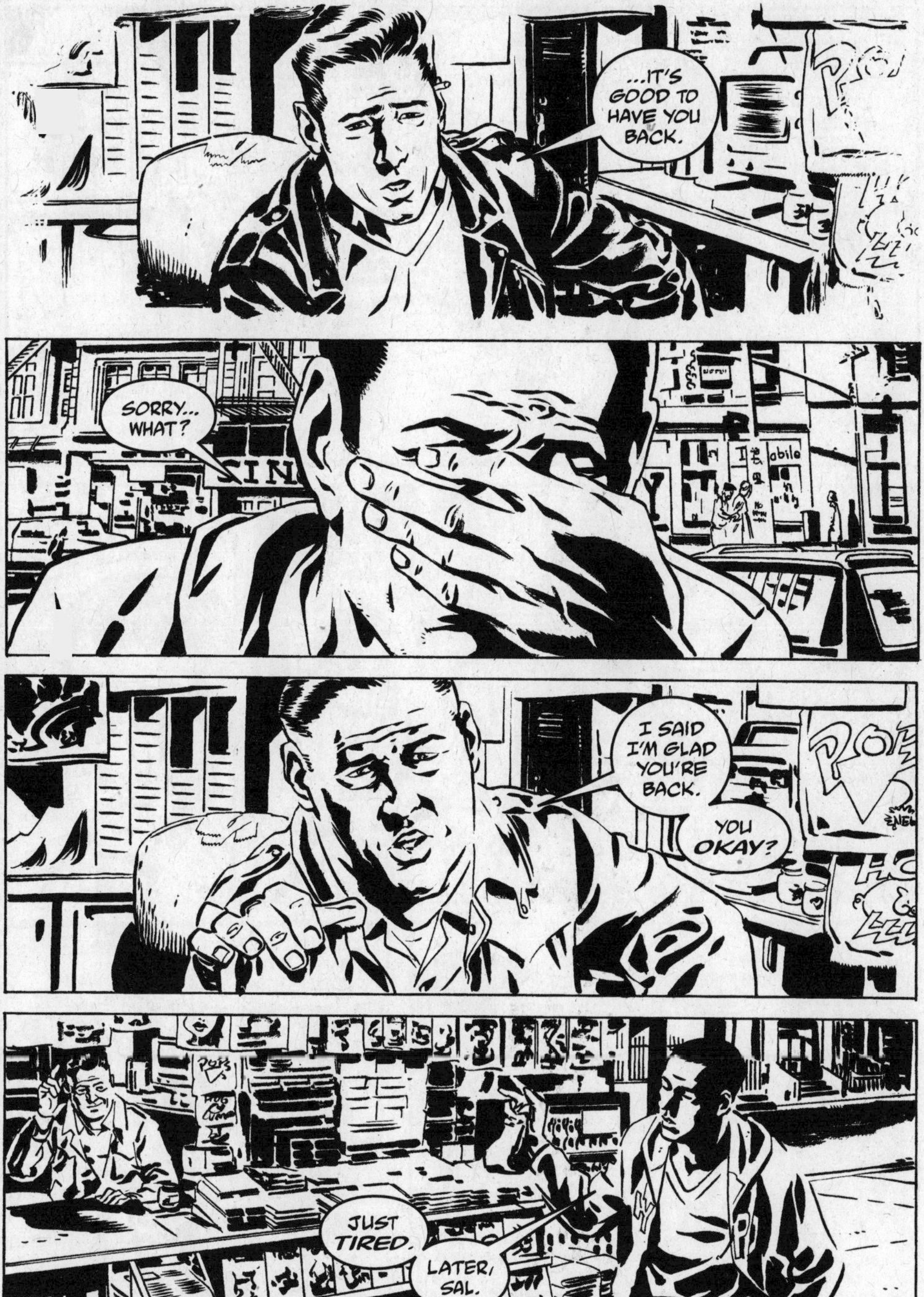
...IT'S GOOD TO HAVE YOU BACK.
SORRY... WHAT?
I SAID I'M GLAD YOU'RE BACK.
YOU OKAY?
JUST TIRED.
LATER, SAL.

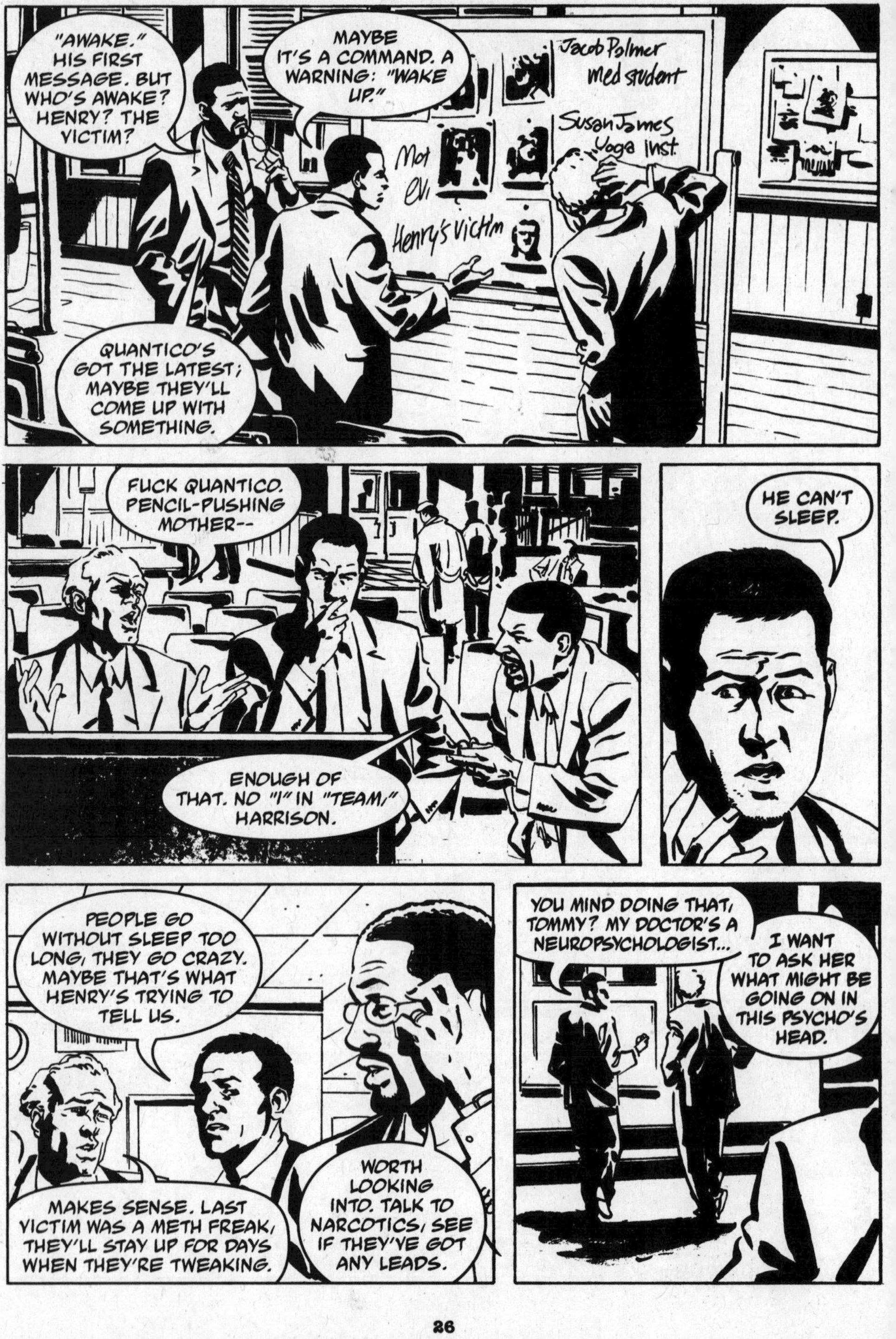
"AWAKE." HIS FIRST MESSAGE. BUT WHO'S AWAKE? HENRY? THE VICTIM?
MAYBE IT'S A COMMAND. A WARNING: "WAKE UP."
Jacob Palmer
med student
Susan James
Yoga inst.
Henry's Victim
QUANTICO'S GOT THE LATEST; MAYBE THEY'LL COME UP WITH SOMETHING.
FUCK QUANTICO. PENCIL-PUSHING MOTHER--
ENOUGH OF THAT. NO "I" IN "TEAM," HARRISON.
HE CAN'T SLEEP.
PEOPLE GO WITHOUT SLEEP TOO LONG, THEY GO CRAZY. MAYBE THAT'S WHAT HENRY'S TRYING TO TELL US.
MAKES SENSE. LAST VICTIM WAS A METH FREAK, THEY'LL STAY UP FOR DAYS WHEN THEY'RE TWEAKING.
WORTH LOOKING INTO. TALK TO NARCOTICS, SEE IF THEY'VE GOT ANY LEADS.
YOU MIND DOING THAT, TOMMY? MY DOCTOR'S A NEUROPSYCHOLOGIST...
I WANT TO ASK HER WHAT MIGHT BE GOING ON IN THIS PSYCHO'S HEAD.

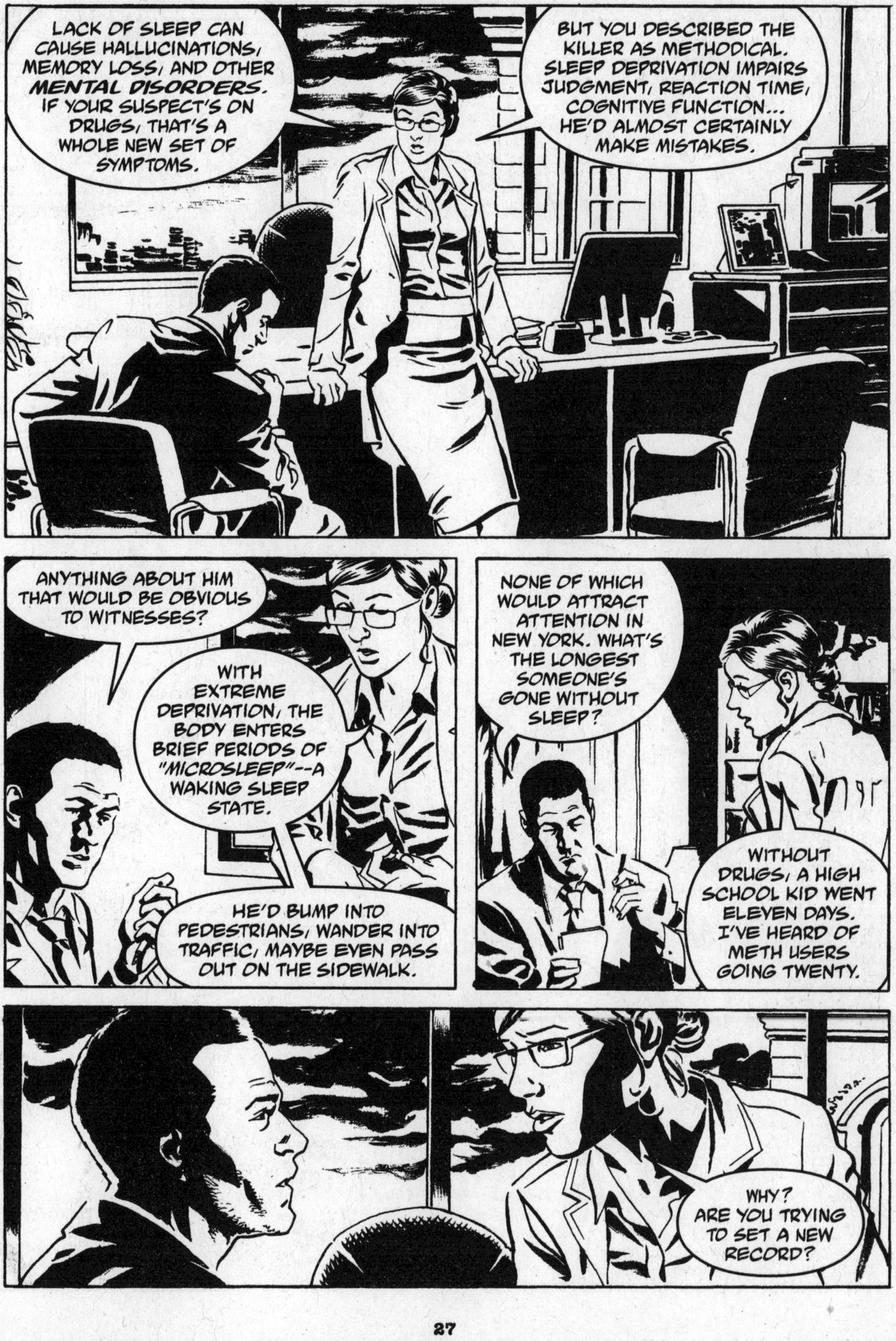
LACK OF SLEEP CAN CAUSE HALLUCINATIONS, MEMORY LOSS, AND OTHER *MENTAL DISORDERS*. IF YOUR SUSPECT'S ON DRUGS, THAT'S A WHOLE NEW SET OF SYMPTOMS.
BUT YOU DESCRIBED THE KILLER AS METHODICAL. SLEEP DEPRIVATION IMPAIRS JUDGMENT, REACTION TIME, COGNITIVE FUNCTION... HE'D ALMOST CERTAINLY MAKE MISTAKES.
ANYTHING ABOUT HIM THAT WOULD BE OBVIOUS TO WITNESSES?
WITH EXTREME DEPRIVATION, THE BODY ENTERS BRIEF PERIODS OF *"MICROSLEEP"*--A WAKING SLEEP STATE.
HE'D BUMP INTO PEDESTRIANS, WANDER INTO TRAFFIC, MAYBE EVEN PASS OUT ON THE SIDEWALK.
NONE OF WHICH WOULD ATTRACT ATTENTION IN NEW YORK. WHAT'S THE LONGEST SOMEONE'S GONE WITHOUT SLEEP?
WITHOUT DRUGS, A HIGH SCHOOL KID WENT ELEVEN DAYS. I'VE HEARD OF METH USERS GOING TWENTY.
WHY? ARE YOU TRYING TO SET A NEW RECORD?

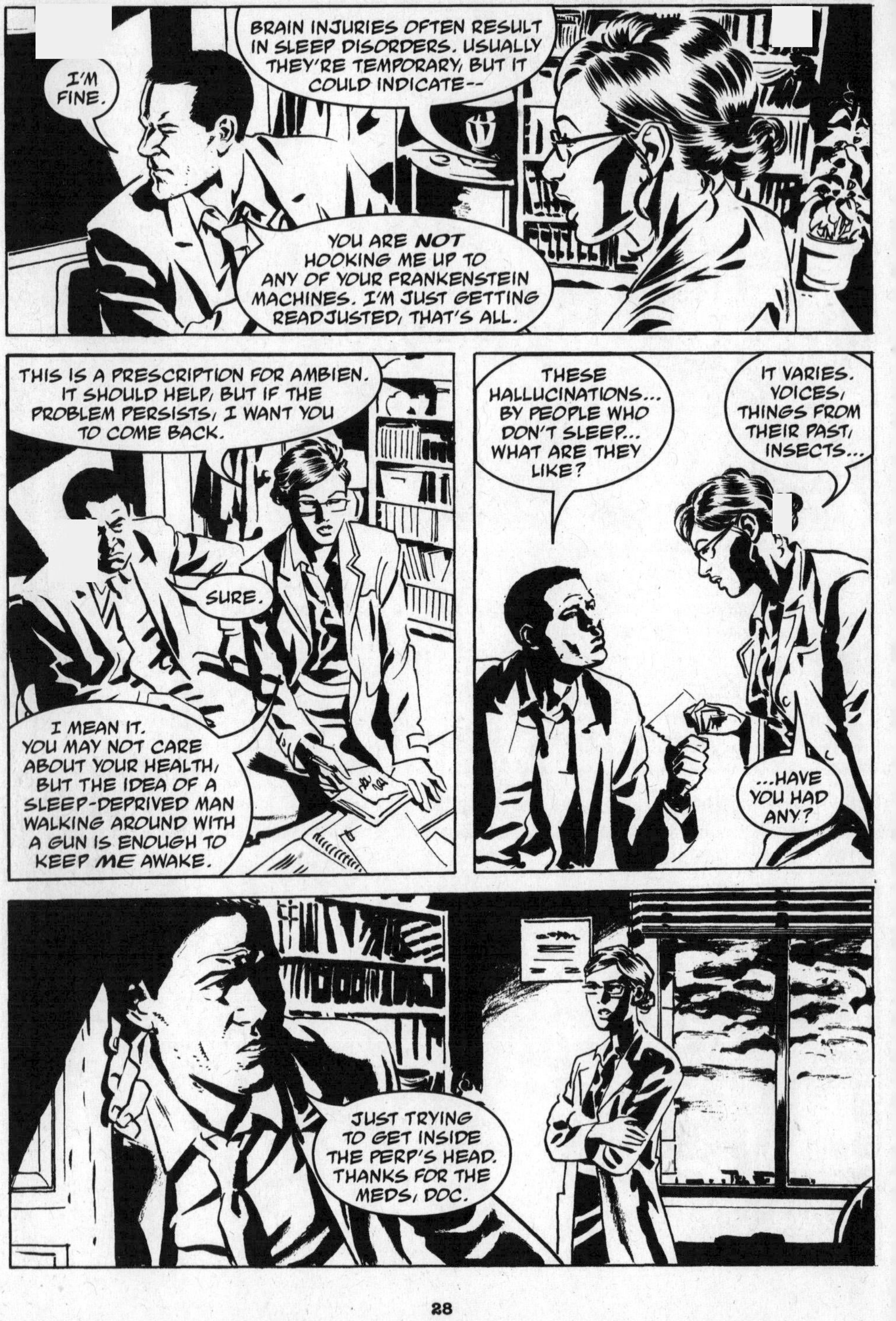

BRAIN INJURIES OFTEN RESULT IN SLEEP DISORDERS. USUALLY THEY'RE TEMPORARY, BUT IT COULD INDICATE--
I'M FINE.
YOU ARE **NOT** HOOKING ME UP TO ANY OF YOUR FRANKENSTEIN MACHINES. I'M JUST GETTING READJUSTED, THAT'S ALL.
THIS IS A PRESCRIPTION FOR AMBIEN. IT SHOULD HELP, BUT IF THE PROBLEM PERSISTS, I WANT YOU TO COME BACK.
SURE.
I MEAN IT. YOU MAY NOT CARE ABOUT YOUR HEALTH, BUT THE IDEA OF A SLEEP-DEPRIVED MAN WALKING AROUND WITH A GUN IS ENOUGH TO KEEP *ME* AWAKE.
THESE HALLUCINATIONS... BY PEOPLE WHO DON'T SLEEP... WHAT ARE THEY LIKE?
IT VARIES. VOICES, THINGS FROM THEIR PAST, INSECTS...
...HAVE YOU HAD ANY?
JUST TRYING TO GET INSIDE THE PERP'S HEAD. THANKS FOR THE MEDS, DOC.

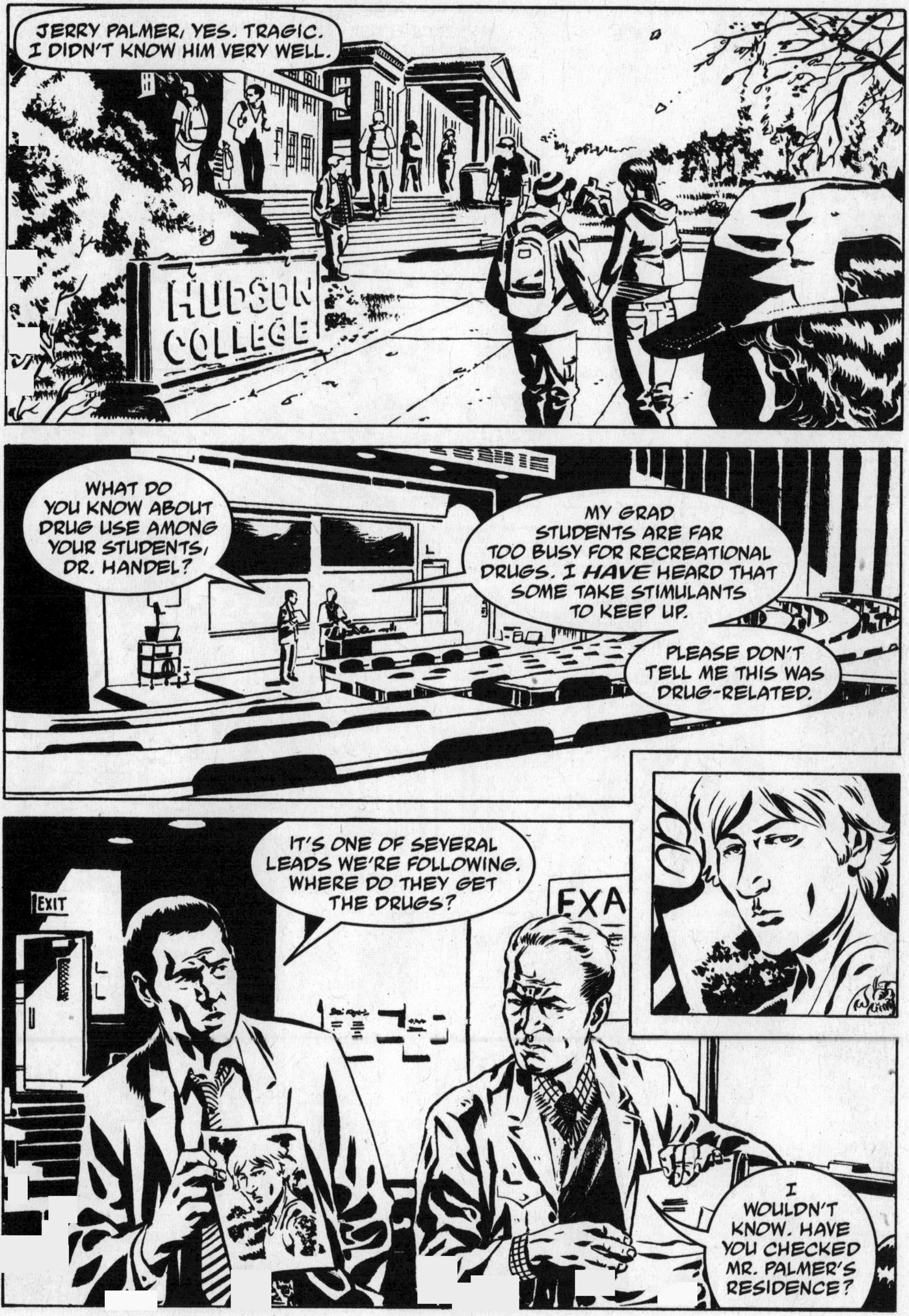
JERRY PALMER, YES. TRAGIC. I DIDN'T KNOW HIM VERY WELL.
HUDSON COLLEGE
WHAT DO YOU KNOW ABOUT DRUG USE AMONG YOUR STUDENTS, DR. HANDEL?
MY GRAD STUDENTS ARE FAR TOO BUSY FOR RECREATIONAL DRUGS. I *HAVE* HEARD THAT SOME TAKE STIMULANTS TO KEEP UP.
PLEASE DON'T TELL ME THIS WAS DRUG-RELATED.
EXIT
IT'S ONE OF SEVERAL LEADS WE'RE FOLLOWING. WHERE DO THEY GET THE DRUGS?
EXA
I WOULDN'T KNOW. HAVE YOU CHECKED MR. PALMER'S RESIDENCE?

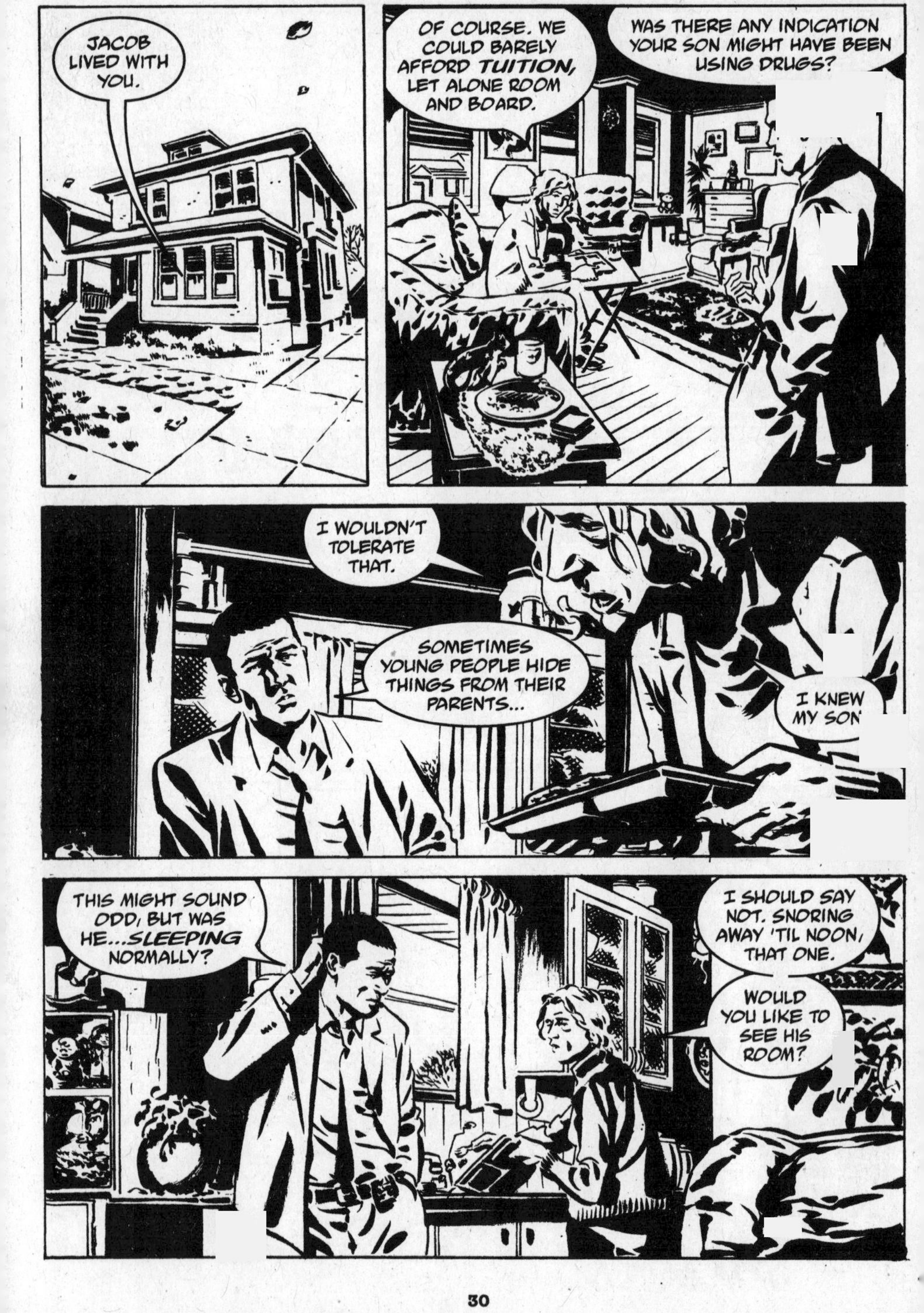
JACOB LIVED WITH YOU.
OF COURSE. WE COULD BARELY AFFORD TUITION, LET ALONE ROOM AND BOARD.
WAS THERE ANY INDICATION YOUR SON MIGHT HAVE BEEN USING DRUGS?
I WOULDN'T TOLERATE THAT.
SOMETIMES YOUNG PEOPLE HIDE THINGS FROM THEIR PARENTS...
I KNEW MY SON
THIS MIGHT SOUND ODD, BUT WAS HE...SLEEPING NORMALLY?
I SHOULD SAY NOT. SNORING AWAY 'TIL NOON, THAT ONE.
WOULD YOU LIKE TO SEE HIS ROOM?

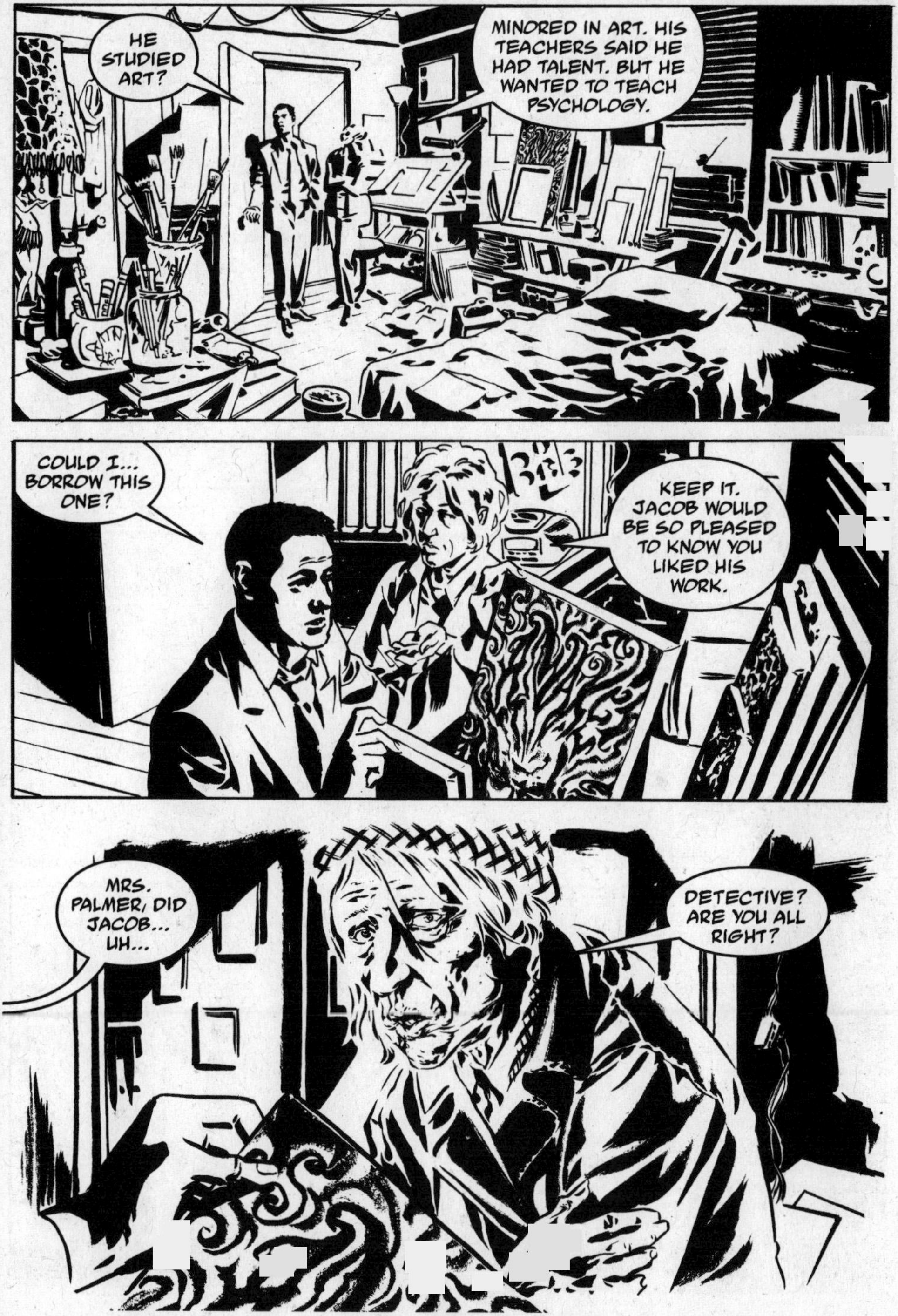
HE STUDIED ART?
MINORED IN ART. HIS TEACHERS SAID HE HAD TALENT. BUT HE WANTED TO TEACH PSYCHOLOGY.
COULD I... BORROW THIS ONE?
KEEP IT. JACOB WOULD BE SO PLEASED TO KNOW YOU LIKED HIS WORK.
MRS. PALMER, DID JACOB... UH...
DETECTIVE? ARE YOU ALL RIGHT?

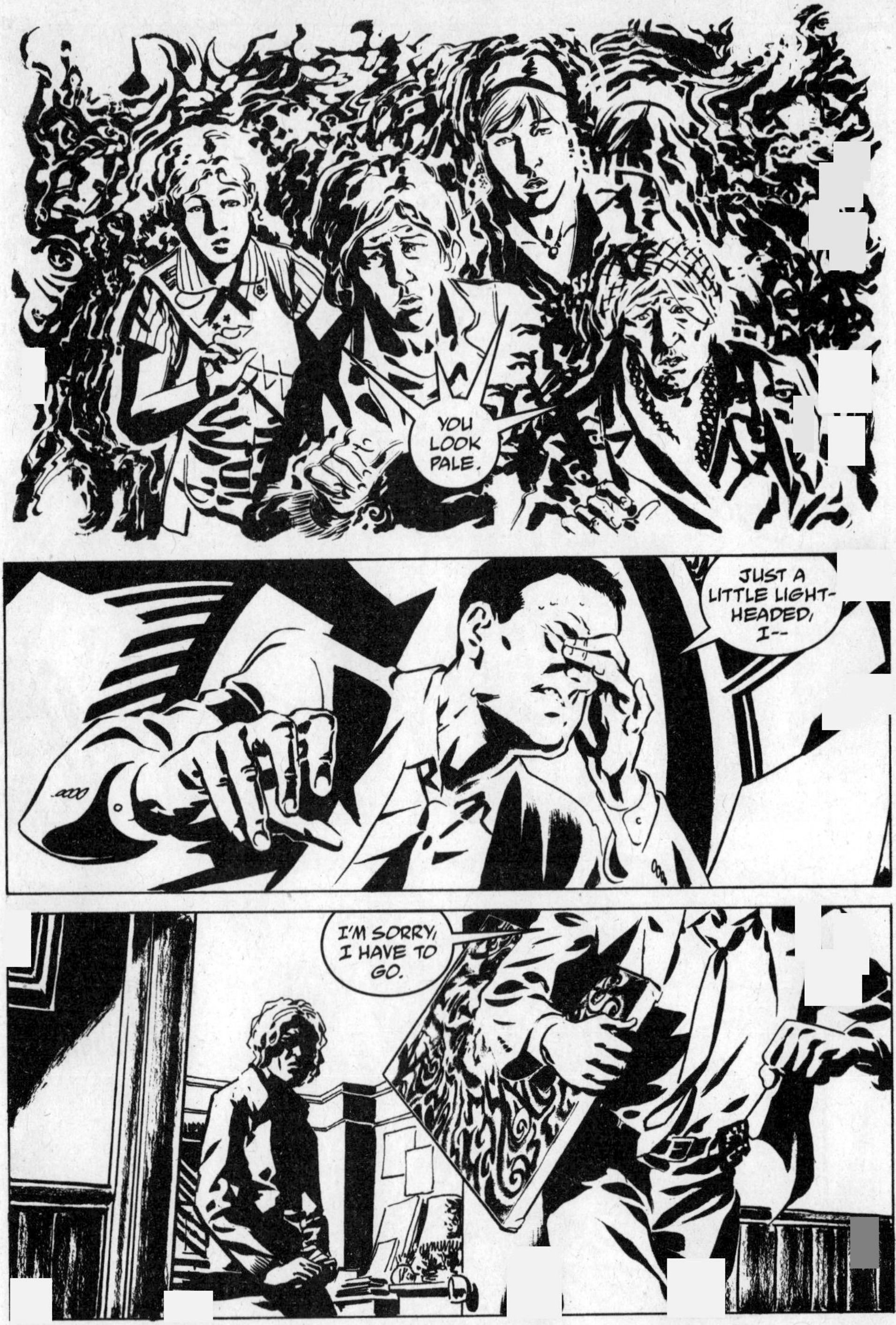
YOU LOOK PALE.
JUST A LITTLE LIGHT-HEADED, I--
I'M SORRY, I HAVE TO GO.

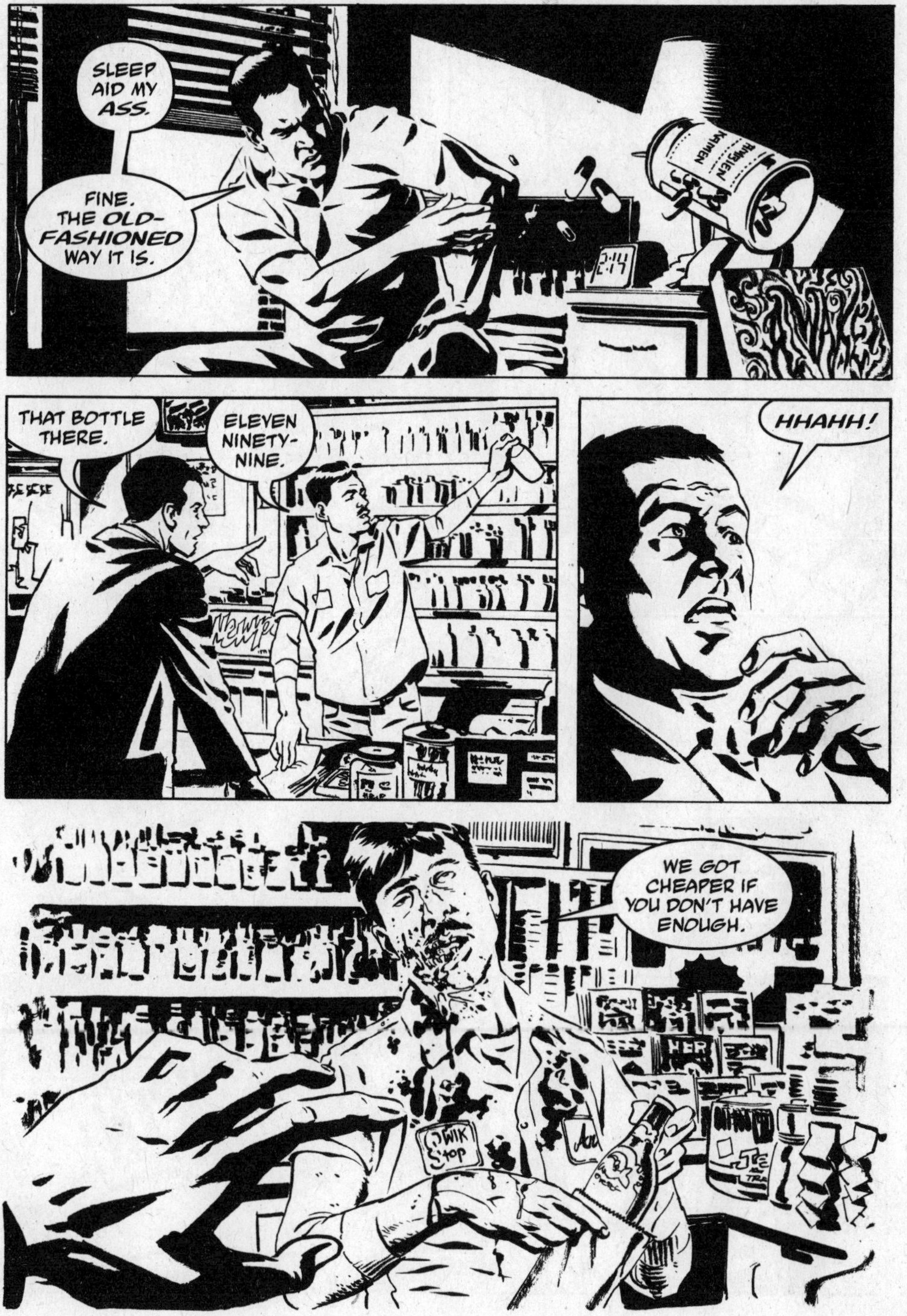
SLEEP AID MY ASS.
FINE. THE OLD-FASHIONED WAY IT IS.
THAT BOTTLE THERE.
ELEVEN NINETY-NINE.
HHAHH!
WE GOT CHEAPER IF YOU DON'T HAVE ENOUGH.

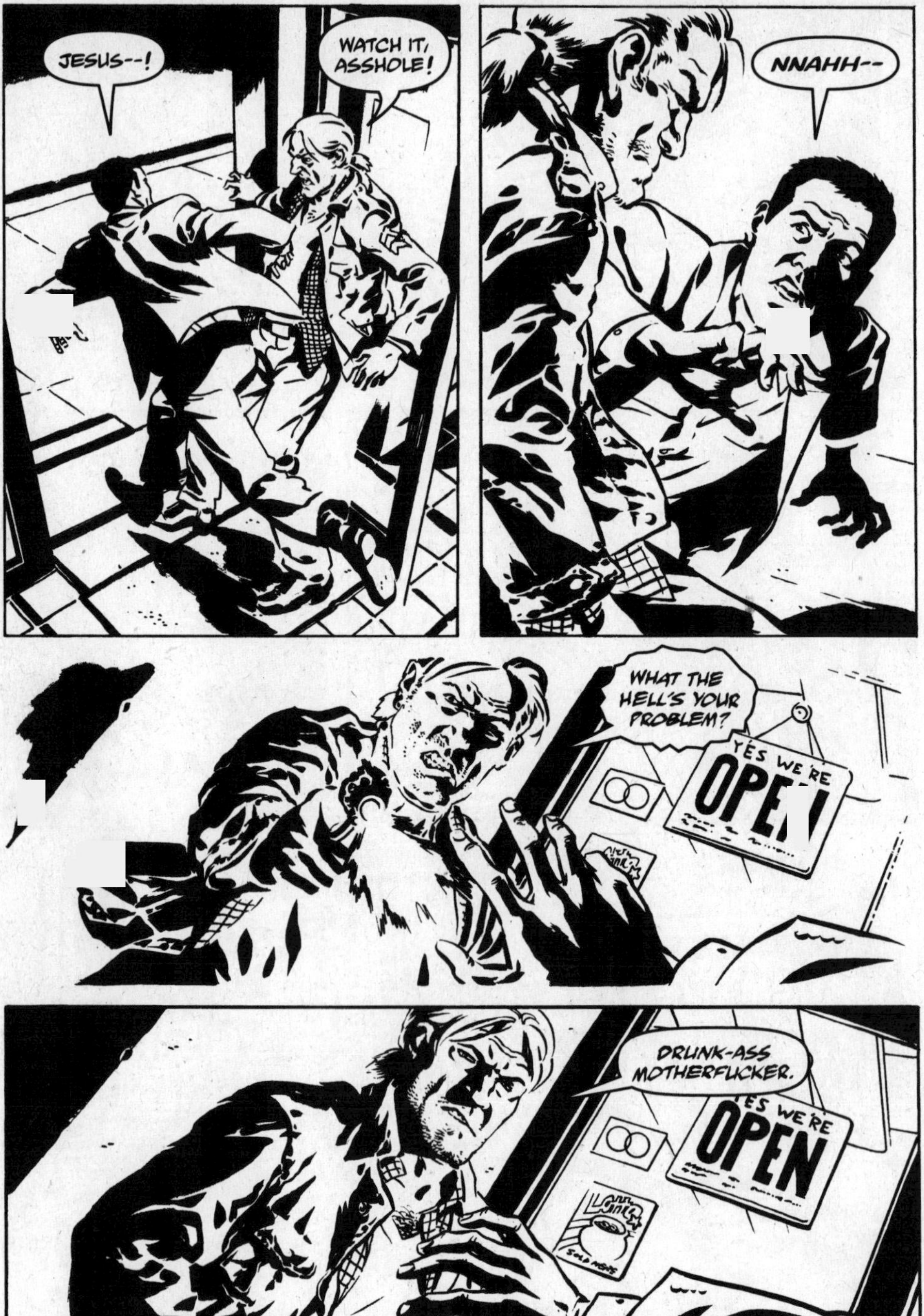
JESUS--!
WATCH IT, ASSHOLE!
NNAHH--
WHAT THE HELL'S YOUR PROBLEM?
YES WE'RE OPEN
DRUNK-ASS MOTHERFUCKER.
YES WE'RE OPEN

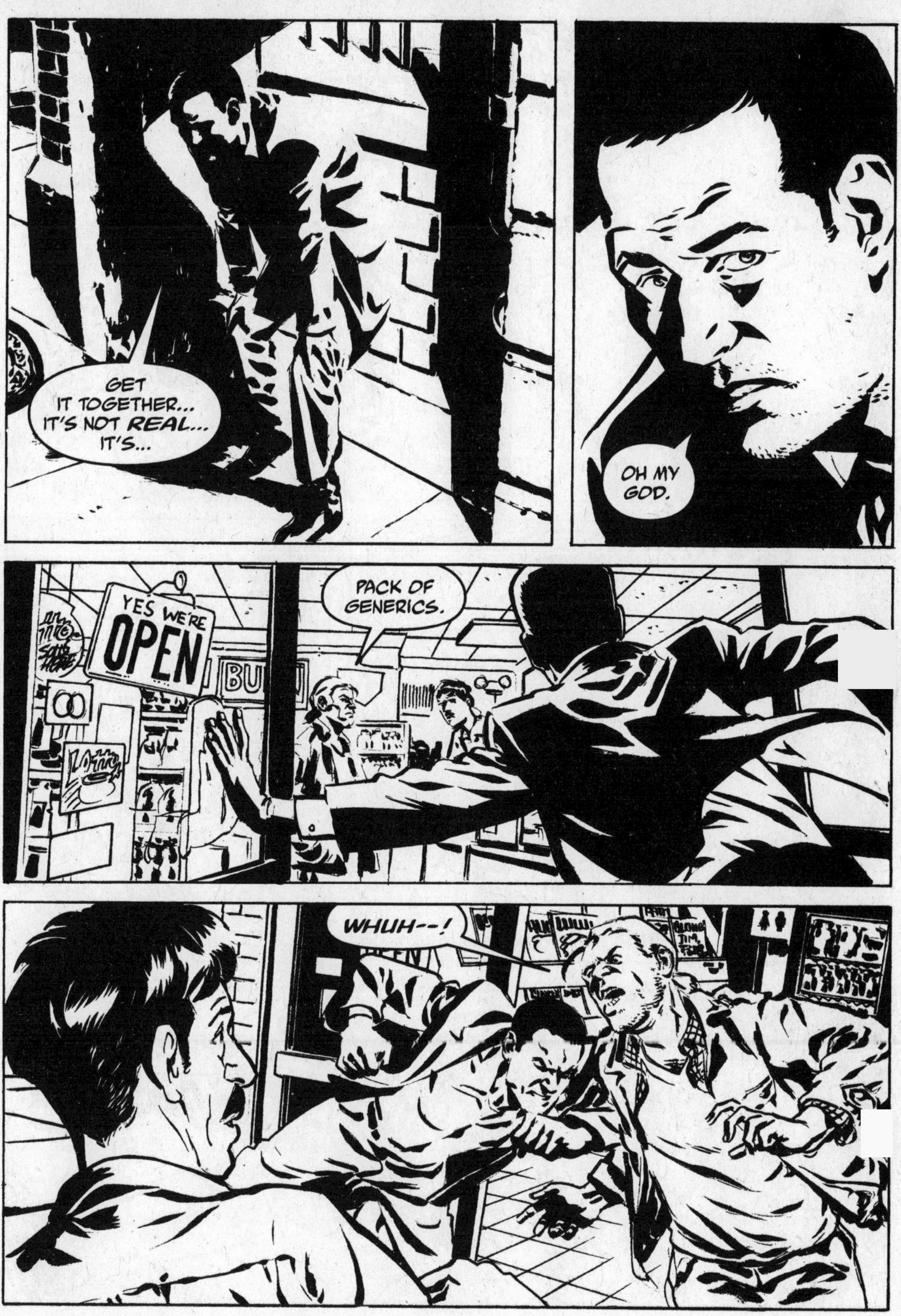
GET IT TOGETHER... IT'S NOT REAL... IT'S...
OH MY GOD.
YES WE'RE OPEN
PACK OF GENERICS.
WHUH--!

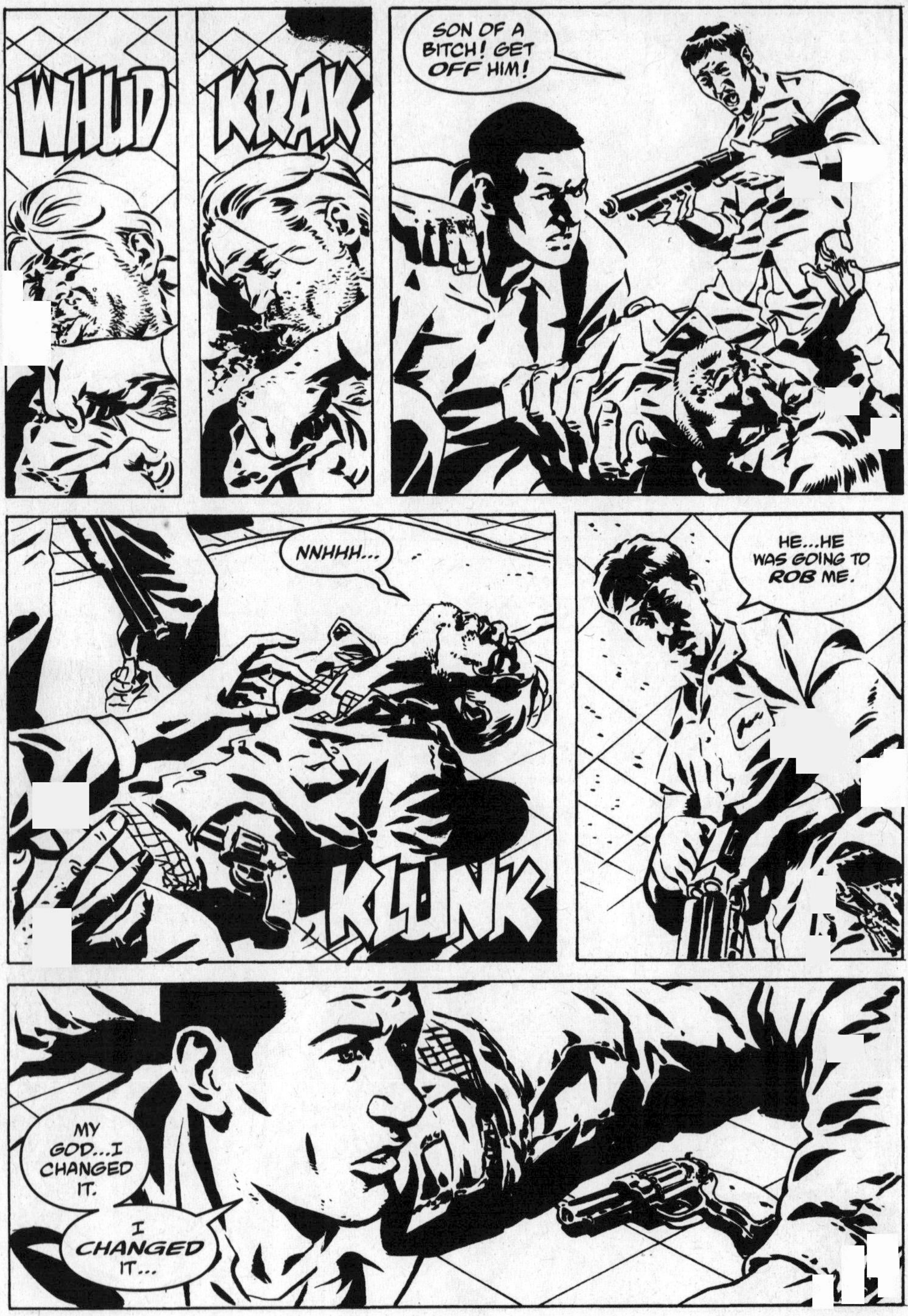
WHUD
KRAK
SON OF A BITCH! GET OFF HIM!
NNHHH...
KLUNK
HE...HE WAS GOING TO ROB ME.
MY GOD...I CHANGED IT.
I CHANGED IT...

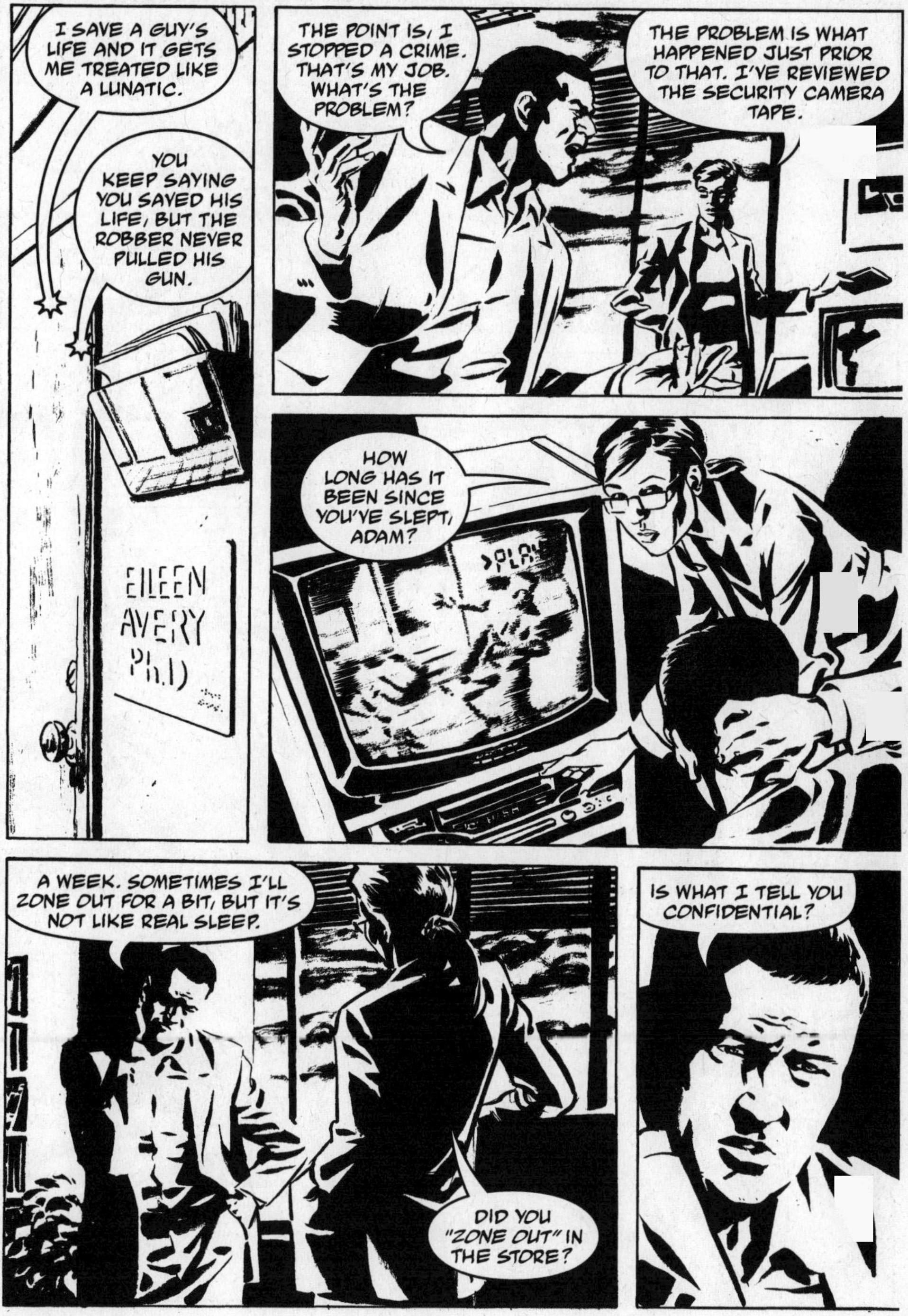

I SAVE A GUY'S LIFE AND IT GETS ME TREATED LIKE A LUNATIC.
YOU KEEP SAYING YOU SAVED HIS LIFE, BUT THE ROBBER NEVER PULLED HIS GUN.
EILEEN AVERY Ph.D
THE POINT IS, I STOPPED A CRIME. THAT'S MY JOB. WHAT'S THE PROBLEM?
THE PROBLEM IS WHAT HAPPENED JUST PRIOR TO THAT. I'VE REVIEWED THE SECURITY CAMERA TAPE.
HOW LONG HAS IT BEEN SINCE YOU'VE SLEPT, ADAM?
>PLAY
A WEEK. SOMETIMES I'LL ZONE OUT FOR A BIT, BUT IT'S NOT LIKE REAL SLEEP.
DID YOU "ZONE OUT" IN THE STORE?
IS WHAT I TELL YOU CONFIDENTIAL?

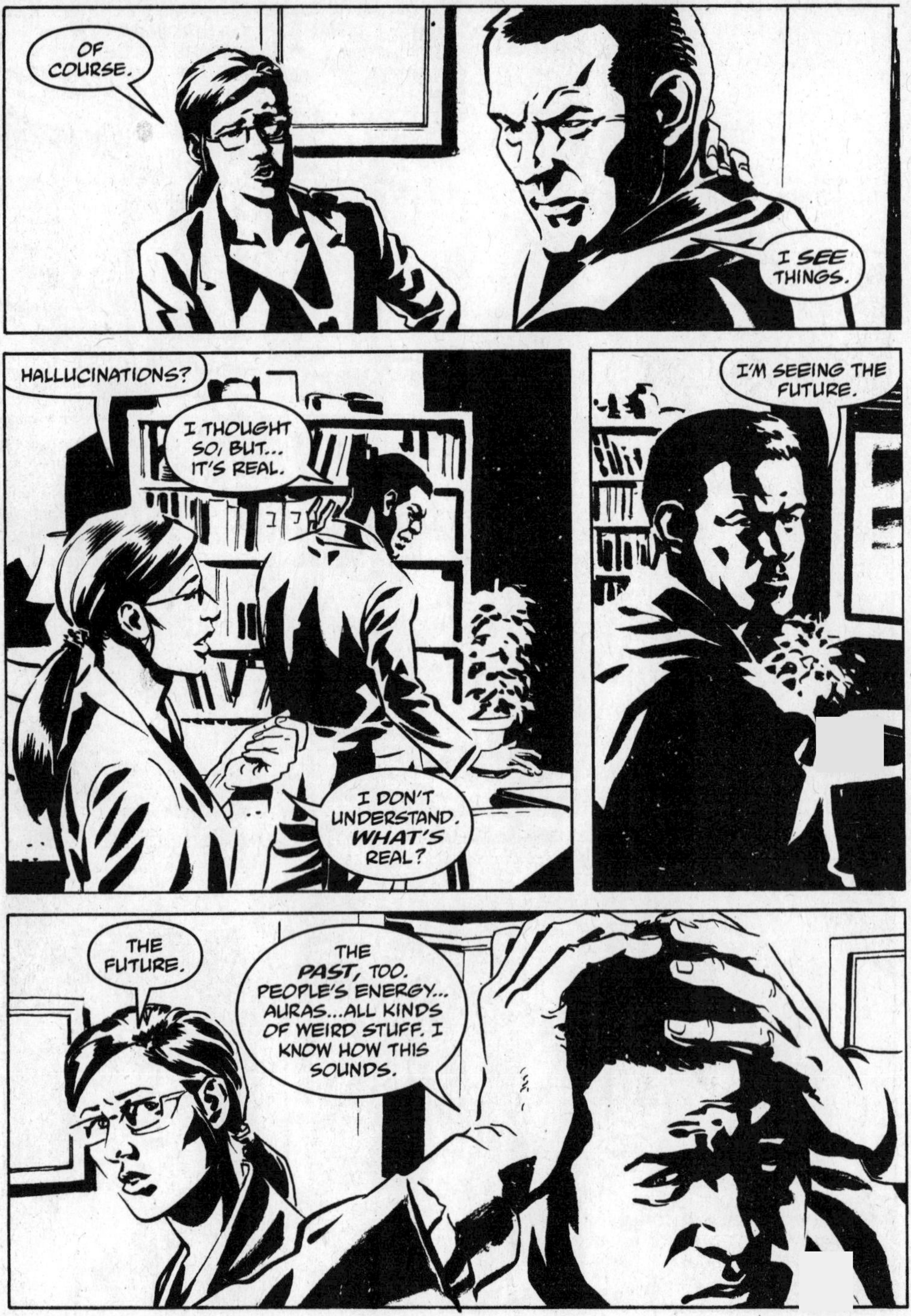
OF COURSE.
I SEE THINGS.
HALLUCINATIONS?
I THOUGHT SO, BUT... IT'S REAL.
I DON'T UNDERSTAND. WHAT'S REAL?
I'M SEEING THE FUTURE.
THE FUTURE.
THE PAST, TOO. PEOPLE'S ENERGY... AURAS...ALL KINDS OF WEIRD STUFF. I KNOW HOW THIS SOUNDS.

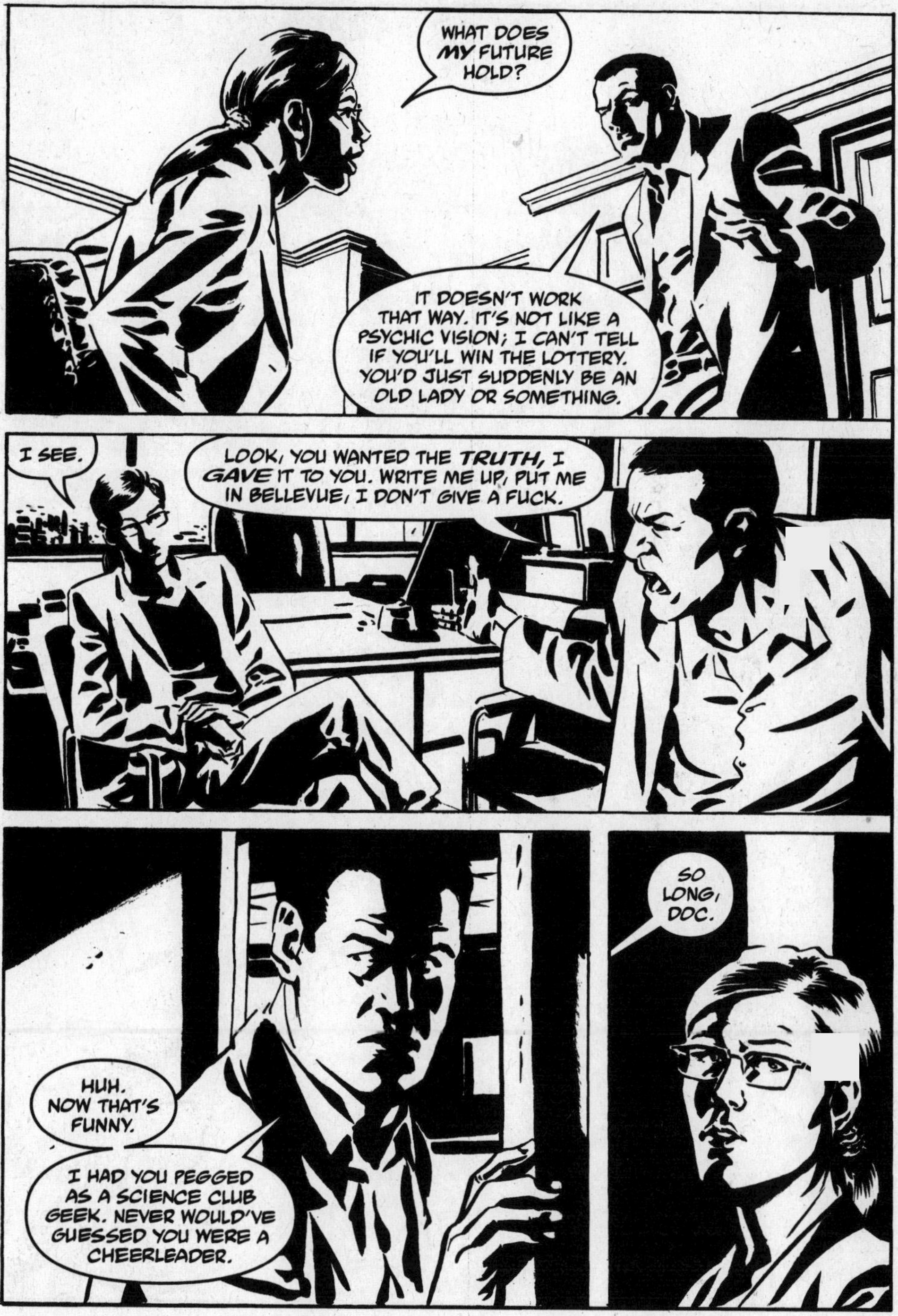
WHAT DOES *MY* FUTURE HOLD?
IT DOESN'T WORK THAT WAY. IT'S NOT LIKE A PSYCHIC VISION; I CAN'T TELL IF YOU'LL WIN THE LOTTERY. YOU'D JUST SUDDENLY BE AN OLD LADY OR SOMETHING.
I SEE.
LOOK, YOU WANTED THE *TRUTH,* I *GAVE* IT TO YOU. WRITE ME UP, PUT ME IN BELLEVUE, I DON'T GIVE A FUCK.
HUH. NOW THAT'S FUNNY.
I HAD YOU PEGGED AS A SCIENCE CLUB GEEK. NEVER WOULD'VE GUESSED YOU WERE A CHEERLEADER.
SO LONG, DOC.

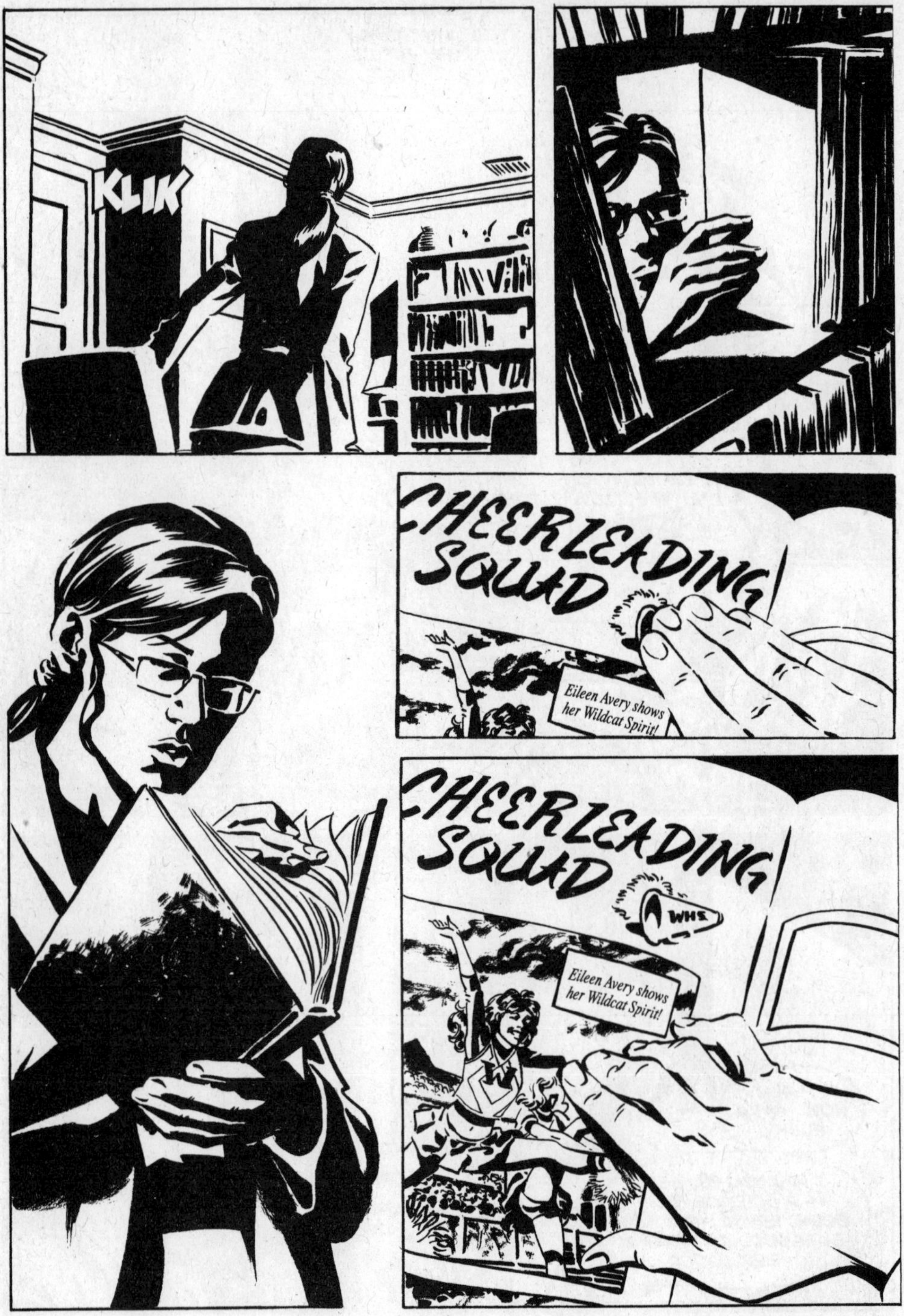
KLIK
CHEERLEADING SQUAD
Eileen Avery shows her Wildcat Spirit!
CHEERLEADING SQUAD
WHS
Eileen Avery shows her Wildcat Spirit!

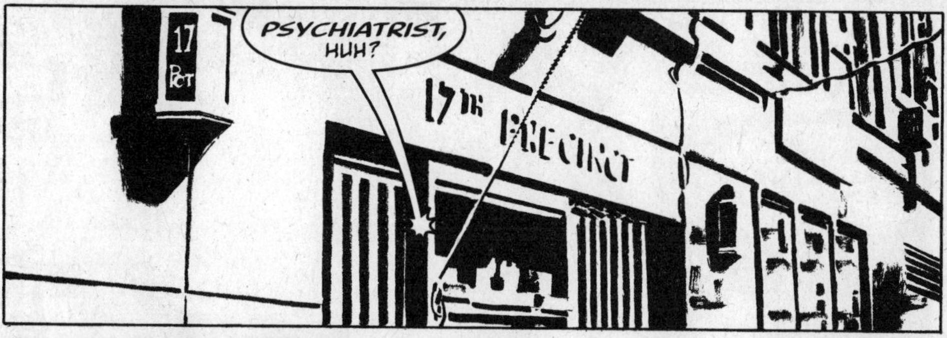
17
PCT
17TH PRECINCT
PSYCHIATRIST, HUH?

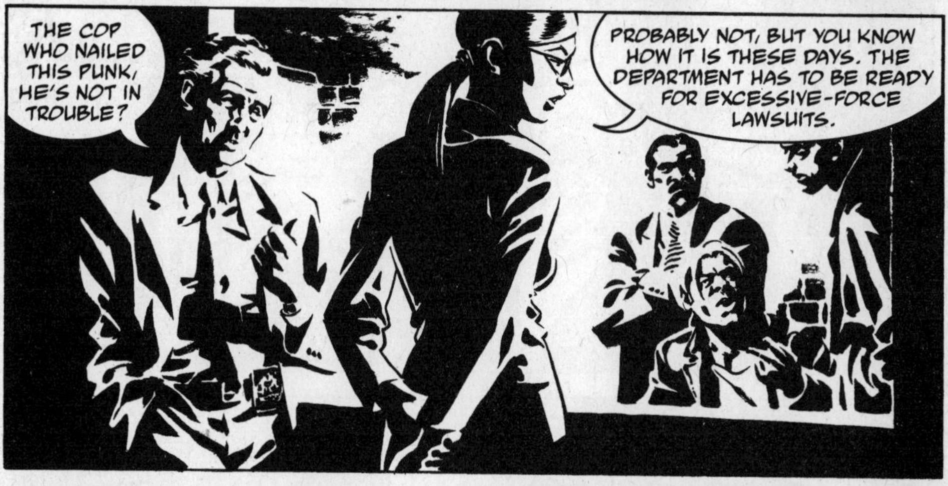
THE COP WHO NAILED THIS PUNK, HE'S NOT IN TROUBLE?
PROBABLY NOT, BUT YOU KNOW HOW IT IS THESE DAYS. THE DEPARTMENT HAS TO BE READY FOR EXCESSIVE-FORCE LAWSUITS.

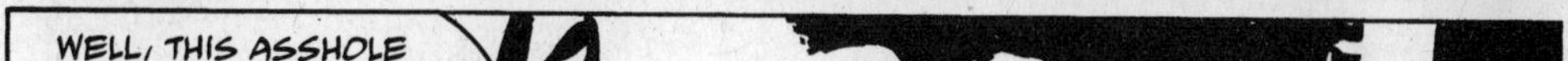
WELL, THIS ASSHOLE *EARNED* HIS BEATING. BETWEEN WITNESSES AND BALLISTICS, WE GOT HIM FOR NINE OTHER ROBBERIES.
BALLISTICS? HE SHOT SOMEONE?

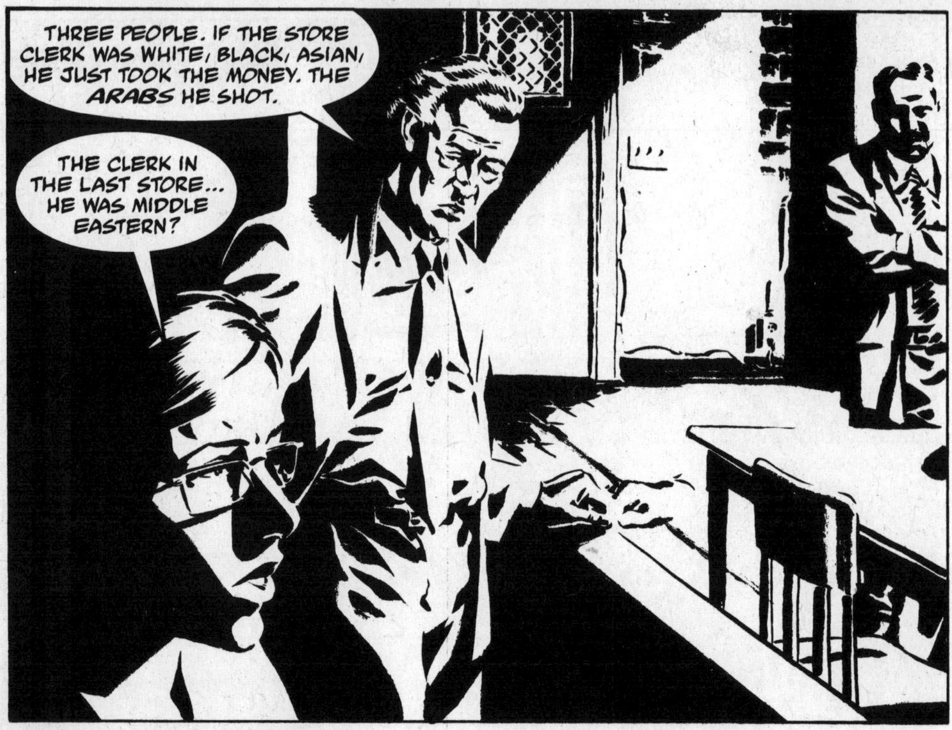
THREE PEOPLE. IF THE STORE CLERK WAS WHITE, BLACK, ASIAN, HE JUST TOOK THE MONEY. THE *ARABS* HE SHOT.
THE CLERK IN THE LAST STORE... HE WAS MIDDLE EASTERN?

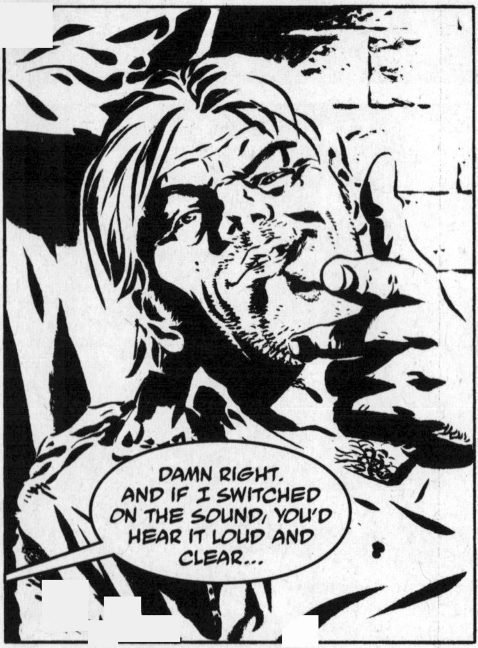
DAMN RIGHT. AND IF I SWITCHED ON THE SOUND, YOU'D HEAR IT LOUD AND CLEAR...

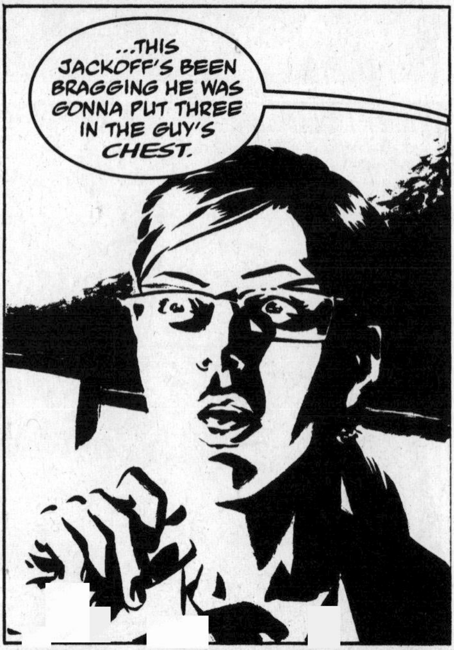
...THIS JACKOFF'S BEEN BRAGGING HE WAS GONNA PUT THREE IN THE GUY'S *CHEST*.

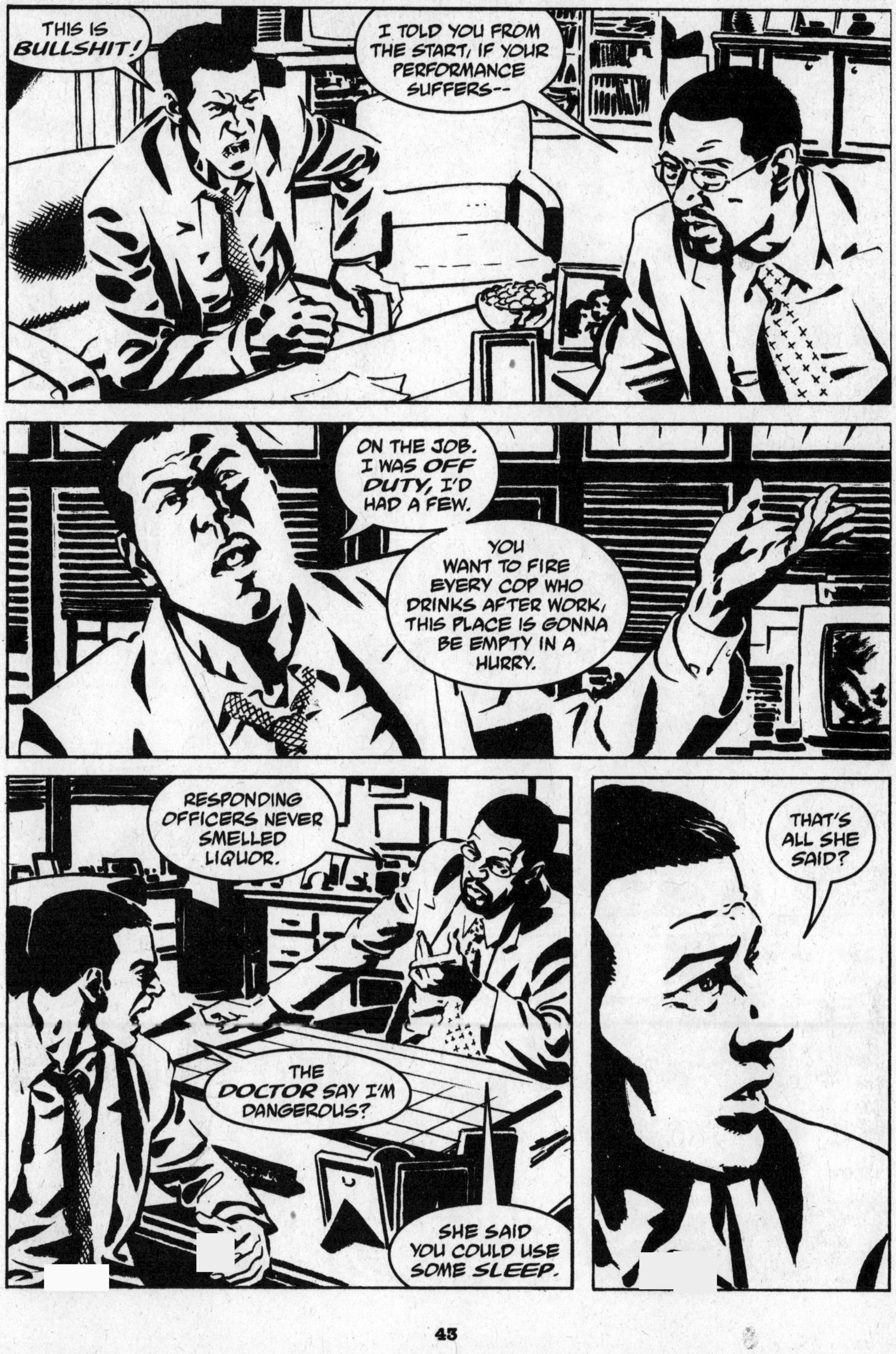
THIS IS BULLSHIT!
I TOLD YOU FROM THE START, IF YOUR PERFORMANCE SUFFERS--
ON THE JOB. I WAS OFF DUTY, I'D HAD A FEW.
YOU WANT TO FIRE EVERY COP WHO DRINKS AFTER WORK, THIS PLACE IS GONNA BE EMPTY IN A HURRY.
RESPONDING OFFICERS NEVER SMELLED LIQUOR.
THE DOCTOR SAY I'M DANGEROUS?
SHE SAID YOU COULD USE SOME SLEEP.
THAT'S ALL SHE SAID?

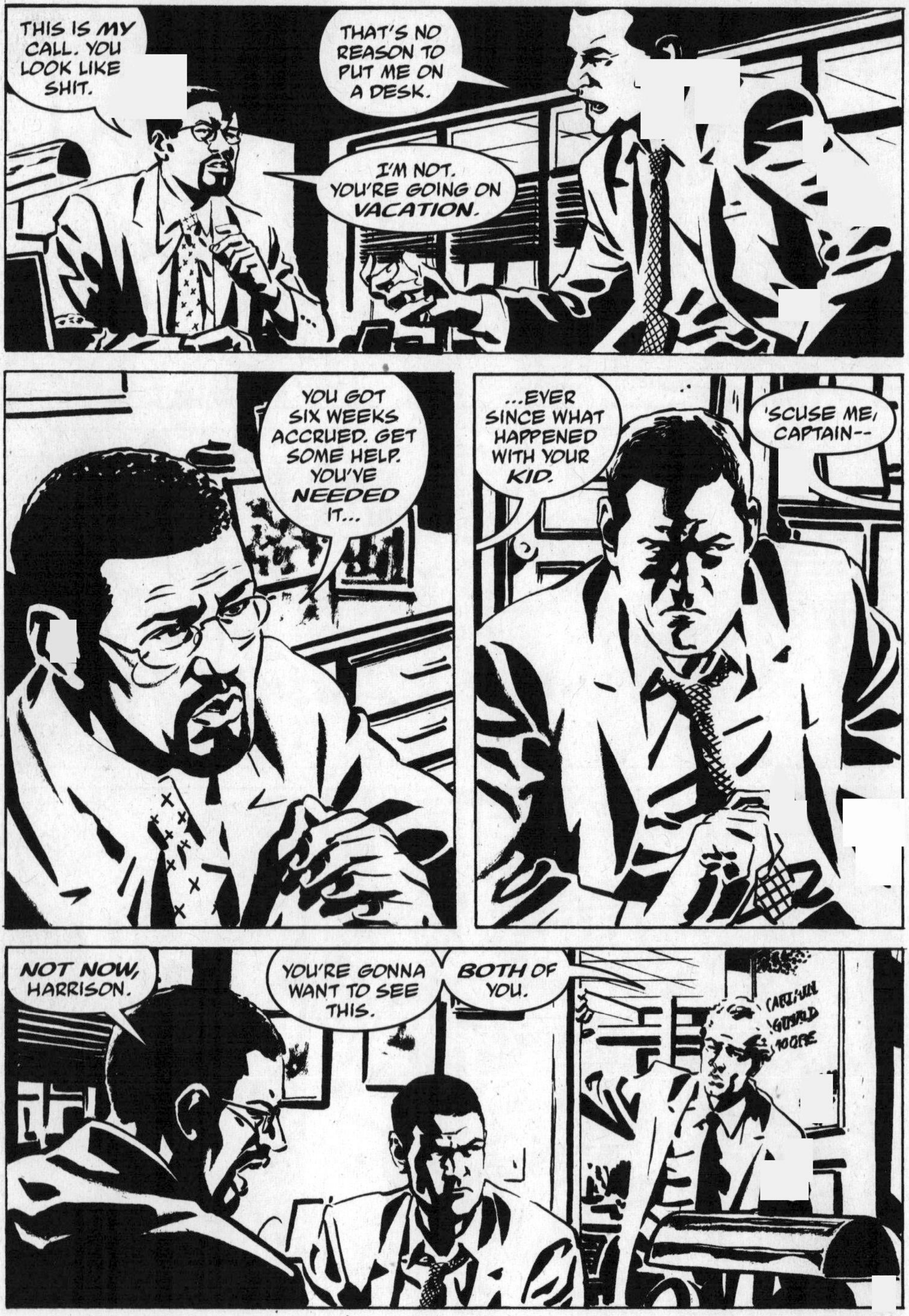
THIS IS MY CALL. YOU LOOK LIKE SHIT.
THAT'S NO REASON TO PUT ME ON A DESK.
I'M NOT. YOU'RE GOING ON VACATION.
YOU GOT SIX WEEKS ACCRUED. GET SOME HELP. YOU'VE NEEDED IT...
...EVER SINCE WHAT HAPPENED WITH YOUR KID.
'SCUSE ME, CAPTAIN--
NOT NOW, HARRISON.
YOU'RE GONNA WANT TO SEE THIS.
BOTH OF YOU.
CAPTAIN GUSTAVO MOORE

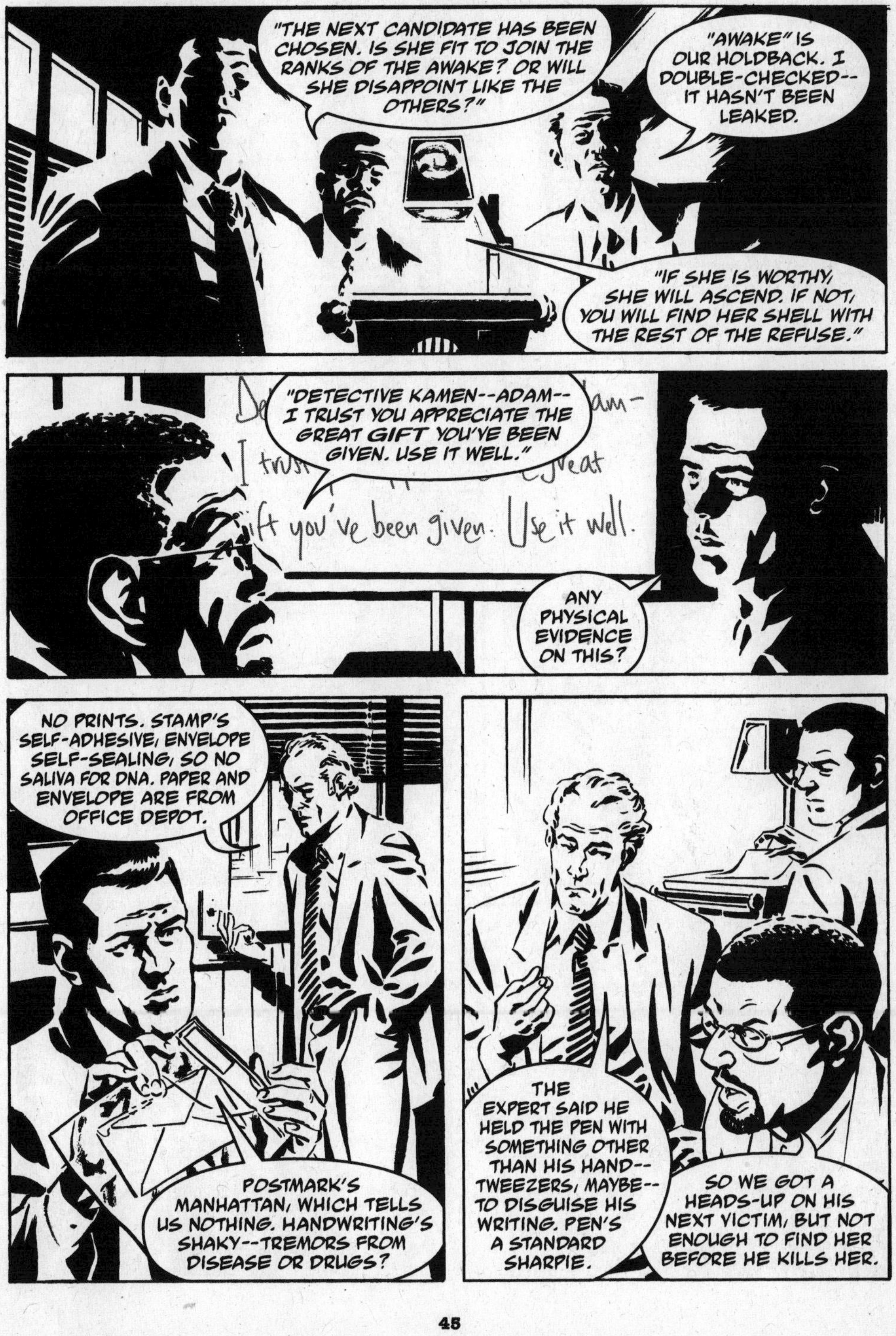
"THE NEXT CANDIDATE HAS BEEN CHOSEN. IS SHE FIT TO JOIN THE RANKS OF THE AWAKE? OR WILL SHE DISAPPOINT LIKE THE OTHERS?"
"AWAKE" IS OUR HOLDBACK. I DOUBLE-CHECKED-- IT HASN'T BEEN LEAKED.
"IF SHE IS WORTHY, SHE WILL ASCEND. IF NOT, YOU WILL FIND HER SHELL WITH THE REST OF THE REFUSE."
"DETECTIVE KAMEN--ADAM-- I TRUST YOU APPRECIATE THE GREAT GIFT YOU'VE BEEN GIVEN. USE IT WELL."
you've been given. Use it well.
ANY PHYSICAL EVIDENCE ON THIS?
NO PRINTS. STAMP'S SELF-ADHESIVE, ENVELOPE SELF-SEALING, SO NO SALIVA FOR DNA. PAPER AND ENVELOPE ARE FROM OFFICE DEPOT.
POSTMARK'S MANHATTAN, WHICH TELLS US NOTHING. HANDWRITING'S SHAKY--TREMORS FROM DISEASE OR DRUGS?
THE EXPERT SAID HE HELD THE PEN WITH SOMETHING OTHER THAN HIS HAND-- TWEEZERS, MAYBE-- TO DISGUISE HIS WRITING. PEN'S A STANDARD SHARPIE.
SO WE GOT A HEADS-UP ON HIS NEXT VICTIM, BUT NOT ENOUGH TO FIND HER BEFORE HE KILLS HER.

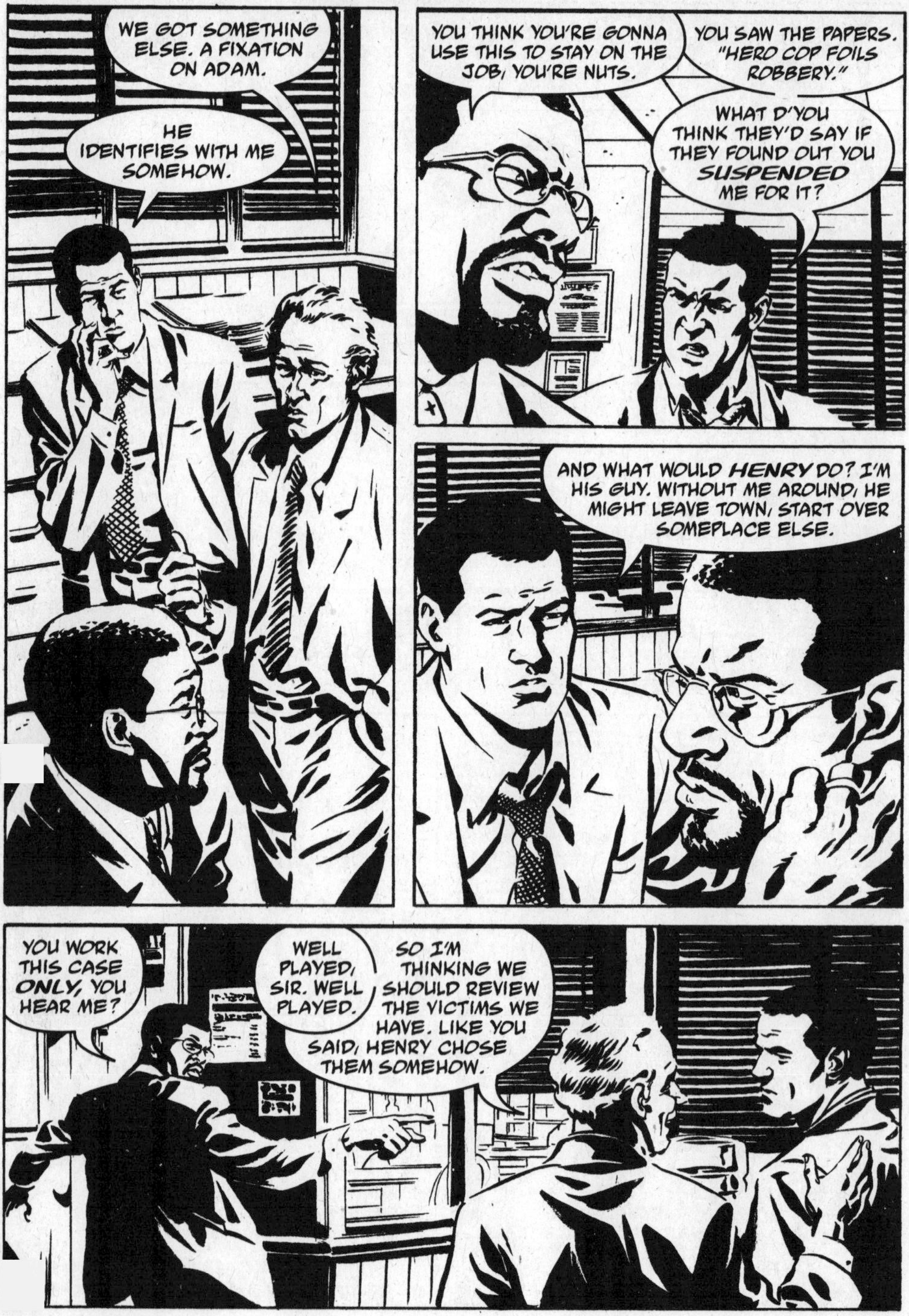
WE GOT SOMETHING ELSE. A FIXATION ON ADAM.
HE IDENTIFIES WITH ME SOMEHOW.
YOU THINK YOU'RE GONNA USE THIS TO STAY ON THE JOB, YOU'RE NUTS.
YOU SAW THE PAPERS. "HERO COP FOILS ROBBERY."
WHAT D'YOU THINK THEY'D SAY IF THEY FOUND OUT YOU SUSPENDED ME FOR IT?
AND WHAT WOULD HENRY DO? I'M HIS GUY. WITHOUT ME AROUND, HE MIGHT LEAVE TOWN, START OVER SOMEPLACE ELSE.
YOU WORK THIS CASE ONLY, YOU HEAR ME?
WELL PLAYED, SIR. WELL PLAYED.
SO I'M THINKING WE SHOULD REVIEW THE VICTIMS WE HAVE. LIKE YOU SAID, HENRY CHOSE THEM SOMEHOW.

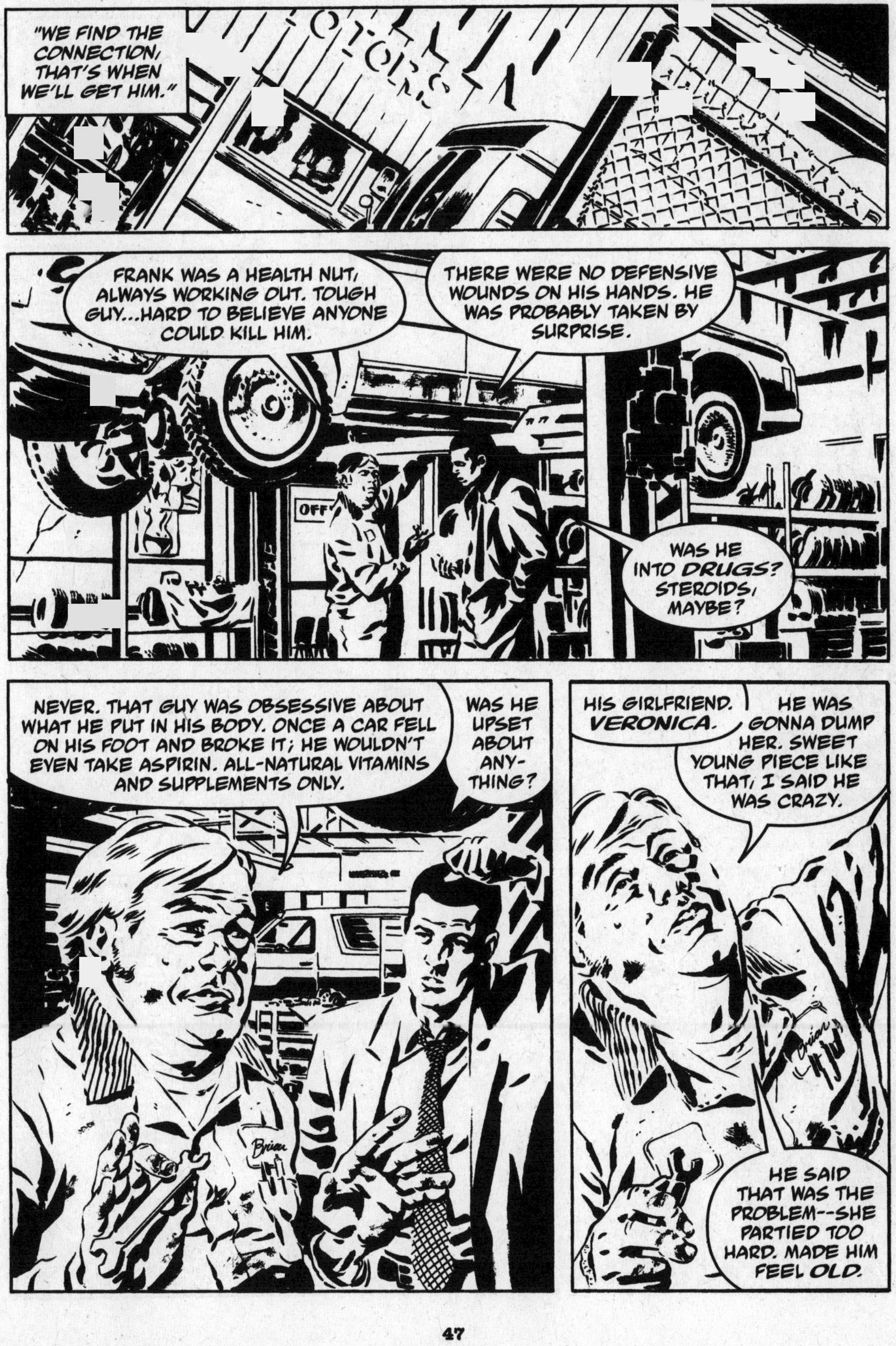
"WE FIND THE CONNECTION, THAT'S WHEN WE'LL GET HIM."
FRANK WAS A HEALTH NUT, ALWAYS WORKING OUT. TOUGH GUY...HARD TO BELIEVE ANYONE COULD KILL HIM.
THERE WERE NO DEFENSIVE WOUNDS ON HIS HANDS. HE WAS PROBABLY TAKEN BY SURPRISE.
OFF
WAS HE INTO *DRUGS*? STEROIDS, MAYBE?
NEVER. THAT GUY WAS OBSESSIVE ABOUT WHAT HE PUT IN HIS BODY. ONCE A CAR FELL ON HIS FOOT AND BROKE IT; HE WOULDN'T EVEN TAKE ASPIRIN. ALL-NATURAL VITAMINS AND SUPPLEMENTS ONLY.
WAS HE UPSET ABOUT ANY-THING?
HIS GIRLFRIEND. *VERONICA*.
HE WAS GONNA DUMP HER. SWEET YOUNG PIECE LIKE THAT, I SAID HE WAS CRAZY.
HE SAID THAT WAS THE PROBLEM--SHE PARTIED TOO HARD. MADE HIM FEEL *OLD*.

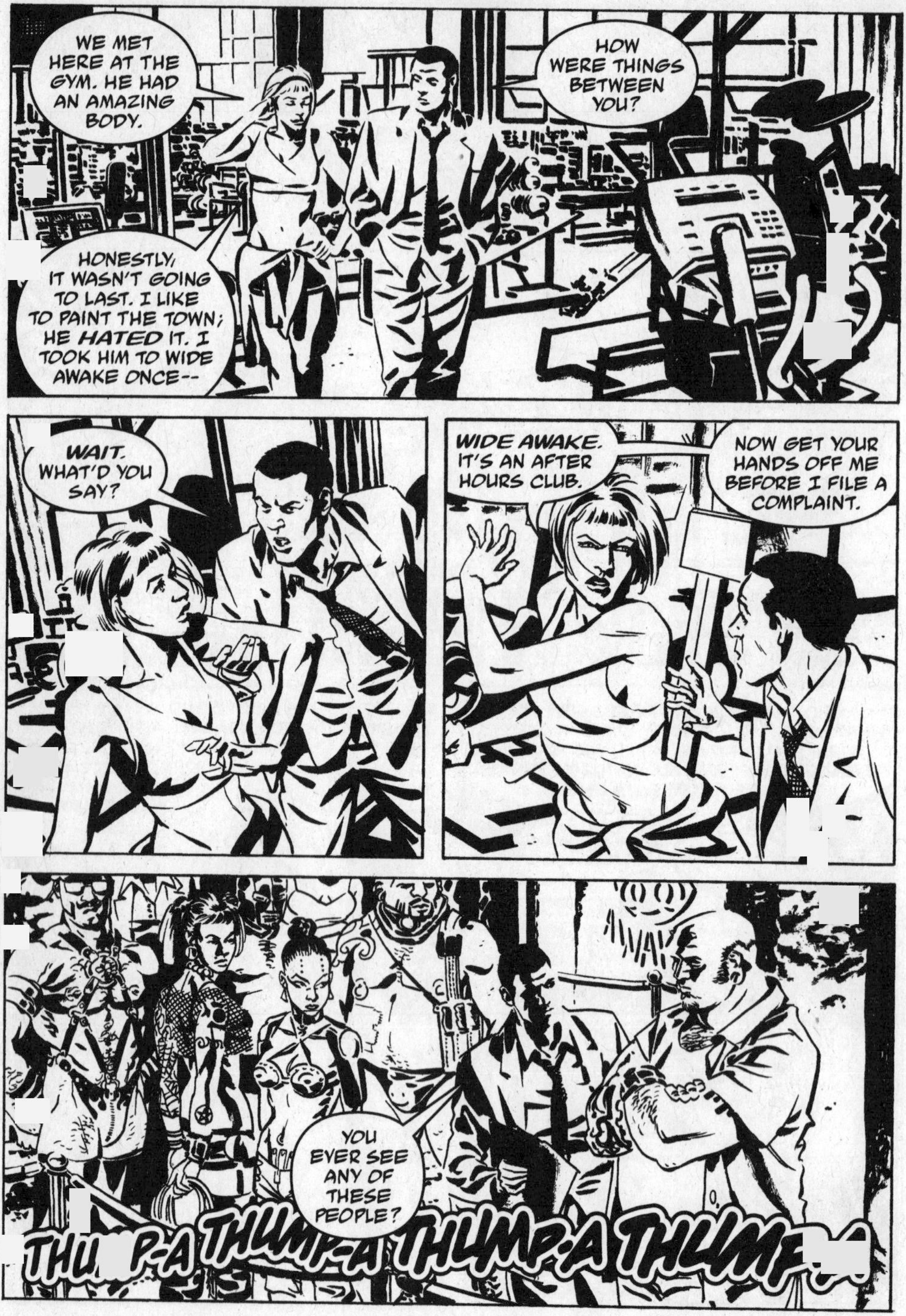

WE MET HERE AT THE GYM. HE HAD AN AMAZING BODY.
HOW WERE THINGS BETWEEN YOU?
HONESTLY, IT WASN'T GOING TO LAST. I LIKE TO PAINT THE TOWN; HE *HATED* IT. I TOOK HIM TO WIDE AWAKE ONCE--
WAIT. WHAT'D YOU SAY?
WIDE AWAKE. IT'S AN AFTER HOURS CLUB.
NOW GET YOUR HANDS OFF ME BEFORE I FILE A COMPLAINT.
YOU EVER SEE ANY OF THESE PEOPLE?
THUMP-A THUMP-A

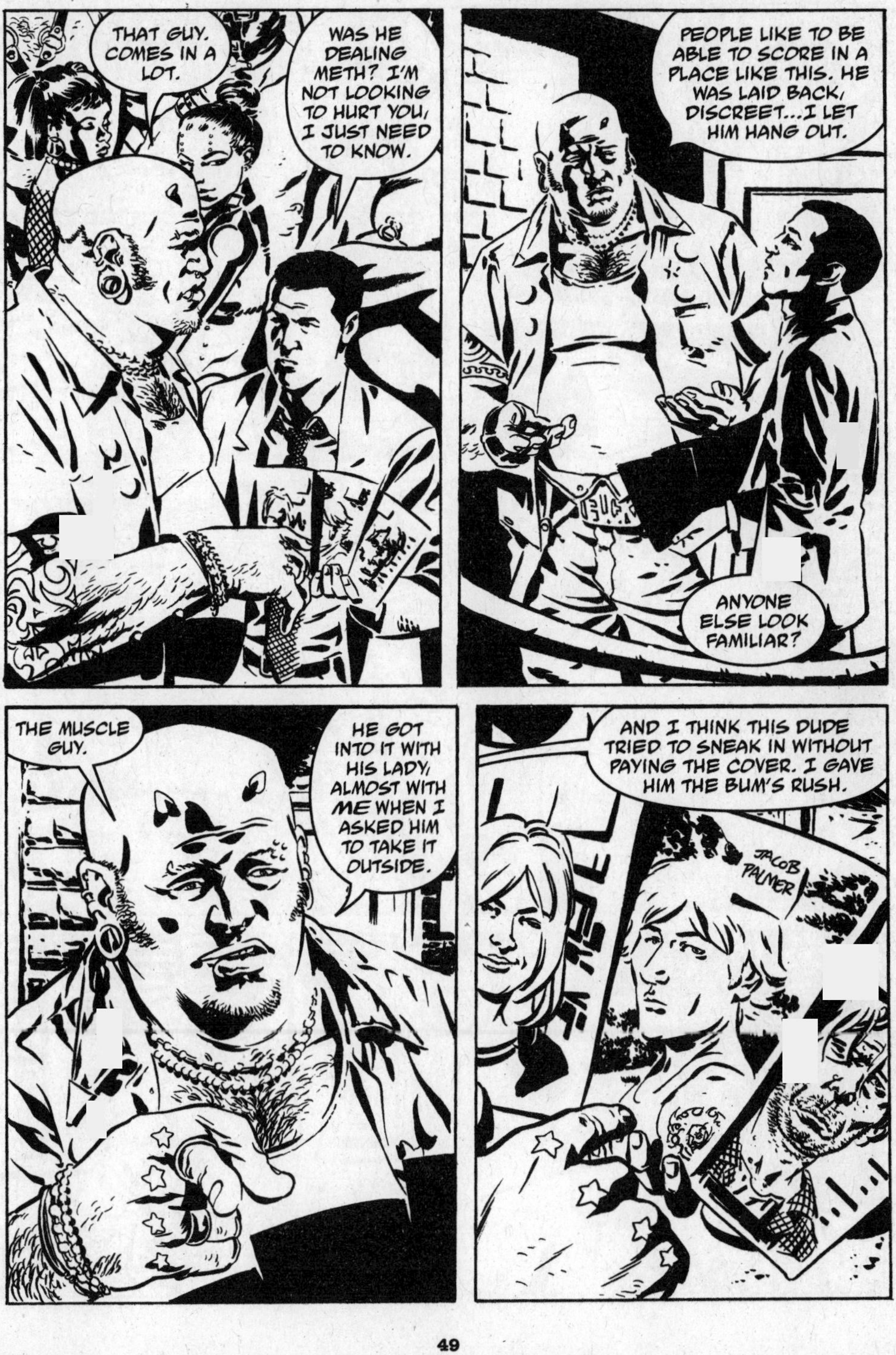
THAT GUY. COMES IN A LOT.
WAS HE DEALING METH? I'M NOT LOOKING TO HURT YOU, I JUST NEED TO KNOW.
PEOPLE LIKE TO BE ABLE TO SCORE IN A PLACE LIKE THIS. HE WAS LAID BACK, DISCREET...I LET HIM HANG OUT.
ANYONE ELSE LOOK FAMILIAR?
THE MUSCLE GUY.
HE GOT INTO IT WITH HIS LADY, ALMOST WITH *ME* WHEN I ASKED HIM TO TAKE IT OUTSIDE.
AND I THINK THIS DUDE TRIED TO SNEAK IN WITHOUT PAYING THE COVER. I GAVE HIM THE BUM'S RUSH.
JACOB PALMER

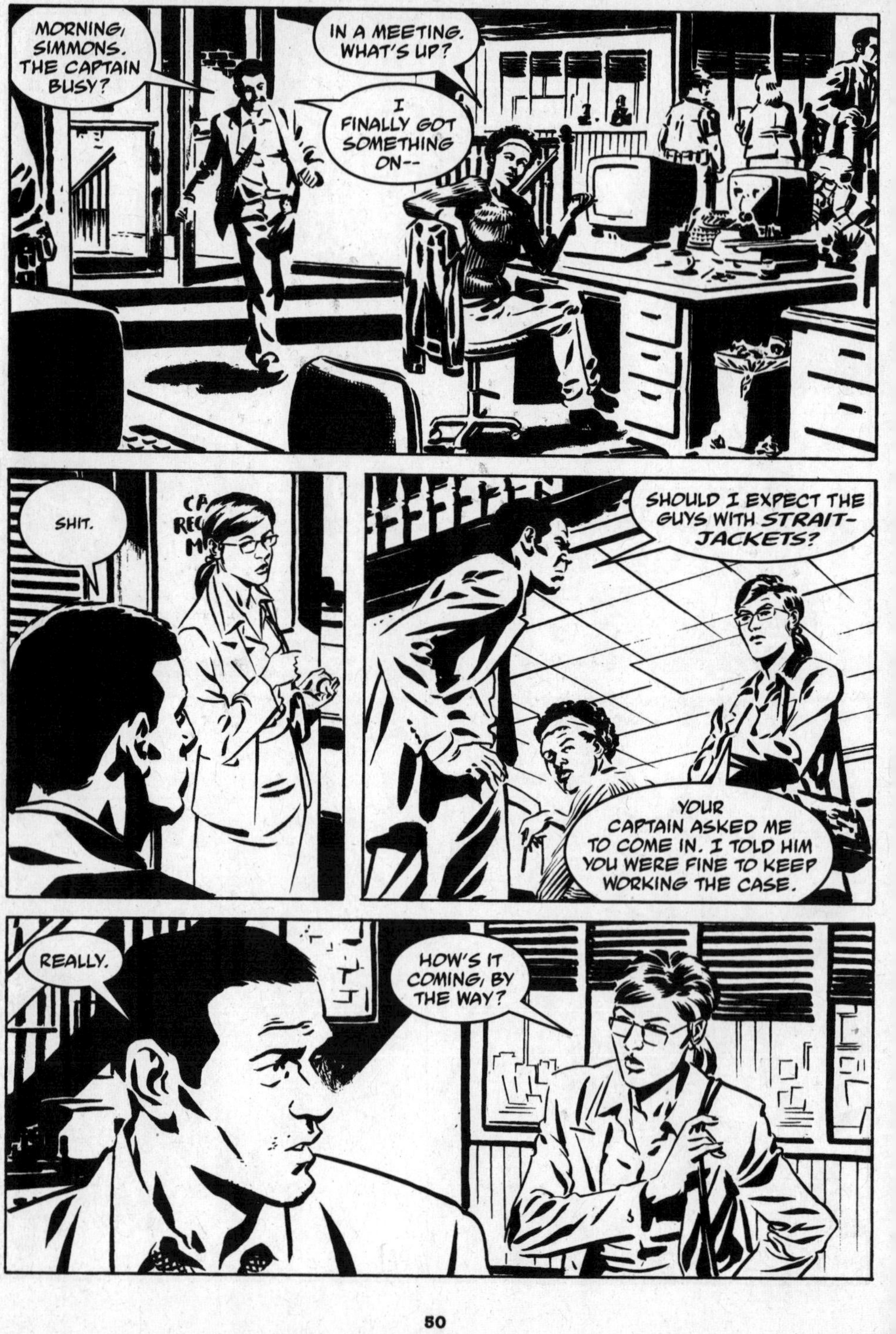
MORNING, SIMMONS. THE CAPTAIN BUSY?
IN A MEETING. WHAT'S UP?
I FINALLY GOT SOMETHING ON--
SHIT.
SHOULD I EXPECT THE GUYS WITH STRAIT-JACKETS?
YOUR CAPTAIN ASKED ME TO COME IN. I TOLD HIM YOU WERE FINE TO KEEP WORKING THE CASE.
REALLY.
HOW'S IT COMING, BY THE WAY?

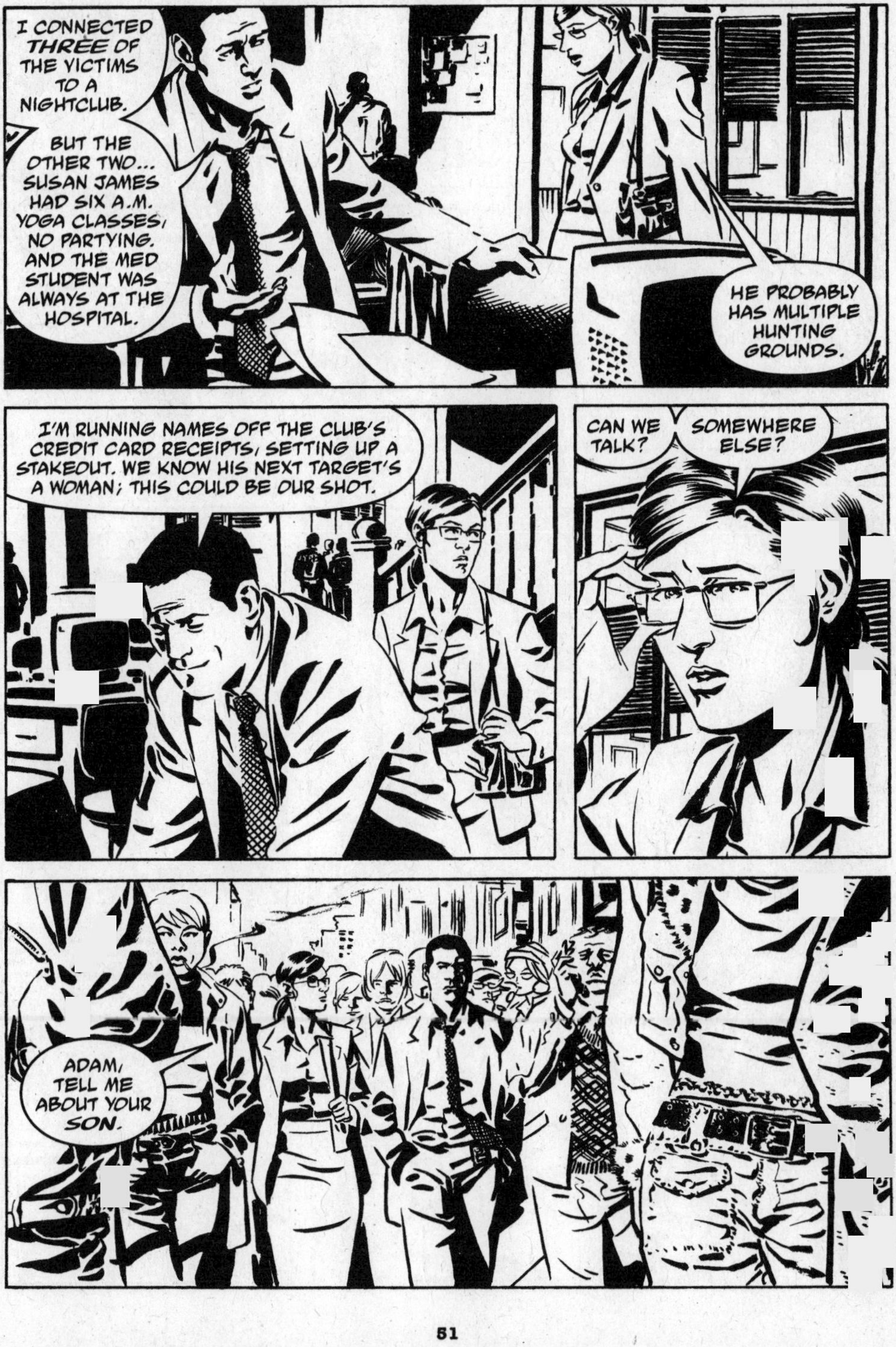
I CONNECTED THREE OF THE VICTIMS TO A NIGHTCLUB.
BUT THE OTHER TWO... SUSAN JAMES HAD SIX A.M. YOGA CLASSES, NO PARTYING. AND THE MED STUDENT WAS ALWAYS AT THE HOSPITAL.
HE PROBABLY HAS MULTIPLE HUNTING GROUNDS.
I'M RUNNING NAMES OFF THE CLUB'S CREDIT CARD RECEIPTS, SETTING UP A STAKEOUT. WE KNOW HIS NEXT TARGET'S A WOMAN; THIS COULD BE OUR SHOT.
CAN WE TALK?
SOMEWHERE ELSE?
ADAM, TELL ME ABOUT YOUR SON.

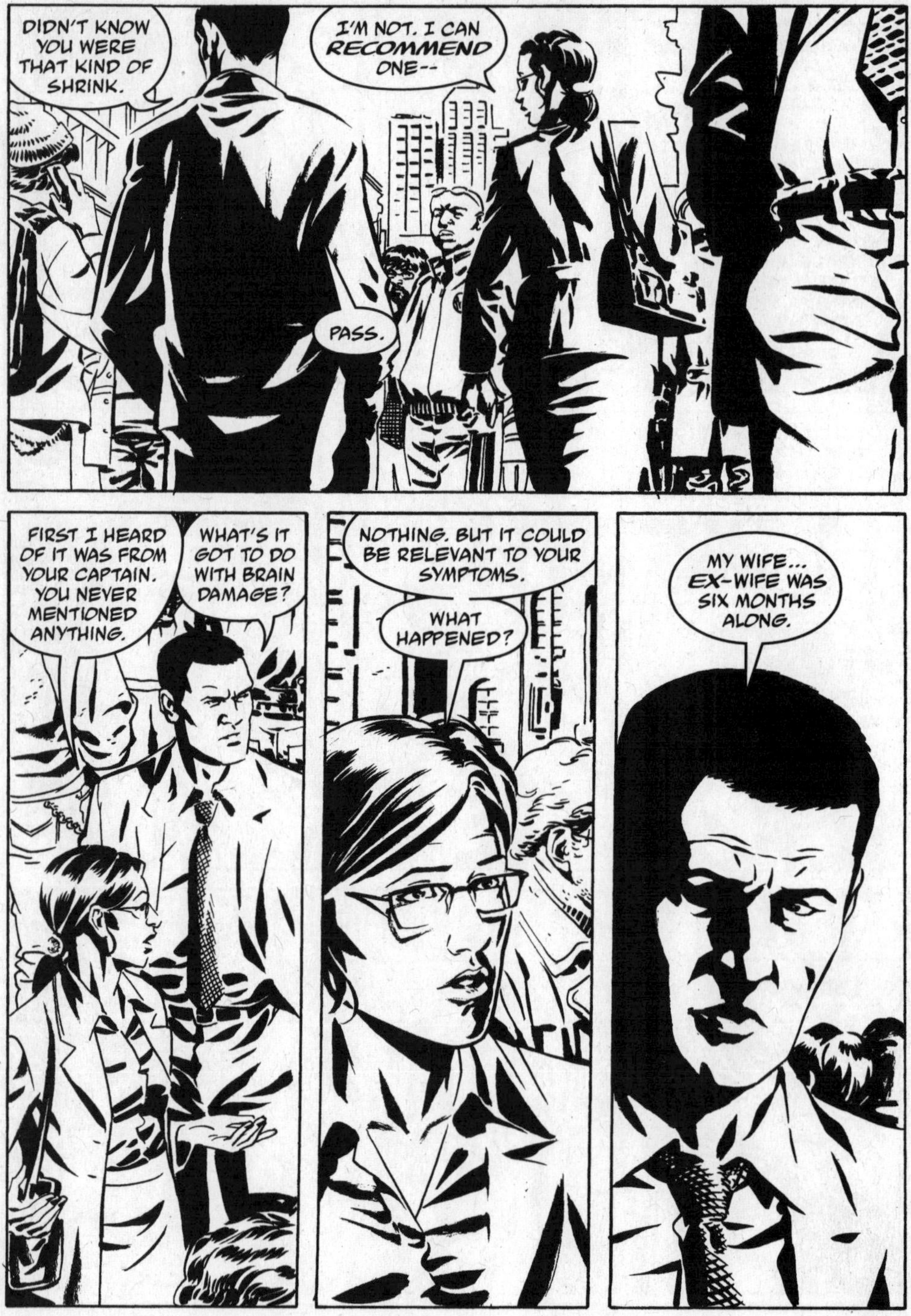
DIDN'T KNOW YOU WERE THAT KIND OF SHRINK.
I'M NOT. I CAN *RECOMMEND* ONE--
PASS.
FIRST I HEARD OF IT WAS FROM YOUR CAPTAIN. YOU NEVER MENTIONED ANYTHING.
WHAT'S IT GOT TO DO WITH BRAIN DAMAGE?
NOTHING. BUT IT COULD BE RELEVANT TO YOUR SYMPTOMS.
WHAT HAPPENED?
MY WIFE... *EX*-WIFE WAS SIX MONTHS ALONG.

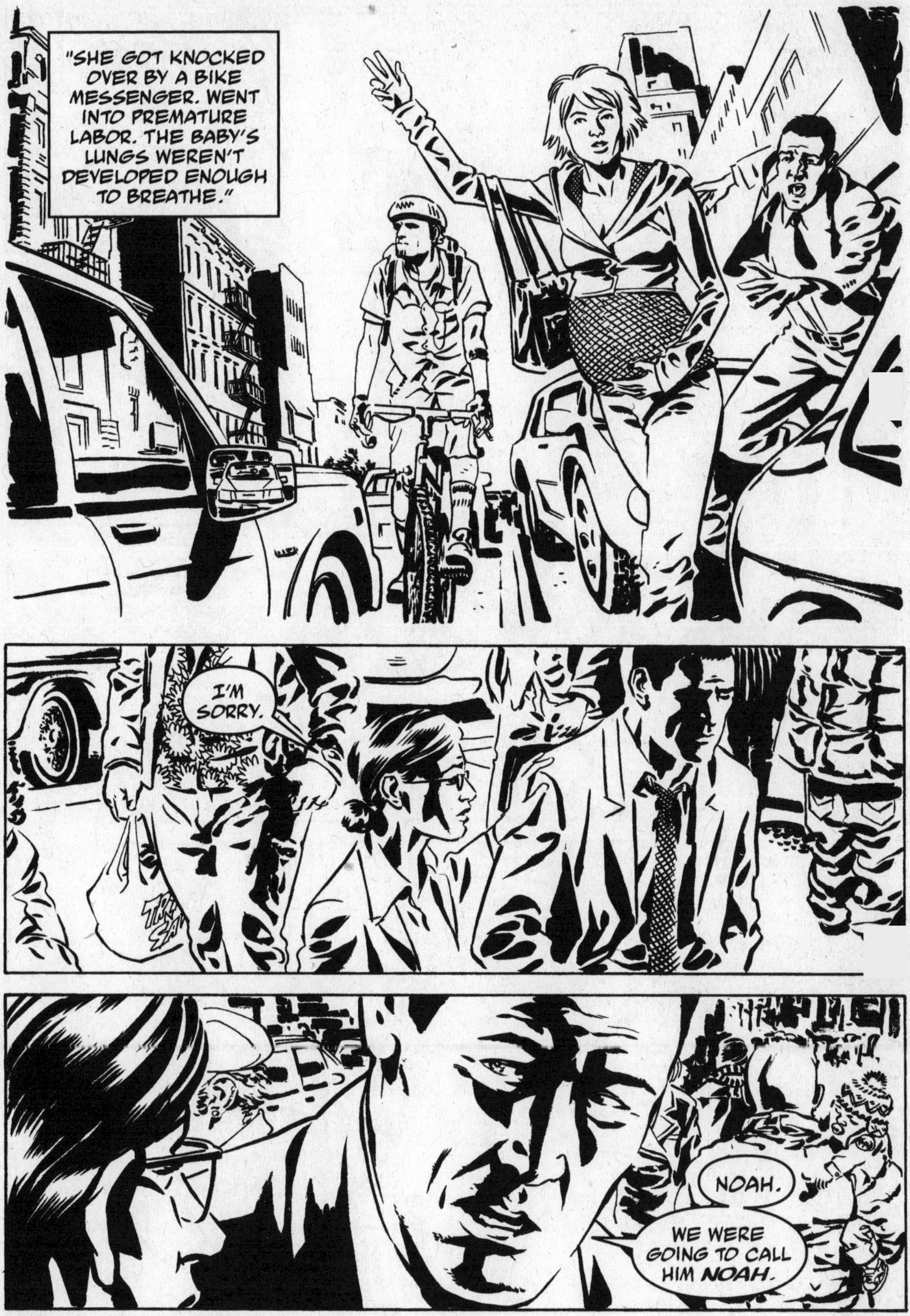
"SHE GOT KNOCKED OVER BY A BIKE MESSENGER. WENT INTO PREMATURE LABOR. THE BABY'S LUNGS WEREN'T DEVELOPED ENOUGH TO BREATHE."
I'M SORRY.
NOAH.
WE WERE GOING TO CALL HIM *NOAH*.

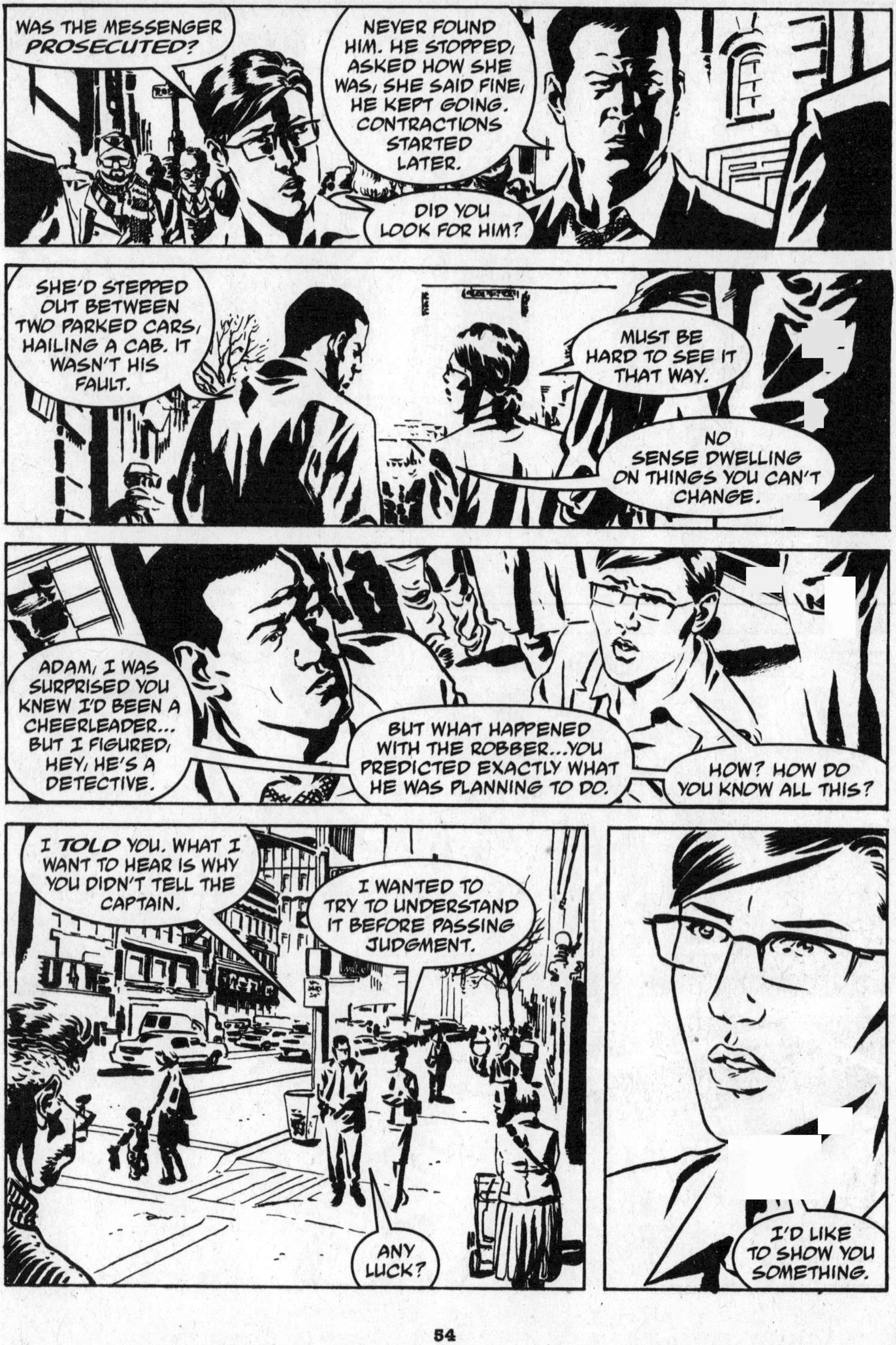
WAS THE MESSENGER *PROSECUTED?*
NEVER FOUND HIM. HE STOPPED, ASKED HOW SHE WAS, SHE SAID FINE, HE KEPT GOING. CONTRACTIONS STARTED LATER.
DID YOU LOOK FOR HIM?
SHE'D STEPPED OUT BETWEEN TWO PARKED CARS, HAILING A CAB. IT WASN'T HIS FAULT.
MUST BE HARD TO SEE IT THAT WAY.
NO SENSE DWELLING ON THINGS YOU CAN'T CHANGE.
ADAM, I WAS SURPRISED YOU KNEW I'D BEEN A CHEERLEADER... BUT I FIGURED, HEY, HE'S A DETECTIVE.
BUT WHAT HAPPENED WITH THE ROBBER...YOU PREDICTED EXACTLY WHAT HE WAS PLANNING TO DO.
HOW? HOW DO YOU KNOW ALL THIS?
I *TOLD* YOU. WHAT I WANT TO HEAR IS WHY YOU DIDN'T TELL THE CAPTAIN.
I WANTED TO TRY TO UNDERSTAND IT BEFORE PASSING JUDGMENT.
ANY LUCK?
I'D LIKE TO SHOW YOU SOMETHING.

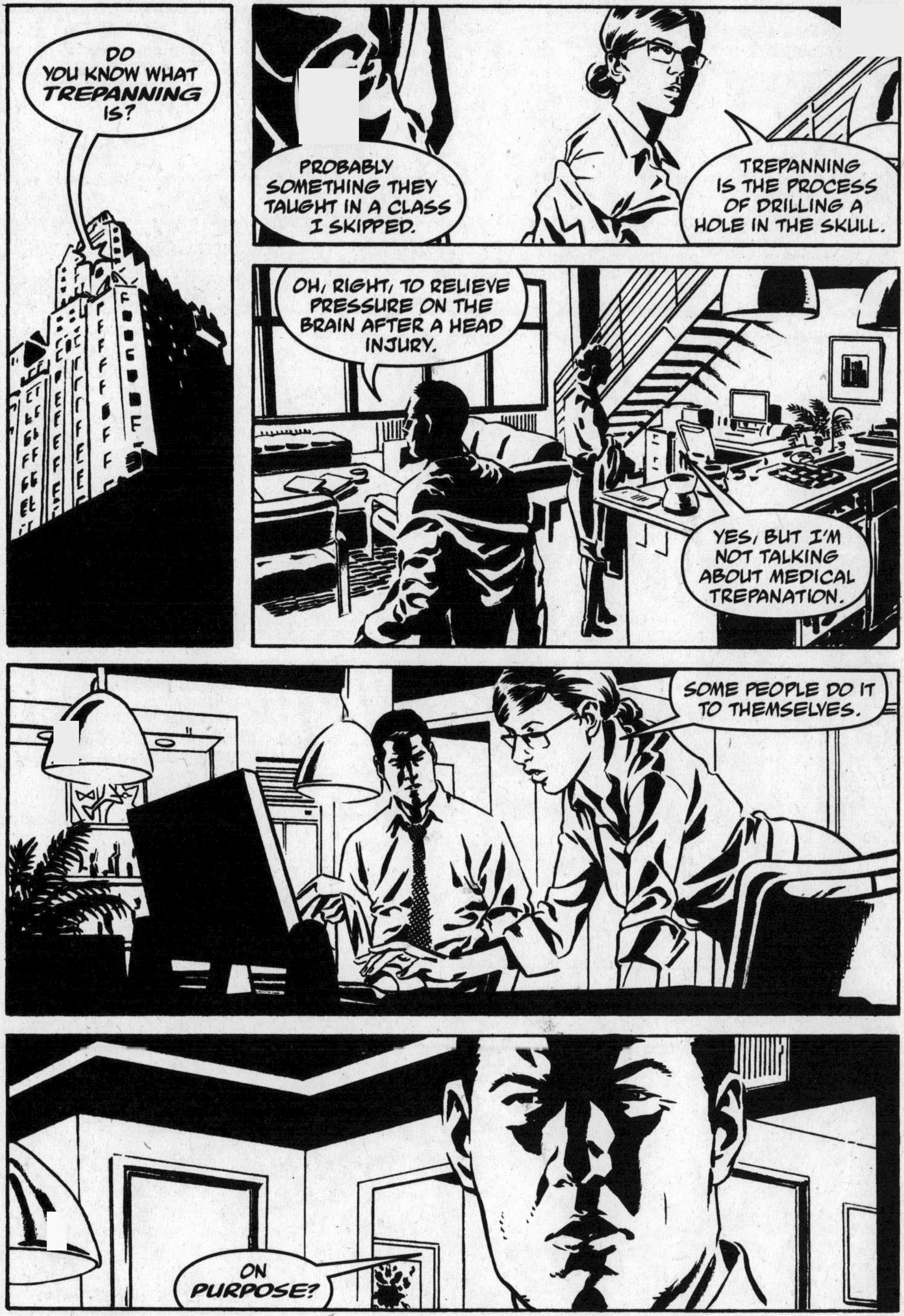
DO YOU KNOW WHAT TREPANNING IS?
PROBABLY SOMETHING THEY TAUGHT IN A CLASS I SKIPPED.
TREPANNING IS THE PROCESS OF DRILLING A HOLE IN THE SKULL.
OH, RIGHT, TO RELIEVE PRESSURE ON THE BRAIN AFTER A HEAD INJURY.
YES, BUT I'M NOT TALKING ABOUT MEDICAL TREPANATION.
SOME PEOPLE DO IT TO THEMSELVES.
ON PURPOSE?

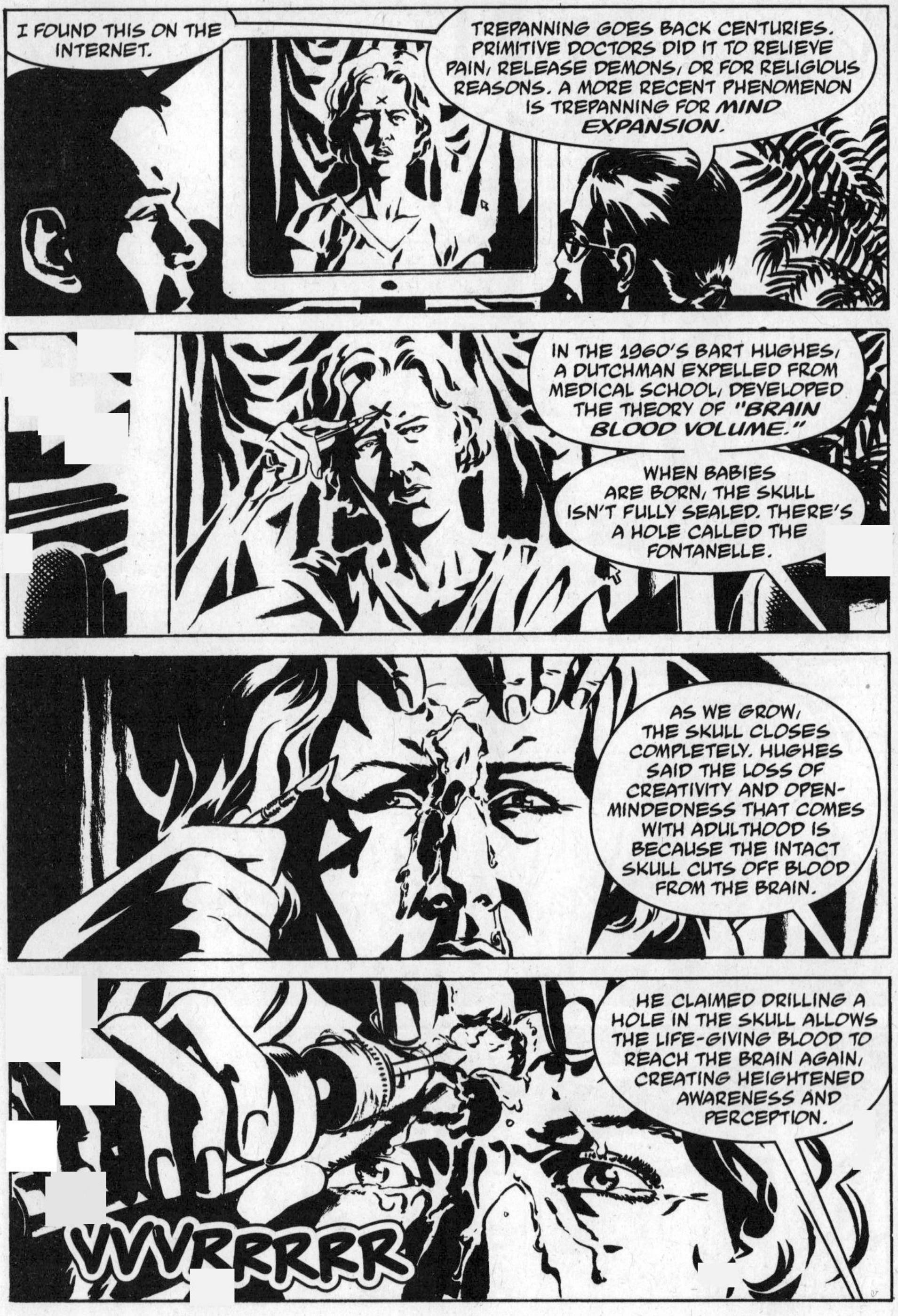
I FOUND THIS ON THE INTERNET.
TREPANNING GOES BACK CENTURIES. PRIMITIVE DOCTORS DID IT TO RELIEVE PAIN, RELEASE DEMONS, OR FOR RELIGIOUS REASONS. A MORE RECENT PHENOMENON IS TREPANNING FOR MIND EXPANSION.
IN THE 1960'S BART HUGHES, A DUTCHMAN EXPELLED FROM MEDICAL SCHOOL, DEVELOPED THE THEORY OF "BRAIN BLOOD VOLUME."
WHEN BABIES ARE BORN, THE SKULL ISN'T FULLY SEALED. THERE'S A HOLE CALLED THE FONTANELLE.
AS WE GROW, THE SKULL CLOSES COMPLETELY. HUGHES SAID THE LOSS OF CREATIVITY AND OPEN-MINDEDNESS THAT COMES WITH ADULTHOOD IS BECAUSE THE INTACT SKULL CUTS OFF BLOOD FROM THE BRAIN.
HE CLAIMED DRILLING A HOLE IN THE SKULL ALLOWS THE LIFE-GIVING BLOOD TO REACH THE BRAIN AGAIN, CREATING HEIGHTENED AWARENESS AND PERCEPTION.
VVVRRRRR

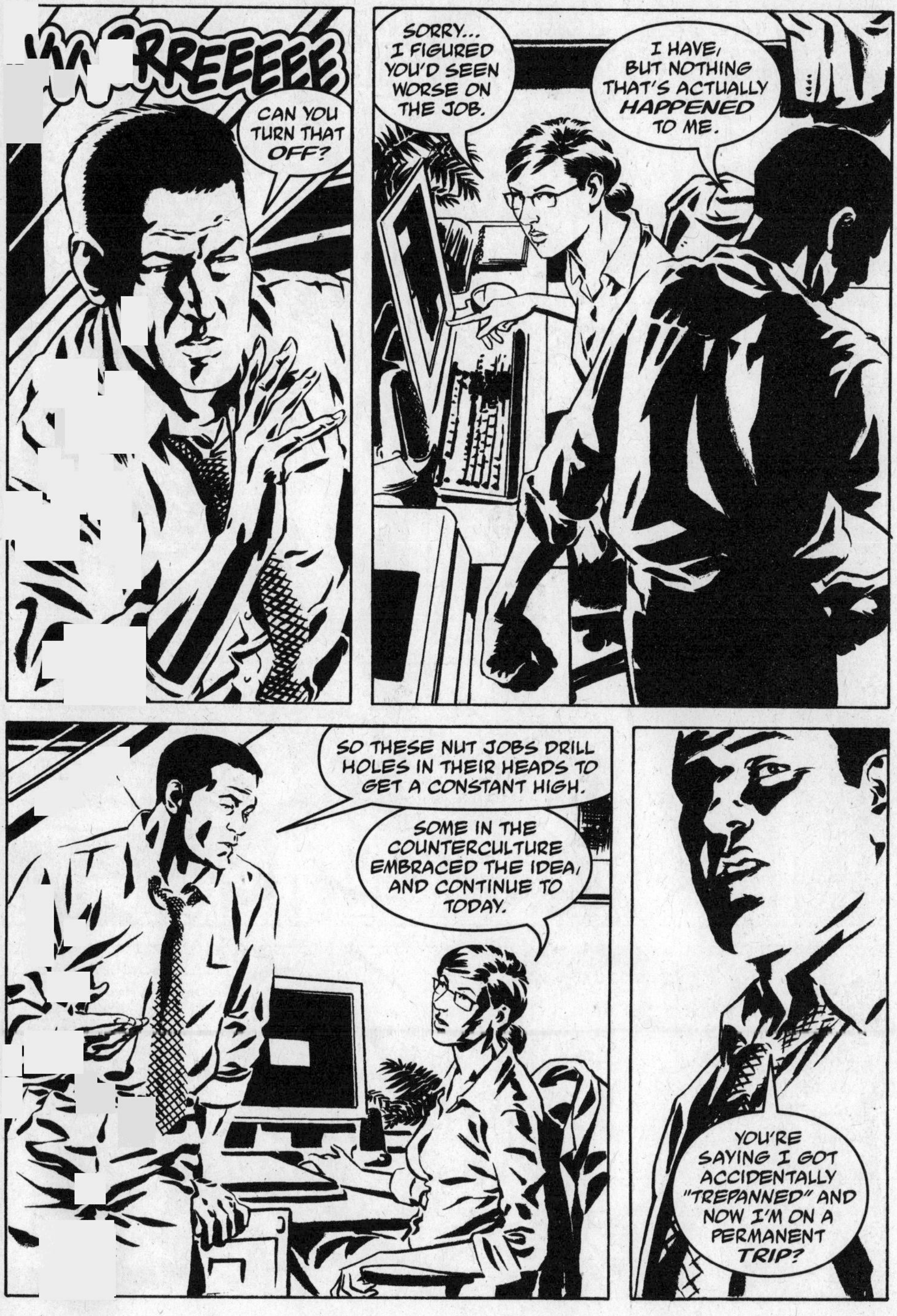
CAN YOU TURN THAT OFF?
SORRY... I FIGURED YOU'D SEEN WORSE ON THE JOB.
I HAVE, BUT NOTHING THAT'S ACTUALLY HAPPENED TO ME.
SO THESE NUT JOBS DRILL HOLES IN THEIR HEADS TO GET A CONSTANT HIGH.
SOME IN THE COUNTERCULTURE EMBRACED THE IDEA, AND CONTINUE TO TODAY.
YOU'RE SAYING I GOT ACCIDENTALLY "TREPANNED" AND NOW I'M ON A PERMANENT TRIP?

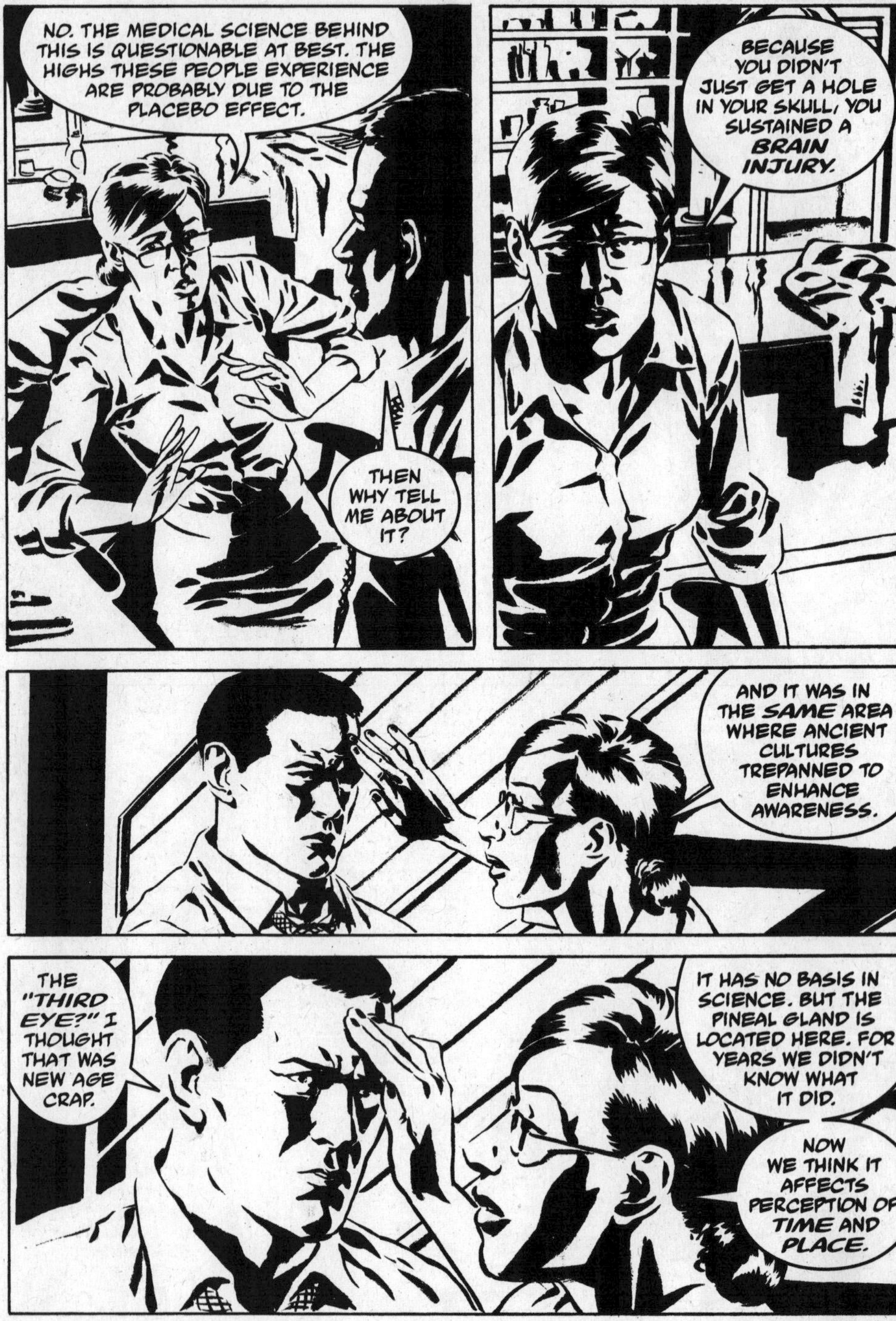
NO. THE MEDICAL SCIENCE BEHIND THIS IS QUESTIONABLE AT BEST. THE HIGHS THESE PEOPLE EXPERIENCE ARE PROBABLY DUE TO THE PLACEBO EFFECT.
THEN WHY TELL ME ABOUT IT?
BECAUSE YOU DIDN'T JUST GET A HOLE IN YOUR SKULL, YOU SUSTAINED A *BRAIN INJURY.*
AND IT WAS IN THE *SAME* AREA WHERE ANCIENT CULTURES TREPANNED TO ENHANCE AWARENESS.
THE *"THIRD EYE?"* I THOUGHT THAT WAS NEW AGE CRAP.
IT HAS NO BASIS IN SCIENCE. BUT THE PINEAL GLAND IS LOCATED HERE. FOR YEARS WE DIDN'T KNOW WHAT IT DID.
NOW WE THINK IT AFFECTS PERCEPTION OF *TIME* AND *PLACE.*

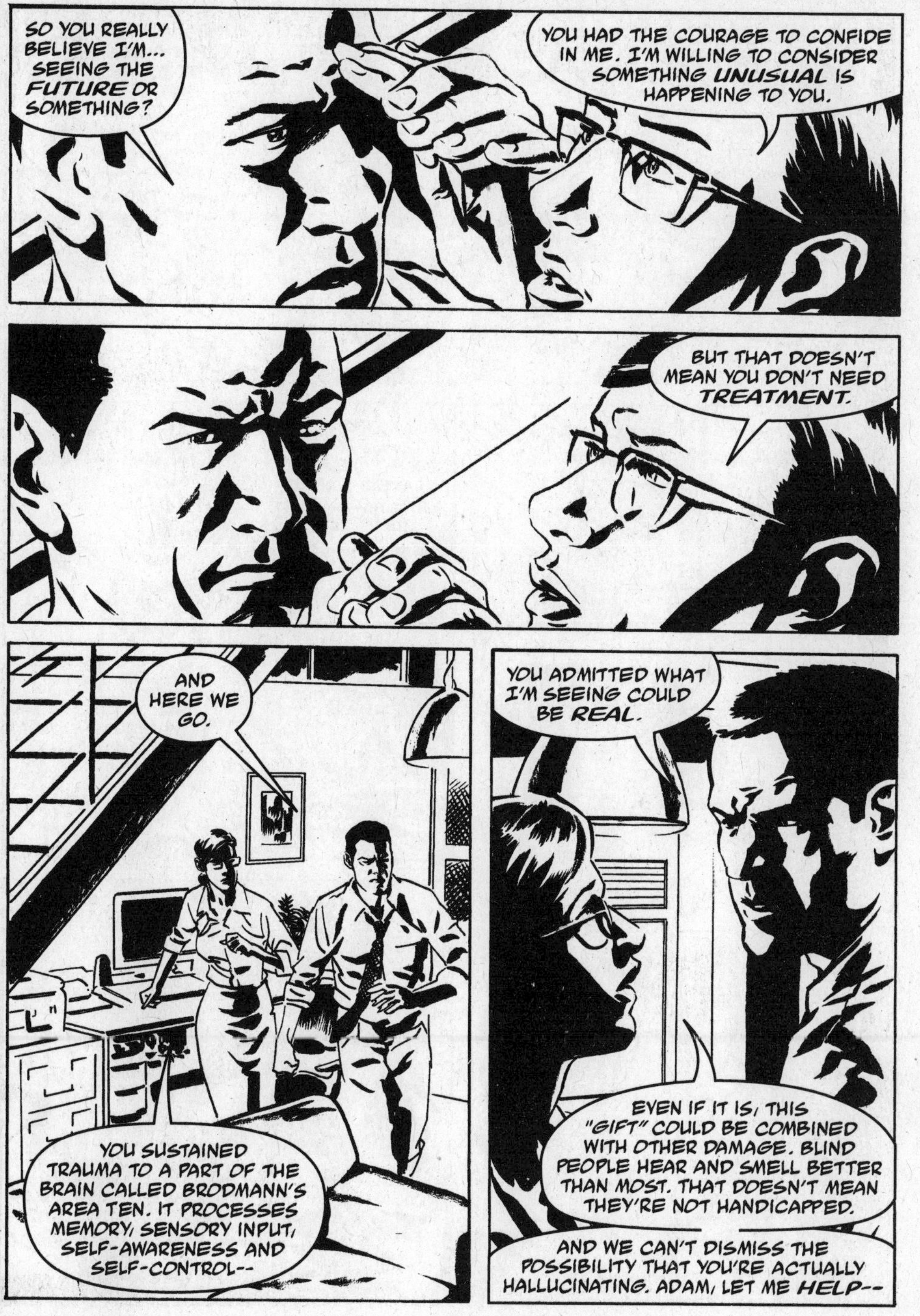
SO YOU REALLY BELIEVE I'M... SEEING THE FUTURE OR SOMETHING?
YOU HAD THE COURAGE TO CONFIDE IN ME. I'M WILLING TO CONSIDER SOMETHING UNUSUAL IS HAPPENING TO YOU.
BUT THAT DOESN'T MEAN YOU DON'T NEED TREATMENT.
AND HERE WE GO.
YOU SUSTAINED TRAUMA TO A PART OF THE BRAIN CALLED BRODMANN'S AREA TEN. IT PROCESSES MEMORY, SENSORY INPUT, SELF-AWARENESS AND SELF-CONTROL--
YOU ADMITTED WHAT I'M SEEING COULD BE REAL.
EVEN IF IT IS, THIS "GIFT" COULD BE COMBINED WITH OTHER DAMAGE. BLIND PEOPLE HEAR AND SMELL BETTER THAN MOST. THAT DOESN'T MEAN THEY'RE NOT HANDICAPPED.
AND WE CAN'T DISMISS THE POSSIBILITY THAT YOU'RE ACTUALLY HALLUCINATING. ADAM, LET ME HELP--

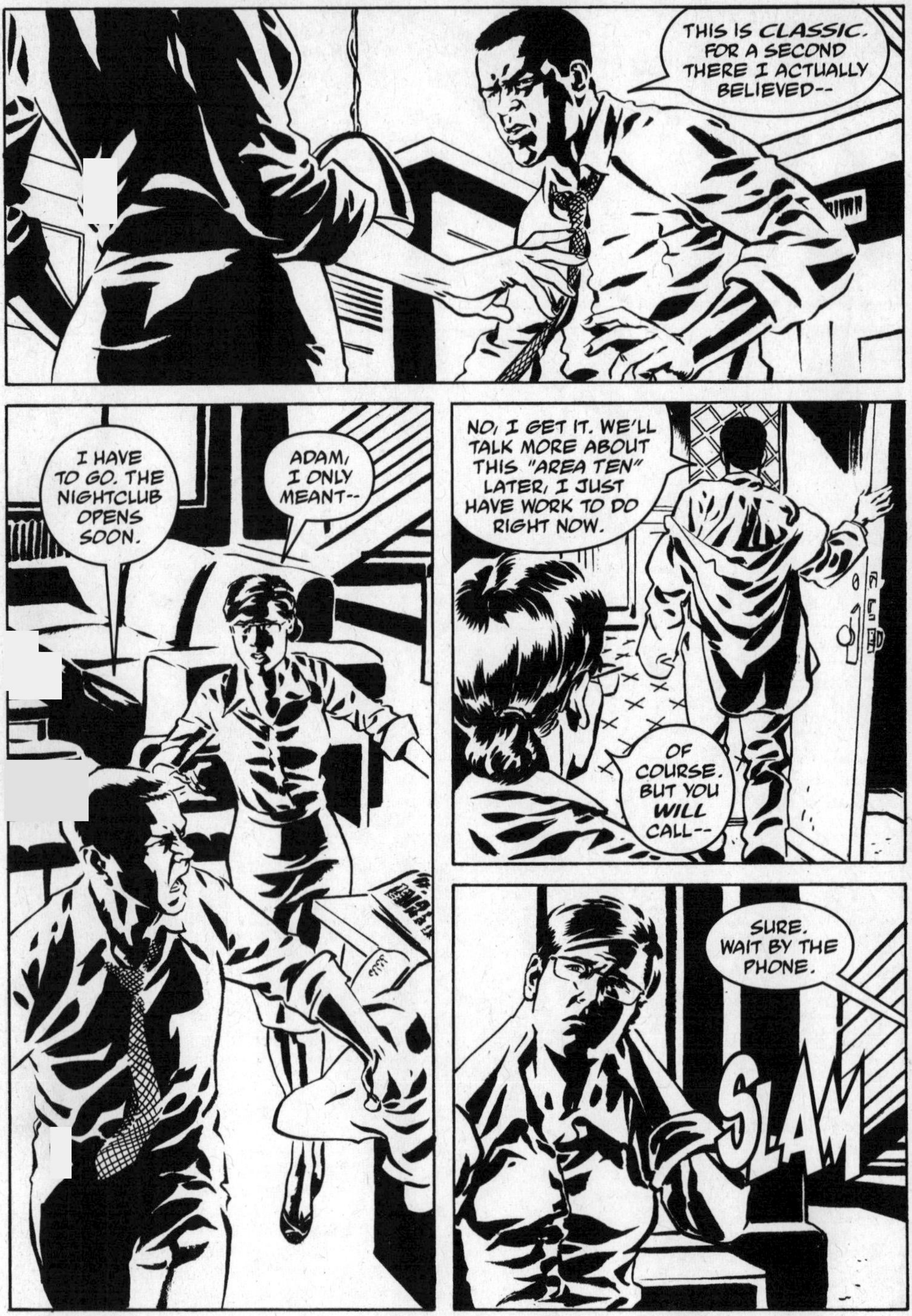
THIS IS CLASSIC. FOR A SECOND THERE I ACTUALLY BELIEVED--
I HAVE TO GO. THE NIGHTCLUB OPENS SOON.
ADAM, I ONLY MEANT--
NO, I GET IT. WE'LL TALK MORE ABOUT THIS "AREA TEN" LATER, I JUST HAVE WORK TO DO RIGHT NOW.
OF COURSE. BUT YOU WILL CALL--
SURE. WAIT BY THE PHONE.
SLAM

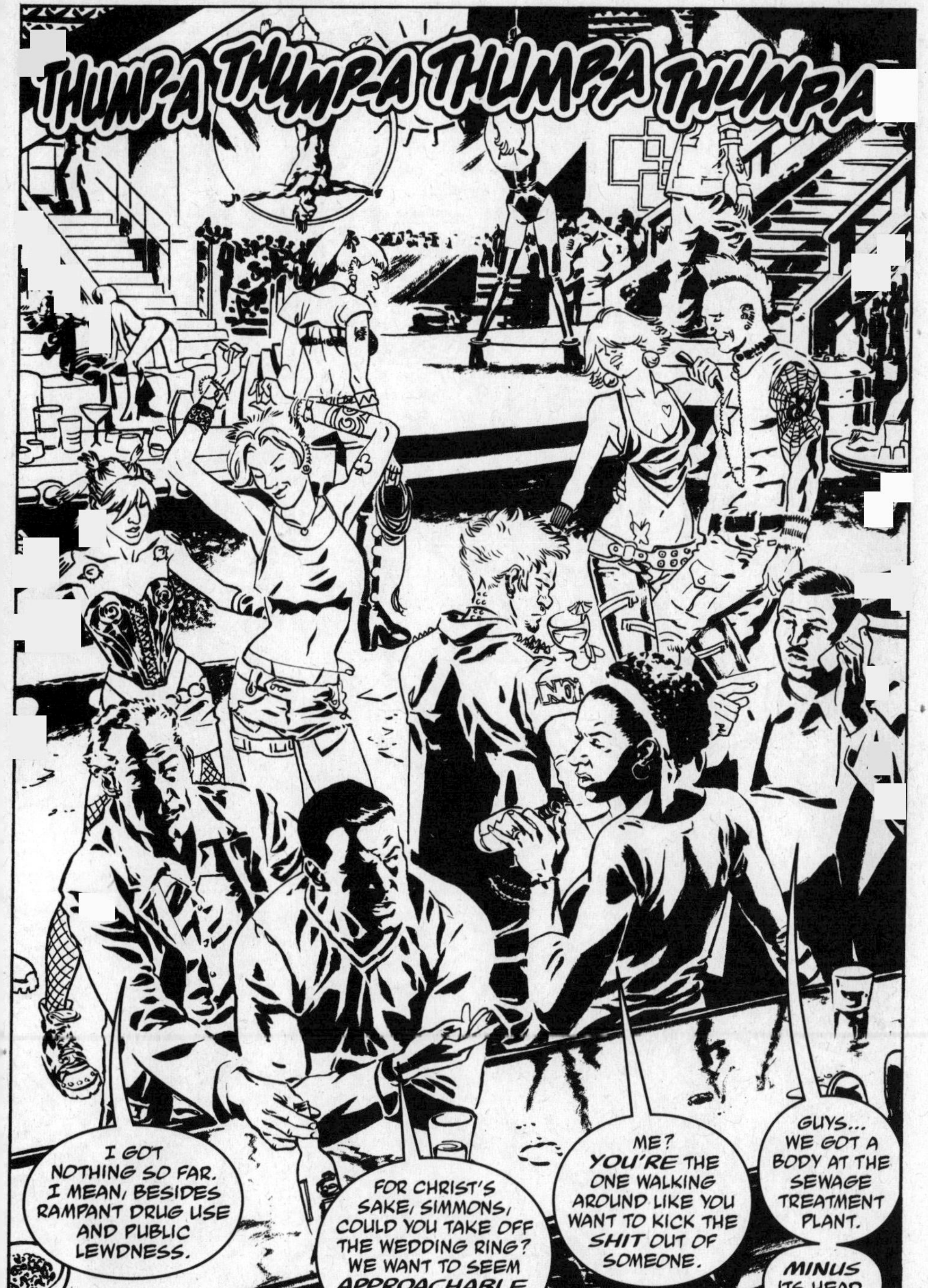
THUMP-A THUMP-A THUMP-A THUMP-A
I GOT NOTHING SO FAR. I MEAN, BESIDES RAMPANT DRUG USE AND PUBLIC LEWDNESS.
FOR CHRIST'S SAKE, SIMMONS, COULD YOU TAKE OFF THE WEDDING RING? WE WANT TO SEEM APPROACHABLE.
ME? YOU'RE THE ONE WALKING AROUND LIKE YOU WANT TO KICK THE SHIT OUT OF SOMEONE.
GUYS... WE GOT A BODY AT THE SEWAGE TREATMENT PLANT.
MINUS ITS HEAD.

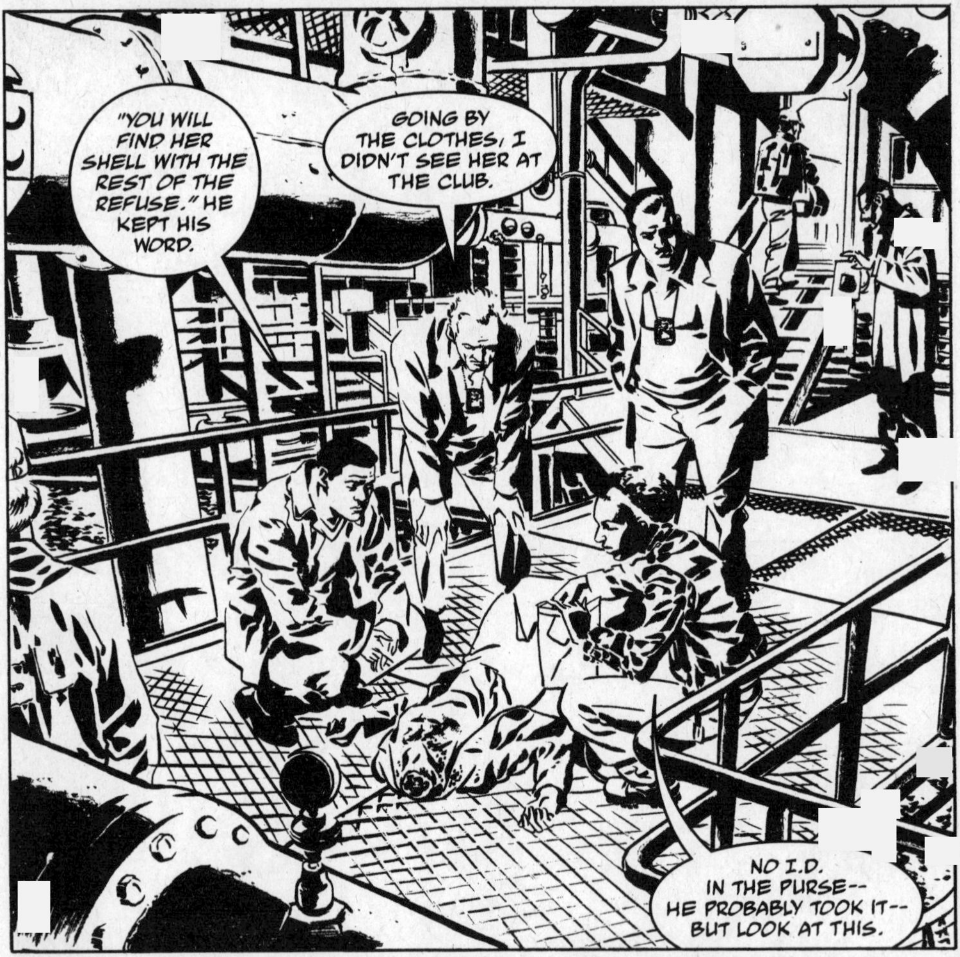
"YOU WILL FIND HER SHELL WITH THE REST OF THE REFUSE." HE KEPT HIS WORD.
GOING BY THE CLOTHES, I DIDN'T SEE HER AT THE CLUB.
NO I.D. IN THE PURSE-- HE PROBABLY TOOK IT-- BUT LOOK AT THIS.

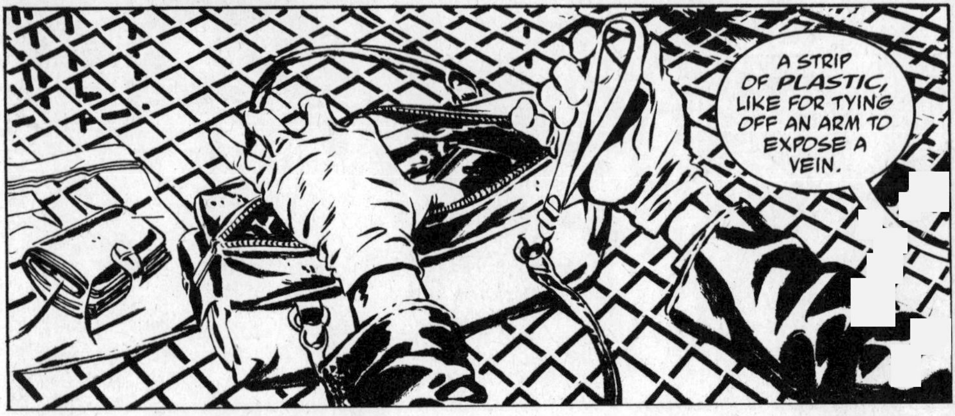
A STRIP OF *PLASTIC,* LIKE FOR TYING OFF AN ARM TO EXPOSE A VEIN.

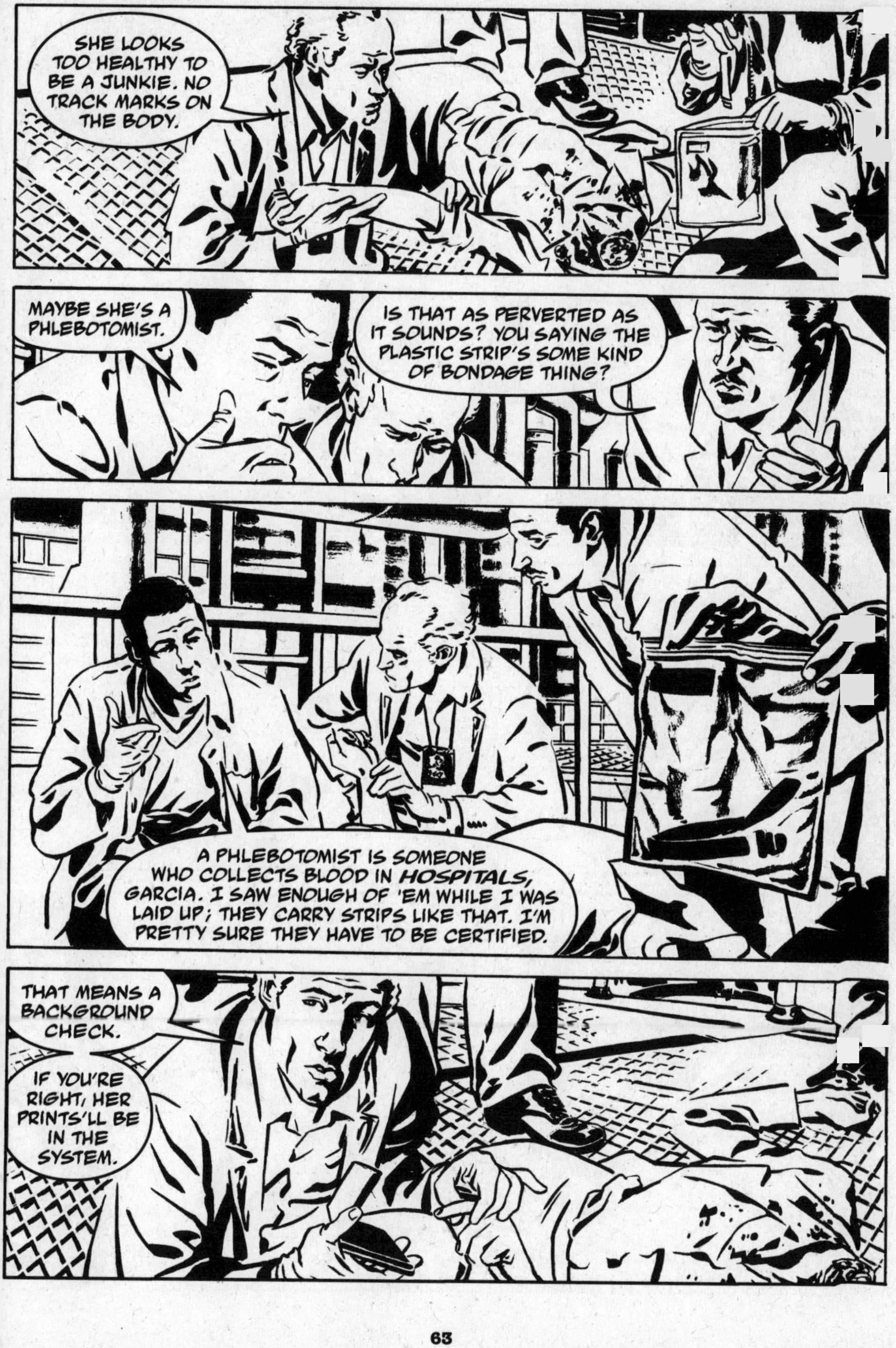
SHE LOOKS TOO HEALTHY TO BE A JUNKIE. NO TRACK MARKS ON THE BODY.
MAYBE SHE'S A PHLEBOTOMIST.
IS THAT AS PERVERTED AS IT SOUNDS? YOU SAYING THE PLASTIC STRIP'S SOME KIND OF BONDAGE THING?
A PHLEBOTOMIST IS SOMEONE WHO COLLECTS BLOOD IN *HOSPITALS*, GARCIA. I SAW ENOUGH OF 'EM WHILE I WAS LAID UP; THEY CARRY STRIPS LIKE THAT. I'M PRETTY SURE THEY HAVE TO BE CERTIFIED.
THAT MEANS A BACKGROUND CHECK.
IF YOU'RE RIGHT, HER PRINTS'LL BE IN THE SYSTEM.

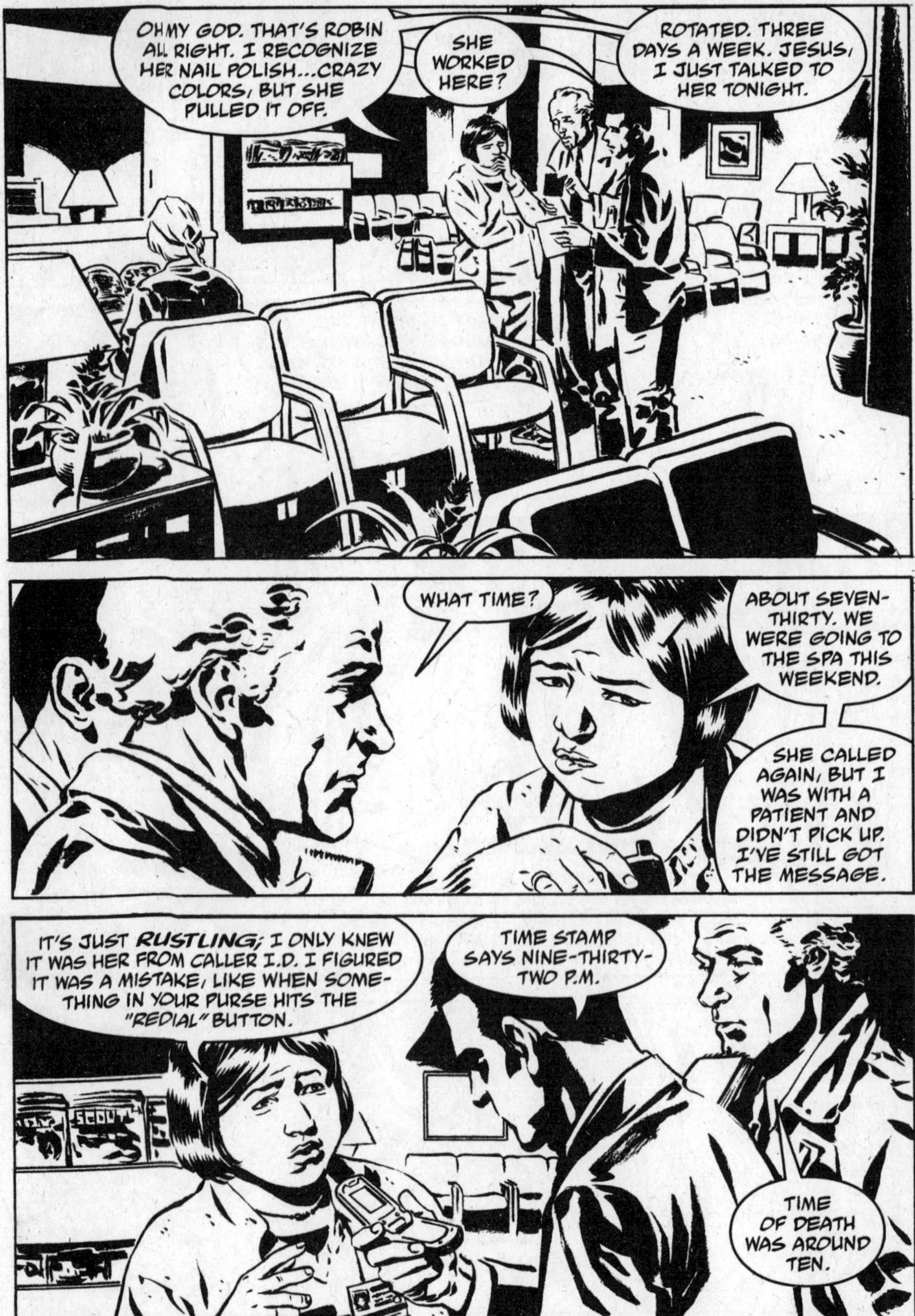
OHMY GOD. THAT'S ROBIN ALL RIGHT. I RECOGNIZE HER NAIL POLISH...CRAZY COLORS, BUT SHE PULLED IT OFF.
SHE WORKED HERE?
ROTATED. THREE DAYS A WEEK. JESUS, I JUST TALKED TO HER TONIGHT.
WHAT TIME?
ABOUT SEVEN-THIRTY. WE WERE GOING TO THE SPA THIS WEEKEND.
SHE CALLED AGAIN, BUT I WAS WITH A PATIENT AND DIDN'T PICK UP. I'VE STILL GOT THE MESSAGE.
IT'S JUST ***RUSTLING;*** I ONLY KNEW IT WAS HER FROM CALLER I.D. I FIGURED IT WAS A MISTAKE, LIKE WHEN SOME-THING IN YOUR PURSE HITS THE *"REDIAL"* BUTTON.
TIME STAMP SAYS NINE-THIRTY-TWO P.M.
TIME OF DEATH WAS AROUND TEN.

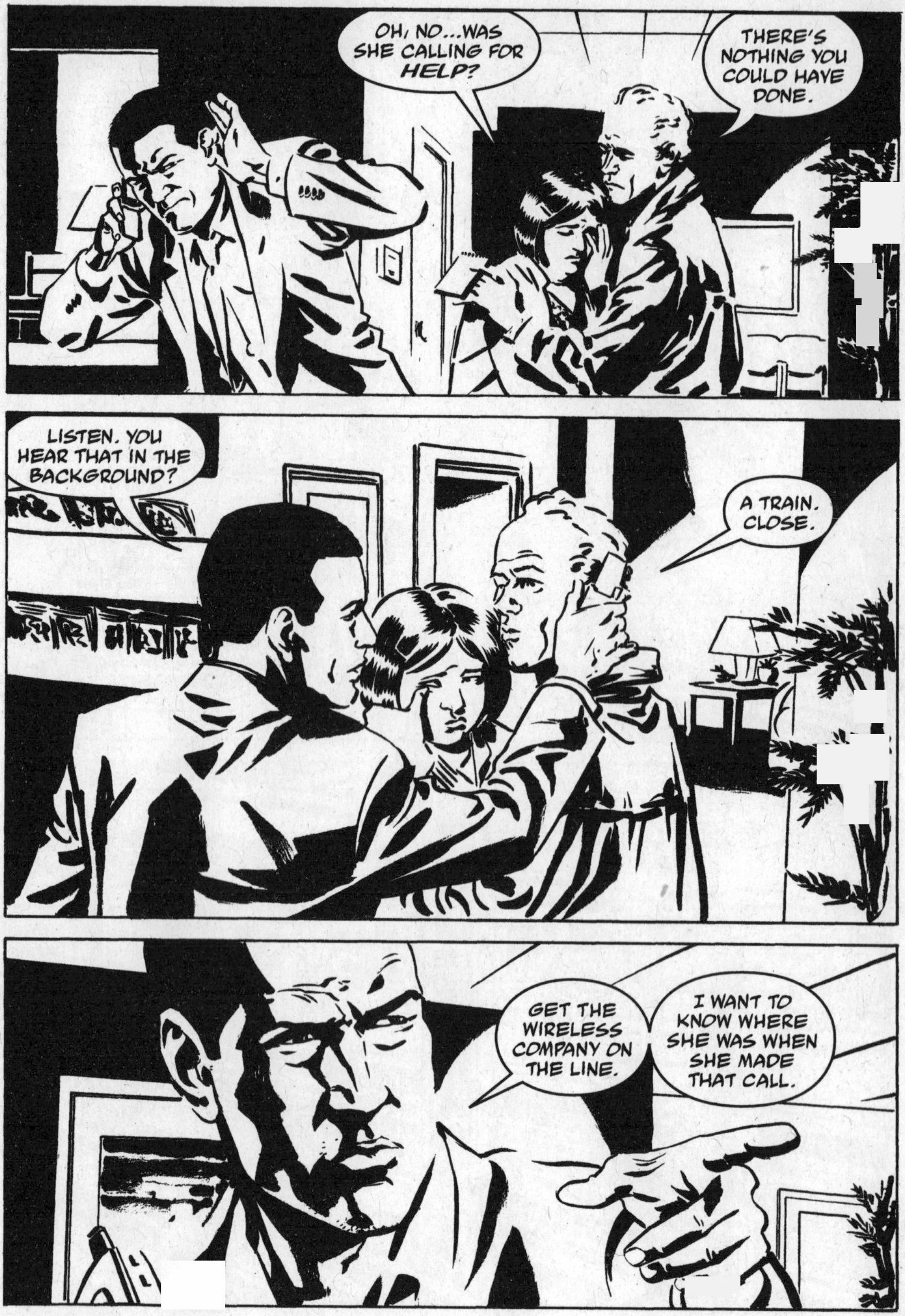
OH, NO...WAS SHE CALLING FOR HELP?
THERE'S NOTHING YOU COULD HAVE DONE.
LISTEN. YOU HEAR THAT IN THE BACKGROUND?
A TRAIN. CLOSE.
GET THE WIRELESS COMPANY ON THE LINE.
I WANT TO KNOW WHERE SHE WAS WHEN SHE MADE THAT CALL.

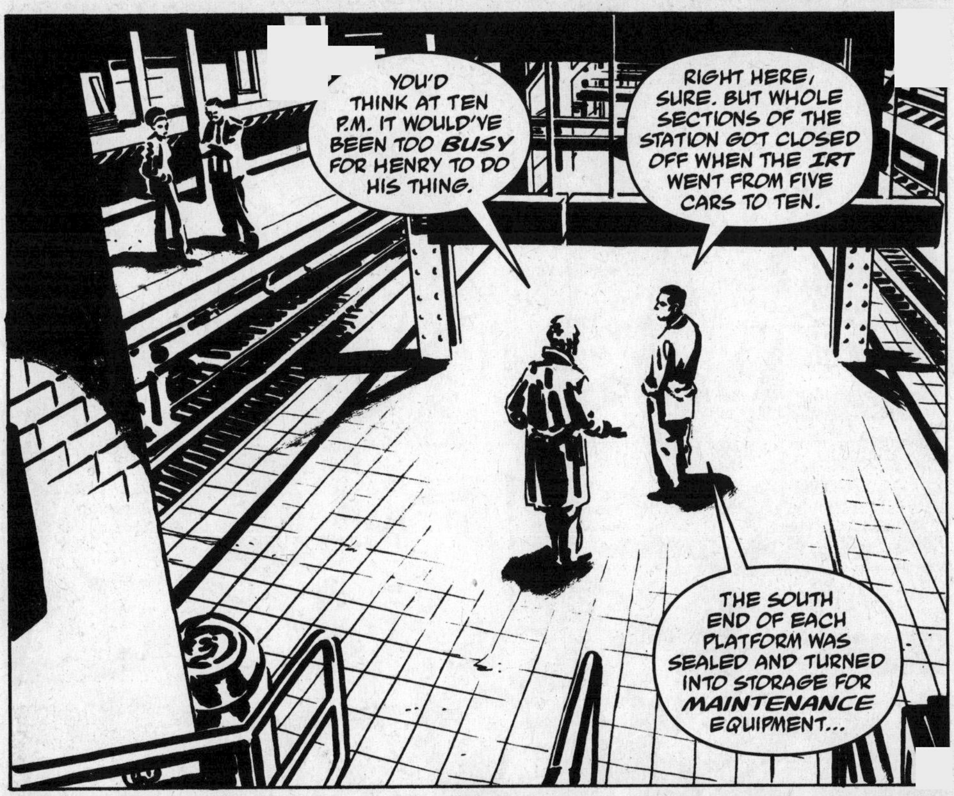
YOU'D THINK AT TEN P.M. IT WOULD'VE BEEN TOO BUSY FOR HENRY TO DO HIS THING.
RIGHT HERE, SURE. BUT WHOLE SECTIONS OF THE STATION GOT CLOSED OFF WHEN THE IRT WENT FROM FIVE CARS TO TEN.
THE SOUTH END OF EACH PLATFORM WAS SEALED AND TURNED INTO STORAGE FOR MAINTENANCE EQUIPMENT...

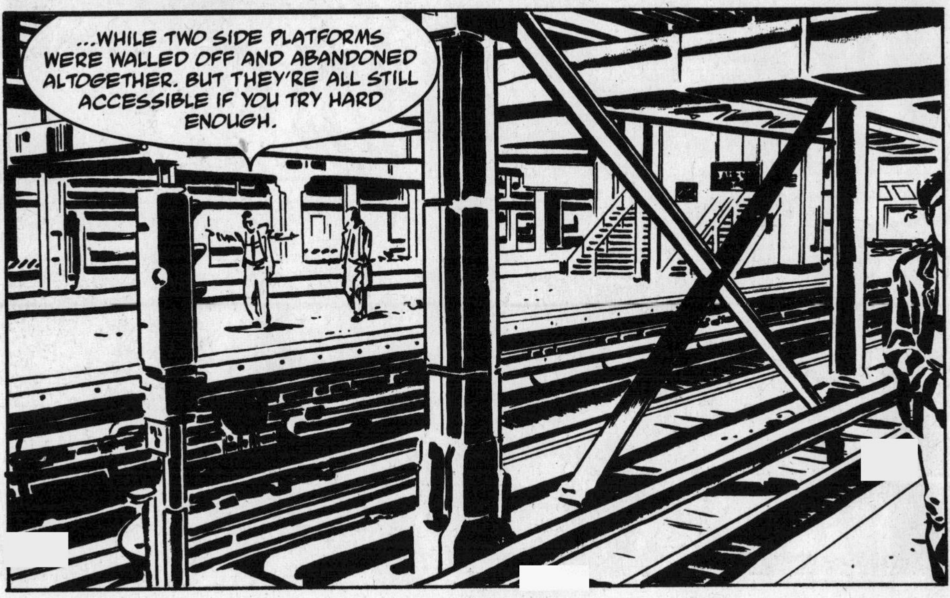
...WHILE TWO SIDE PLATFORMS WERE WALLED OFF AND ABANDONED ALTOGETHER. BUT THEY'RE ALL STILL ACCESSIBLE IF YOU TRY HARD ENOUGH.

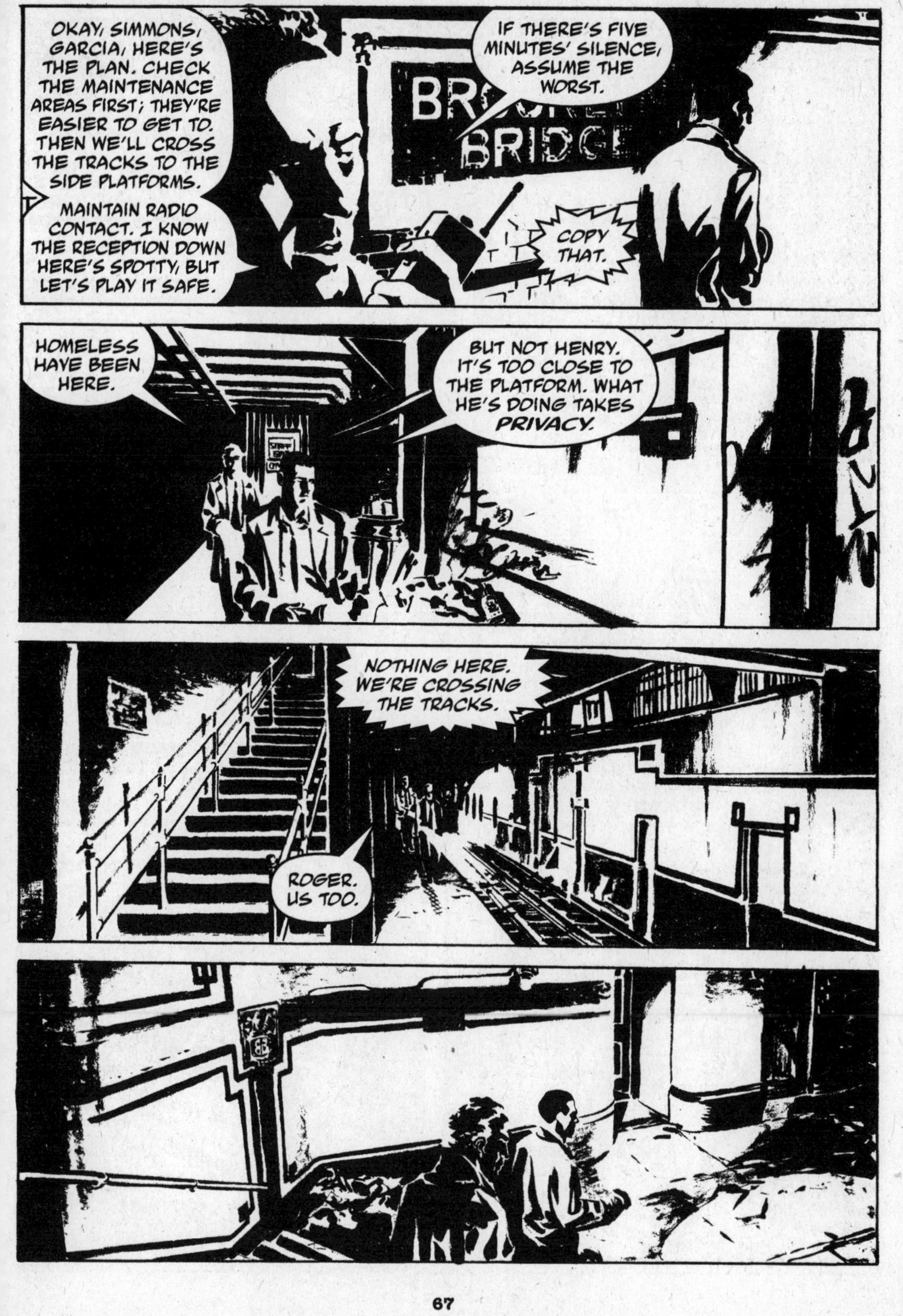
OKAY, SIMMONS, GARCIA, HERE'S THE PLAN. CHECK THE MAINTENANCE AREAS FIRST; THEY'RE EASIER TO GET TO. THEN WE'LL CROSS THE TRACKS TO THE SIDE PLATFORMS.
MAINTAIN RADIO CONTACT. I KNOW THE RECEPTION DOWN HERE'S SPOTTY, BUT LET'S PLAY IT SAFE.
IF THERE'S FIVE MINUTES' SILENCE, ASSUME THE WORST.
COPY THAT.
HOMELESS HAVE BEEN HERE.
BUT NOT HENRY. IT'S TOO CLOSE TO THE PLATFORM. WHAT HE'S DOING TAKES *PRIVACY.*
NOTHING HERE. WE'RE CROSSING THE TRACKS.
ROGER. US TOO.

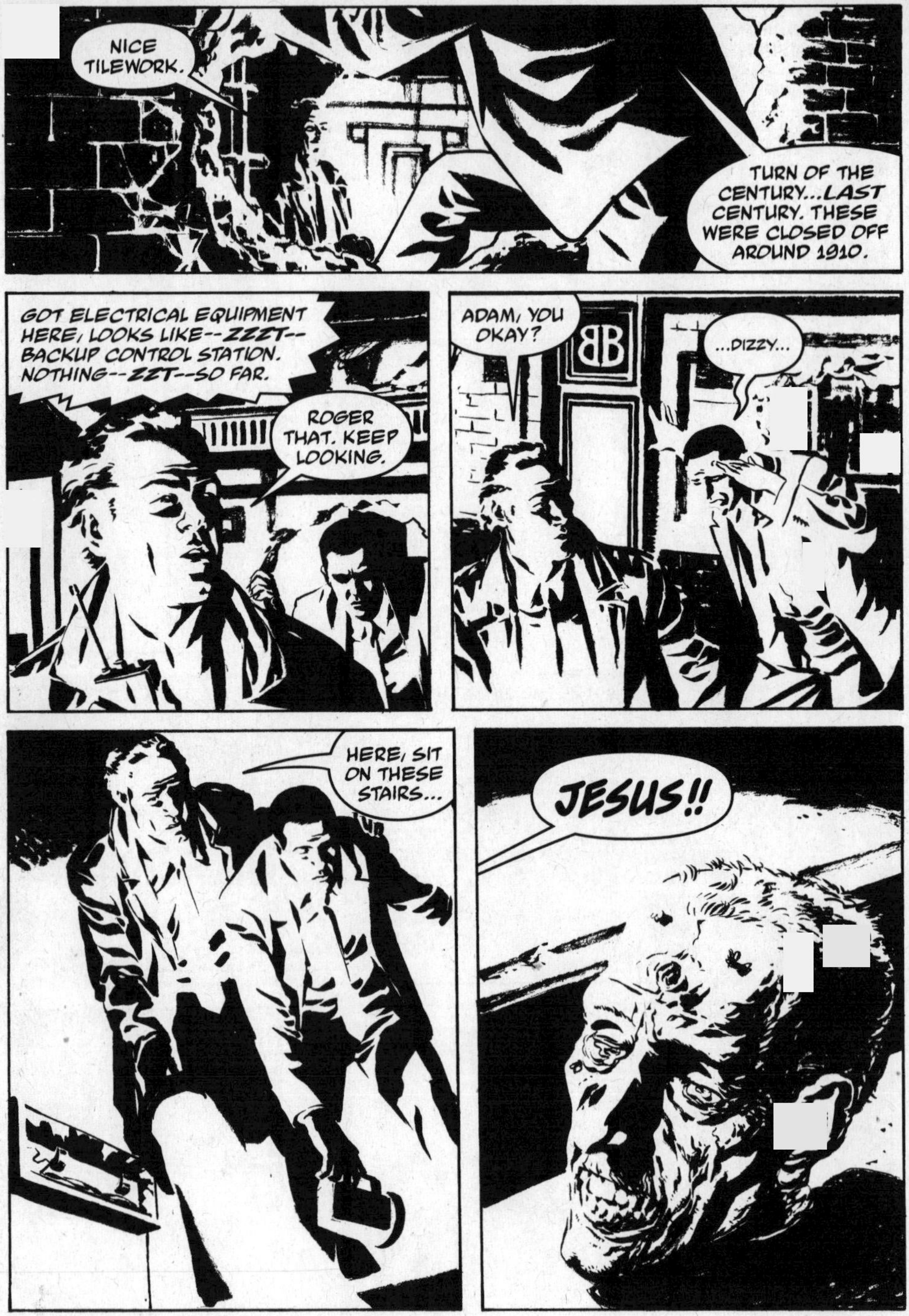
NICE TILEWORK.
TURN OF THE CENTURY...LAST CENTURY. THESE WERE CLOSED OFF AROUND 1910.
GOT ELECTRICAL EQUIPMENT HERE, LOOKS LIKE--ZZZT--BACKUP CONTROL STATION. NOTHING--ZZT--SO FAR.
ROGER THAT. KEEP LOOKING.
ADAM, YOU OKAY?
...DIZZY...
HERE, SIT ON THESE STAIRS...
JESUS!!

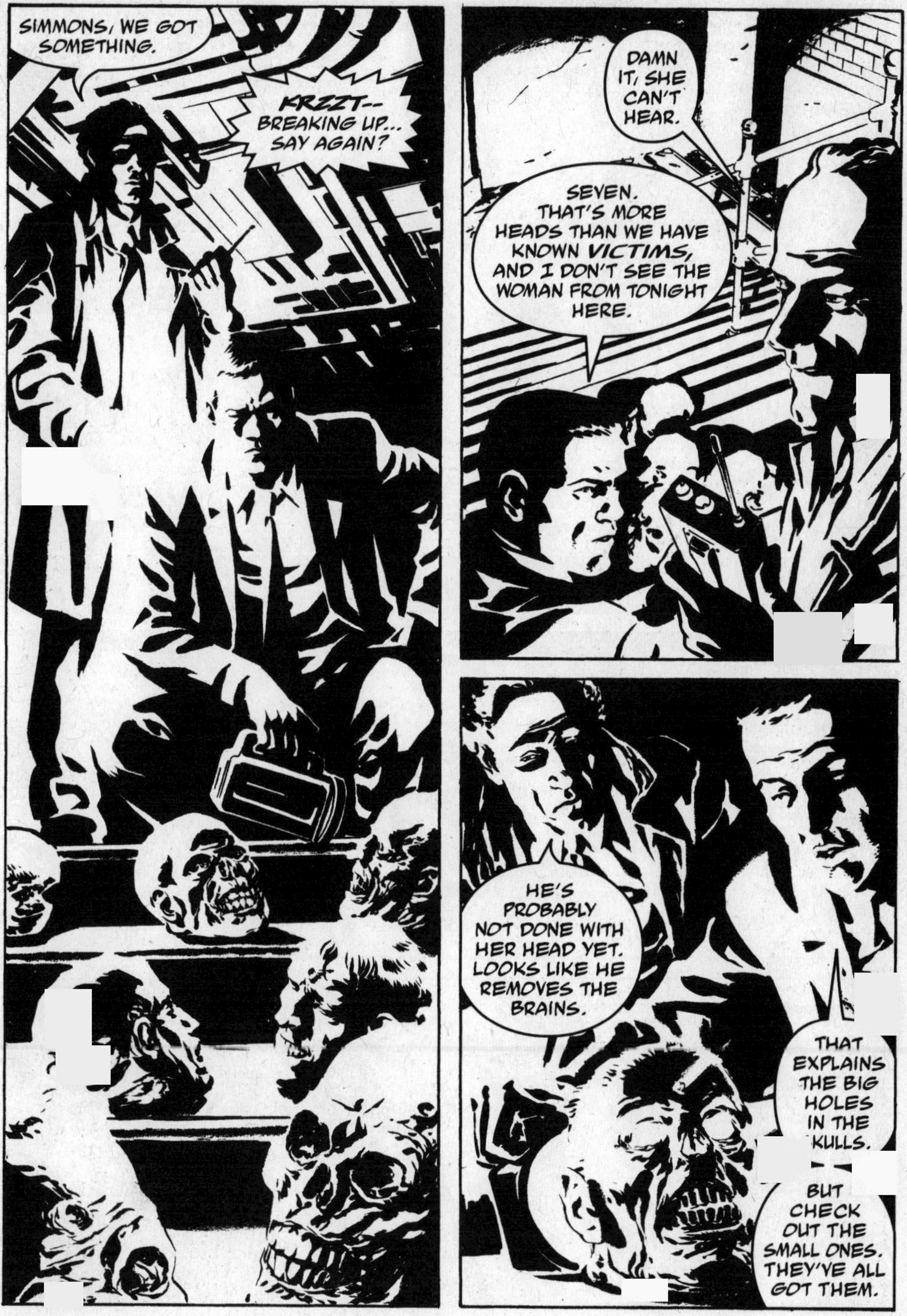
SIMMONS, WE GOT SOMETHING.
KRZZT-- BREAKING UP... SAY AGAIN?
DAMN IT, SHE CAN'T HEAR.
SEVEN. THAT'S MORE HEADS THAN WE HAVE KNOWN VICTIMS, AND I DON'T SEE THE WOMAN FROM TONIGHT HERE.
HE'S PROBABLY NOT DONE WITH HER HEAD YET. LOOKS LIKE HE REMOVES THE BRAINS.
THAT EXPLAINS THE BIG HOLES IN THE KULLS.
BUT CHECK OUT THE SMALL ONES. THEY'VE ALL GOT THEM.

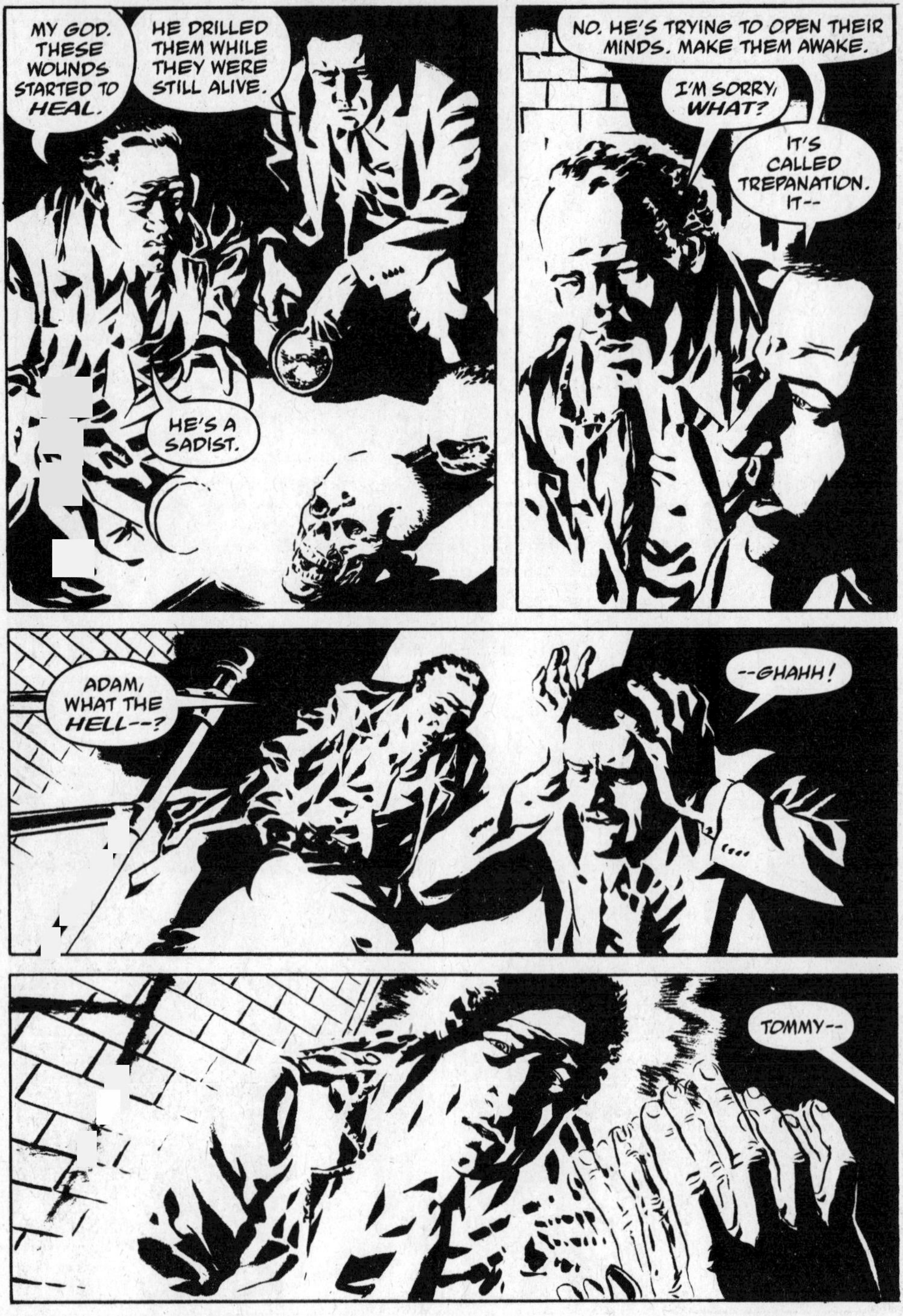
MY GOD. THESE WOUNDS STARTED TO HEAL.
HE DRILLED THEM WHILE THEY WERE STILL ALIVE.
HE'S A SADIST.
NO. HE'S TRYING TO OPEN THEIR MINDS. MAKE THEM AWAKE.
I'M SORRY, WHAT?
IT'S CALLED TREPANATION. IT--
ADAM, WHAT THE HELL--?
--GHAHH!
TOMMY--

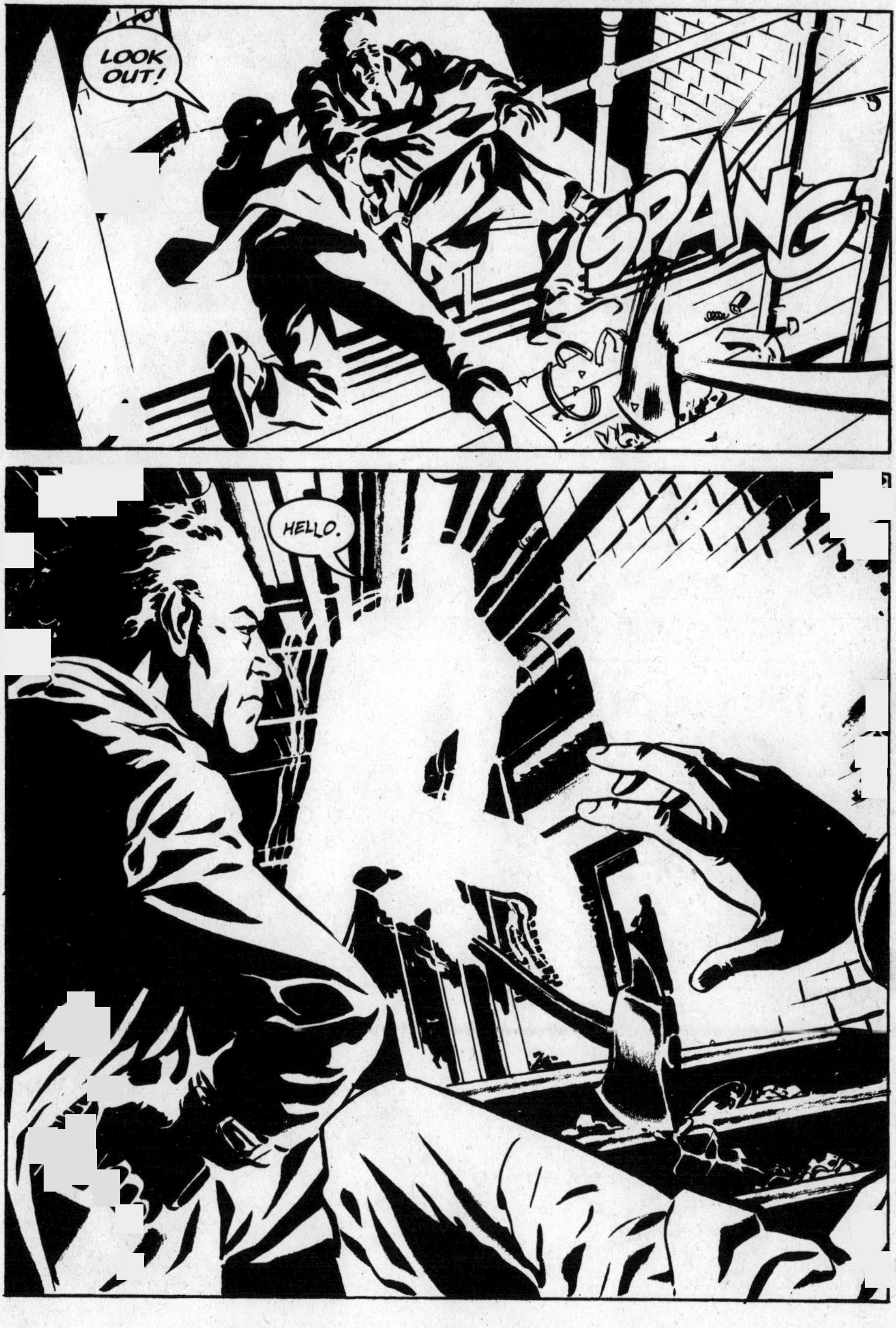
LOOK OUT!
SPANG
HELLO.

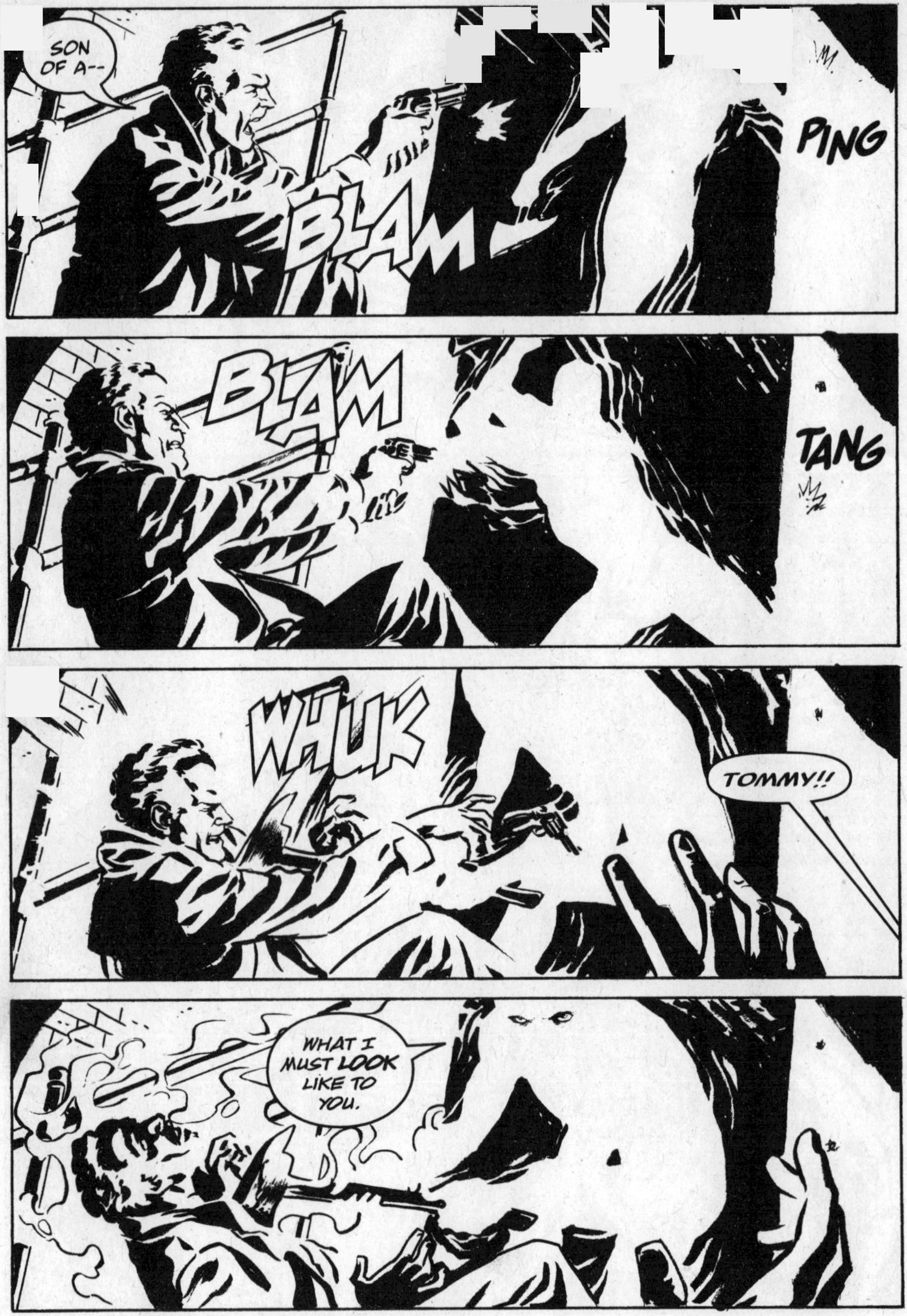
SON OF A--
BLAM
PING
BLAM
TANG
WHUK
TOMMY!!
WHAT I MUST LOOK LIKE TO YOU.

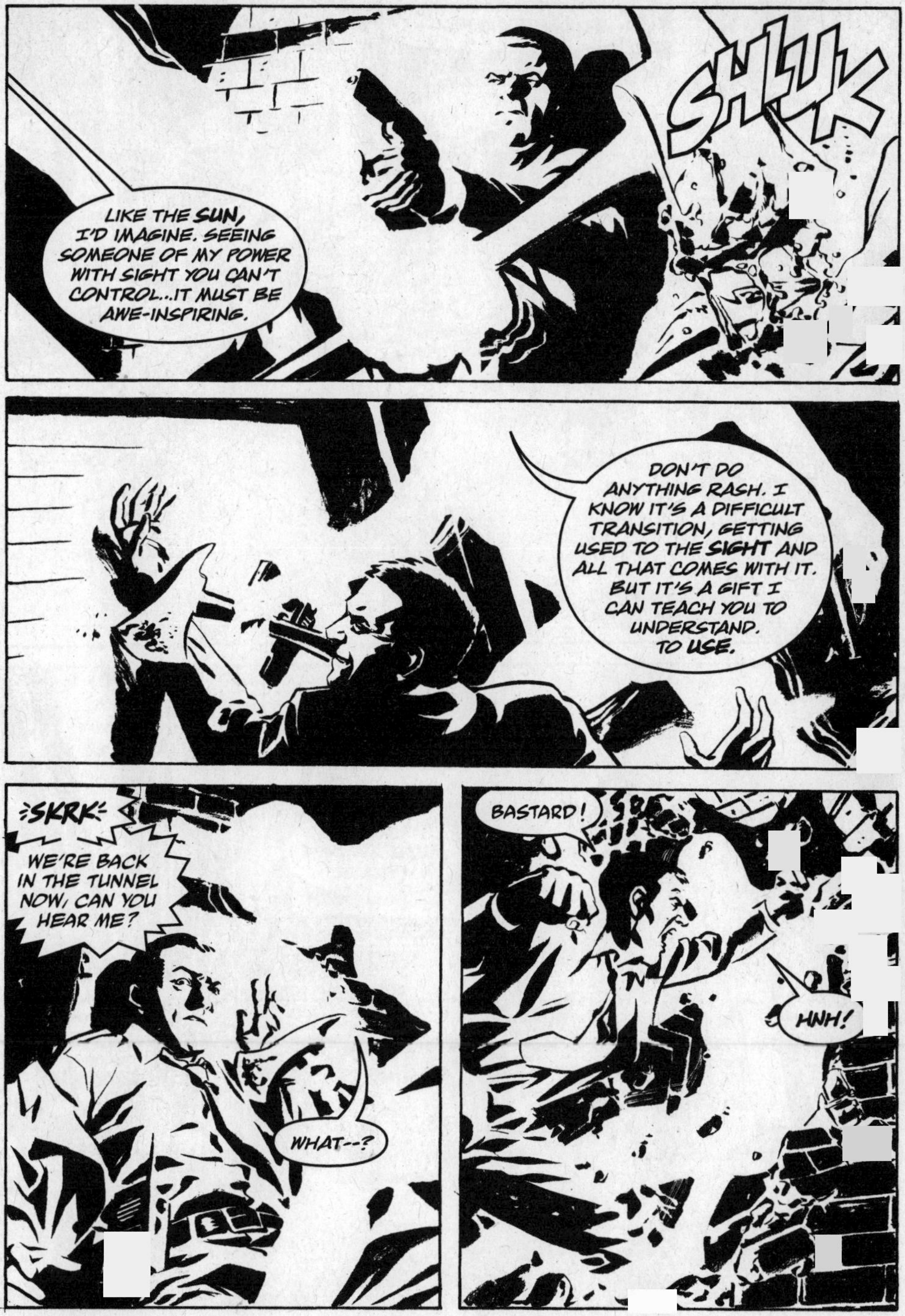
SHUK
LIKE THE SUN, I'D IMAGINE. SEEING SOMEONE OF MY POWER WITH SIGHT YOU CAN'T CONTROL...IT MUST BE AWE-INSPIRING.
DON'T DO ANYTHING RASH. I KNOW IT'S A DIFFICULT TRANSITION, GETTING USED TO THE SIGHT AND ALL THAT COMES WITH IT. BUT IT'S A GIFT I CAN TEACH YOU TO UNDERSTAND. TO USE.
SKRK
WE'RE BACK IN THE TUNNEL NOW, CAN YOU HEAR ME?
WHAT--?
BASTARD!
HNH!

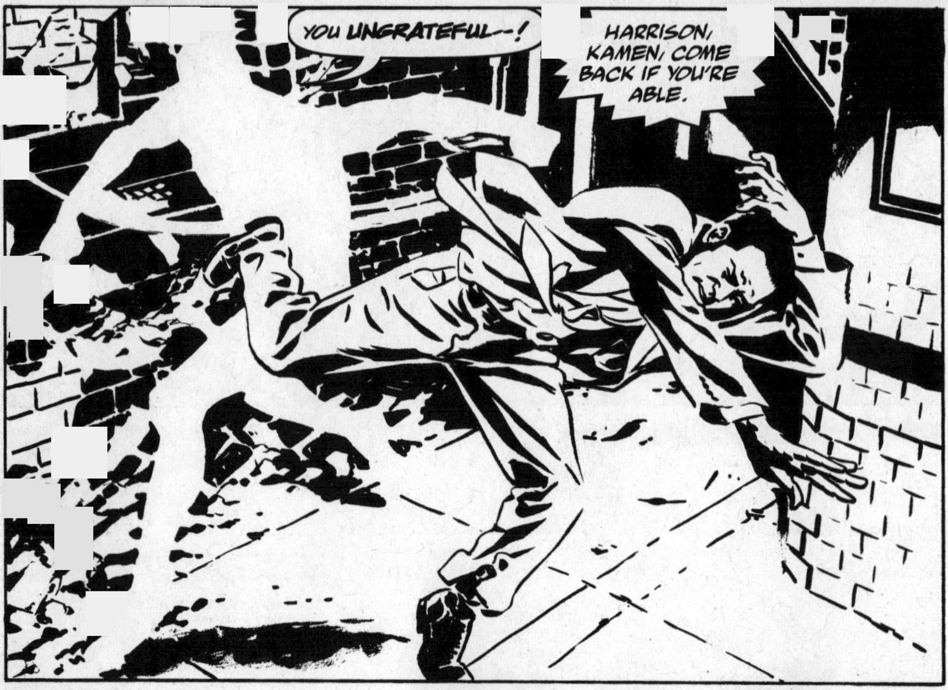
YOU UNGRATEFUL--!
HARRISON, KAMEN, COME BACK IF YOU'RE ABLE.

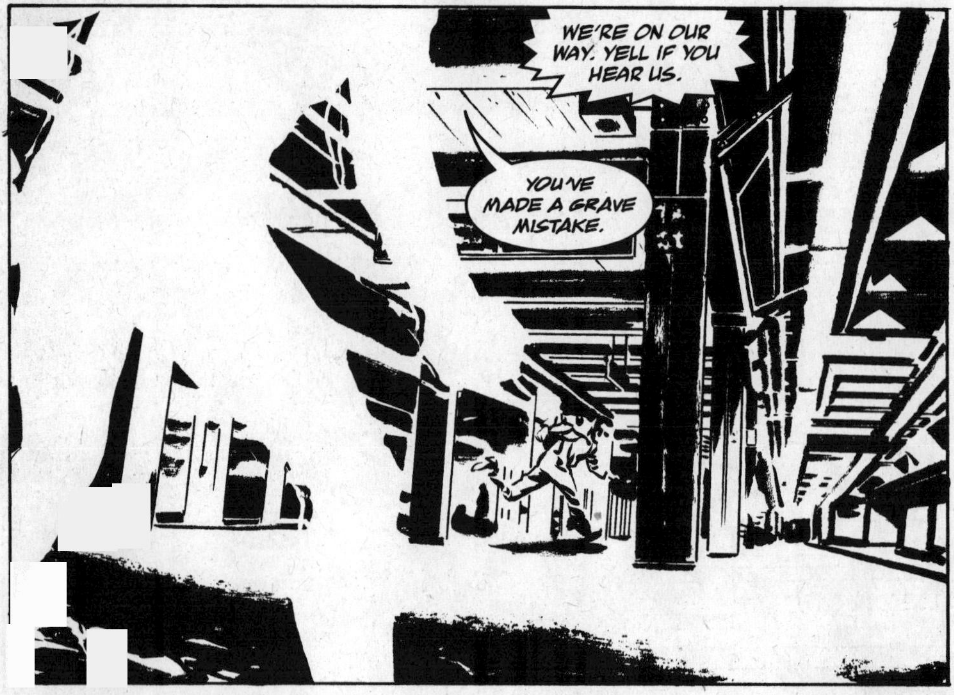
WE'RE ON OUR WAY. YELL IF YOU HEAR US.
YOU'VE MADE A GRAVE MISTAKE.

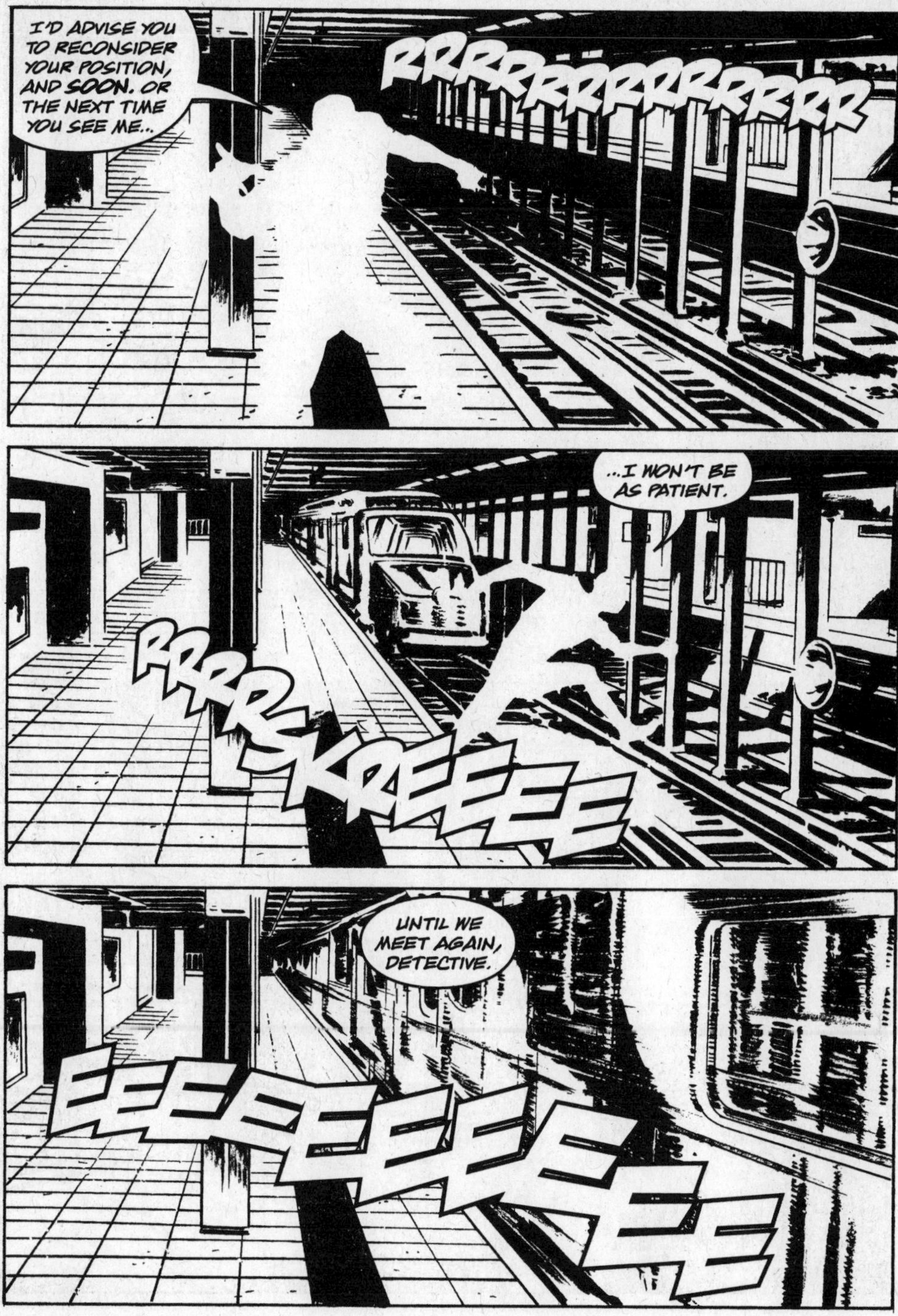
I'D ADVISE YOU TO RECONSIDER YOUR POSITION, AND SOON. OR THE NEXT TIME YOU SEE ME...
RRRRRRRRRRRRRRR
...I WON'T BE AS PATIENT.
RRRRSKREEEEE
UNTIL WE MEET AGAIN, DETECTIVE.
EEEEEEEEEEE

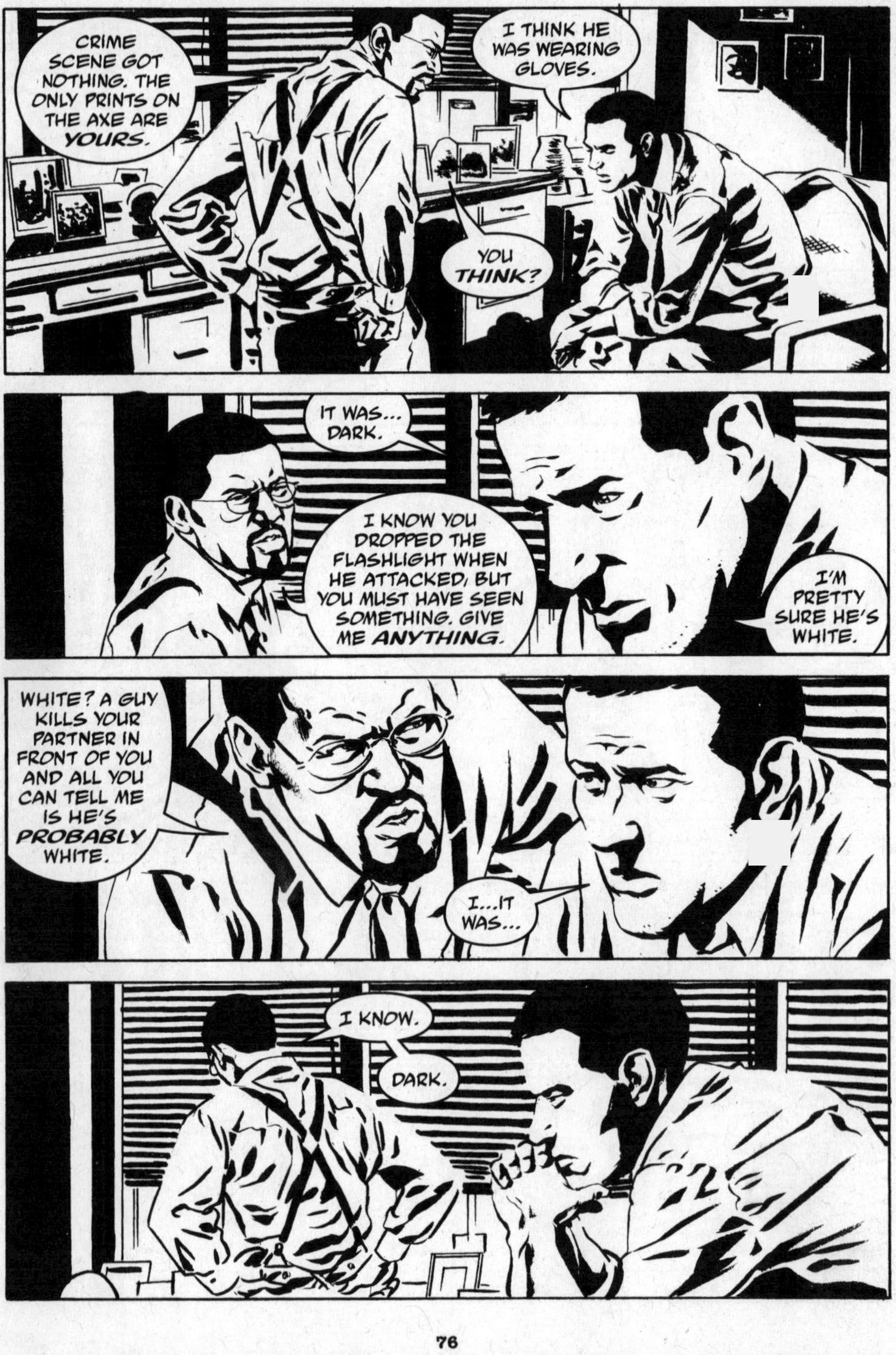
CRIME SCENE GOT NOTHING. THE ONLY PRINTS ON THE AXE ARE YOURS.
I THINK HE WAS WEARING GLOVES.
YOU THINK?
IT WAS... DARK.
I KNOW YOU DROPPED THE FLASHLIGHT WHEN HE ATTACKED, BUT YOU MUST HAVE SEEN SOMETHING. GIVE ME ANYTHING.
I'M PRETTY SURE HE'S WHITE.
WHITE? A GUY KILLS YOUR PARTNER IN FRONT OF YOU AND ALL YOU CAN TELL ME IS HE'S PROBABLY WHITE.
I...IT WAS...
I KNOW.
DARK.

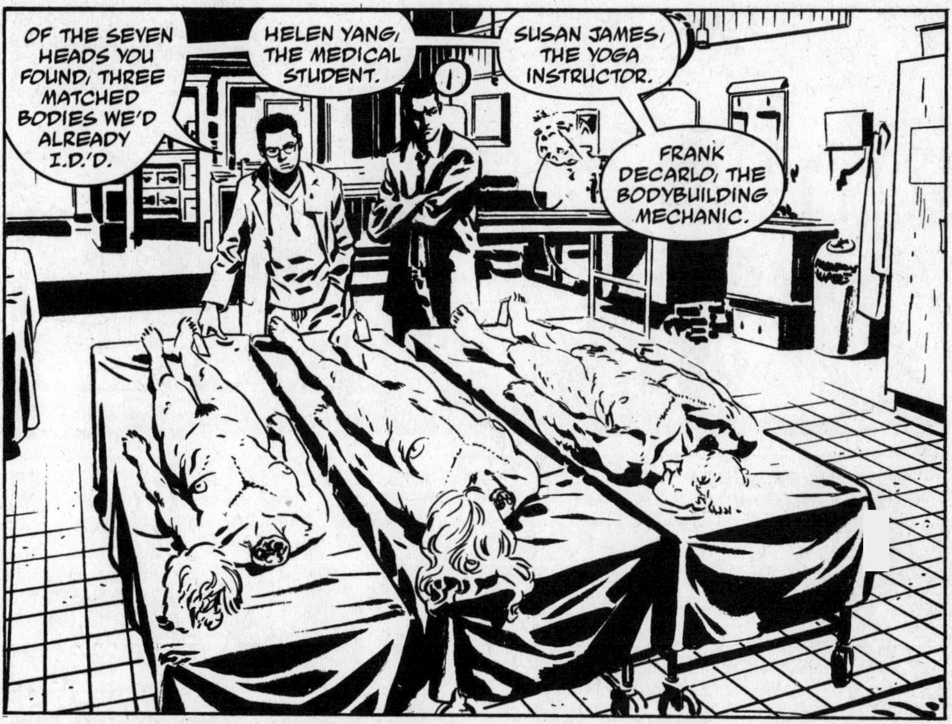
OF THE SEVEN HEADS YOU FOUND, THREE MATCHED BODIES WE'D ALREADY I.D.'D.
HELEN YANG, THE MEDICAL STUDENT.
SUSAN JAMES, THE YOGA INSTRUCTOR.
FRANK DECARLO, THE BODYBUILDING MECHANIC.

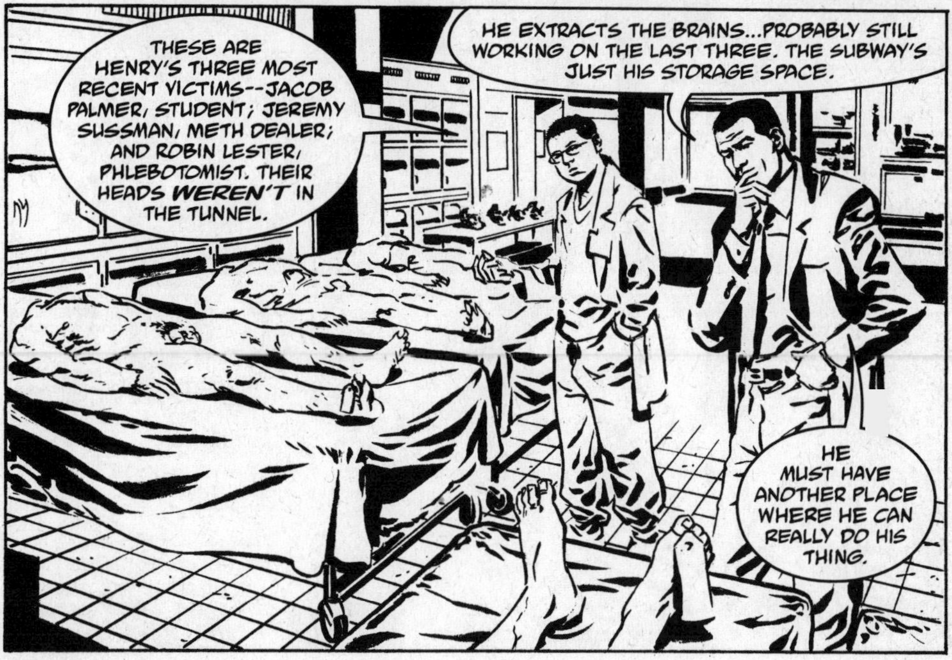
THESE ARE HENRY'S THREE MOST RECENT VICTIMS--JACOB PALMER, STUDENT; JEREMY SUSSMAN, METH DEALER; AND ROBIN LESTER, PHLEBOTOMIST. THEIR HEADS ***WEREN'T*** IN THE TUNNEL.
HE EXTRACTS THE BRAINS...PROBABLY STILL WORKING ON THE LAST THREE. THE SUBWAY'S JUST HIS STORAGE SPACE.
HE MUST HAVE ANOTHER PLACE WHERE HE CAN REALLY DO HIS THING.

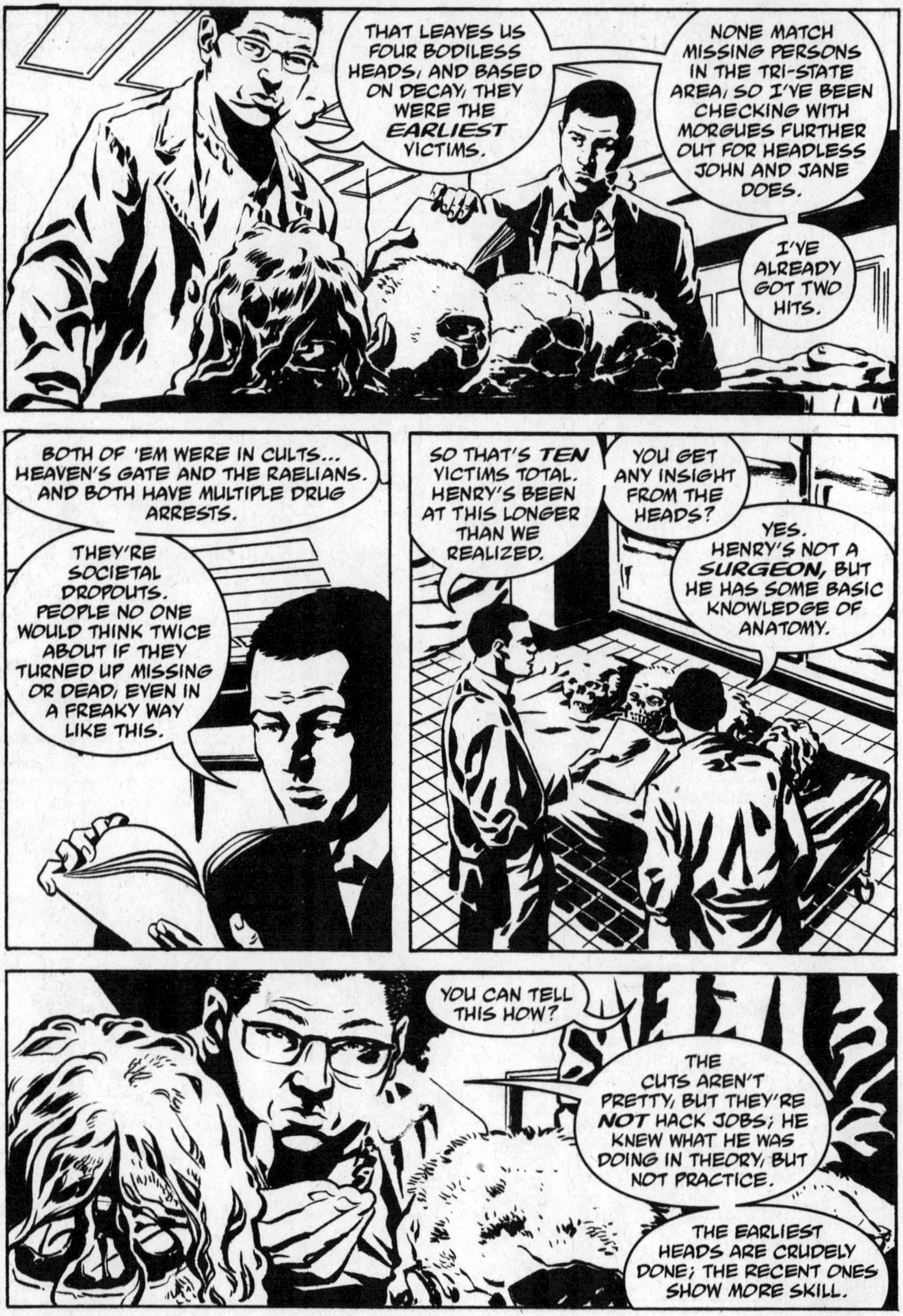
THAT LEAVES US FOUR BODILESS HEADS, AND BASED ON DECAY, THEY WERE THE *EARLIEST* VICTIMS.
NONE MATCH MISSING PERSONS IN THE TRI-STATE AREA, SO I'VE BEEN CHECKING WITH MORGUES FURTHER OUT FOR HEADLESS JOHN AND JANE DOES.
I'VE ALREADY GOT TWO HITS.
BOTH OF 'EM WERE IN CULTS... HEAVEN'S GATE AND THE RAELIANS. AND BOTH HAVE MULTIPLE DRUG ARRESTS.
THEY'RE SOCIETAL DROPOUTS. PEOPLE NO ONE WOULD THINK TWICE ABOUT IF THEY TURNED UP MISSING OR DEAD, EVEN IN A FREAKY WAY LIKE THIS.
SO THAT'S *TEN* VICTIMS TOTAL. HENRY'S BEEN AT THIS LONGER THAN WE REALIZED.
YOU GET ANY INSIGHT FROM THE HEADS?
YES. HENRY'S NOT A *SURGEON,* BUT HE HAS SOME BASIC KNOWLEDGE OF ANATOMY.
YOU CAN TELL THIS HOW?
THE CUTS AREN'T PRETTY, BUT THEY'RE *NOT* HACK JOBS; HE KNEW WHAT HE WAS DOING IN THEORY, BUT NOT PRACTICE.
THE EARLIEST HEADS ARE CRUDELY DONE; THE RECENT ONES SHOW MORE SKILL.

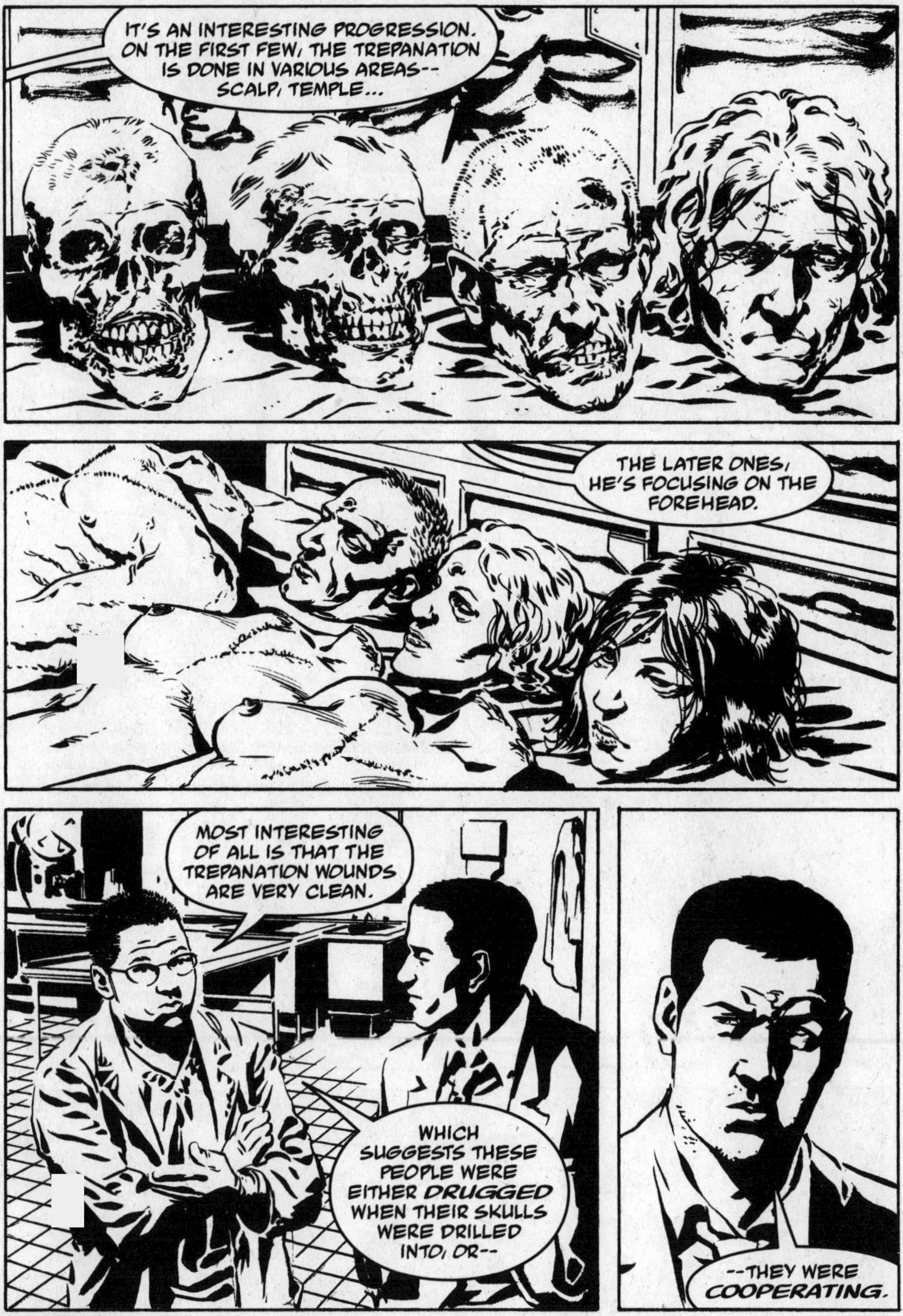
IT'S AN INTERESTING PROGRESSION. ON THE FIRST FEW, THE TREPANATION IS DONE IN VARIOUS AREAS-- SCALP, TEMPLE...
THE LATER ONES, HE'S FOCUSING ON THE FOREHEAD.
MOST INTERESTING OF ALL IS THAT THE TREPANATION WOUNDS ARE VERY CLEAN.
WHICH SUGGESTS THESE PEOPLE WERE EITHER *DRUGGED* WHEN THEIR SKULLS WERE DRILLED INTO, OR--
--THEY WERE *COOPERATING.*

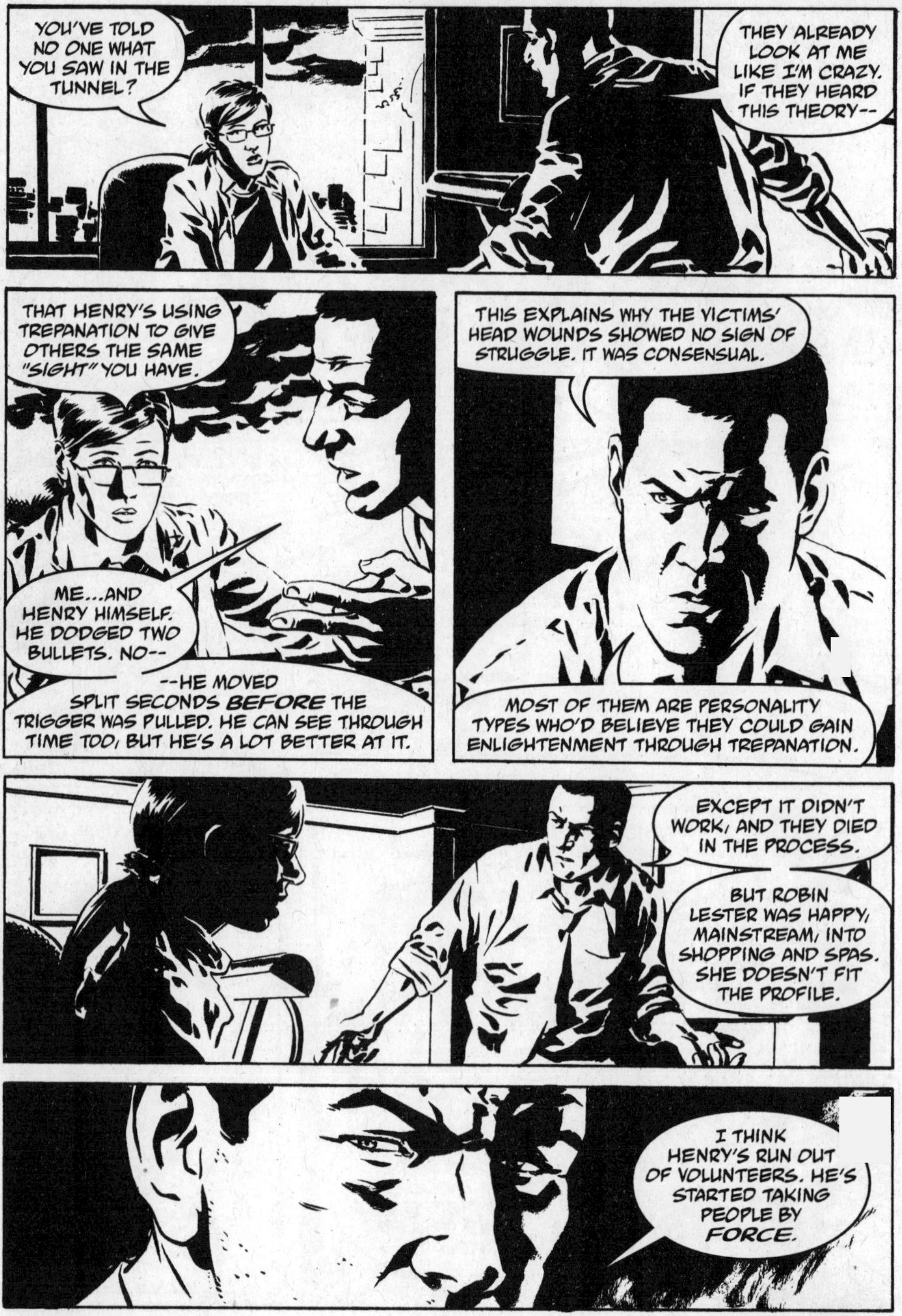
YOU'VE TOLD NO ONE WHAT YOU SAW IN THE TUNNEL?
THEY ALREADY LOOK AT ME LIKE I'M CRAZY. IF THEY HEARD THIS THEORY--
THAT HENRY'S USING TREPANATION TO GIVE OTHERS THE SAME "SIGHT" YOU HAVE.
ME...AND HENRY HIMSELF. HE DODGED TWO BULLETS. NO--
--HE MOVED SPLIT SECONDS BEFORE THE TRIGGER WAS PULLED. HE CAN SEE THROUGH TIME TOO, BUT HE'S A LOT BETTER AT IT.
THIS EXPLAINS WHY THE VICTIMS' HEAD WOUNDS SHOWED NO SIGN OF STRUGGLE. IT WAS CONSENSUAL.
MOST OF THEM ARE PERSONALITY TYPES WHO'D BELIEVE THEY COULD GAIN ENLIGHTENMENT THROUGH TREPANATION.
EXCEPT IT DIDN'T WORK, AND THEY DIED IN THE PROCESS.
BUT ROBIN LESTER WAS HAPPY, MAINSTREAM, INTO SHOPPING AND SPAS. SHE DOESN'T FIT THE PROFILE.
I THINK HENRY'S RUN OUT OF VOLUNTEERS. HE'S STARTED TAKING PEOPLE BY FORCE.

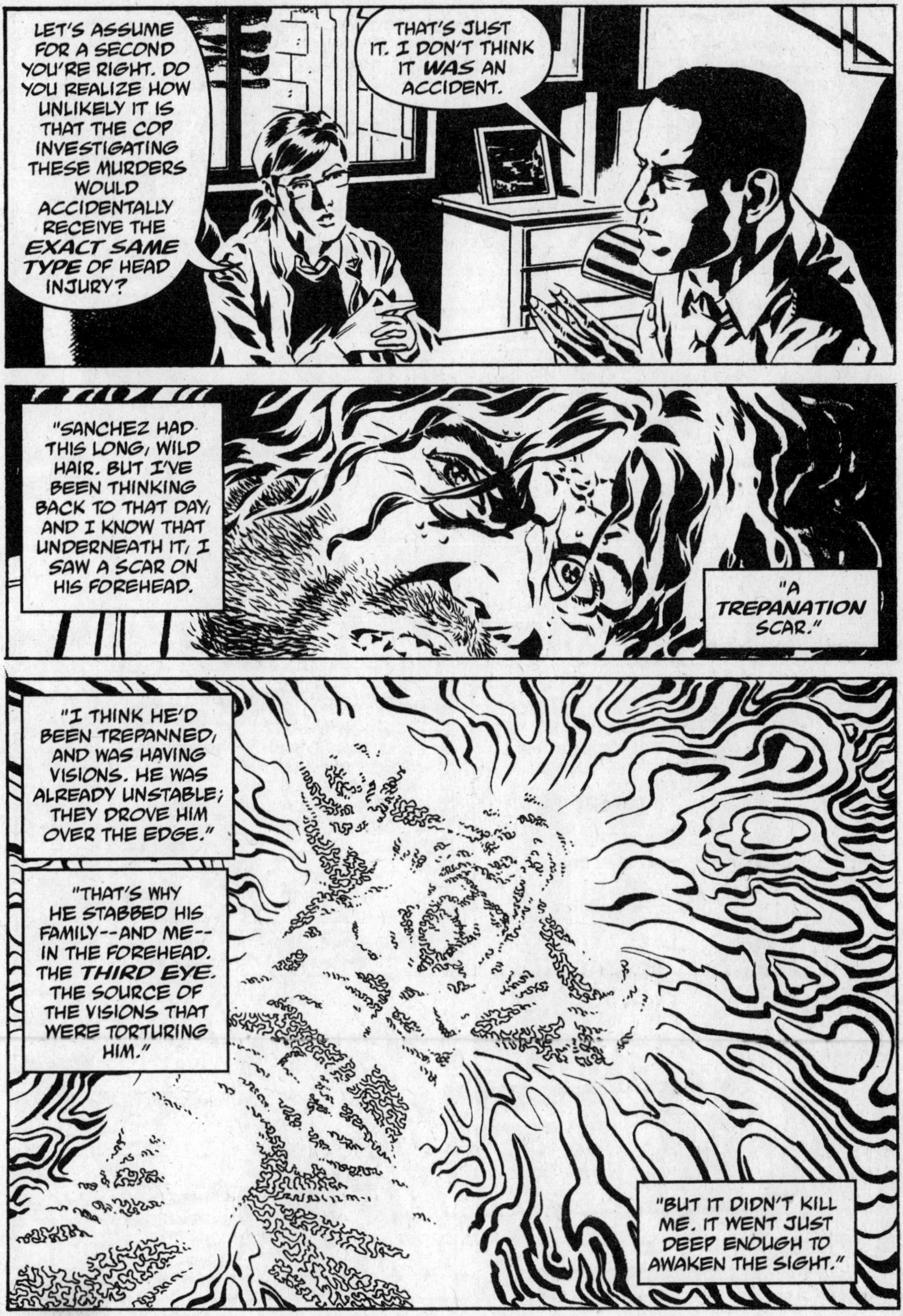
LET'S ASSUME FOR A SECOND YOU'RE RIGHT. DO YOU REALIZE HOW UNLIKELY IT IS THAT THE COP INVESTIGATING THESE MURDERS WOULD ACCIDENTALLY RECEIVE THE *EXACT SAME TYPE* OF HEAD INJURY?
THAT'S JUST IT. I DON'T THINK IT *WAS* AN ACCIDENT.
"SANCHEZ HAD THIS LONG, WILD HAIR. BUT I'VE BEEN THINKING BACK TO THAT DAY, AND I KNOW THAT UNDERNEATH IT, I SAW A SCAR ON HIS FOREHEAD.
"A *TREPANATION* SCAR."
"I THINK HE'D BEEN TREPANNED, AND WAS HAVING VISIONS. HE WAS ALREADY UNSTABLE; THEY DROVE HIM OVER THE EDGE."
"THAT'S WHY HE STABBED HIS FAMILY--AND ME--IN THE FOREHEAD. THE *THIRD EYE*. THE SOURCE OF THE VISIONS THAT WERE TORTURING HIM."
"BUT IT DIDN'T KILL ME. IT WENT JUST DEEP ENOUGH TO AWAKEN THE SIGHT."

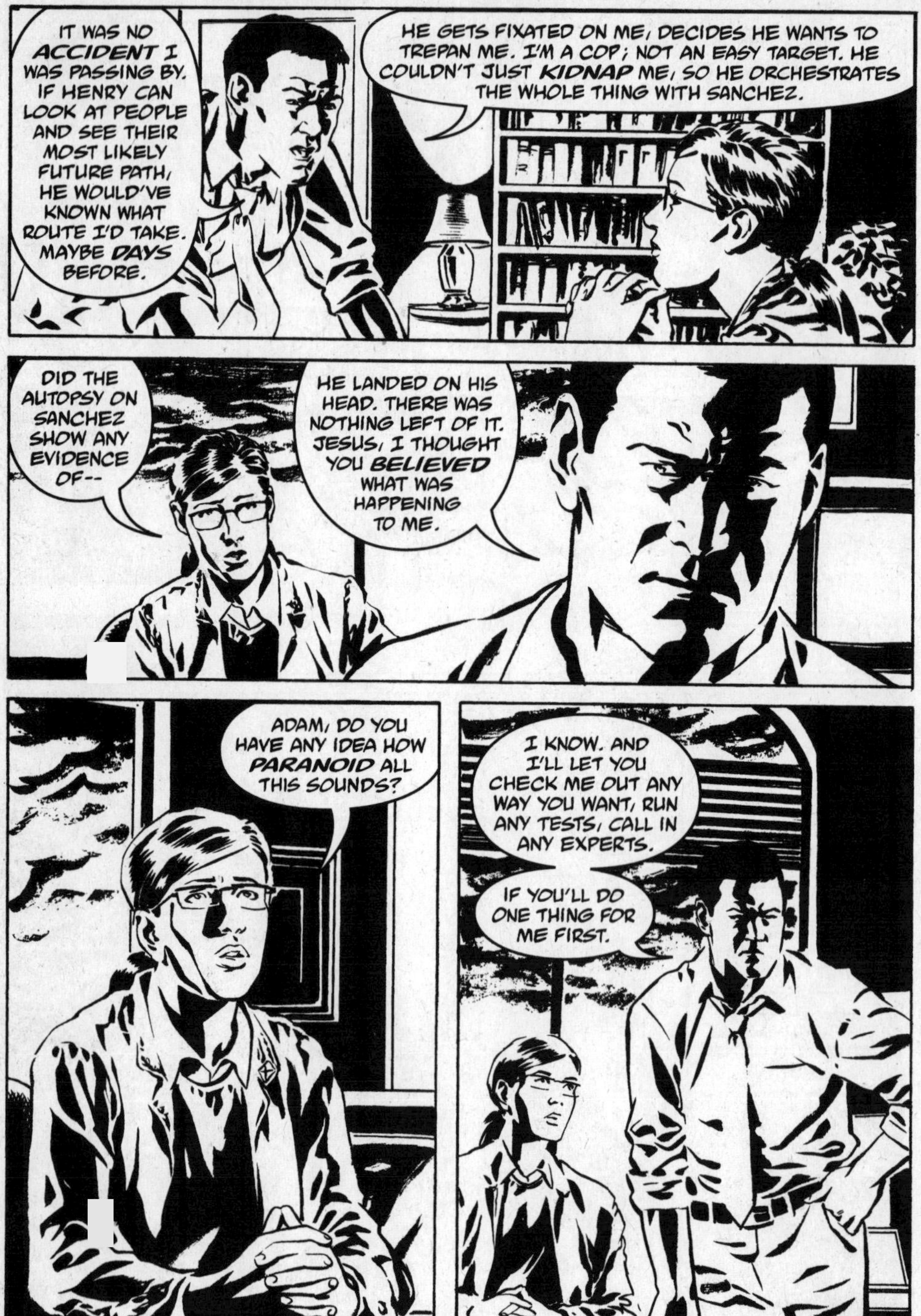
IT WAS NO ACCIDENT I WAS PASSING BY. IF HENRY CAN LOOK AT PEOPLE AND SEE THEIR MOST LIKELY FUTURE PATH, HE WOULD'VE KNOWN WHAT ROUTE I'D TAKE. MAYBE DAYS BEFORE.
HE GETS FIXATED ON ME, DECIDES HE WANTS TO TREPAN ME. I'M A COP; NOT AN EASY TARGET. HE COULDN'T JUST KIDNAP ME, SO HE ORCHESTRATES THE WHOLE THING WITH SANCHEZ.
DID THE AUTOPSY ON SANCHEZ SHOW ANY EVIDENCE OF--
HE LANDED ON HIS HEAD. THERE WAS NOTHING LEFT OF IT. JESUS, I THOUGHT YOU BELIEVED WHAT WAS HAPPENING TO ME.
ADAM, DO YOU HAVE ANY IDEA HOW PARANOID ALL THIS SOUNDS?
I KNOW. AND I'LL LET YOU CHECK ME OUT ANY WAY YOU WANT, RUN ANY TESTS, CALL IN ANY EXPERTS.
IF YOU'LL DO ONE THING FOR ME FIRST.

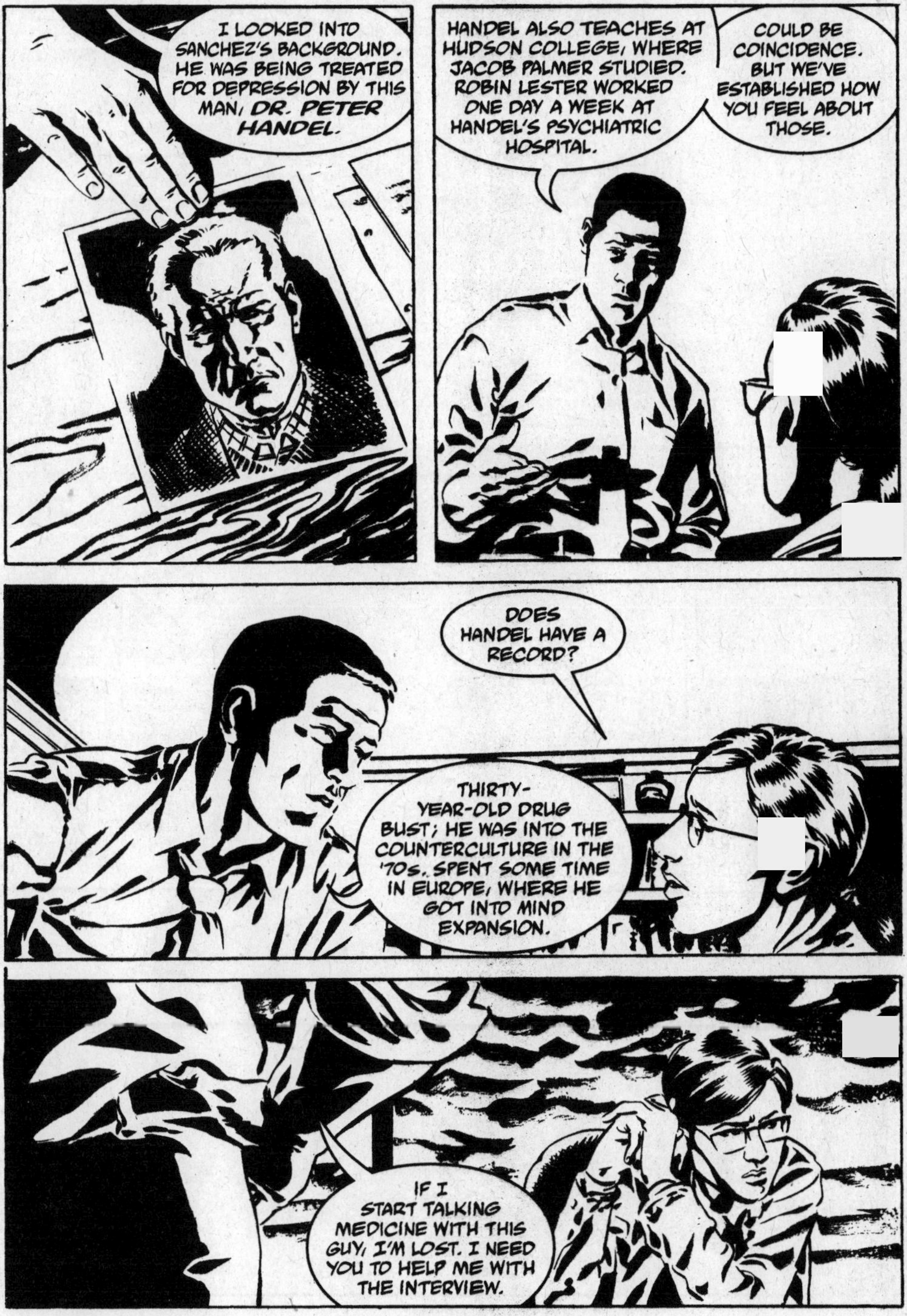
I LOOKED INTO SANCHEZ'S BACKGROUND. HE WAS BEING TREATED FOR DEPRESSION BY THIS MAN, DR. PETER HANDEL.
HANDEL ALSO TEACHES AT HUDSON COLLEGE, WHERE JACOB PALMER STUDIED. ROBIN LESTER WORKED ONE DAY A WEEK AT HANDEL'S PSYCHIATRIC HOSPITAL.
COULD BE COINCIDENCE. BUT WE'VE ESTABLISHED HOW YOU FEEL ABOUT THOSE.
DOES HANDEL HAVE A RECORD?
THIRTY-YEAR-OLD DRUG BUST; HE WAS INTO THE COUNTERCULTURE IN THE '70s. SPENT SOME TIME IN EUROPE, WHERE HE GOT INTO MIND EXPANSION.
IF I START TALKING MEDICINE WITH THIS GUY, I'M LOST. I NEED YOU TO HELP ME WITH THE INTERVIEW.

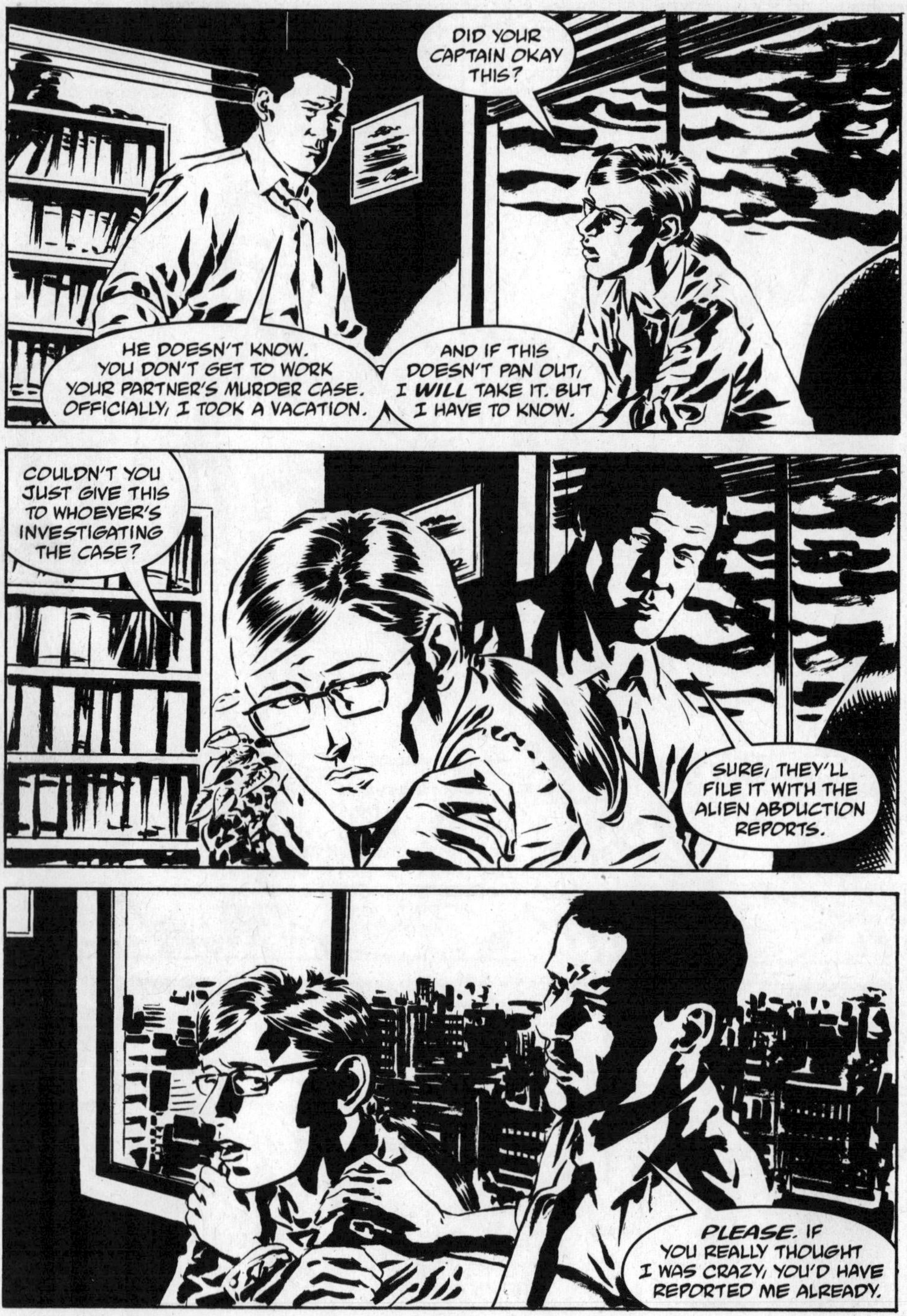
DID YOUR CAPTAIN OKAY THIS?
HE DOESN'T KNOW. YOU DON'T GET TO WORK YOUR PARTNER'S MURDER CASE. OFFICIALLY, I TOOK A VACATION.
AND IF THIS DOESN'T PAN OUT, I **WILL** TAKE IT. BUT I HAVE TO KNOW.
COULDN'T YOU JUST GIVE THIS TO WHOEVER'S INVESTIGATING THE CASE?
SURE, THEY'LL FILE IT WITH THE ALIEN ABDUCTION REPORTS.
PLEASE. IF YOU REALLY THOUGHT I WAS CRAZY, YOU'D HAVE REPORTED ME ALREADY.

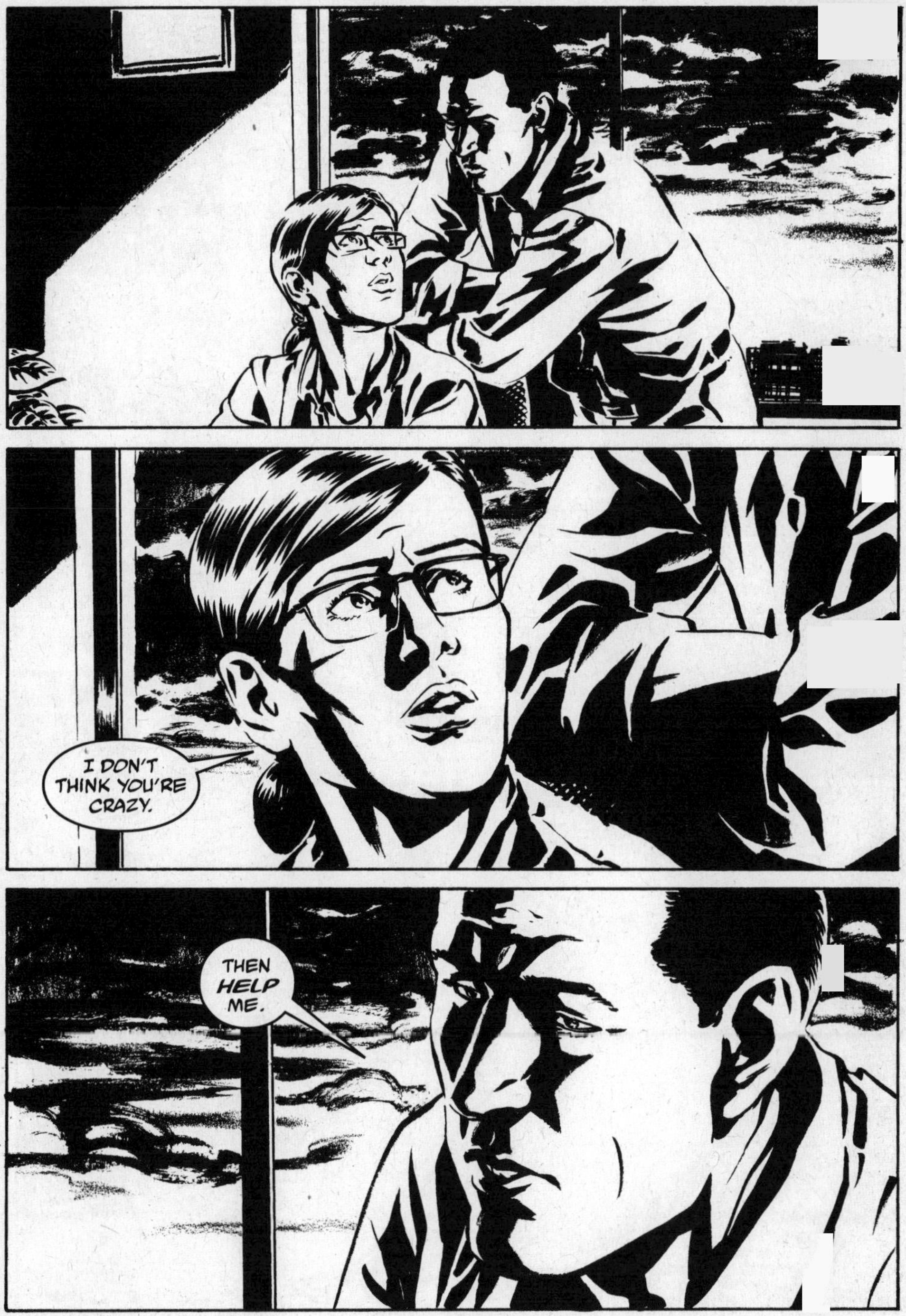
I DON'T THINK YOU'RE CRAZY.
THEN HELP ME.

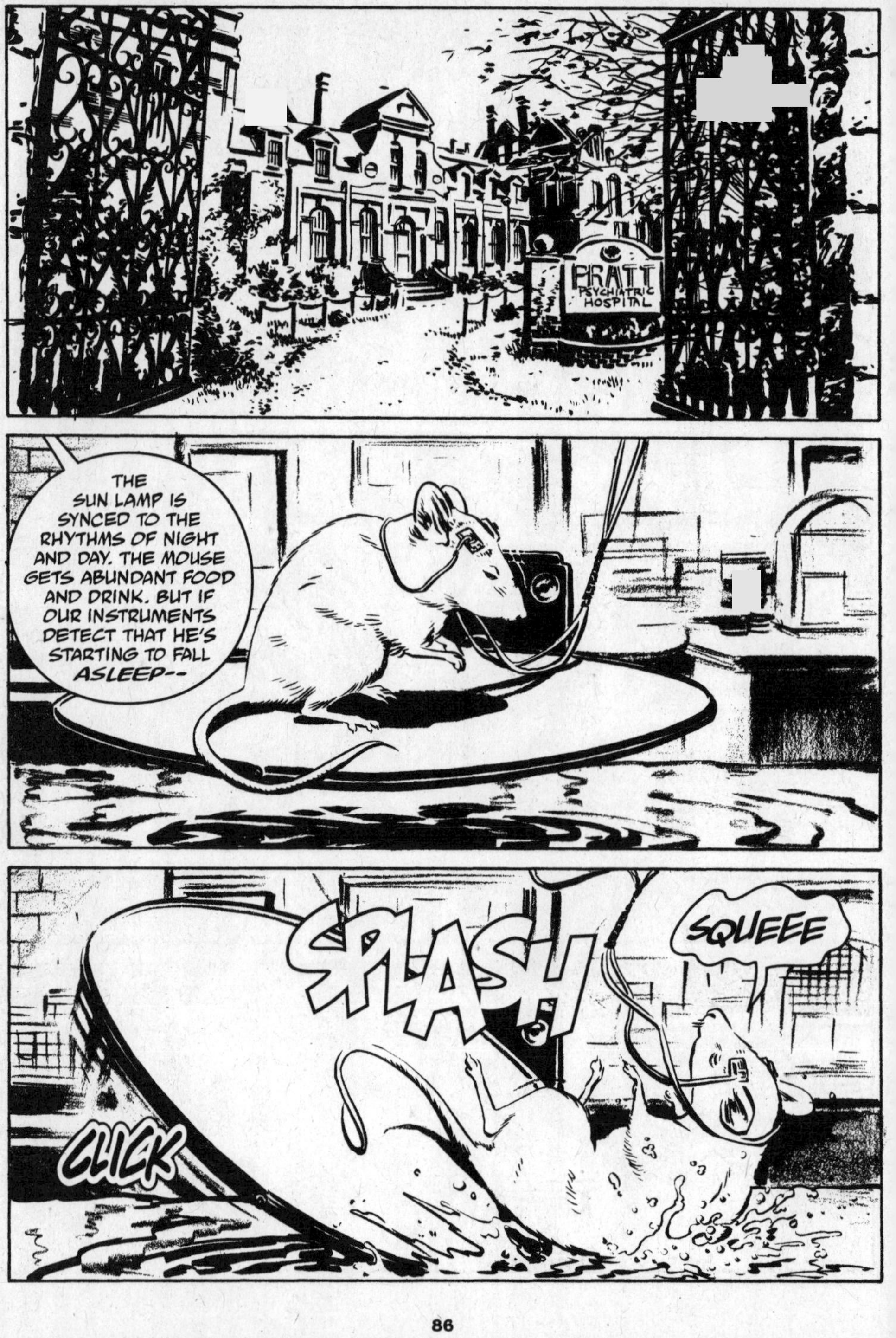
PRATT
PSYCHIATRIC
HOSPITAL
THE SUN LAMP IS SYNCED TO THE RHYTHMS OF NIGHT AND DAY. THE MOUSE GETS ABUNDANT FOOD AND DRINK. BUT IF OUR INSTRUMENTS DETECT THAT HE'S STARTING TO FALL *ASLEEP*--
SPLASH!
SQUEEEE
CLICK

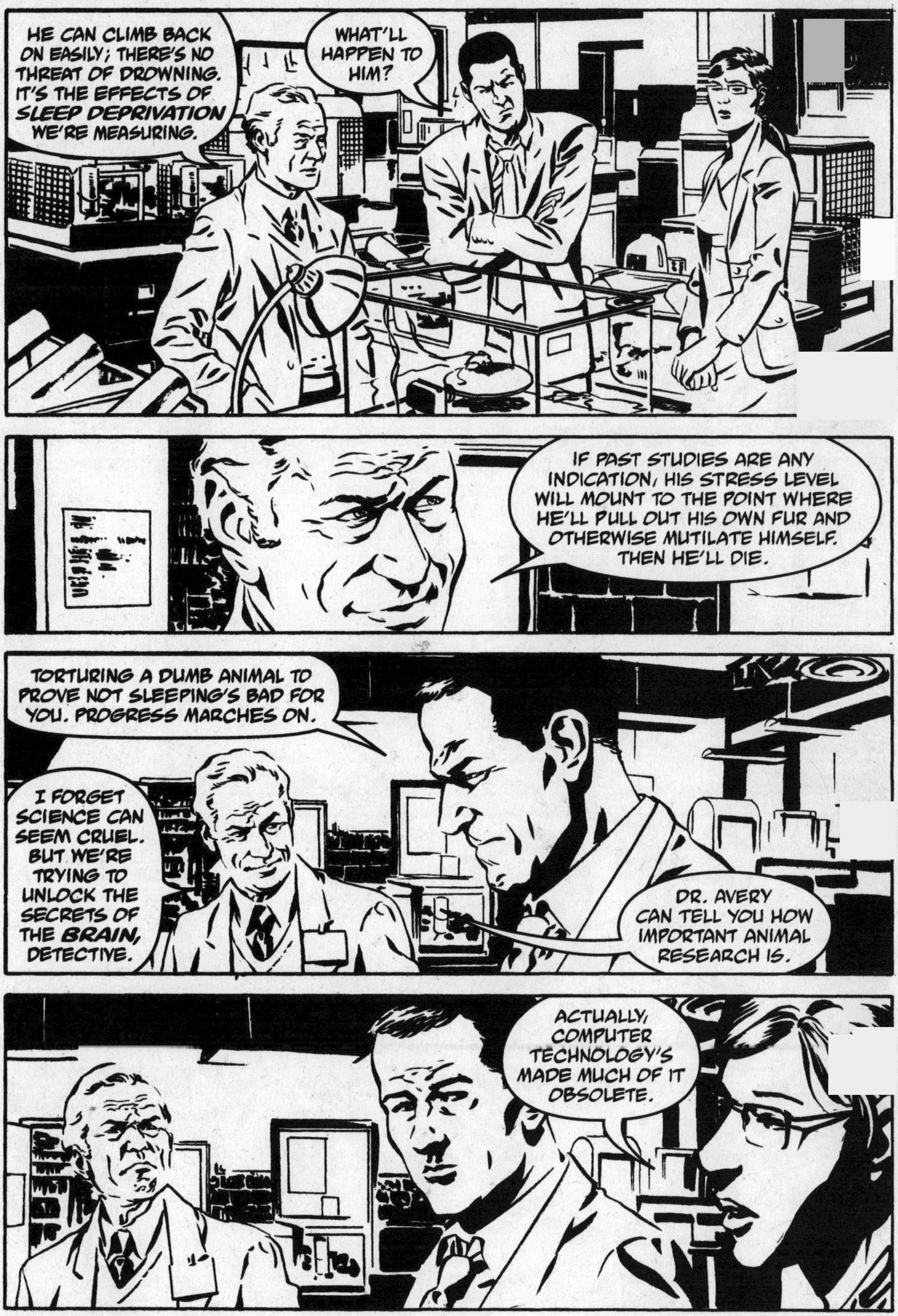
HE CAN CLIMB BACK ON EASILY; THERE'S NO THREAT OF DROWNING. IT'S THE EFFECTS OF *SLEEP DEPRIVATION* WE'RE MEASURING.
WHAT'LL HAPPEN TO HIM?
IF PAST STUDIES ARE ANY INDICATION, HIS STRESS LEVEL WILL MOUNT TO THE POINT WHERE HE'LL PULL OUT HIS OWN FUR AND OTHERWISE MUTILATE HIMSELF. THEN HE'LL DIE.
TORTURING A DUMB ANIMAL TO PROVE NOT SLEEPING'S BAD FOR YOU. PROGRESS MARCHES ON.
I FORGET SCIENCE CAN SEEM CRUEL. BUT WE'RE TRYING TO UNLOCK THE SECRETS OF THE *BRAIN*, DETECTIVE.
DR. AVERY CAN TELL YOU HOW IMPORTANT ANIMAL RESEARCH IS.
ACTUALLY, COMPUTER TECHNOLOGY'S MADE MUCH OF IT OBSOLETE.

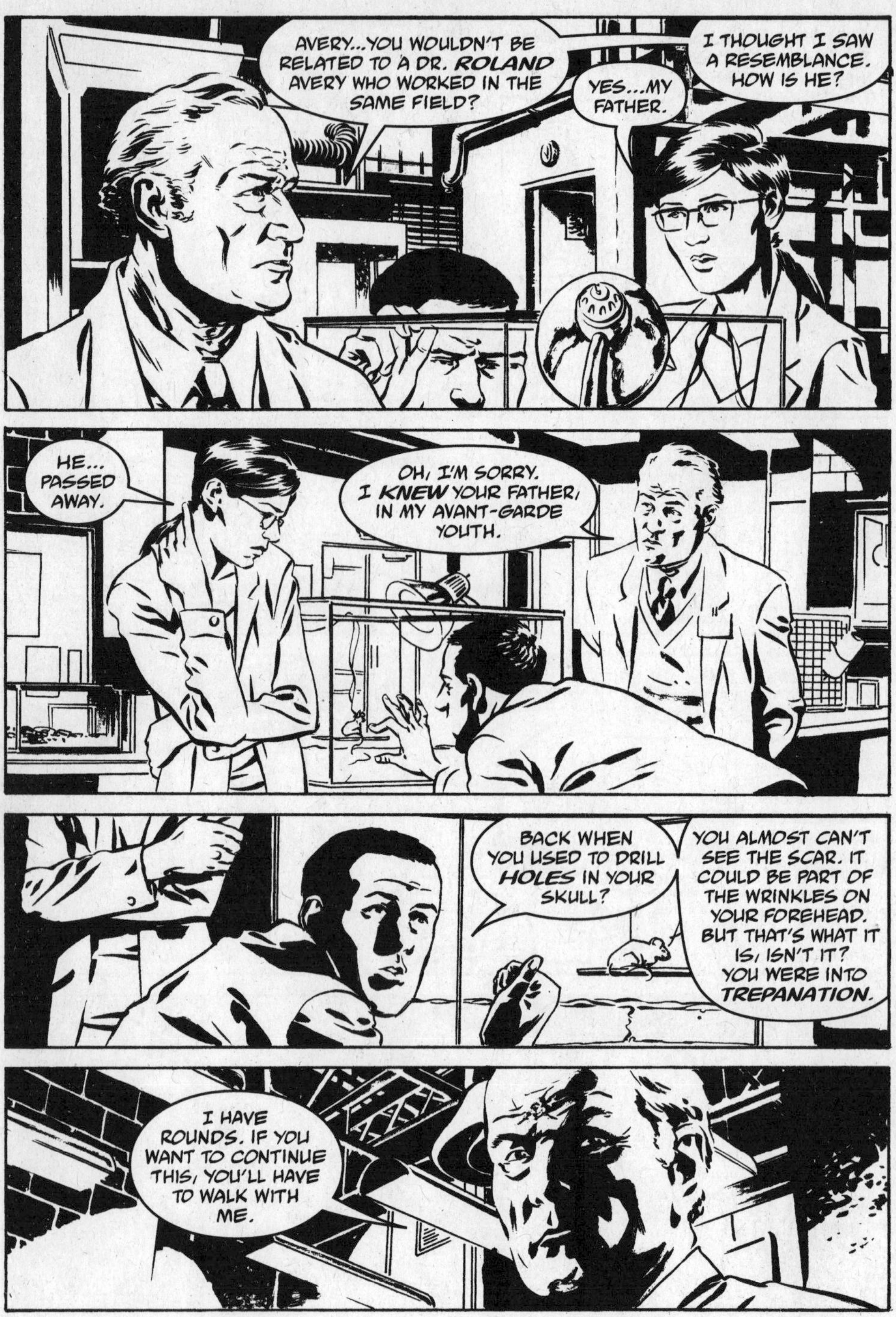
AVERY...YOU WOULDN'T BE RELATED TO A DR. ROLAND AVERY WHO WORKED IN THE SAME FIELD?
YES...MY FATHER.
I THOUGHT I SAW A RESEMBLANCE. HOW IS HE?
HE... PASSED AWAY.
OH, I'M SORRY. I KNEW YOUR FATHER, IN MY AVANT-GARDE YOUTH.
BACK WHEN YOU USED TO DRILL HOLES IN YOUR SKULL?
YOU ALMOST CAN'T SEE THE SCAR. IT COULD BE PART OF THE WRINKLES ON YOUR FOREHEAD. BUT THAT'S WHAT IT IS, ISN'T IT? YOU WERE INTO TREPANATION.
I HAVE ROUNDS. IF YOU WANT TO CONTINUE THIS, YOU'LL HAVE TO WALK WITH ME.

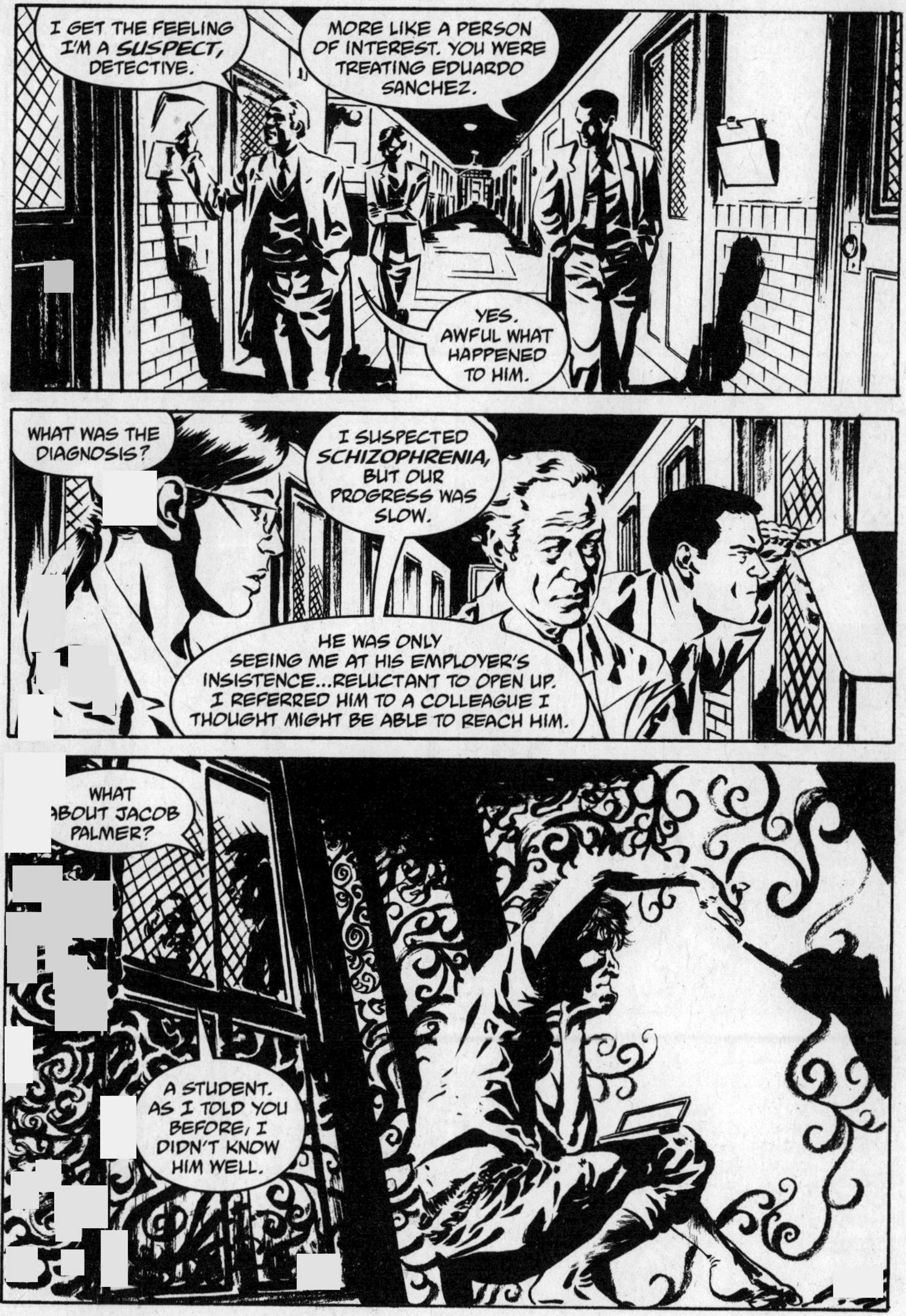
I GET THE FEELING I'M A *SUSPECT*, DETECTIVE.
MORE LIKE A PERSON OF INTEREST. YOU WERE TREATING EDUARDO SANCHEZ.
YES. AWFUL WHAT HAPPENED TO HIM.
WHAT WAS THE DIAGNOSIS?
I SUSPECTED *SCHIZOPHRENIA*, BUT OUR PROGRESS WAS SLOW.
HE WAS ONLY SEEING ME AT HIS EMPLOYER'S INSISTENCE...RELUCTANT TO OPEN UP. I REFERRED HIM TO A COLLEAGUE I THOUGHT MIGHT BE ABLE TO REACH HIM.
WHAT ABOUT JACOB PALMER?
A STUDENT. AS I TOLD YOU BEFORE, I DIDN'T KNOW HIM WELL.

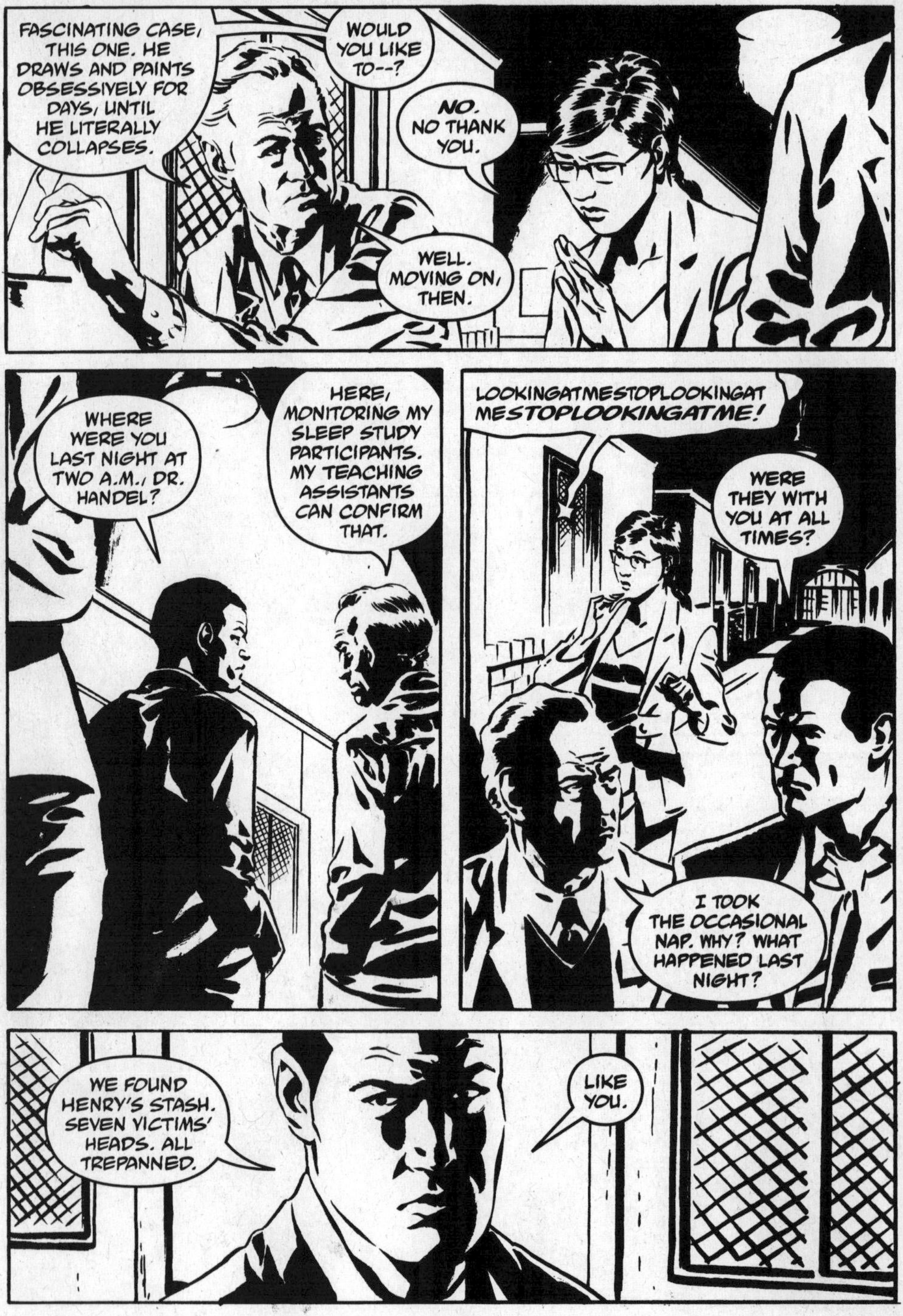
FASCINATING CASE, THIS ONE. HE DRAWS AND PAINTS OBSESSIVELY FOR DAYS, UNTIL HE LITERALLY COLLAPSES.
WOULD YOU LIKE TO--?
NO. NO THANK YOU.
WELL. MOVING ON, THEN.
WHERE WERE YOU LAST NIGHT AT TWO A.M., DR. HANDEL?
HERE, MONITORING MY SLEEP STUDY PARTICIPANTS. MY TEACHING ASSISTANTS CAN CONFIRM THAT.
LOOKINGATMESTOPLOOKINGAT MESTOPLOOKINGATME!
WERE THEY WITH YOU AT ALL TIMES?
I TOOK THE OCCASIONAL NAP. WHY? WHAT HAPPENED LAST NIGHT?
WE FOUND HENRY'S STASH. SEVEN VICTIMS' HEADS. ALL TREPANNED.
LIKE YOU.

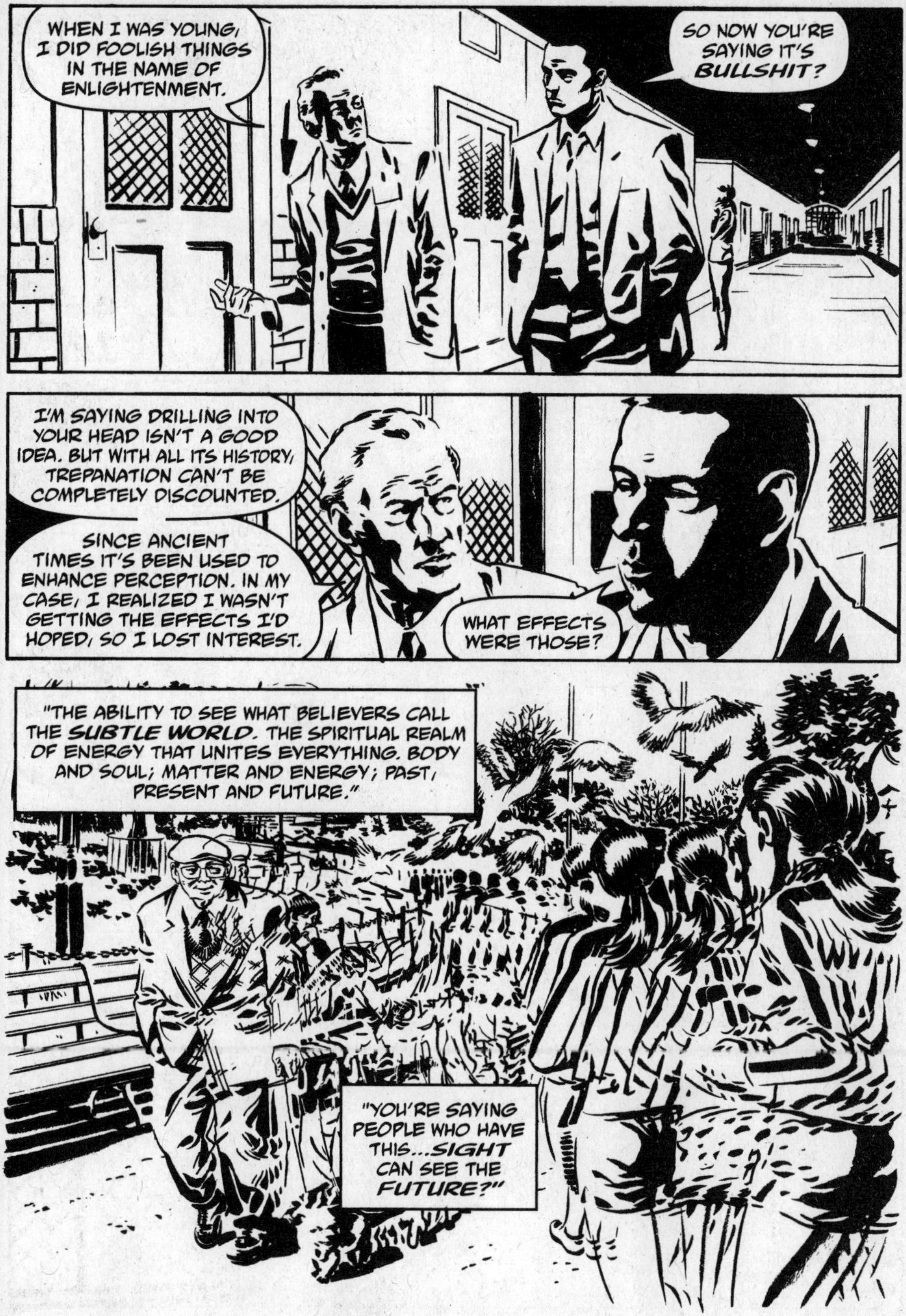
WHEN I WAS YOUNG, I DID FOOLISH THINGS IN THE NAME OF ENLIGHTENMENT.
SO NOW YOU'RE SAYING IT'S BULLSHIT?
I'M SAYING DRILLING INTO YOUR HEAD ISN'T A GOOD IDEA. BUT WITH ALL ITS HISTORY, TREPANATION CAN'T BE COMPLETELY DISCOUNTED.
SINCE ANCIENT TIMES IT'S BEEN USED TO ENHANCE PERCEPTION. IN MY CASE, I REALIZED I WASN'T GETTING THE EFFECTS I'D HOPED, SO I LOST INTEREST.
WHAT EFFECTS WERE THOSE?
"THE ABILITY TO SEE WHAT BELIEVERS CALL THE SUBTLE WORLD. THE SPIRITUAL REALM OF ENERGY THAT UNITES EVERYTHING. BODY AND SOUL; MATTER AND ENERGY; PAST, PRESENT AND FUTURE."
"YOU'RE SAYING PEOPLE WHO HAVE THIS...SIGHT CAN SEE THE FUTURE?"

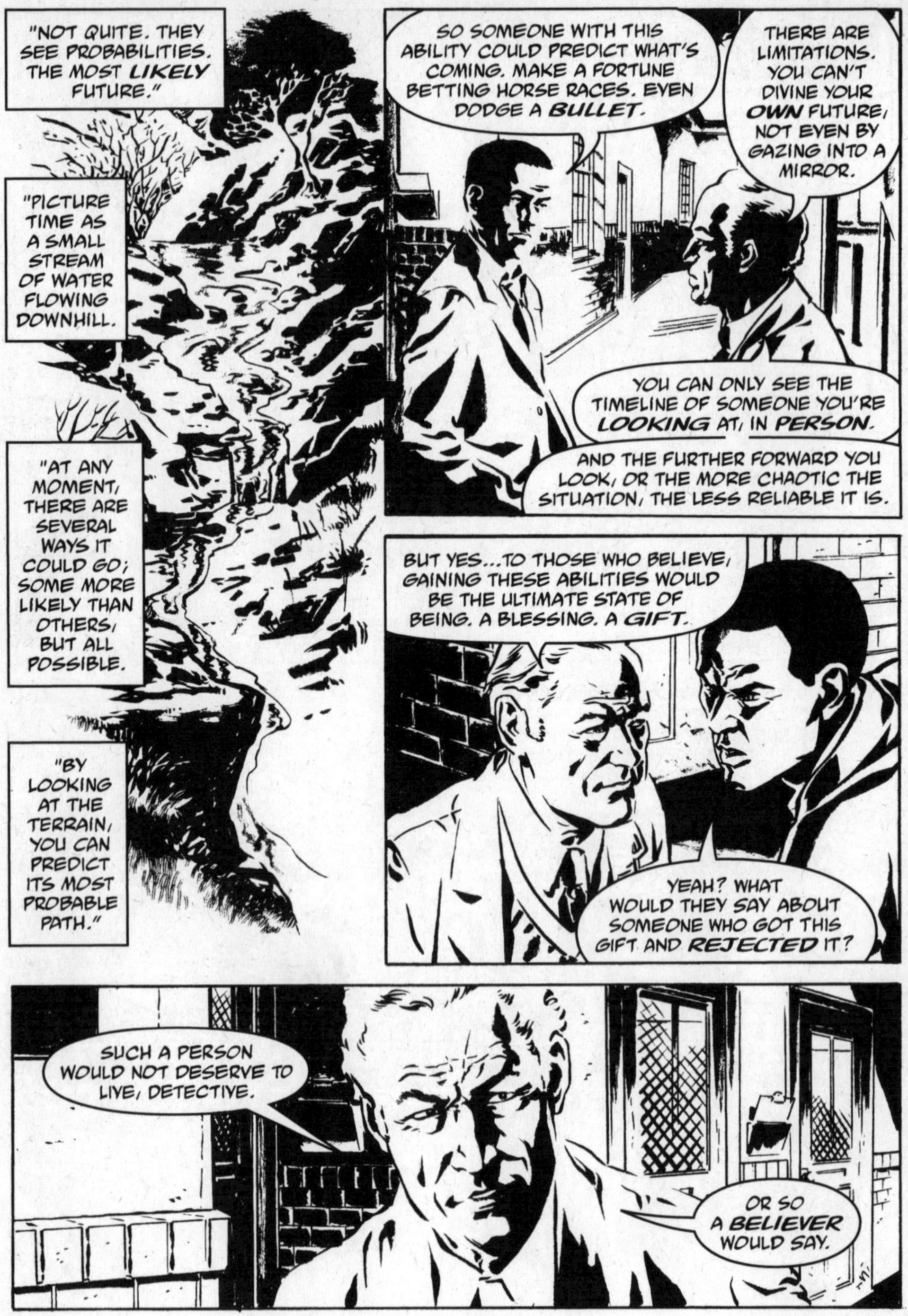
"NOT QUITE. THEY SEE PROBABILITIES. THE MOST LIKELY FUTURE."
"PICTURE TIME AS A SMALL STREAM OF WATER FLOWING DOWNHILL.
"AT ANY MOMENT, THERE ARE SEVERAL WAYS IT COULD GO; SOME MORE LIKELY THAN OTHERS, BUT ALL POSSIBLE.
"BY LOOKING AT THE TERRAIN, YOU CAN PREDICT ITS MOST PROBABLE PATH."
SO SOMEONE WITH THIS ABILITY COULD PREDICT WHAT'S COMING. MAKE A FORTUNE BETTING HORSE RACES. EVEN DODGE A BULLET.
THERE ARE LIMITATIONS. YOU CAN'T DIVINE YOUR OWN FUTURE, NOT EVEN BY GAZING INTO A MIRROR.
YOU CAN ONLY SEE THE TIMELINE OF SOMEONE YOU'RE LOOKING AT, IN PERSON.
AND THE FURTHER FORWARD YOU LOOK, OR THE MORE CHAOTIC THE SITUATION, THE LESS RELIABLE IT IS.
BUT YES...TO THOSE WHO BELIEVE, GAINING THESE ABILITIES WOULD BE THE ULTIMATE STATE OF BEING. A BLESSING. A GIFT.
YEAH? WHAT WOULD THEY SAY ABOUT SOMEONE WHO GOT THIS GIFT AND REJECTED IT?
SUCH A PERSON WOULD NOT DESERVE TO LIVE, DETECTIVE.
OR SO A BELIEVER WOULD SAY.

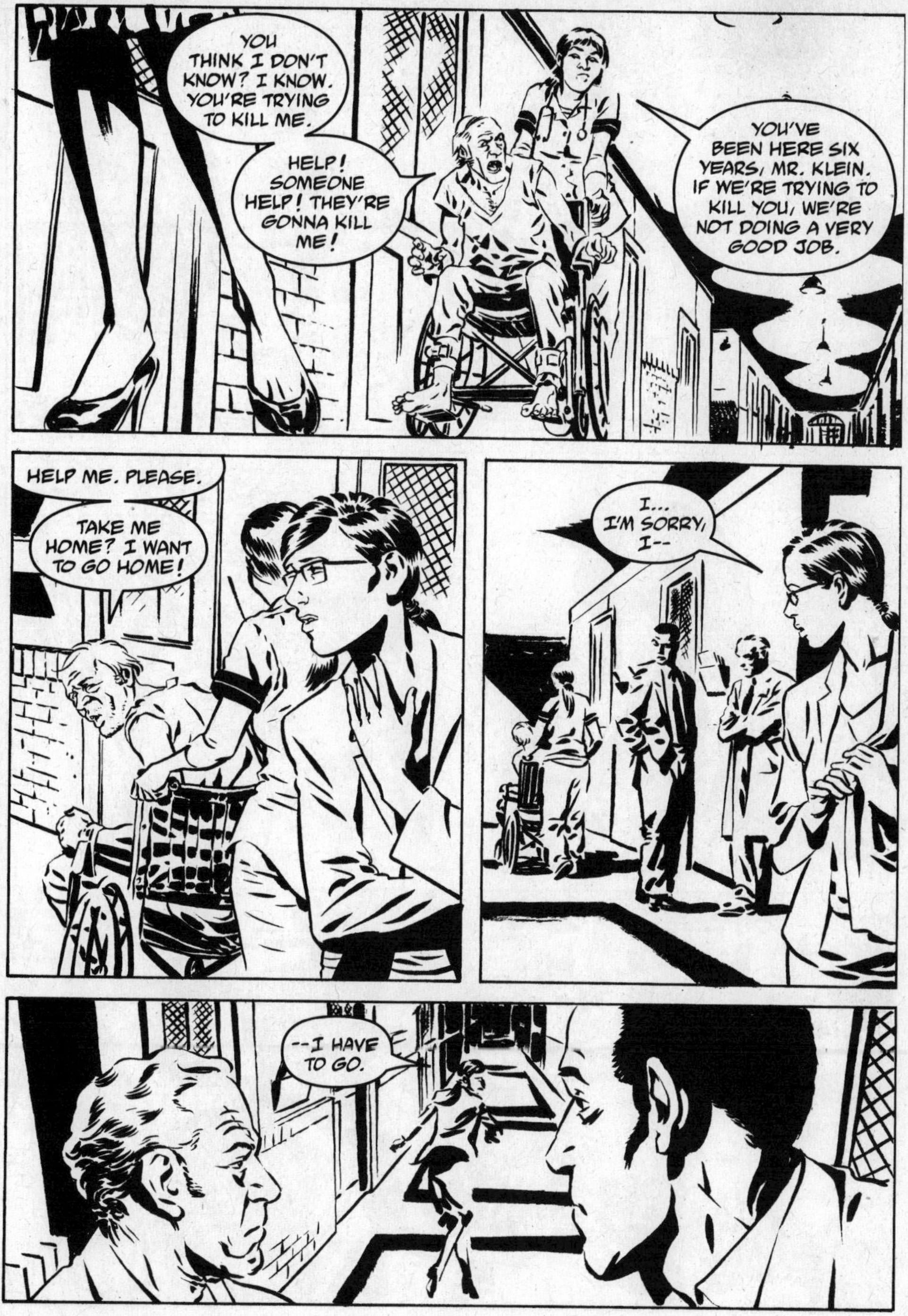
YOU THINK I DON'T KNOW? I KNOW. YOU'RE TRYING TO KILL ME.
HELP! SOMEONE HELP! THEY'RE GONNA KILL ME!
YOU'VE BEEN HERE SIX YEARS, MR. KLEIN. IF WE'RE TRYING TO KILL YOU, WE'RE NOT DOING A VERY GOOD JOB.
HELP ME. PLEASE.
TAKE ME HOME? I WANT TO GO HOME!
I... I'M SORRY, I--
--I HAVE TO GO.

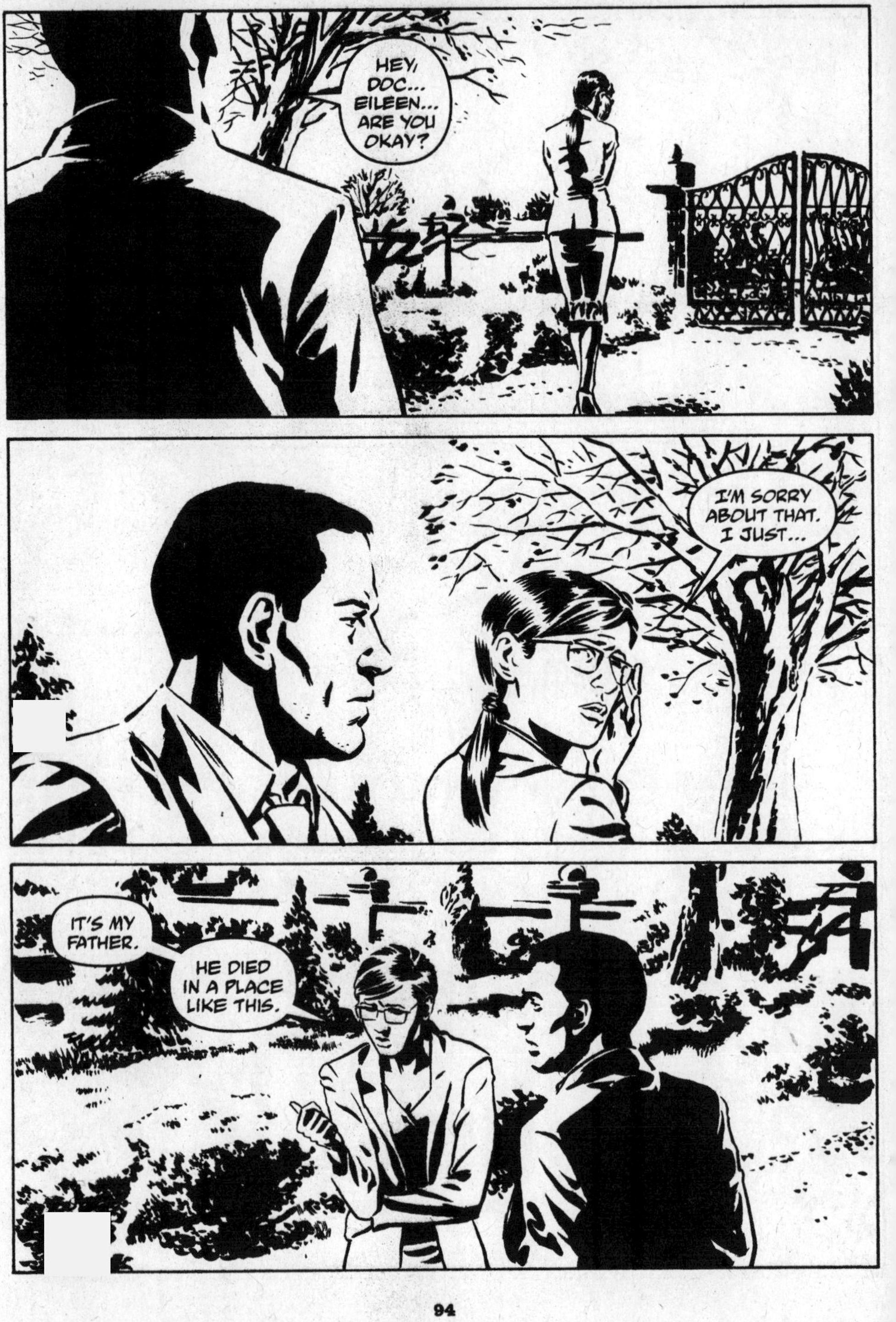
HEY, DOC... EILEEN... ARE YOU OKAY?
I'M SORRY ABOUT THAT. I JUST...
IT'S MY FATHER.
HE DIED IN A PLACE LIKE THIS.

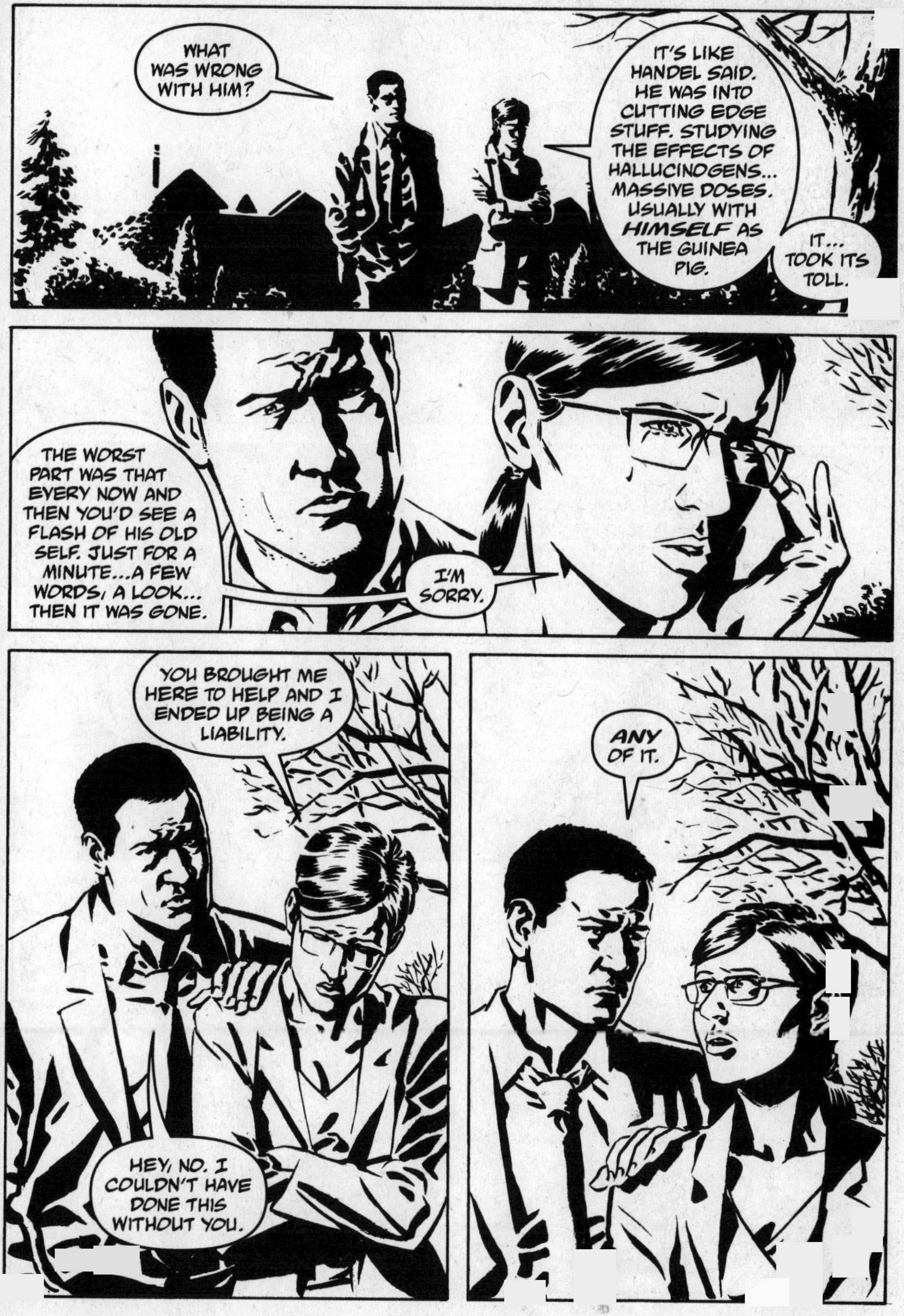
WHAT WAS WRONG WITH HIM?
IT'S LIKE HANDEL SAID. HE WAS INTO CUTTING EDGE STUFF. STUDYING THE EFFECTS OF HALLUCINOGENS... MASSIVE DOSES. USUALLY WITH *HIMSELF* AS THE GUINEA PIG.
IT... TOOK ITS TOLL.
THE WORST PART WAS THAT EVERY NOW AND THEN YOU'D SEE A FLASH OF HIS OLD SELF. JUST FOR A MINUTE...A FEW WORDS, A LOOK... THEN IT WAS GONE.
I'M SORRY.
YOU BROUGHT ME HERE TO HELP AND I ENDED UP BEING A LIABILITY.
HEY, NO. I COULDN'T HAVE DONE THIS WITHOUT YOU.
ANY OF IT.

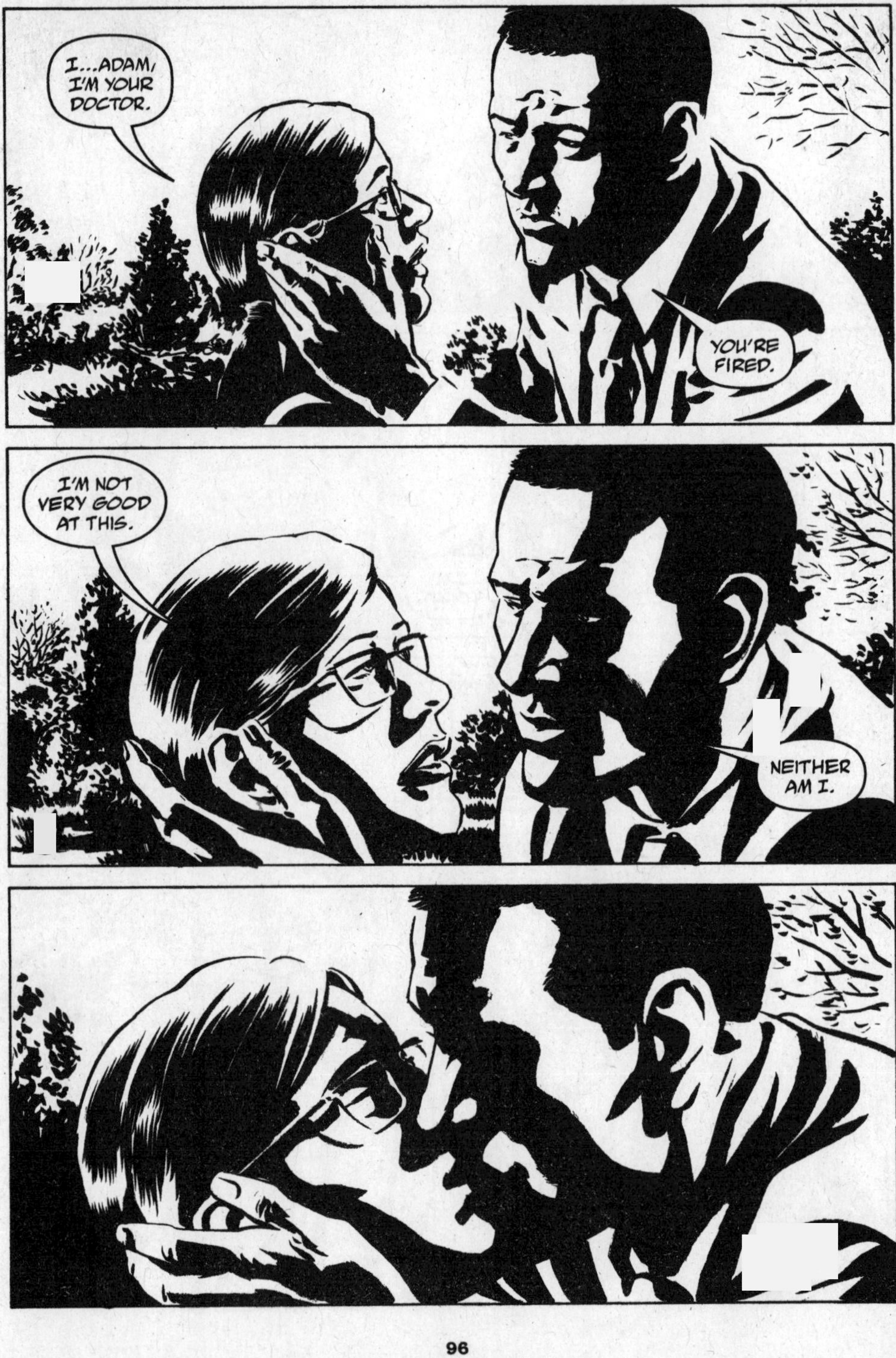
I...ADAM, I'M YOUR DOCTOR.
YOU'RE FIRED.
I'M NOT VERY GOOD AT THIS.
NEITHER AM I.

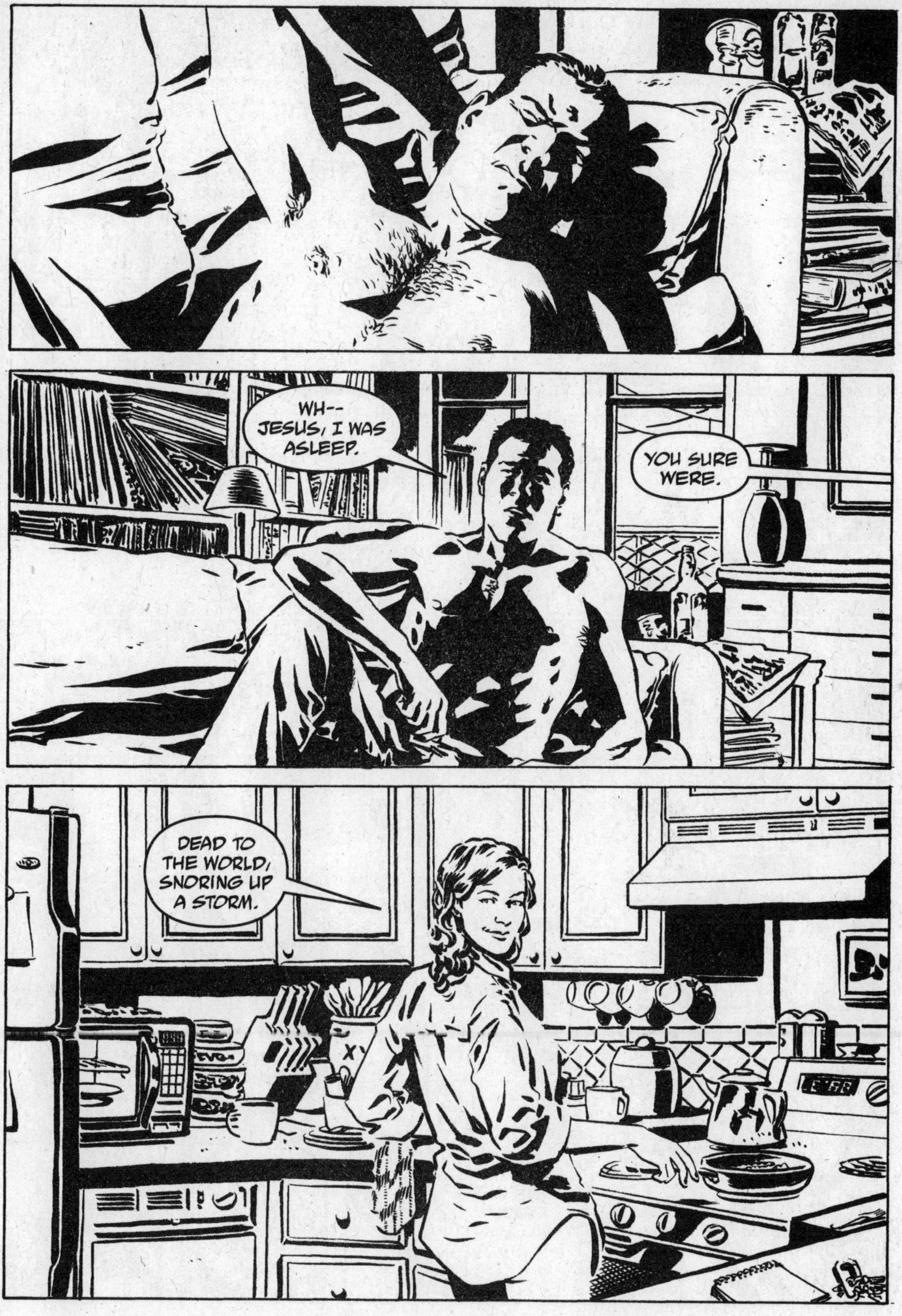
WH-- JESUS, I WAS ASLEEP.
YOU SURE WERE.
DEAD TO THE WORLD, SNORING UP A STORM.

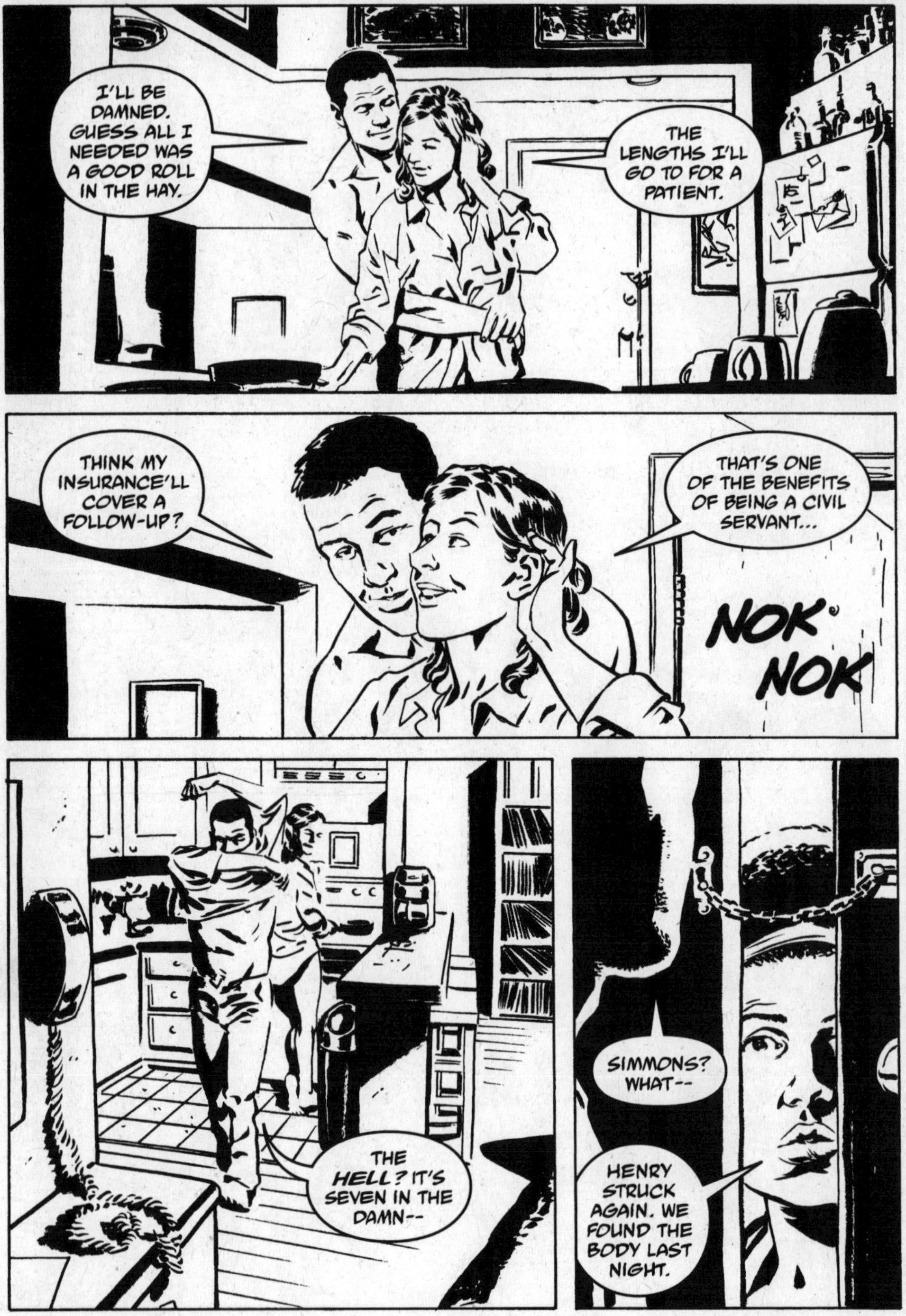
I'LL BE DAMNED. GUESS ALL I NEEDED WAS A GOOD ROLL IN THE HAY.
THE LENGTHS I'LL GO TO FOR A PATIENT.
THINK MY INSURANCE'LL COVER A FOLLOW-UP?
THAT'S ONE OF THE BENEFITS OF BEING A CIVIL SERVANT...
NOK NOK
THE *HELL?* IT'S SEVEN IN THE DAMN--
SIMMONS? WHAT--
HENRY STRUCK AGAIN. WE FOUND THE BODY LAST NIGHT.

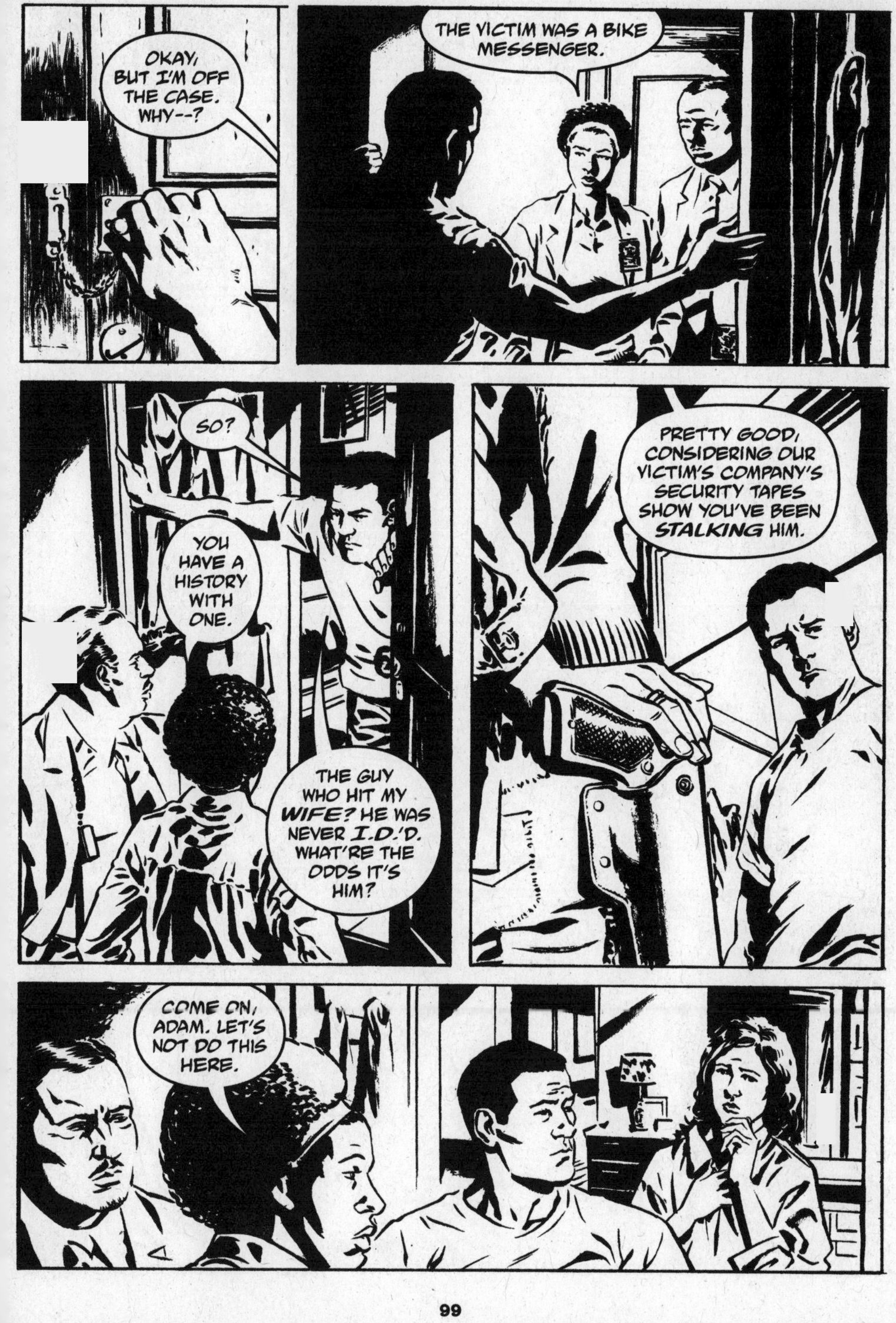
OKAY, BUT I'M OFF THE CASE. WHY--?
THE VICTIM WAS A BIKE MESSENGER.
SO?
YOU HAVE A HISTORY WITH ONE.
THE GUY WHO HIT MY WIFE? HE WAS NEVER I.D.'D. WHAT'RE THE ODDS IT'S HIM?
PRETTY GOOD, CONSIDERING OUR VICTIM'S COMPANY'S SECURITY TAPES SHOW YOU'VE BEEN STALKING HIM.
COME ON, ADAM. LET'S NOT DO THIS HERE.

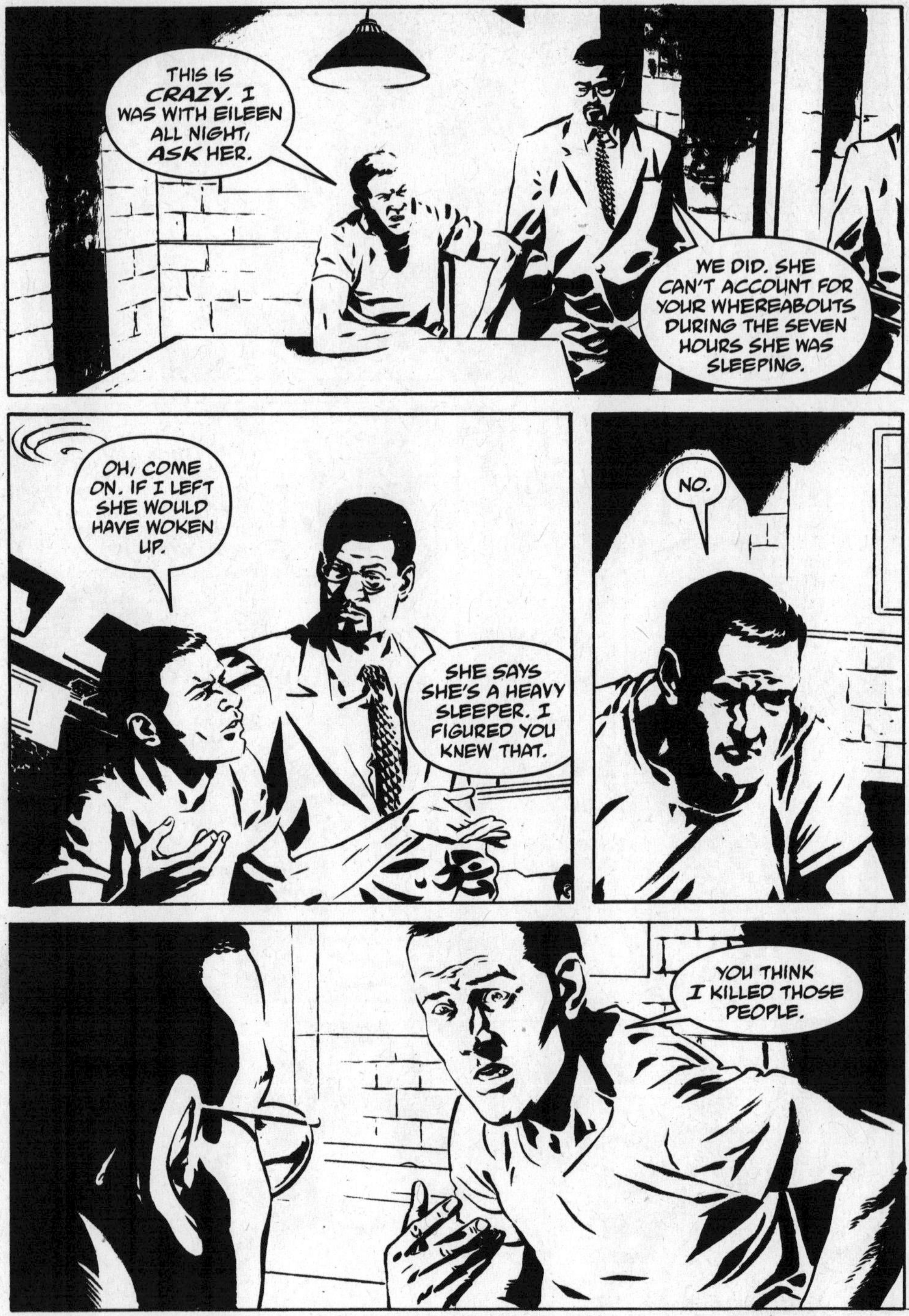
THIS IS *CRAZY*. I WAS WITH EILEEN ALL NIGHT, *ASK* HER.
WE DID. SHE CAN'T ACCOUNT FOR YOUR WHEREABOUTS DURING THE SEVEN HOURS SHE WAS SLEEPING.
OH, COME ON. IF I LEFT SHE WOULD HAVE WOKEN UP.
SHE SAYS SHE'S A HEAVY SLEEPER. I FIGURED YOU KNEW THAT.
NO.
YOU THINK *I* KILLED THOSE PEOPLE.

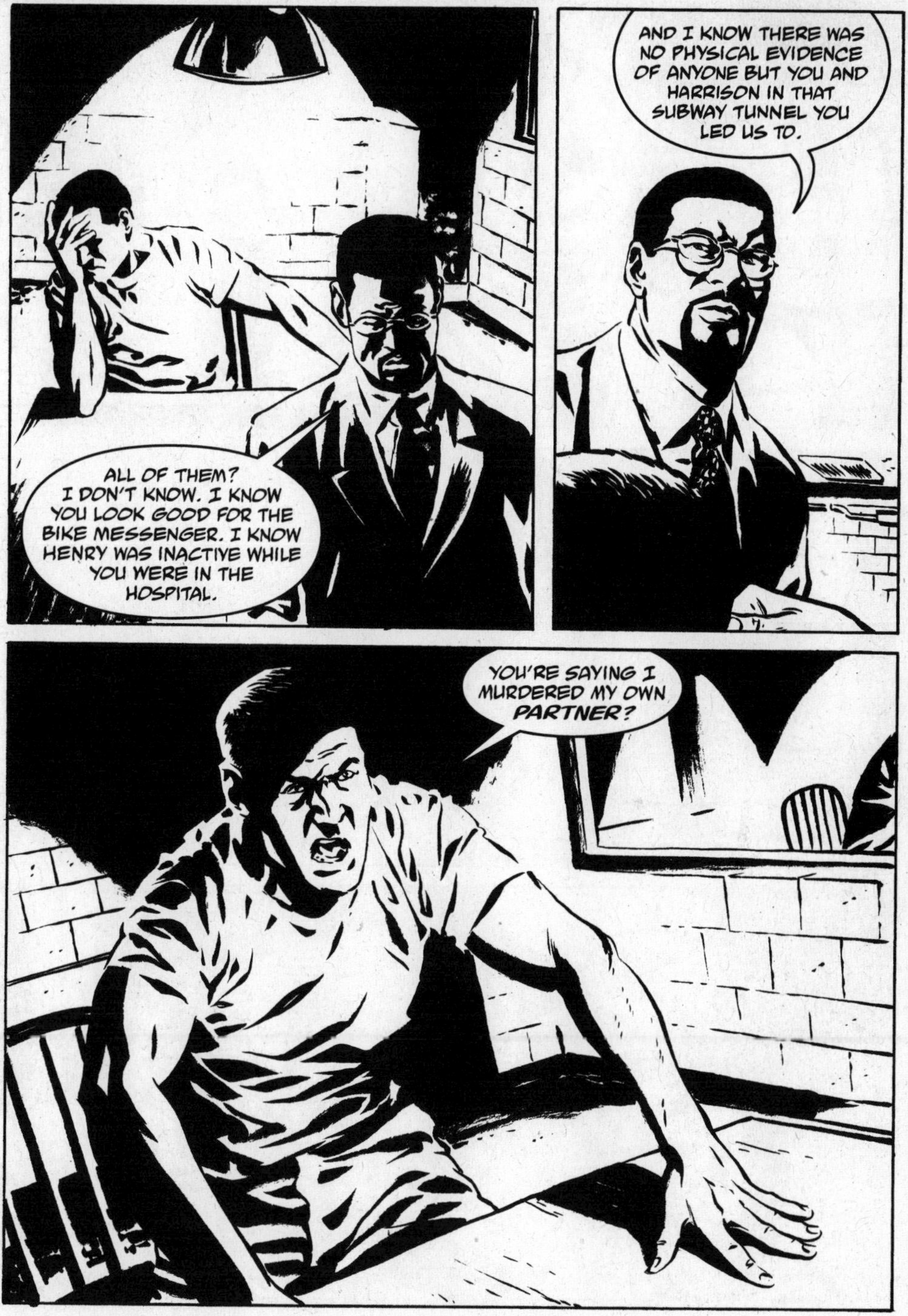
ALL OF THEM? I DON'T KNOW. I KNOW YOU LOOK GOOD FOR THE BIKE MESSENGER. I KNOW HENRY WAS INACTIVE WHILE YOU WERE IN THE HOSPITAL.
AND I KNOW THERE WAS NO PHYSICAL EVIDENCE OF ANYONE BUT YOU AND HARRISON IN THAT SUBWAY TUNNEL YOU LED US TO.
YOU'RE SAYING I MURDERED MY OWN *PARTNER*?

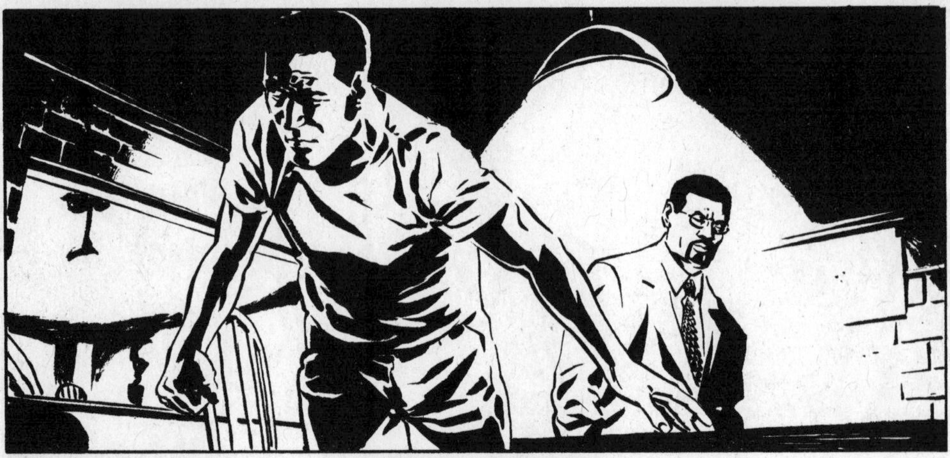

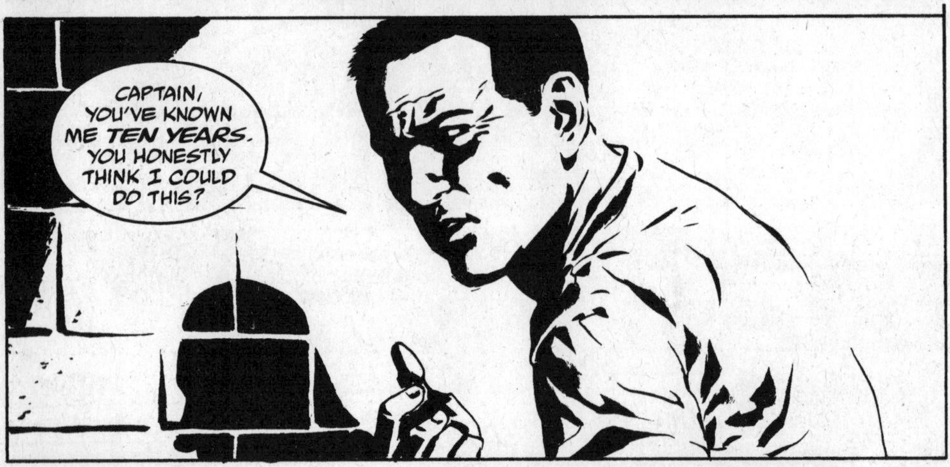
CAPTAIN, YOU'VE KNOWN ME TEN YEARS. YOU HONESTLY THINK I COULD DO THIS?

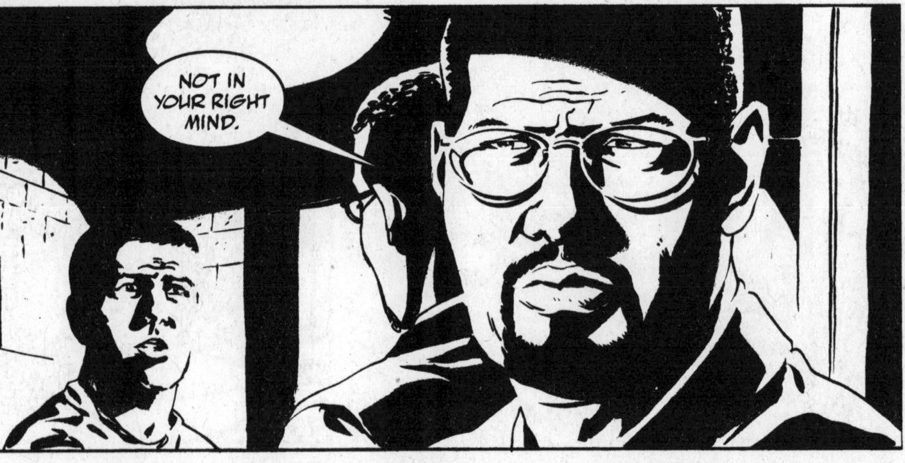
NOT IN YOUR RIGHT MIND.

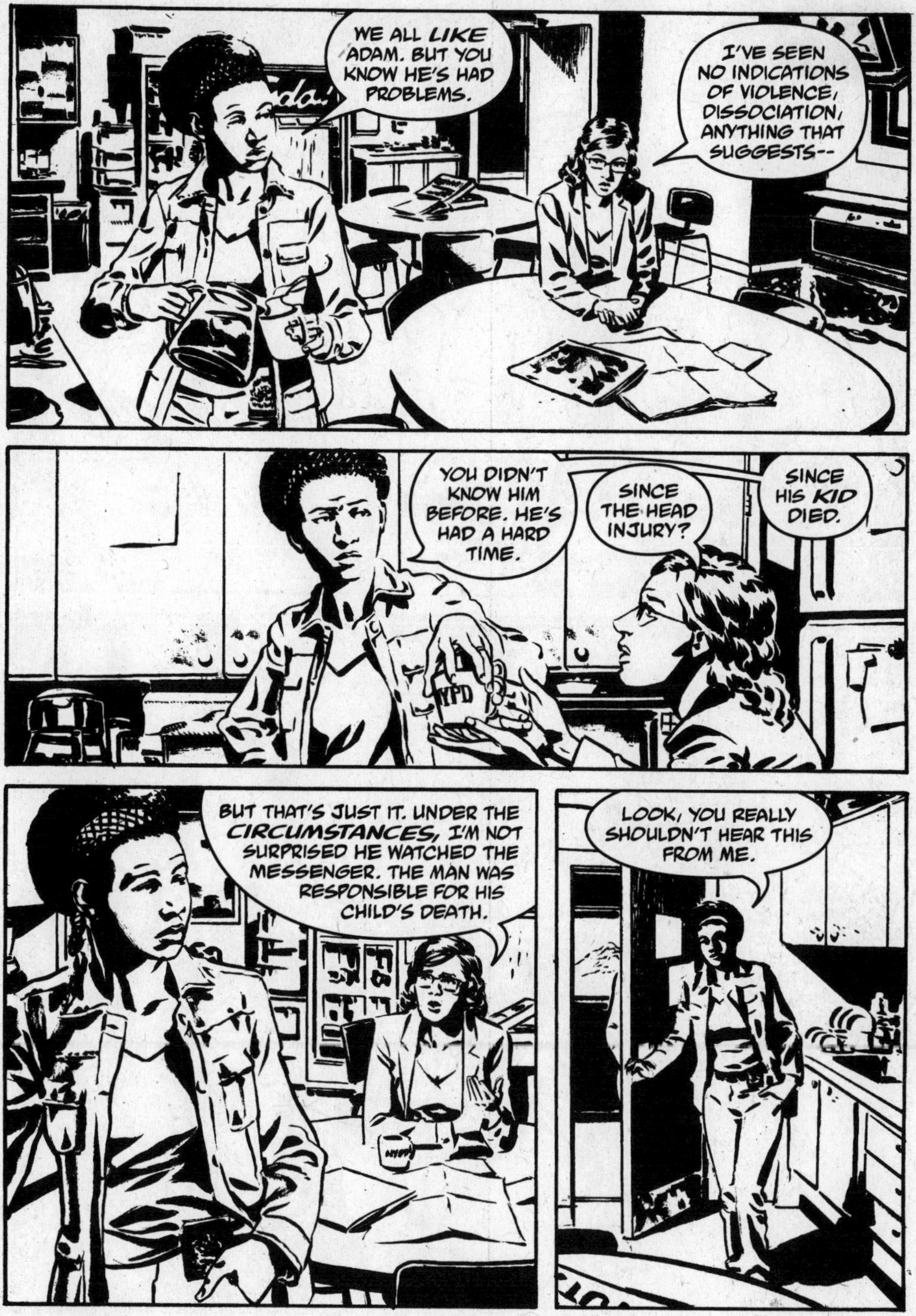
WE ALL LIKE ADAM. BUT YOU KNOW HE'S HAD PROBLEMS.
I'VE SEEN NO INDICATIONS OF VIOLENCE, DISSOCIATION, ANYTHING THAT SUGGESTS--
YOU DIDN'T KNOW HIM BEFORE. HE'S HAD A HARD TIME.
SINCE THE HEAD INJURY?
SINCE HIS KID DIED.
NYPD
BUT THAT'S JUST IT. UNDER THE CIRCUMSTANCES, I'M NOT SURPRISED HE WATCHED THE MESSENGER. THE MAN WAS RESPONSIBLE FOR HIS CHILD'S DEATH.
LOOK, YOU REALLY SHOULDN'T HEAR THIS FROM ME.

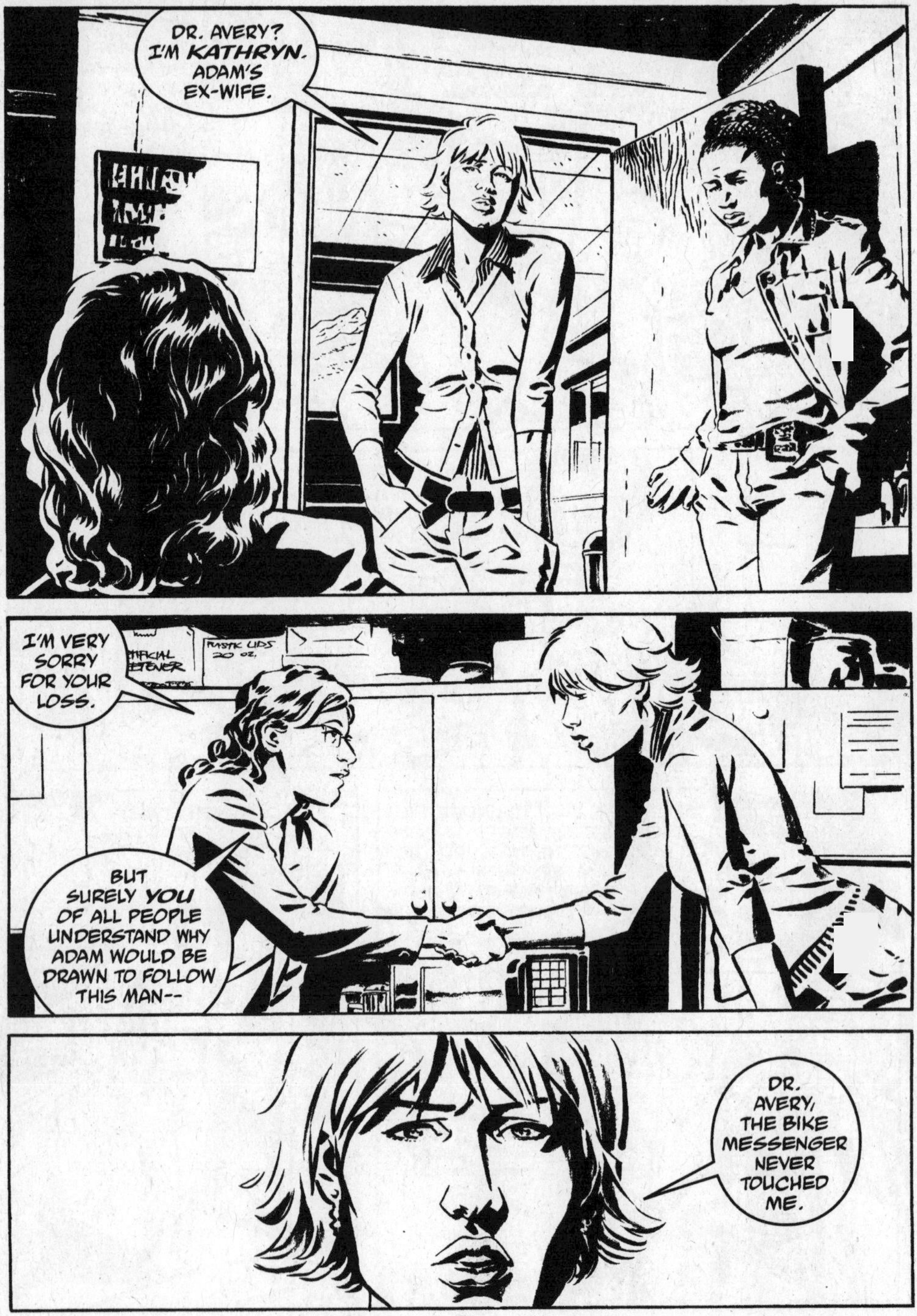
DR. AVERY? I'M KATHRYN. ADAM'S EX-WIFE.
I'M VERY SORRY FOR YOUR LOSS.
BUT SURELY YOU OF ALL PEOPLE UNDERSTAND WHY ADAM WOULD BE DRAWN TO FOLLOW THIS MAN--
DR. AVERY, THE BIKE MESSENGER NEVER TOUCHED ME.

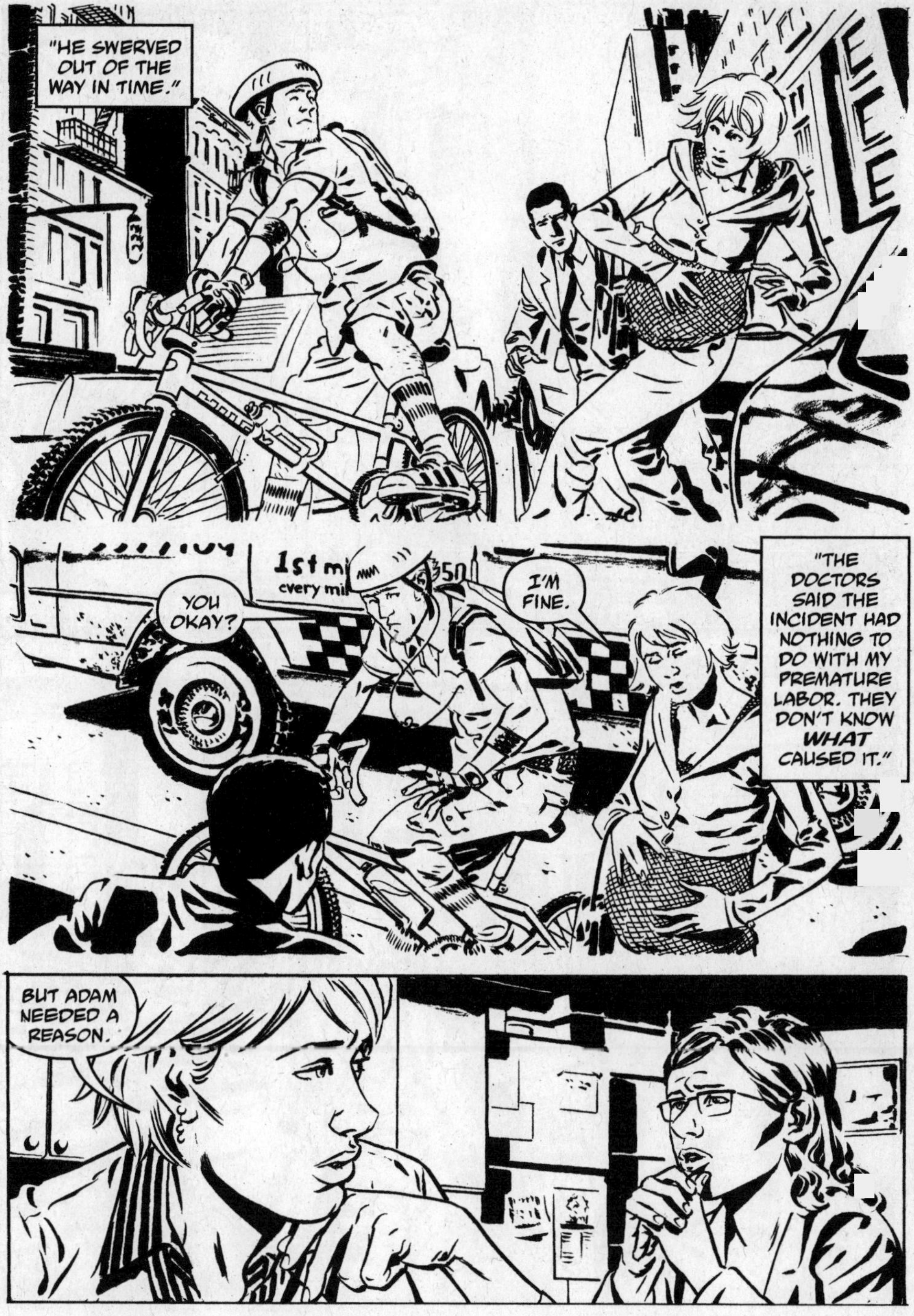
"HE SWERVED OUT OF THE WAY IN TIME."
YOU OKAY?
I'M FINE.
"THE DOCTORS SAID THE INCIDENT HAD NOTHING TO DO WITH MY PREMATURE LABOR. THEY DON'T KNOW *WHAT* CAUSED IT."
BUT ADAM NEEDED A REASON.

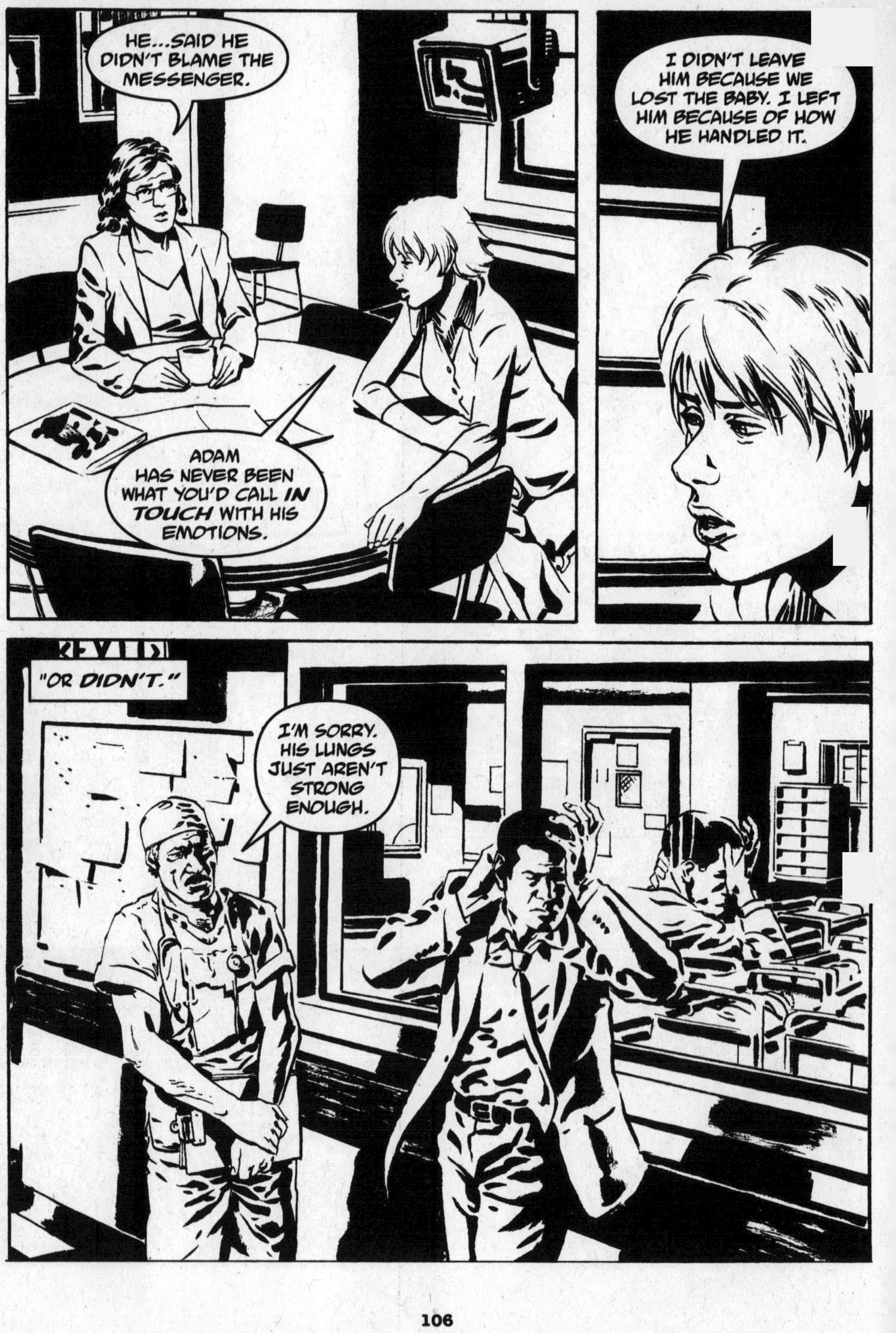
HE...SAID HE DIDN'T BLAME THE MESSENGER.
ADAM HAS NEVER BEEN WHAT YOU'D CALL *IN TOUCH* WITH HIS EMOTIONS.
I DIDN'T LEAVE HIM BECAUSE WE LOST THE BABY. I LEFT HIM BECAUSE OF HOW HE HANDLED IT.
"OR *DIDN'T*."
I'M SORRY. HIS LUNGS JUST AREN'T STRONG ENOUGH.

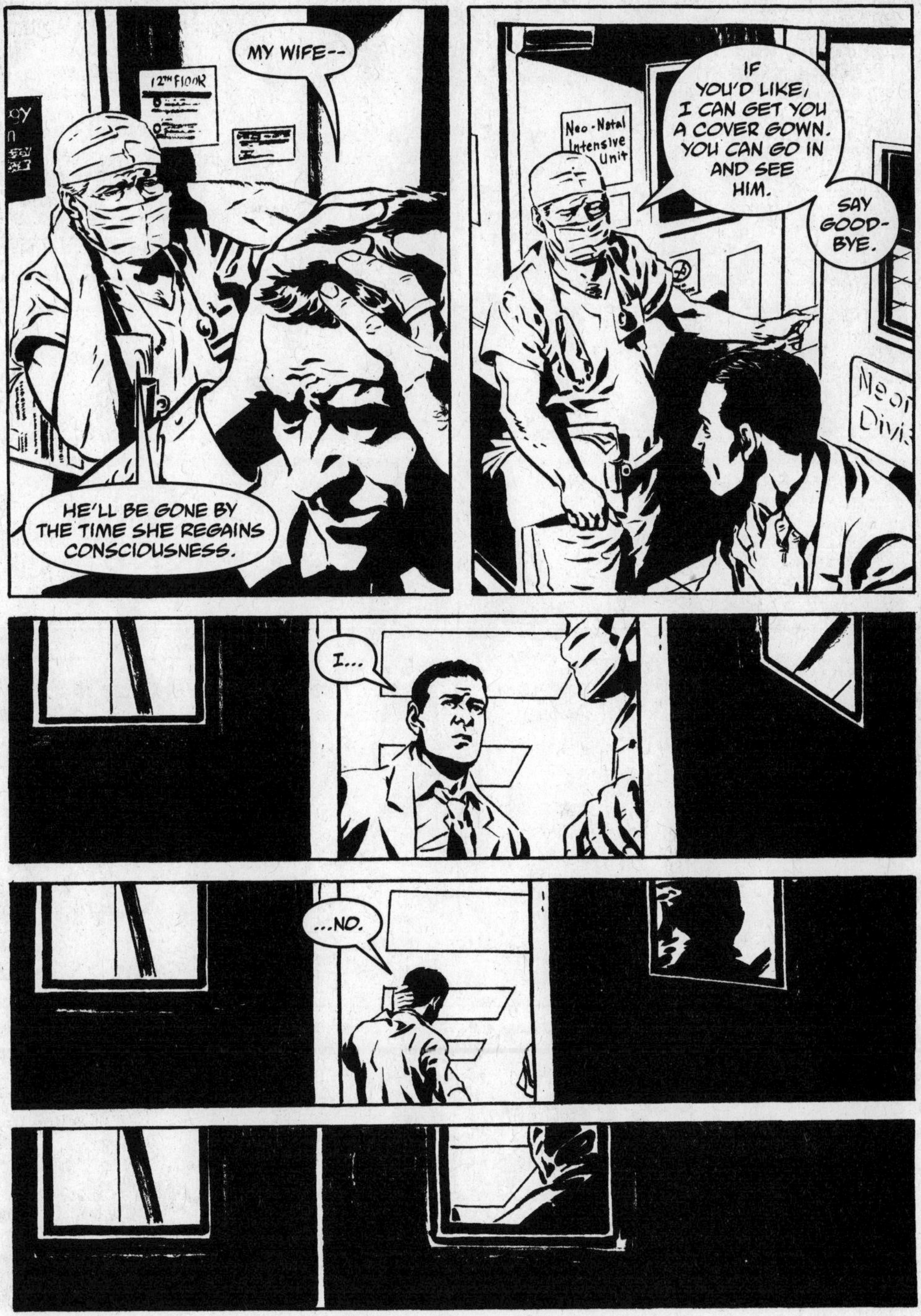
MY WIFE--
12TH FLOOR
HE'LL BE GONE BY THE TIME SHE REGAINS CONSCIOUSNESS.
Neo-Natal Intensive Unit
IF YOU'D LIKE, I CAN GET YOU A COVER GOWN. YOU CAN GO IN AND SEE HIM.
SAY GOOD-BYE.
I...
...NO.

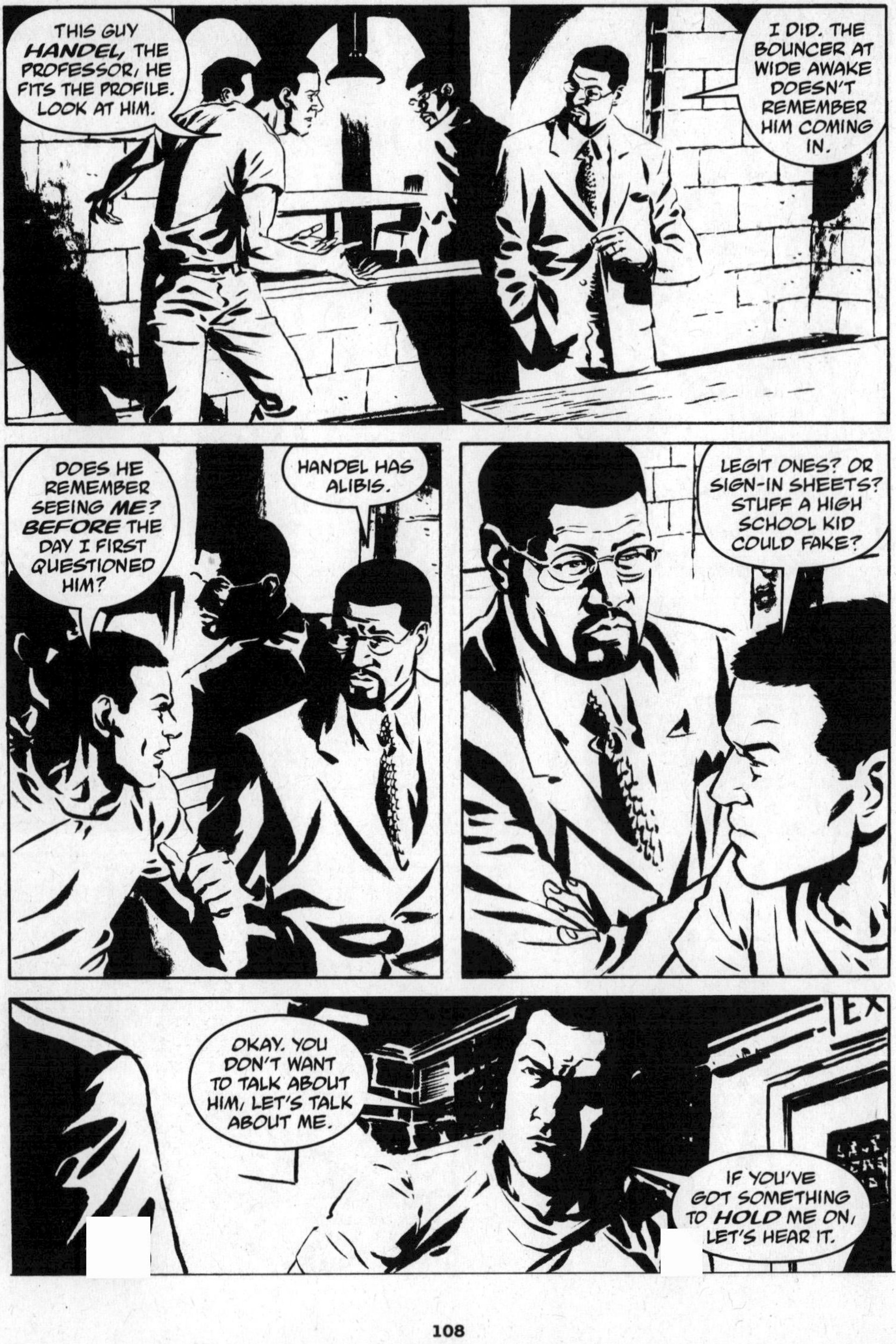
THIS GUY HANDEL, THE PROFESSOR, HE FITS THE PROFILE. LOOK AT HIM.
I DID. THE BOUNCER AT WIDE AWAKE DOESN'T REMEMBER HIM COMING IN.
DOES HE REMEMBER SEEING ME? BEFORE THE DAY I FIRST QUESTIONED HIM?
HANDEL HAS ALIBIS.
LEGIT ONES? OR SIGN-IN SHEETS? STUFF A HIGH SCHOOL KID COULD FAKE?
OKAY. YOU DON'T WANT TO TALK ABOUT HIM, LET'S TALK ABOUT ME.
IF YOU'VE GOT SOMETHING TO HOLD ME ON, LET'S HEAR IT.
EX

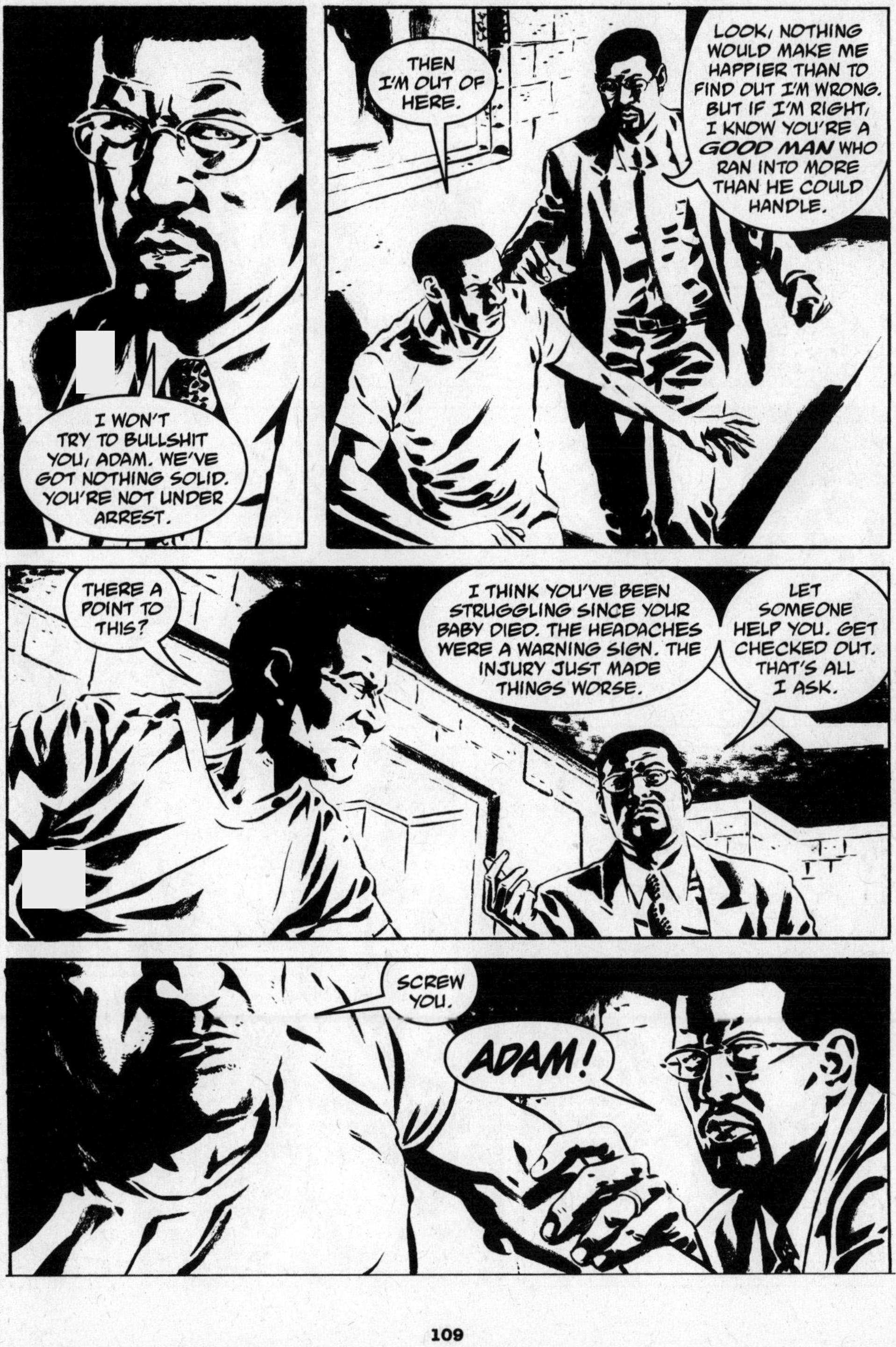
I WON'T TRY TO BULLSHIT YOU, ADAM. WE'VE GOT NOTHING SOLID. YOU'RE NOT UNDER ARREST.
THEN I'M OUT OF HERE.
LOOK, NOTHING WOULD MAKE ME HAPPIER THAN TO FIND OUT I'M WRONG. BUT IF I'M RIGHT, I KNOW YOU'RE A GOOD MAN WHO RAN INTO MORE THAN HE COULD HANDLE.
THERE A POINT TO THIS?
I THINK YOU'VE BEEN STRUGGLING SINCE YOUR BABY DIED. THE HEADACHES WERE A WARNING SIGN. THE INJURY JUST MADE THINGS WORSE.
LET SOMEONE HELP YOU. GET CHECKED OUT. THAT'S ALL I ASK.
SCREW YOU.
ADAM!

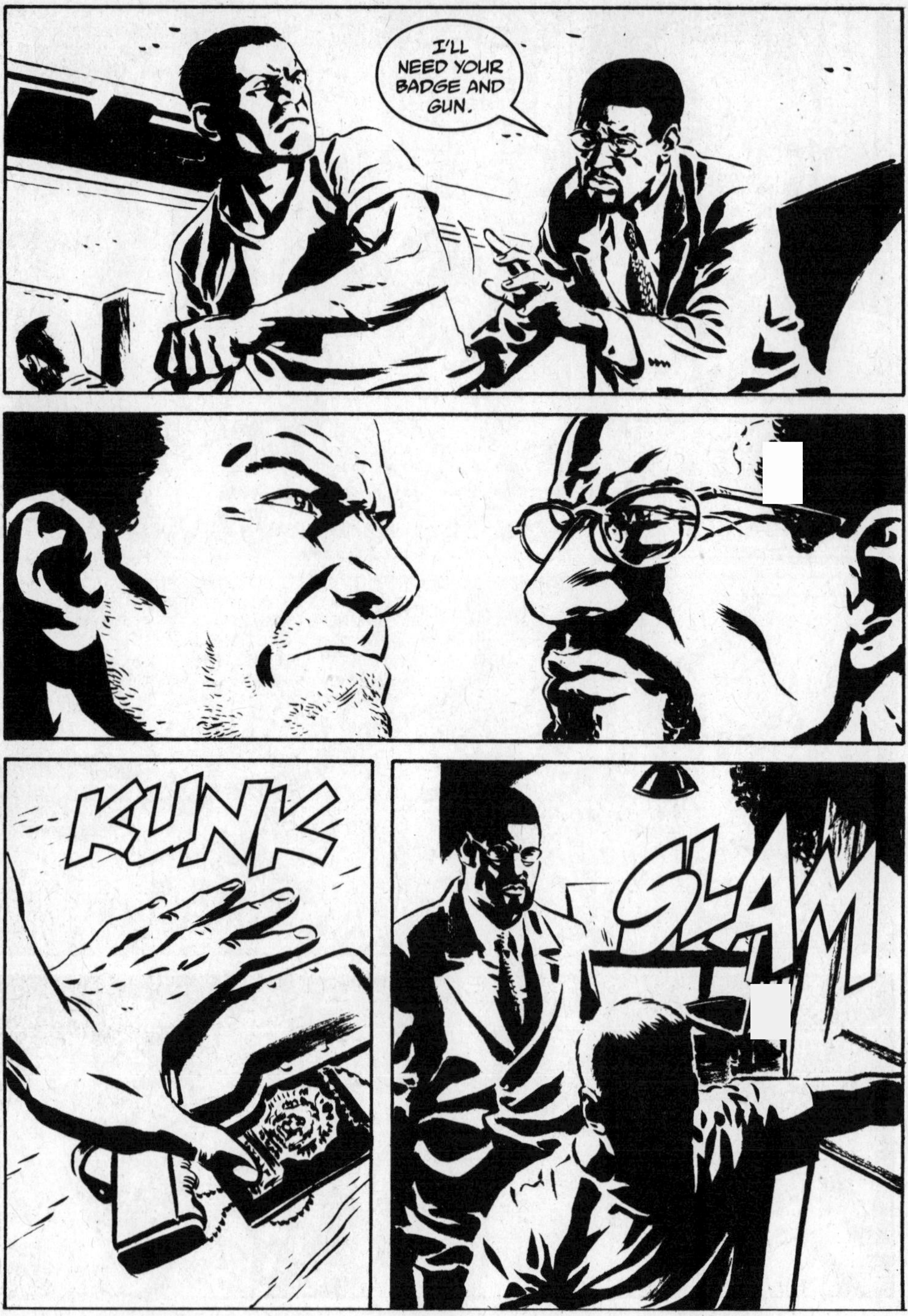

I'LL NEED YOUR BADGE AND GUN.
KUNK
SLAM

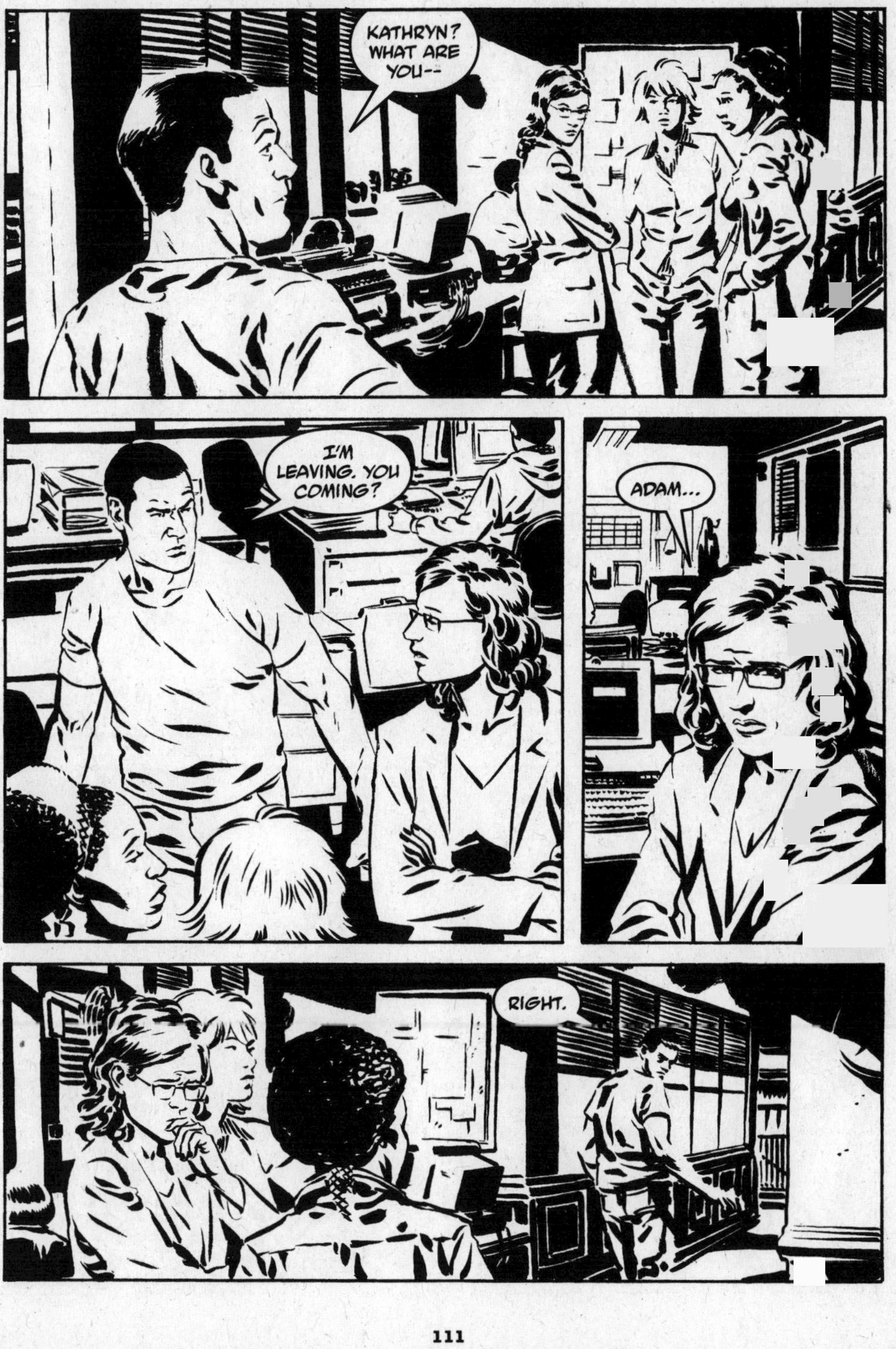
KATHRYN? WHAT ARE YOU--
I'M LEAVING. YOU COMING?
ADAM...
RIGHT.

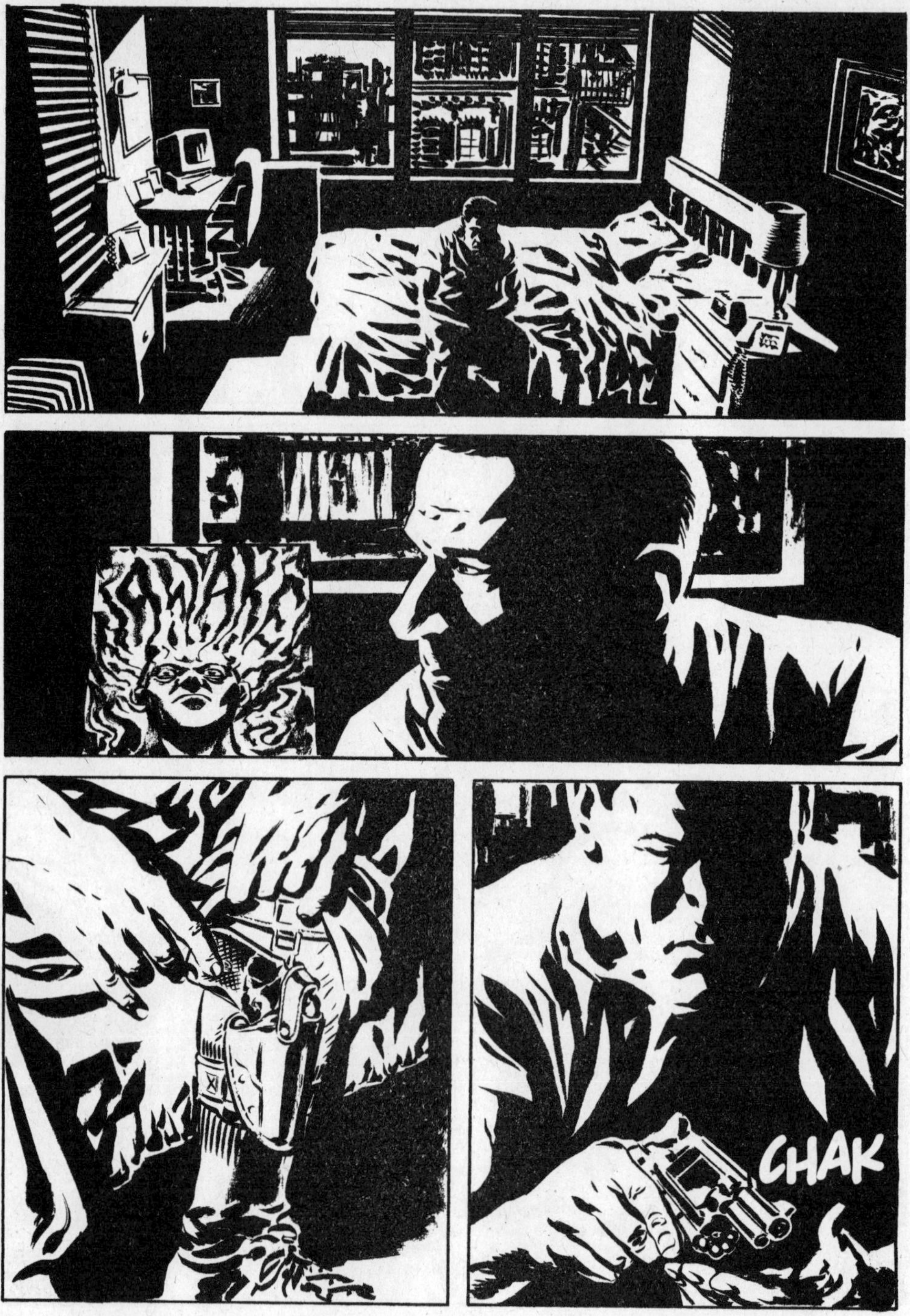
CHAK

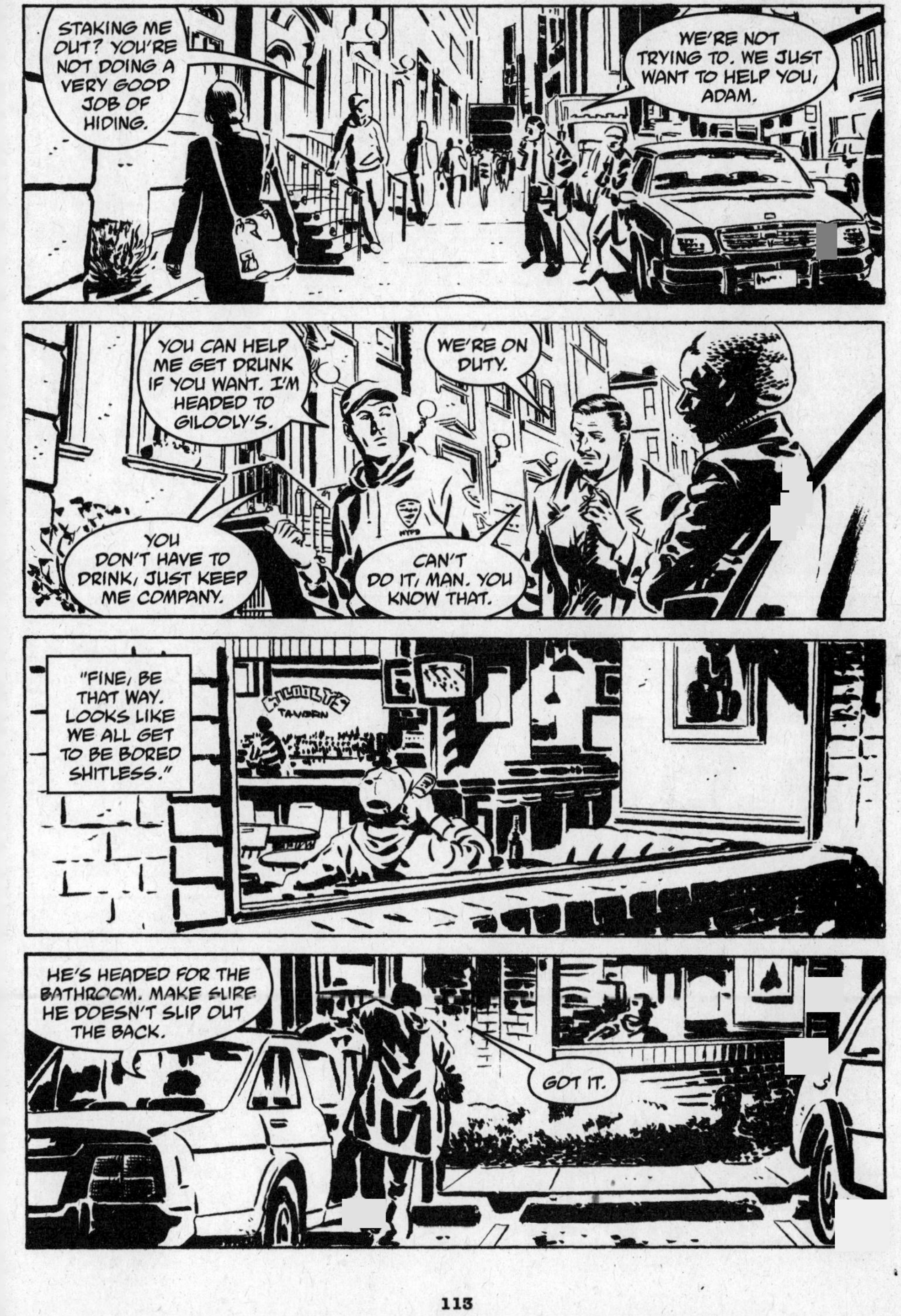
STAKING ME OUT? YOU'RE NOT DOING A VERY GOOD JOB OF HIDING.
WE'RE NOT TRYING TO. WE JUST WANT TO HELP YOU, ADAM.
YOU CAN HELP ME GET DRUNK IF YOU WANT. I'M HEADED TO GILOOLY'S.
WE'RE ON DUTY.
YOU DON'T HAVE TO DRINK, JUST KEEP ME COMPANY.
CAN'T DO IT, MAN. YOU KNOW THAT.
"FINE, BE THAT WAY. LOOKS LIKE WE ALL GET TO BE BORED SHITLESS."
TAVERN
HE'S HEADED FOR THE BATHROOM. MAKE SURE HE DOESN'T SLIP OUT THE BACK.
GOT IT.

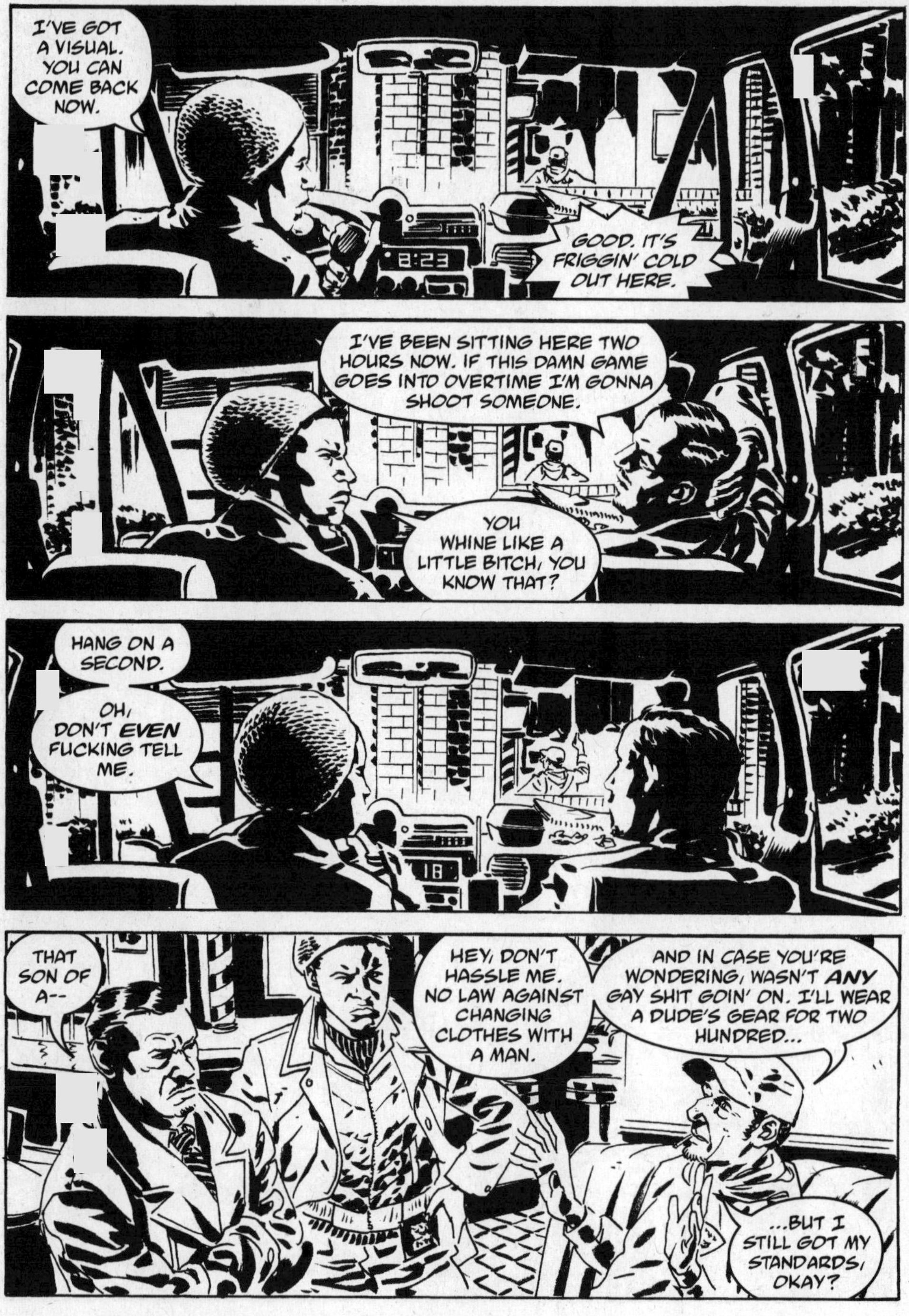
I'VE GOT A VISUAL. YOU CAN COME BACK NOW.
GOOD. IT'S FRIGGIN' COLD OUT HERE.
8:23
I'VE BEEN SITTING HERE TWO HOURS NOW. IF THIS DAMN GAME GOES INTO OVERTIME I'M GONNA SHOOT SOMEONE.
YOU WHINE LIKE A LITTLE BITCH, YOU KNOW THAT?
HANG ON A SECOND.
OH, DON'T *EVEN* FUCKING TELL ME.
THAT SON OF A--
HEY, DON'T HASSLE ME. NO LAW AGAINST CHANGING CLOTHES WITH A MAN.
AND IN CASE YOU'RE WONDERING, WASN'T *ANY* GAY SHIT GOIN' ON. I'LL WEAR A DUDE'S GEAR FOR TWO HUNDRED...
...BUT I STILL GOT MY STANDARDS, OKAY?

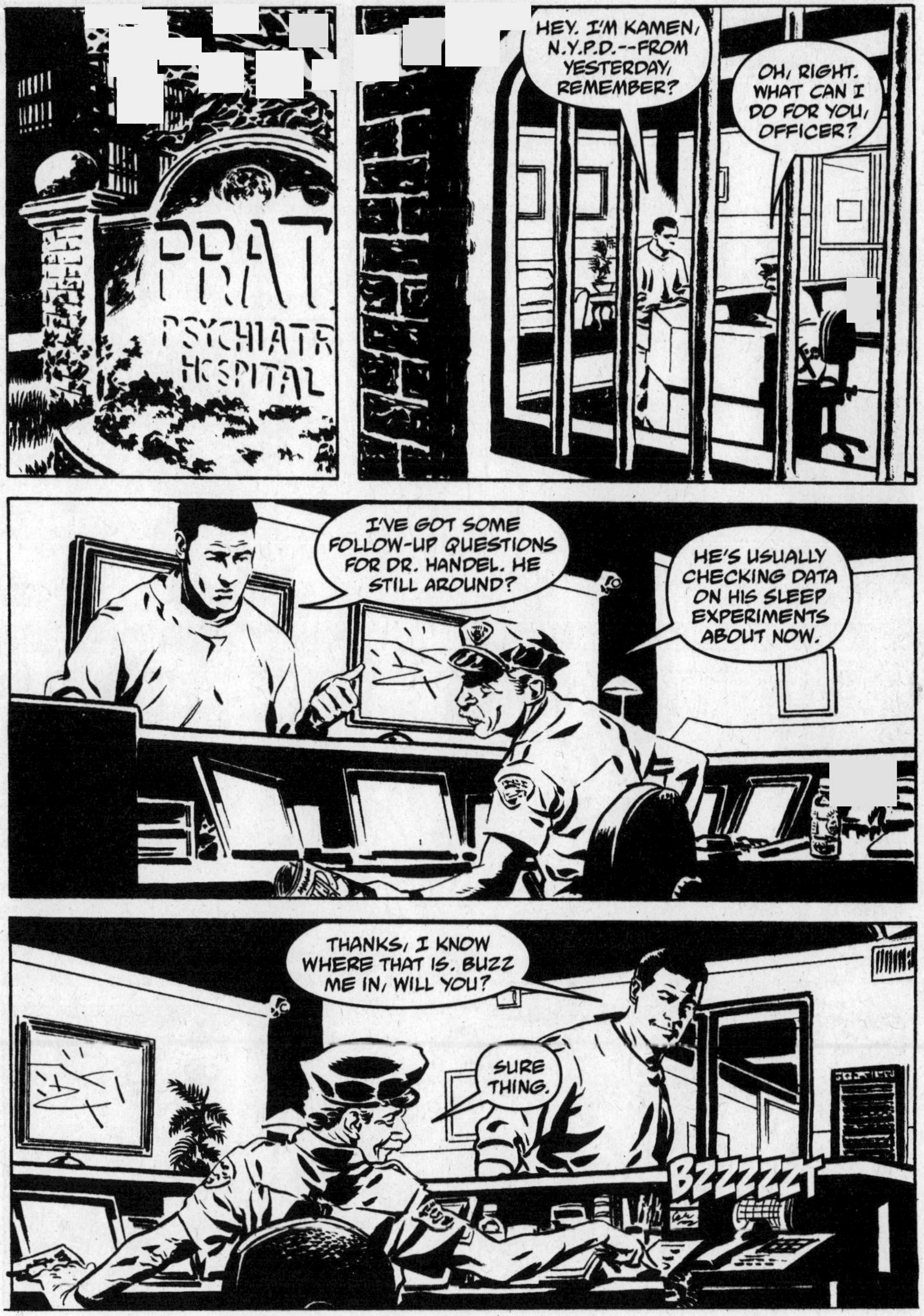
PRAT
PSYCHIATR
HOSPITAL
HEY. I'M KAMEN, N.Y.P.D.--FROM YESTERDAY, REMEMBER?
OH, RIGHT. WHAT CAN I DO FOR YOU, OFFICER?
I'VE GOT SOME FOLLOW-UP QUESTIONS FOR DR. HANDEL. HE STILL AROUND?
HE'S USUALLY CHECKING DATA ON HIS SLEEP EXPERIMENTS ABOUT NOW.
THANKS, I KNOW WHERE THAT IS. BUZZ ME IN, WILL YOU?
SURE THING.
BZZZZZT

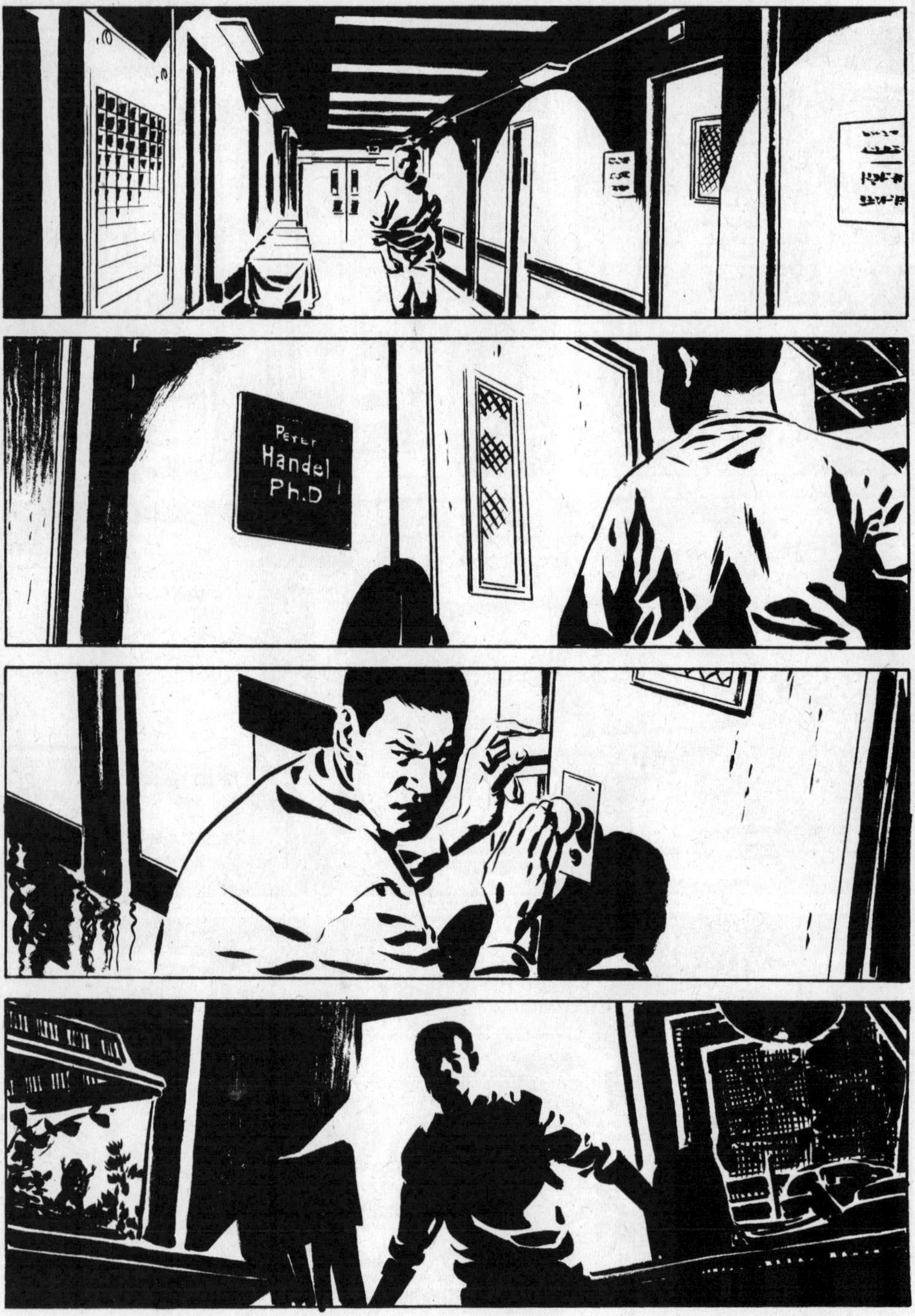
Peter
Handel
Ph.D

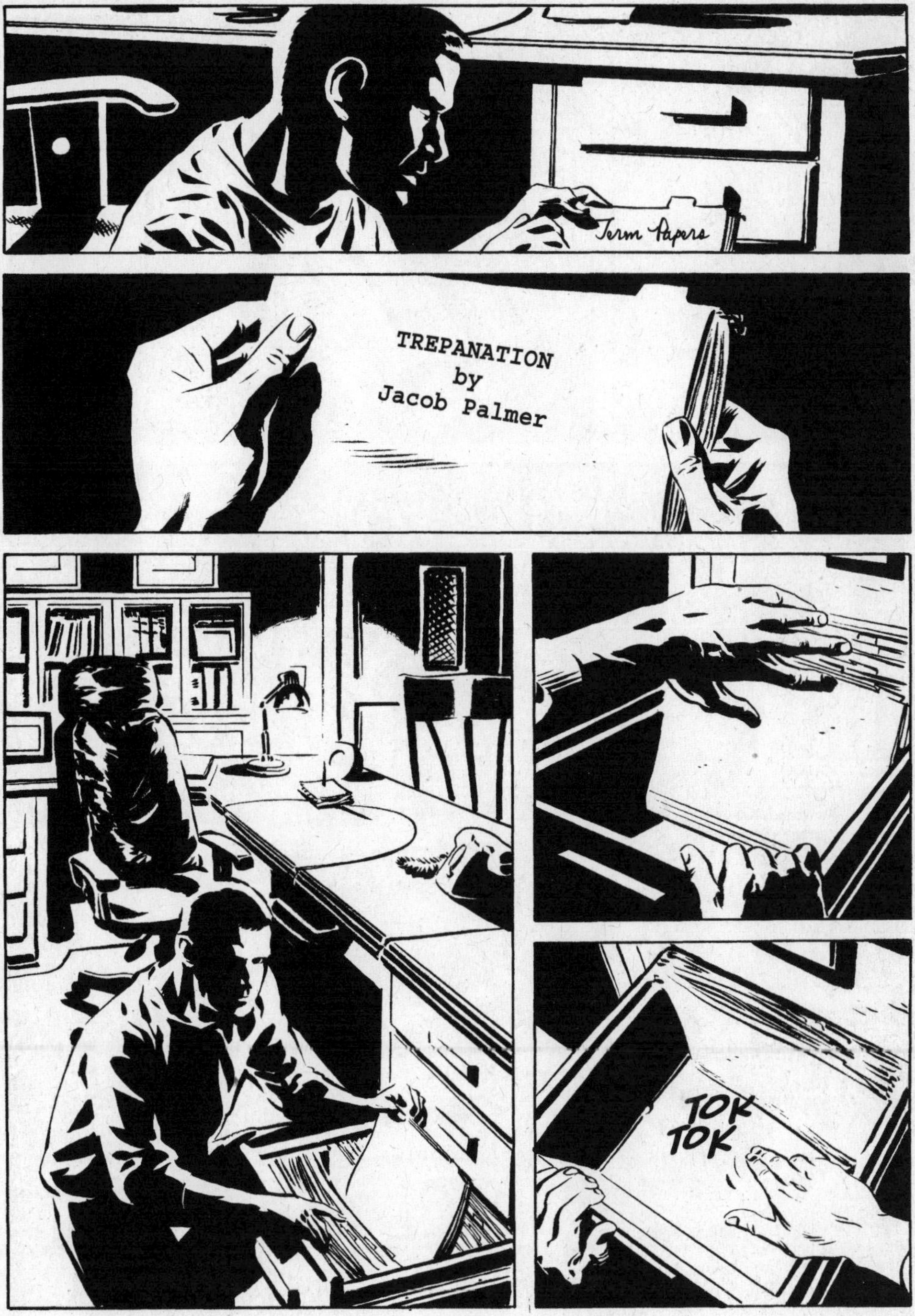
Term Papers
TREPANATION
by
Jacob Palmer
TOK
TOK

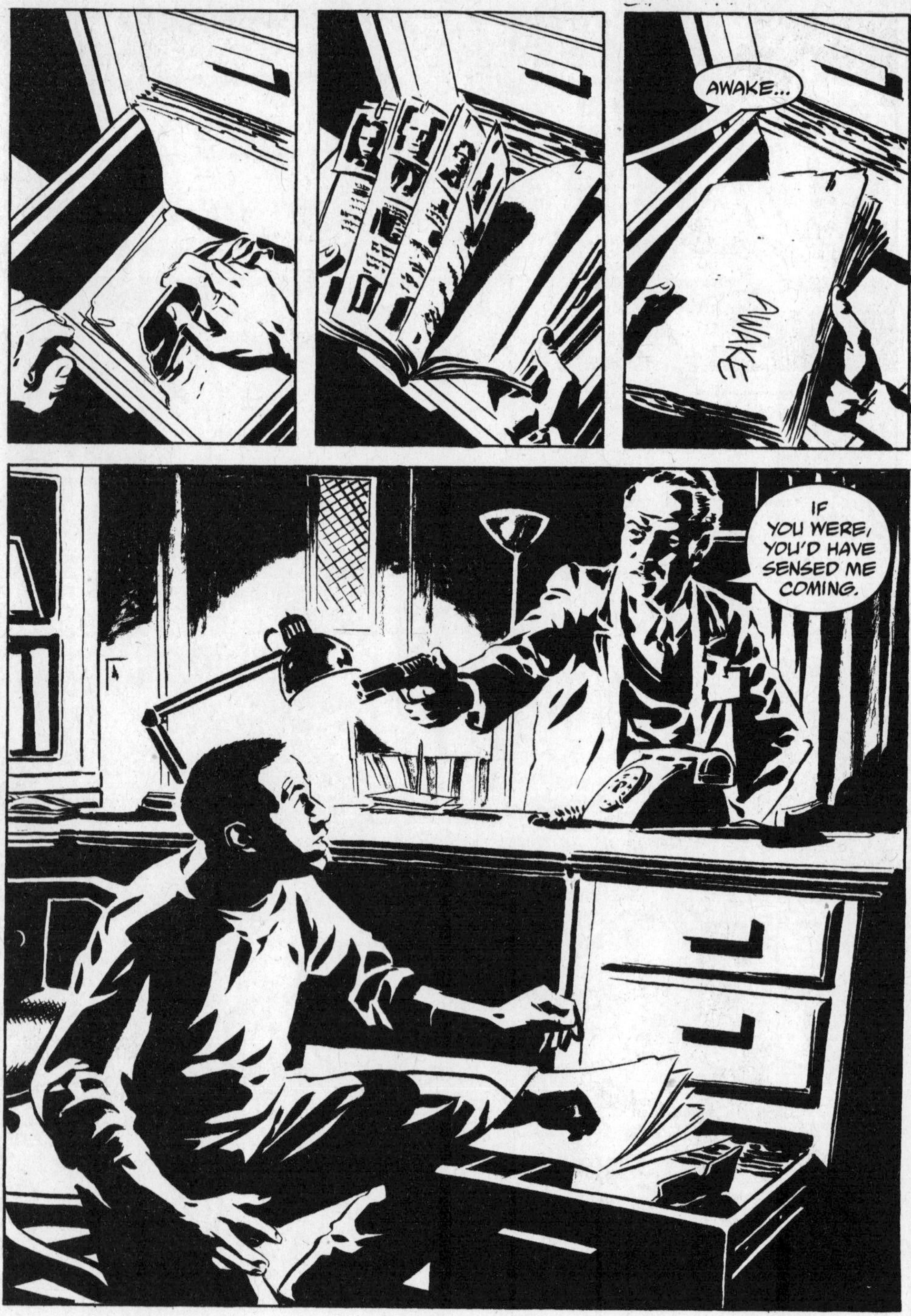
AWAKE...
AWAKE
IF YOU WERE, YOU'D HAVE SENSED ME COMING.

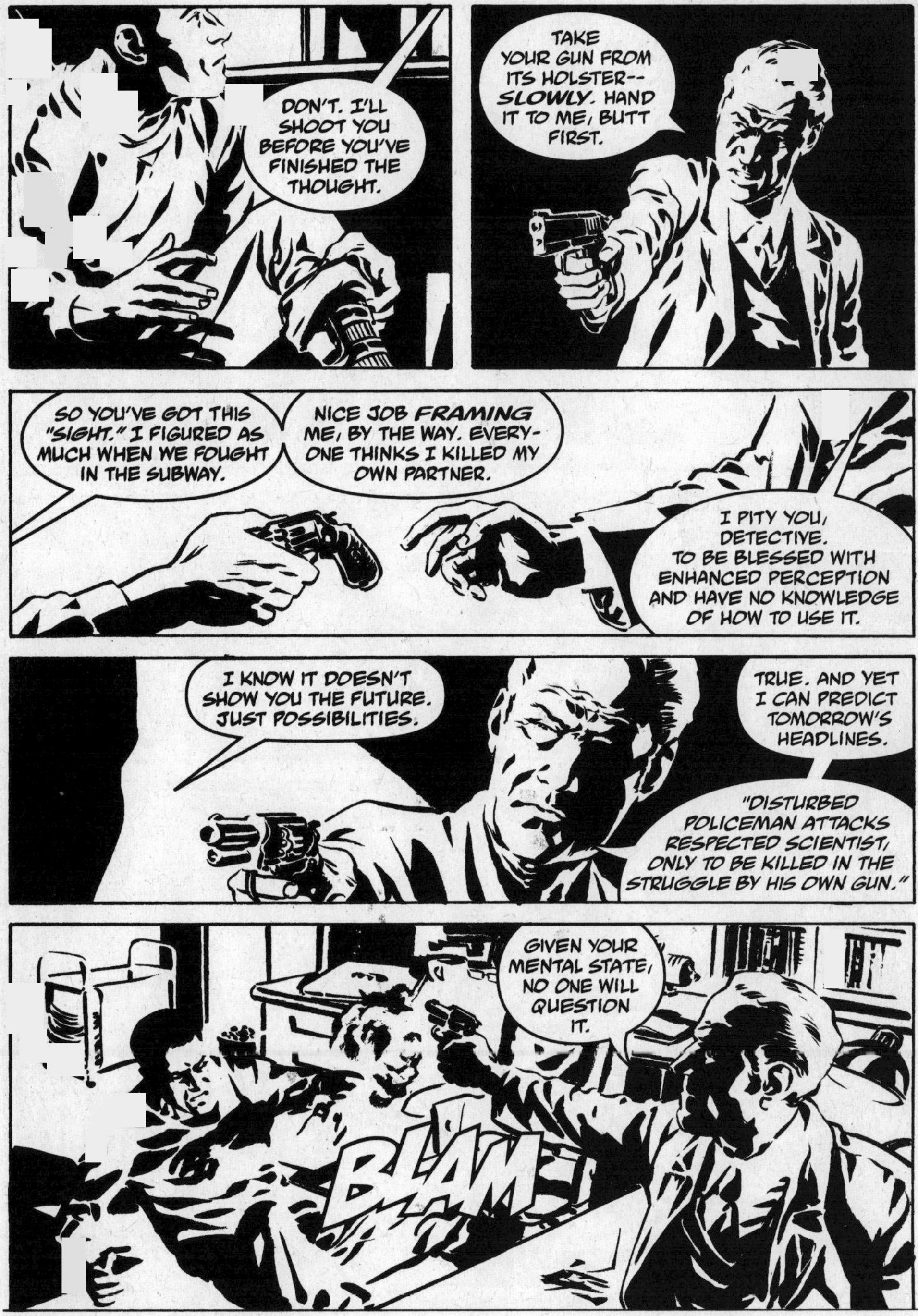
DON'T. I'LL SHOOT YOU BEFORE YOU'VE FINISHED THE THOUGHT.
TAKE YOUR GUN FROM ITS HOLSTER-- SLOWLY. HAND IT TO ME, BUTT FIRST.
SO YOU'VE GOT THIS "SIGHT." I FIGURED AS MUCH WHEN WE FOUGHT IN THE SUBWAY.
NICE JOB FRAMING ME, BY THE WAY. EVERY-ONE THINKS I KILLED MY OWN PARTNER.
I PITY YOU, DETECTIVE. TO BE BLESSED WITH ENHANCED PERCEPTION AND HAVE NO KNOWLEDGE OF HOW TO USE IT.
I KNOW IT DOESN'T SHOW YOU THE FUTURE. JUST POSSIBILITIES.
TRUE. AND YET I CAN PREDICT TOMORROW'S HEADLINES.
"DISTURBED POLICEMAN ATTACKS RESPECTED SCIENTIST, ONLY TO BE KILLED IN THE STRUGGLE BY HIS OWN GUN."
GIVEN YOUR MENTAL STATE, NO ONE WILL QUESTION IT.
BLAM

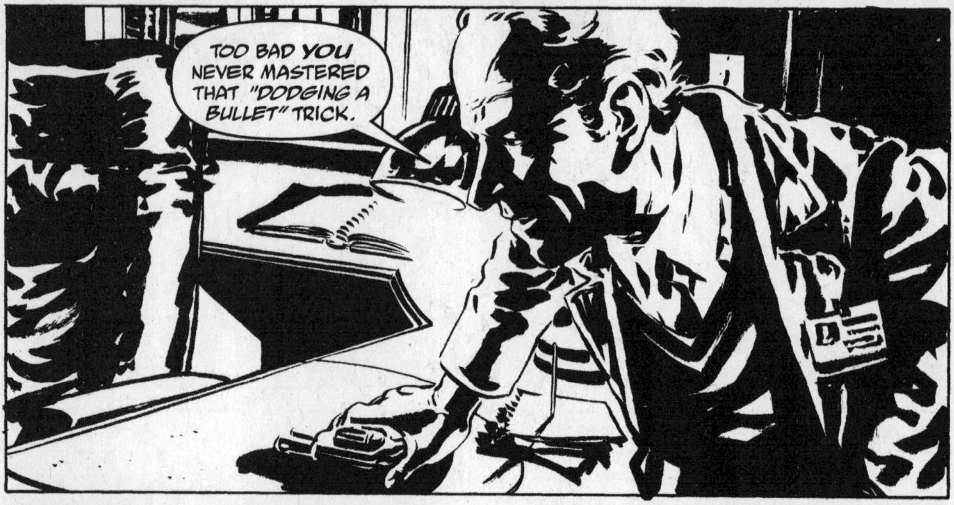
TOO BAD YOU NEVER MASTERED THAT "DODGING A BULLET" TRICK.
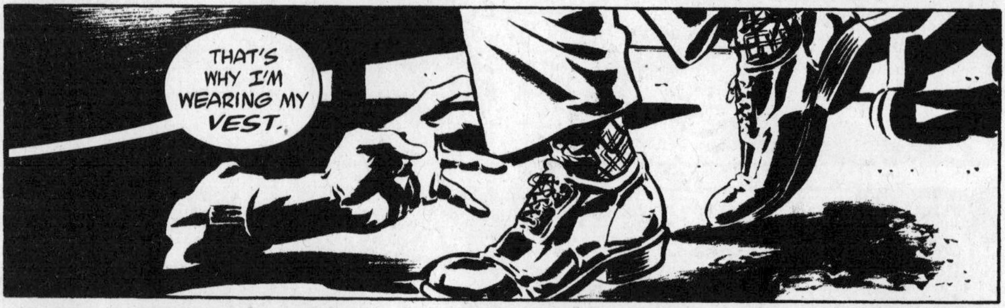
THAT'S WHY I'M WEARING MY VEST.
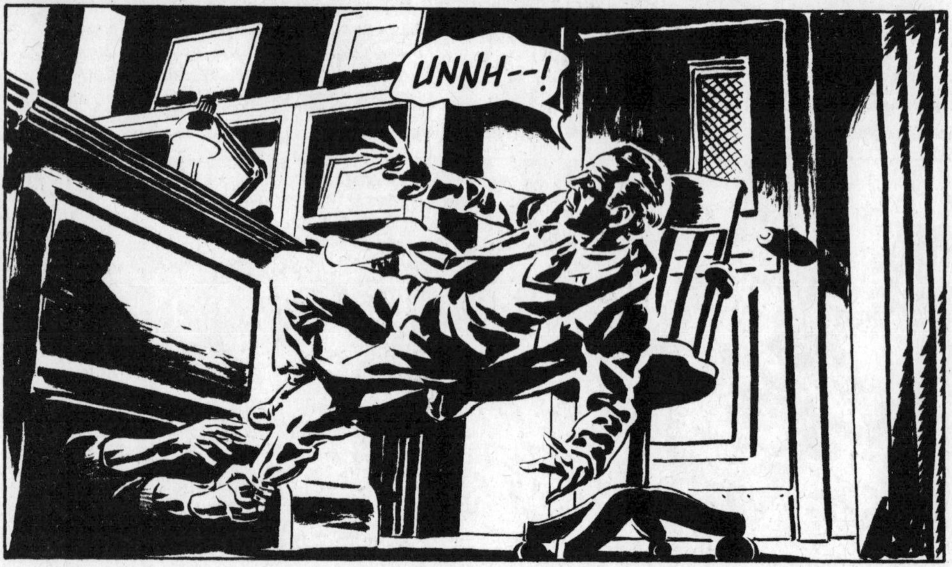
UNNH--!

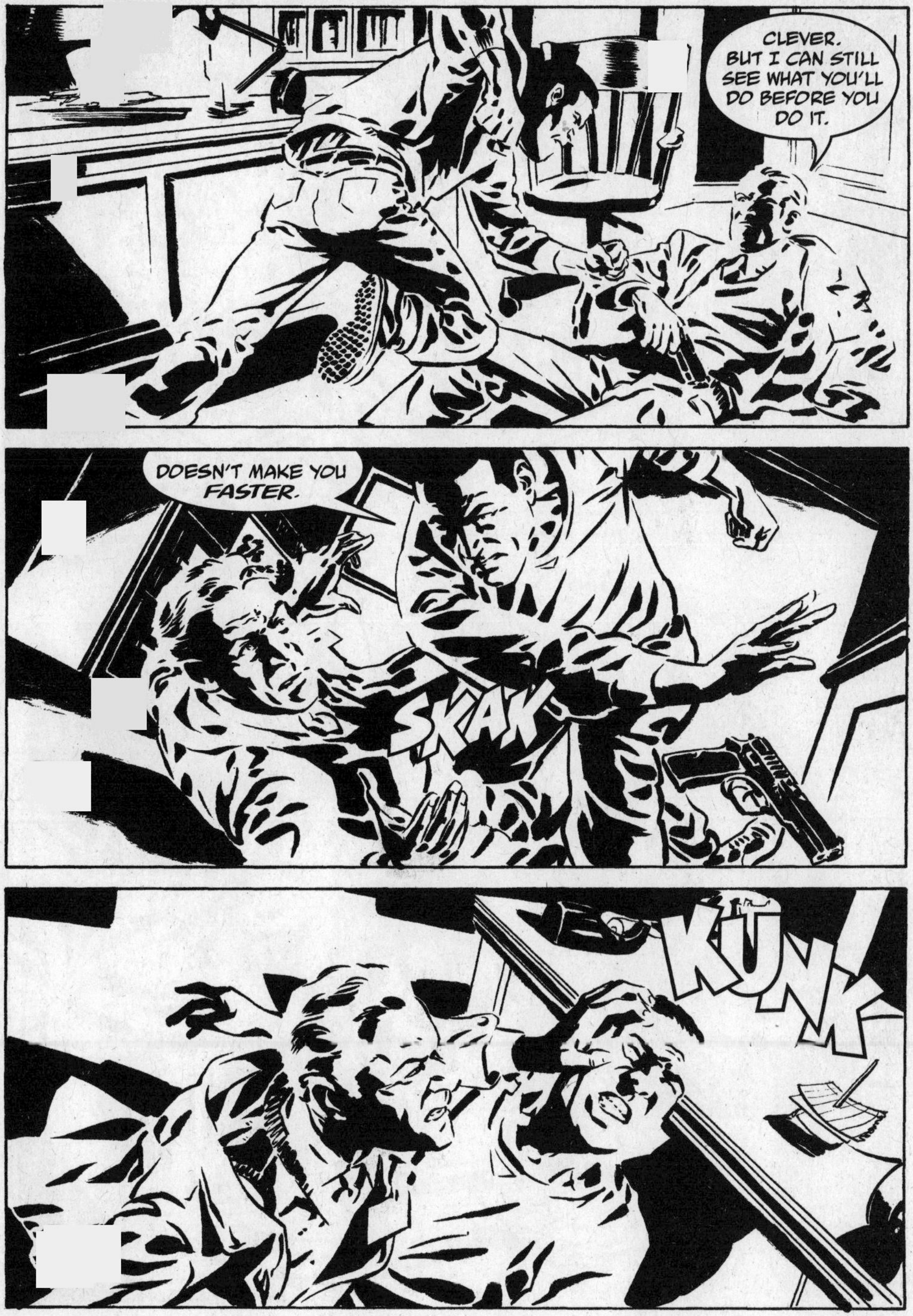
CLEVER. BUT I CAN STILL SEE WHAT YOU'LL DO BEFORE YOU DO IT.
DOESN'T MAKE YOU FASTER.
SKAK
KUNK

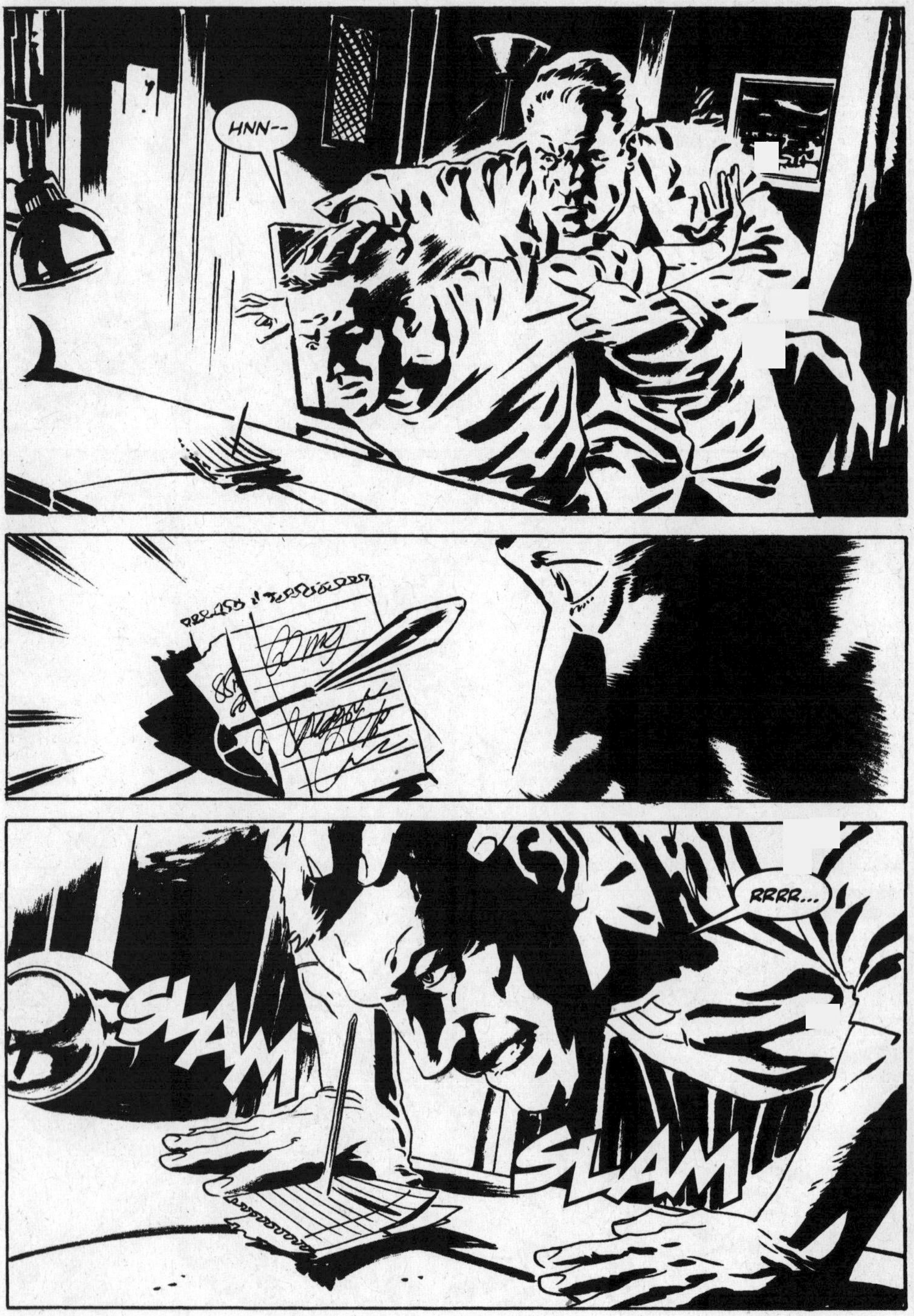
HNN--
RRRR...
SLAM
SLAM

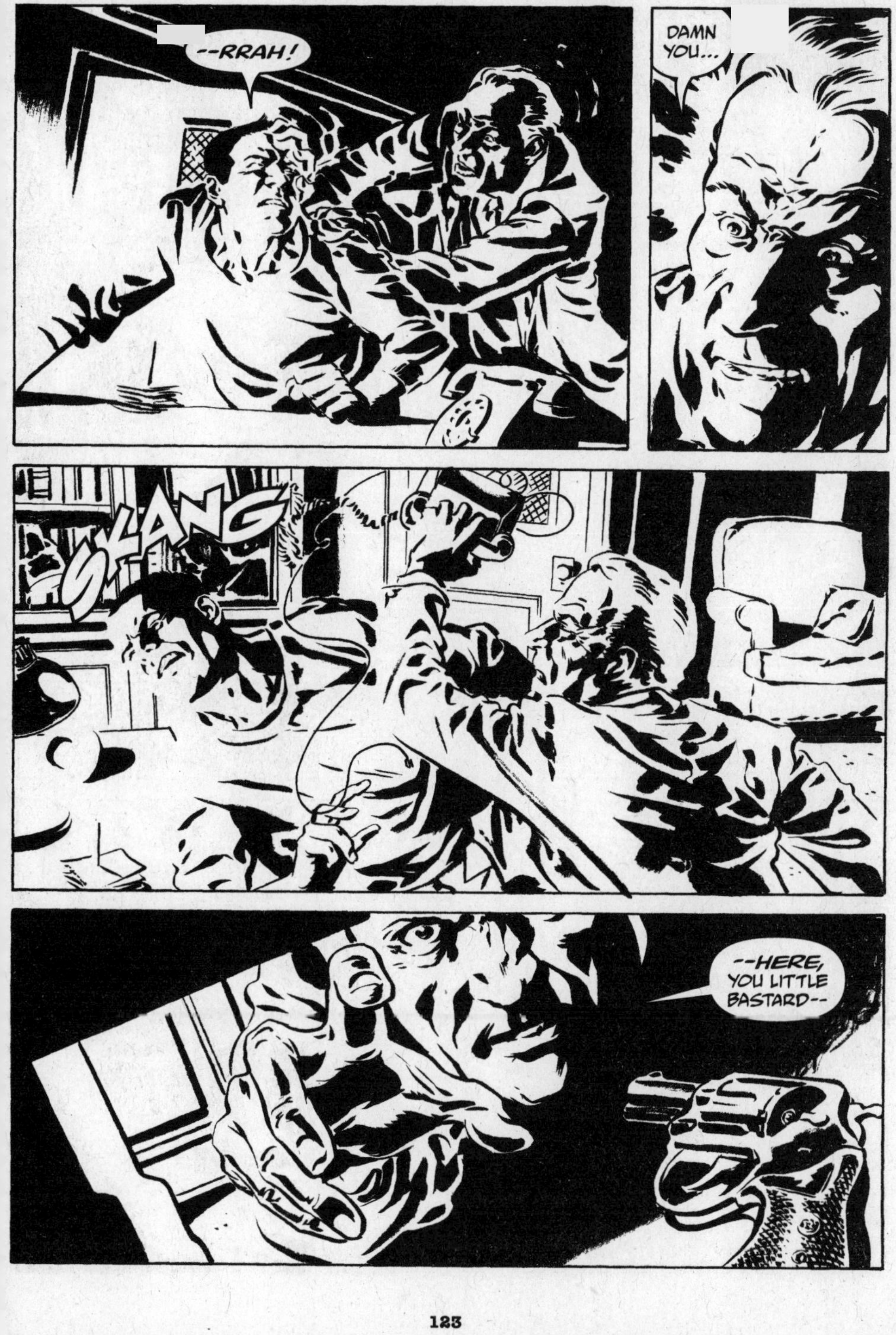
--RRAH!
DAMN YOU...
SKLANG
--HERE, YOU LITTLE BASTARD--

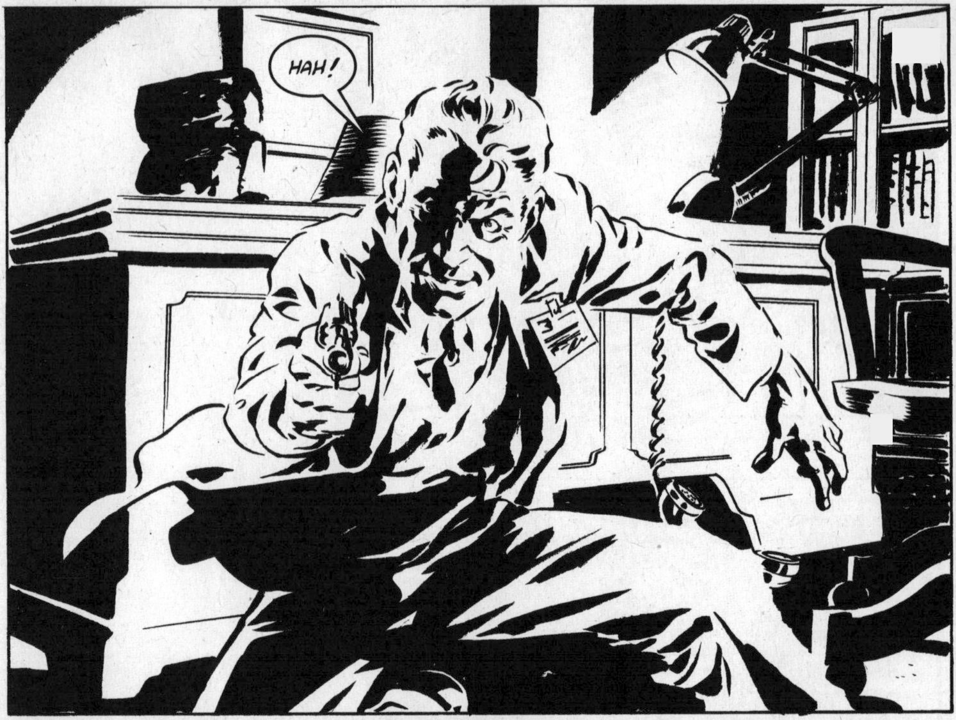
HAH!

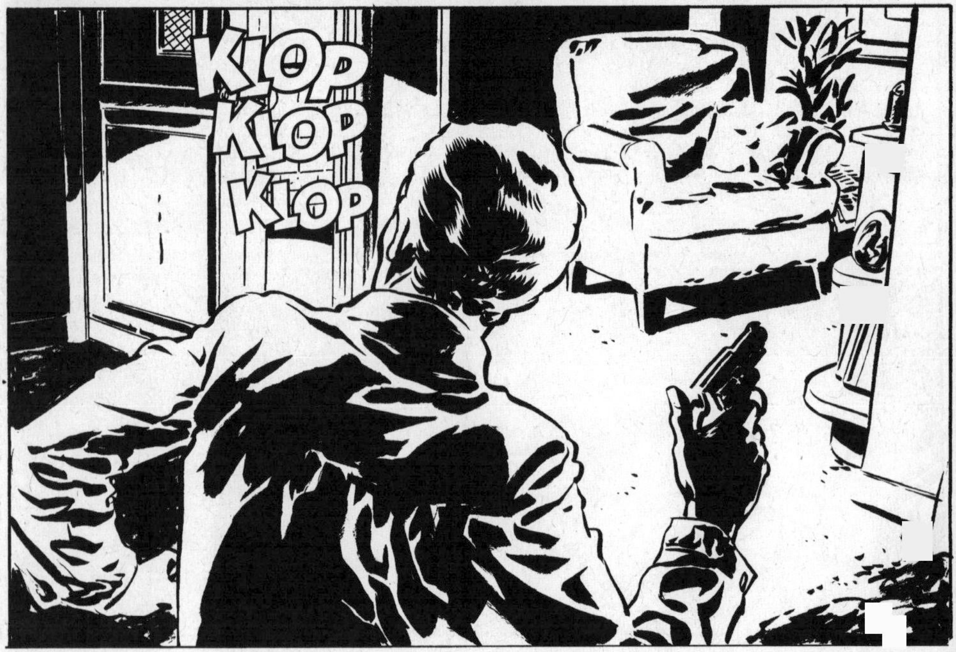
KLOP
KLOP
KLOP

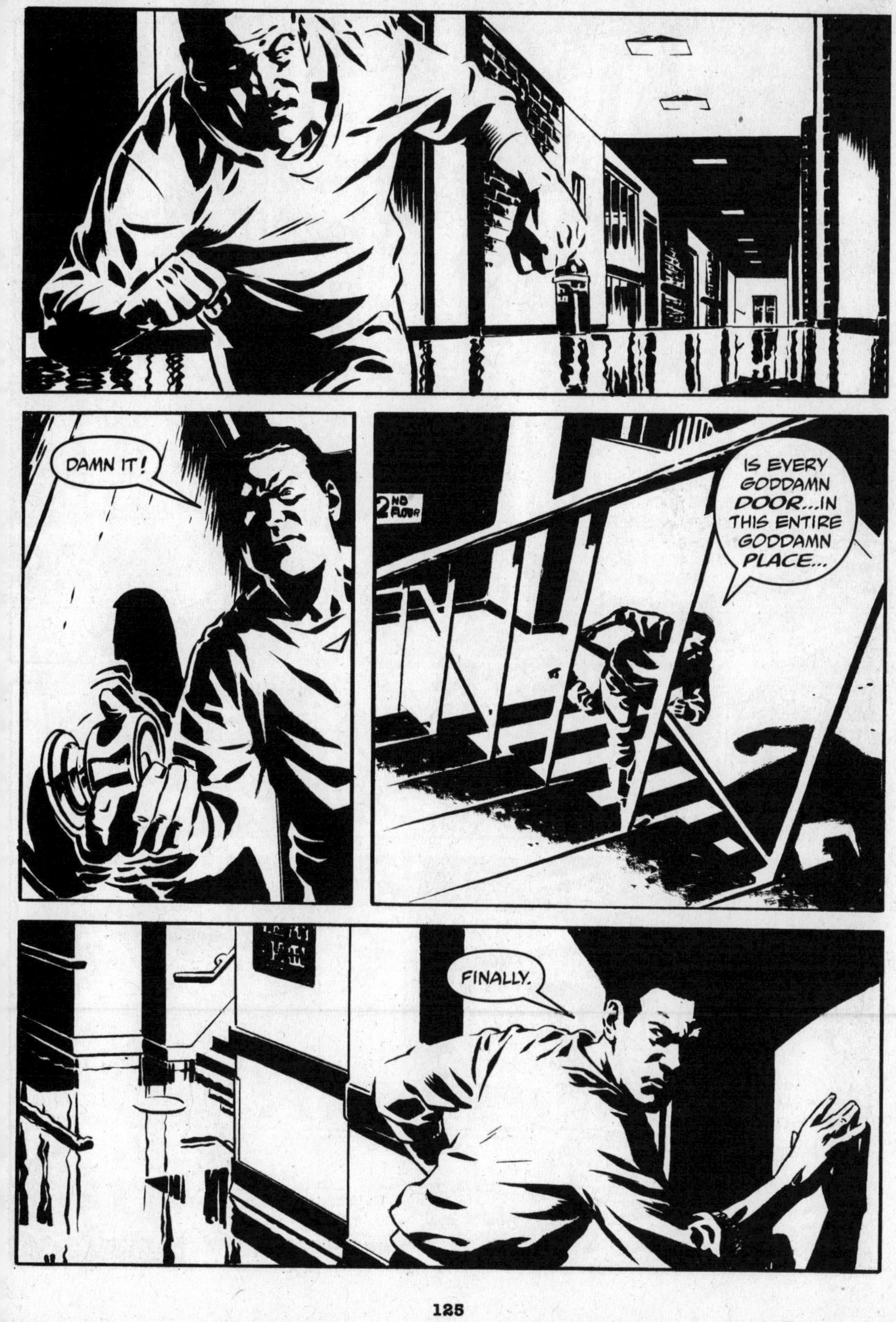
DAMN IT!
IS EVERY GODDAMN DOOR...IN THIS ENTIRE GODDAMN PLACE...
FINALLY.

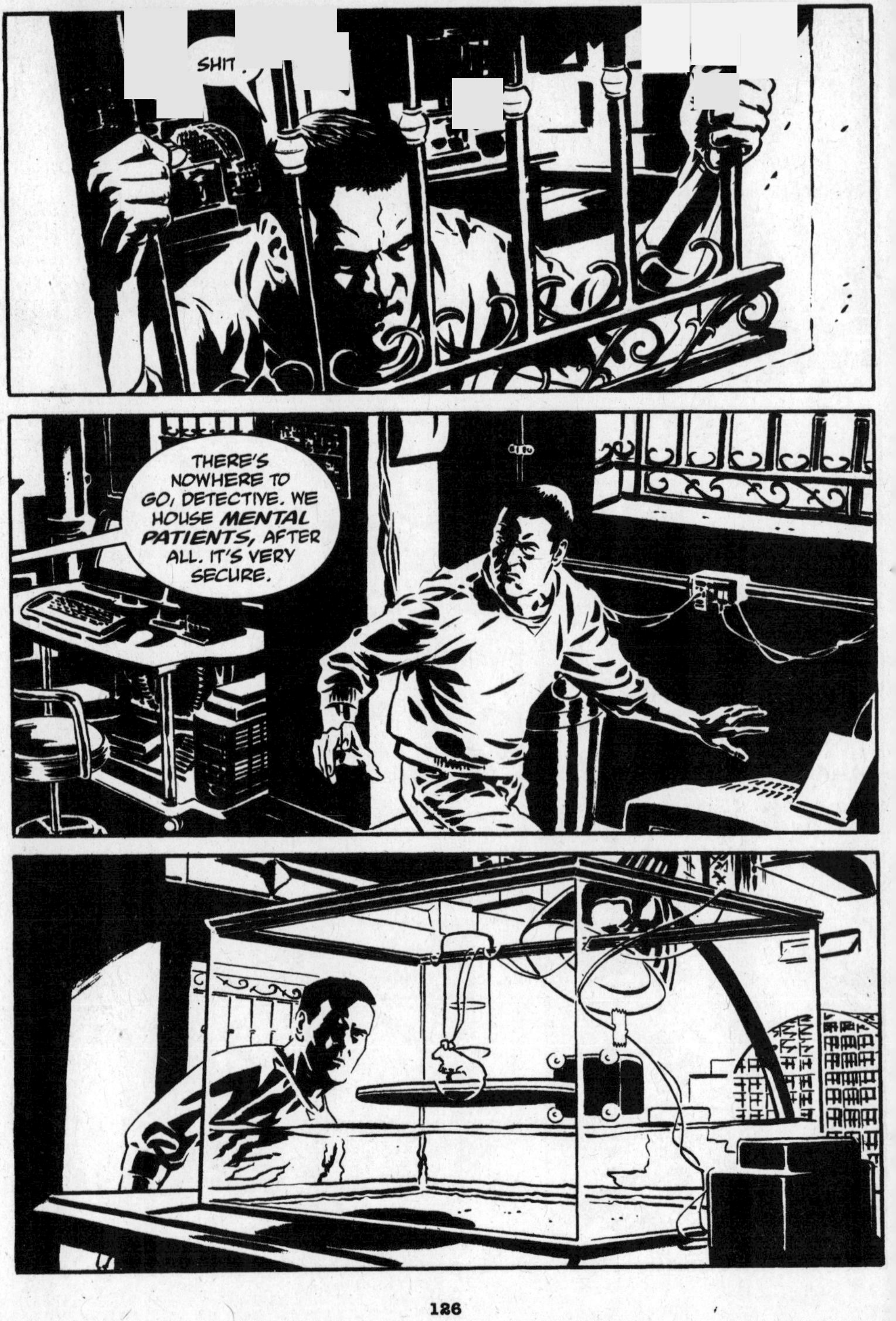
SHIT.
THERE'S NOWHERE TO GO, DETECTIVE. WE HOUSE *MENTAL PATIENTS,* AFTER ALL. IT'S VERY SECURE.

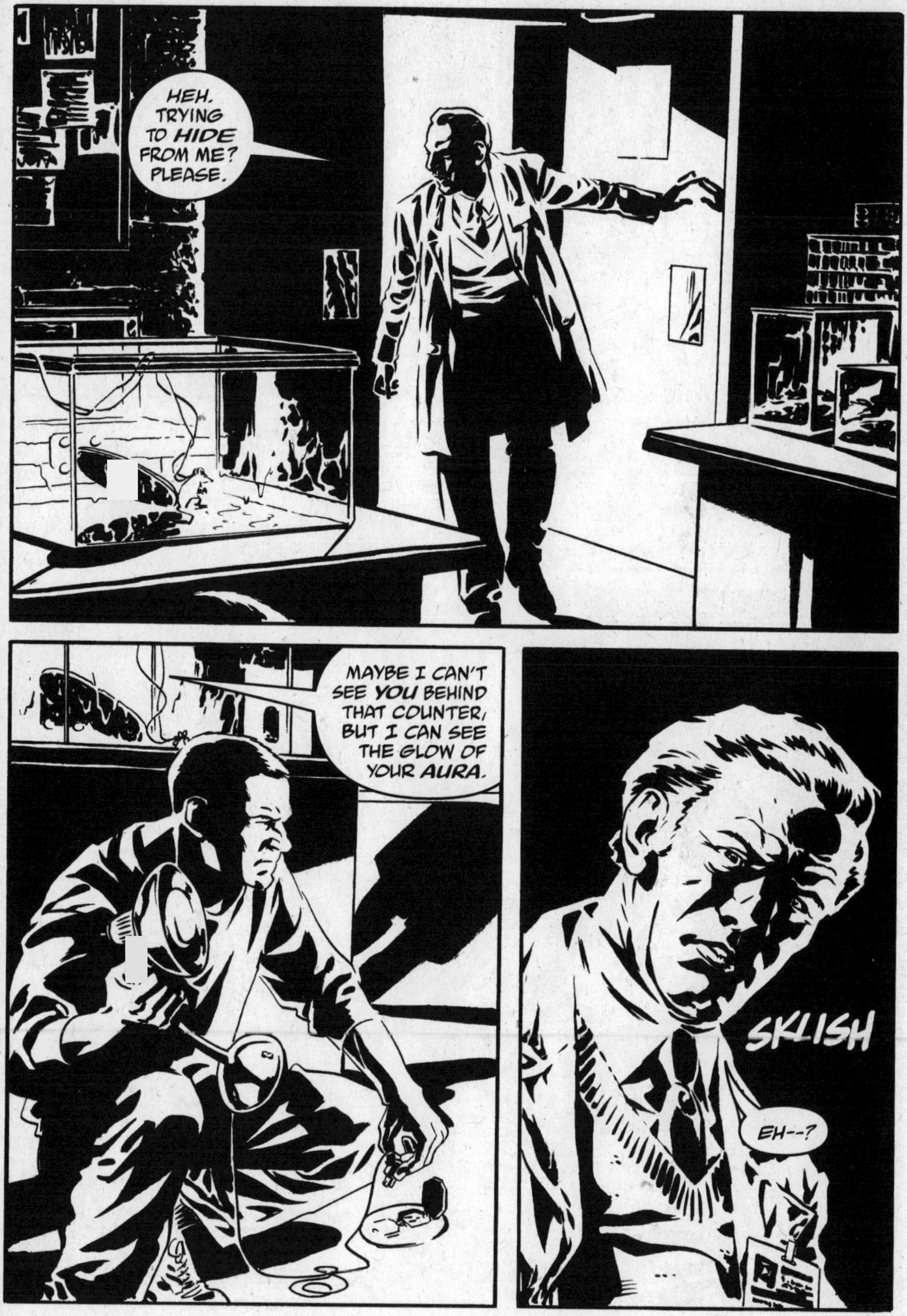
HEH. TRYING TO HIDE FROM ME? PLEASE.
MAYBE I CAN'T SEE YOU BEHIND THAT COUNTER, BUT I CAN SEE THE GLOW OF YOUR AURA.
SKLISH
EH--?

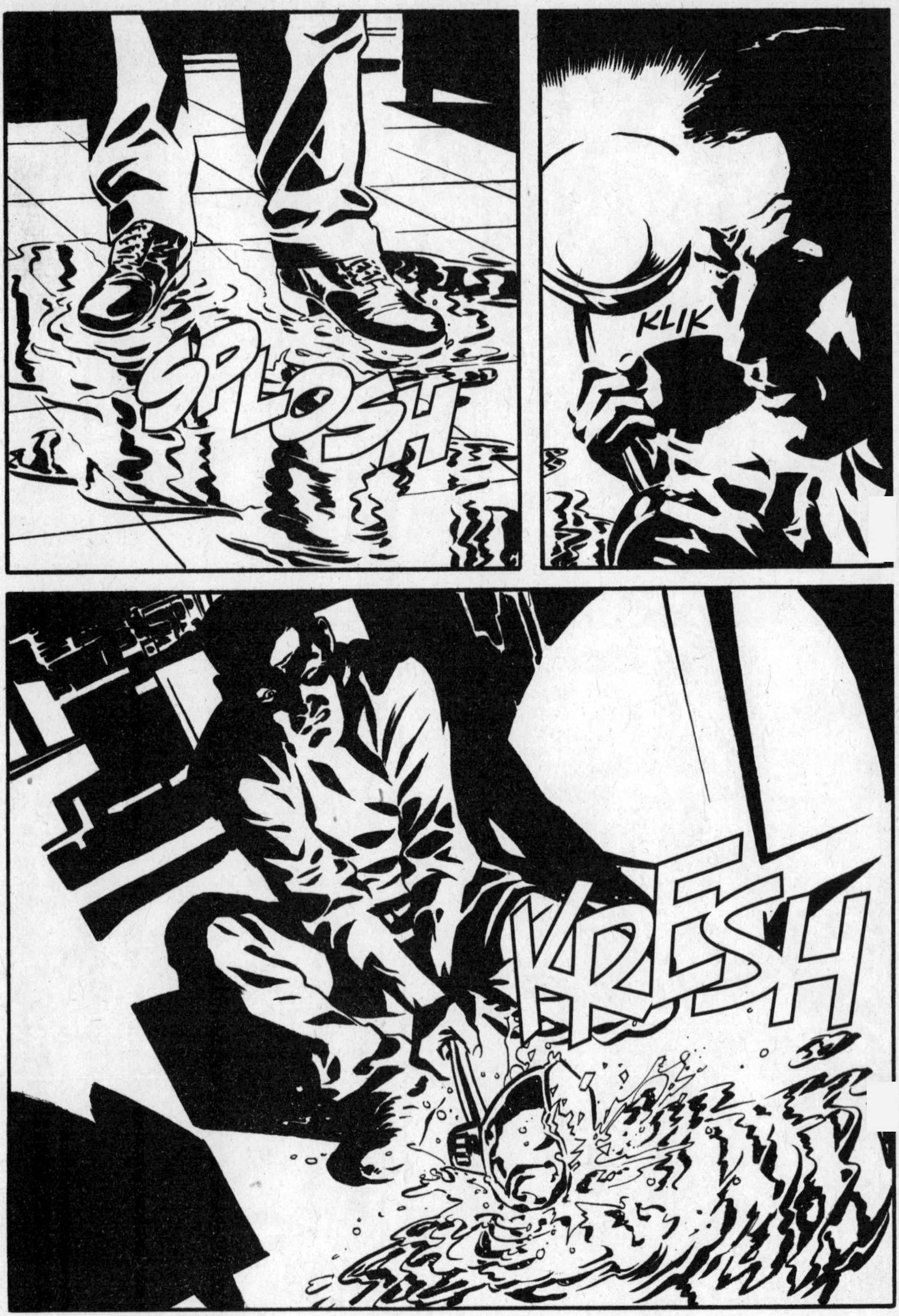
SPLOSH
KLIK
KRESH

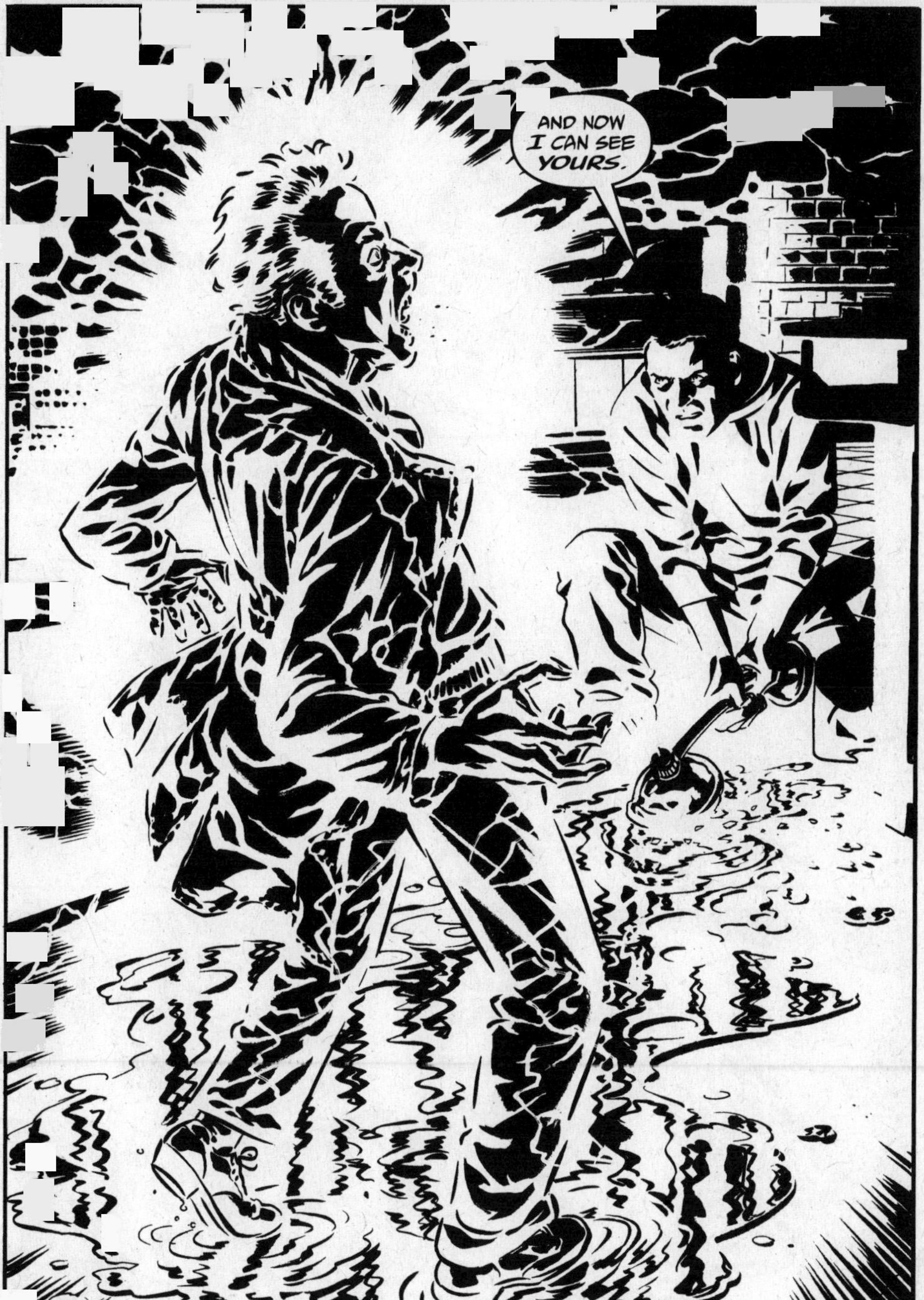
AND NOW I CAN SEE YOURS.

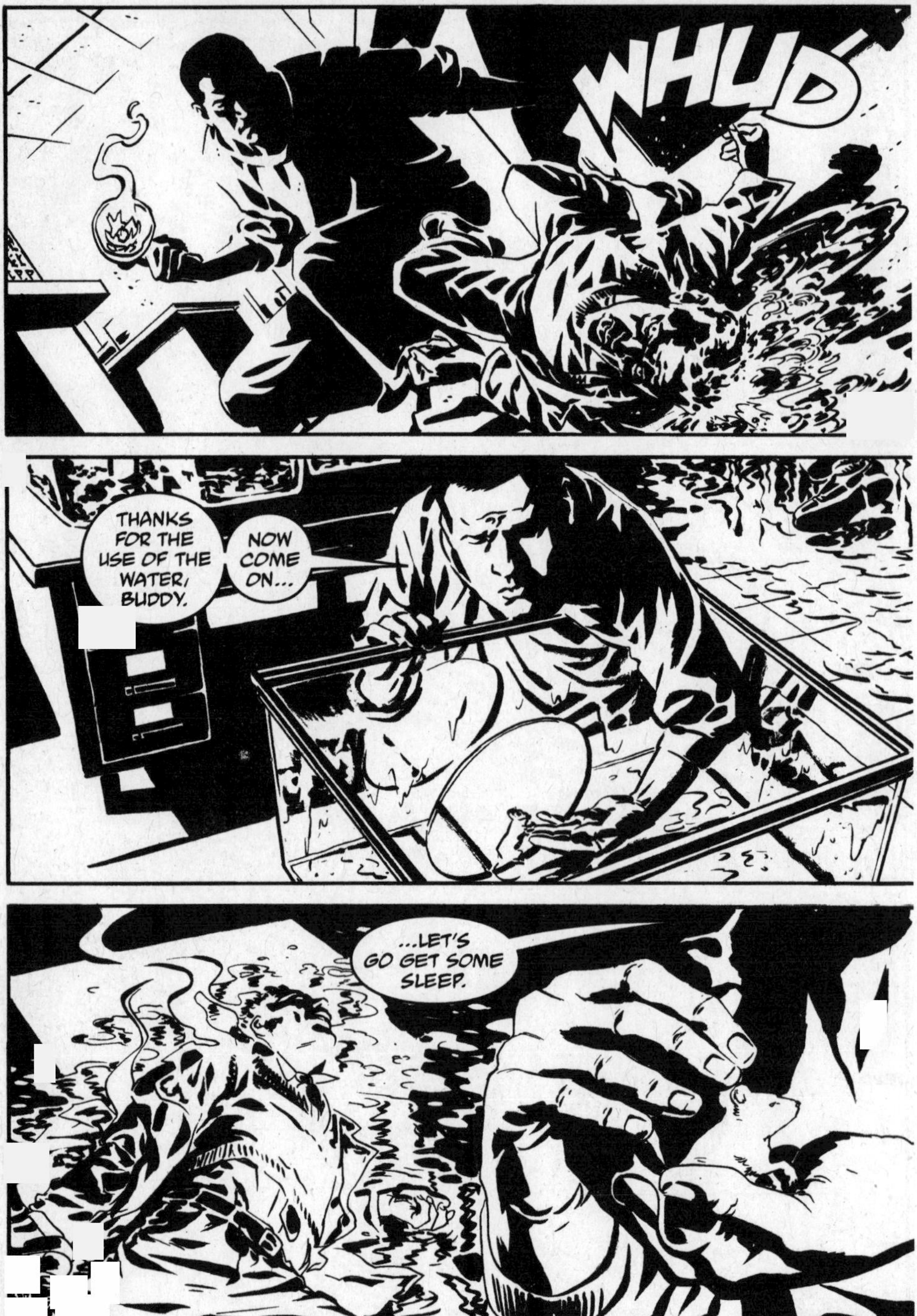
WHUD
THANKS FOR THE USE OF THE WATER, BUDDY.
NOW COME ON...
...LET'S GO GET SOME SLEEP.

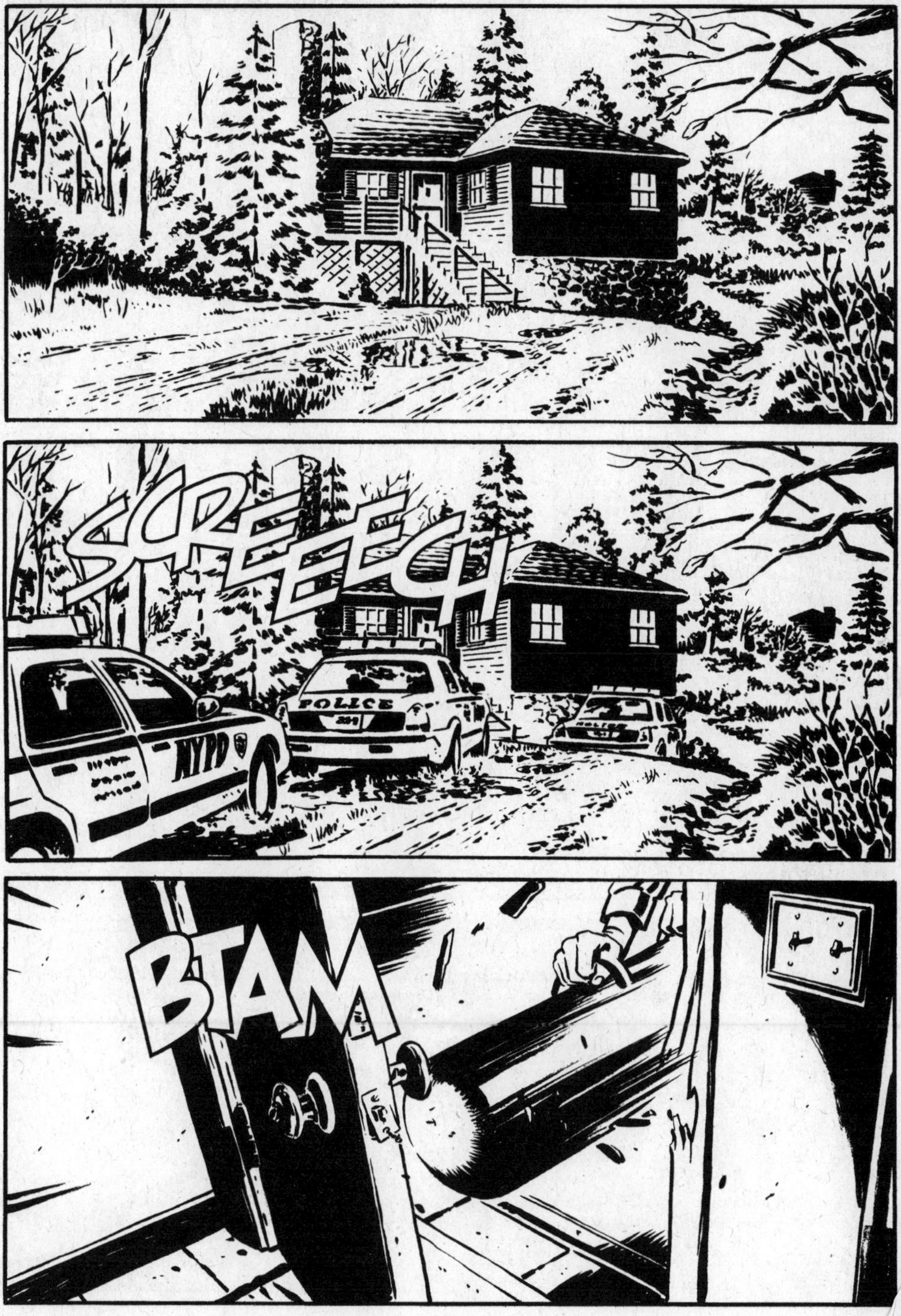
SCREEECH
NYPD
POLICE
BTAM

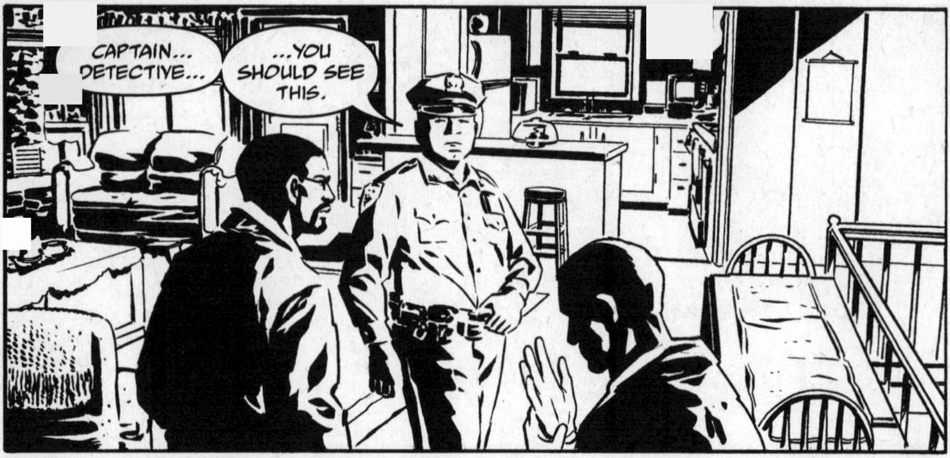
CAPTAIN... DETECTIVE...
...YOU SHOULD SEE THIS.

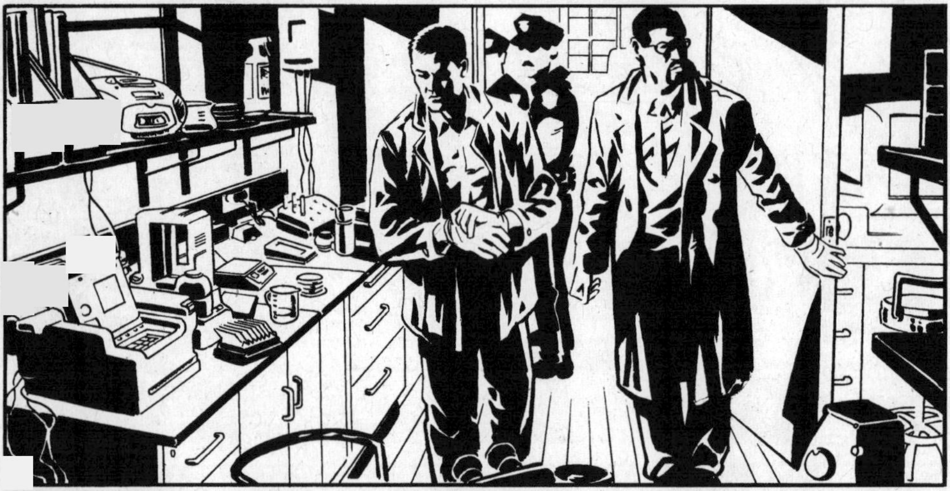

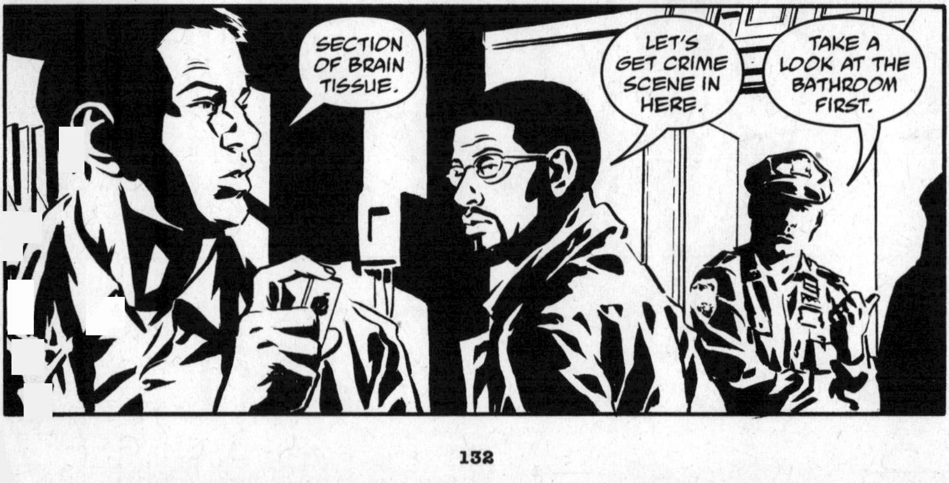
SECTION OF BRAIN TISSUE.
LET'S GET CRIME SCENE IN HERE.
TAKE A LOOK AT THE BATHROOM FIRST.

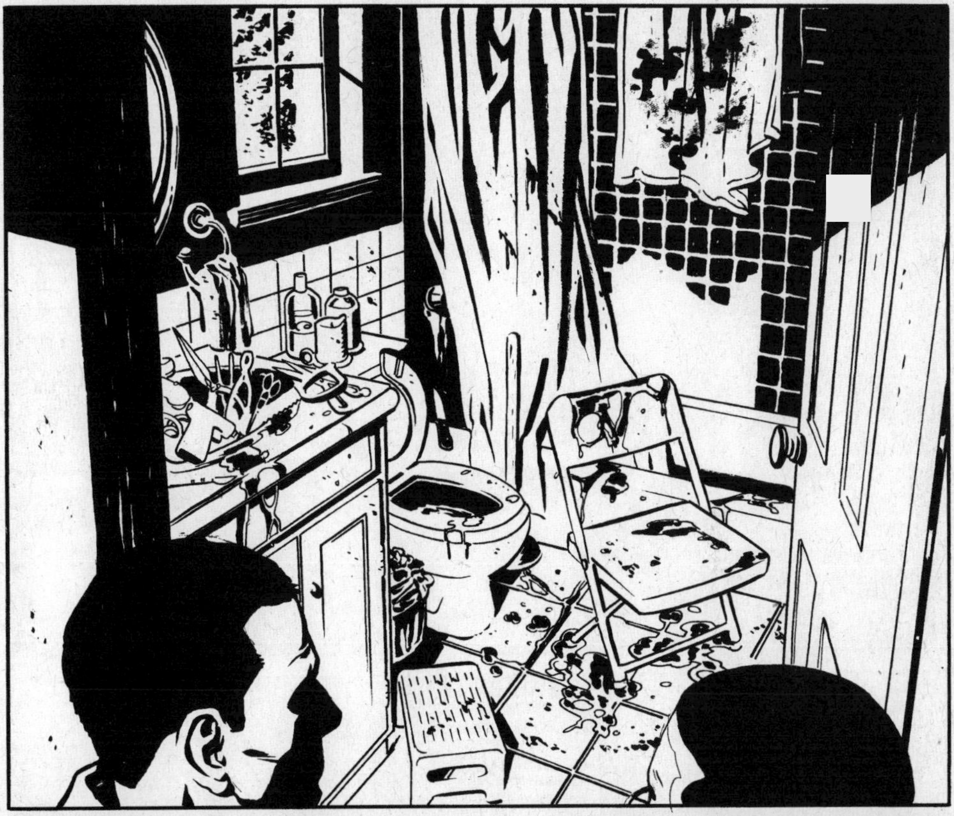

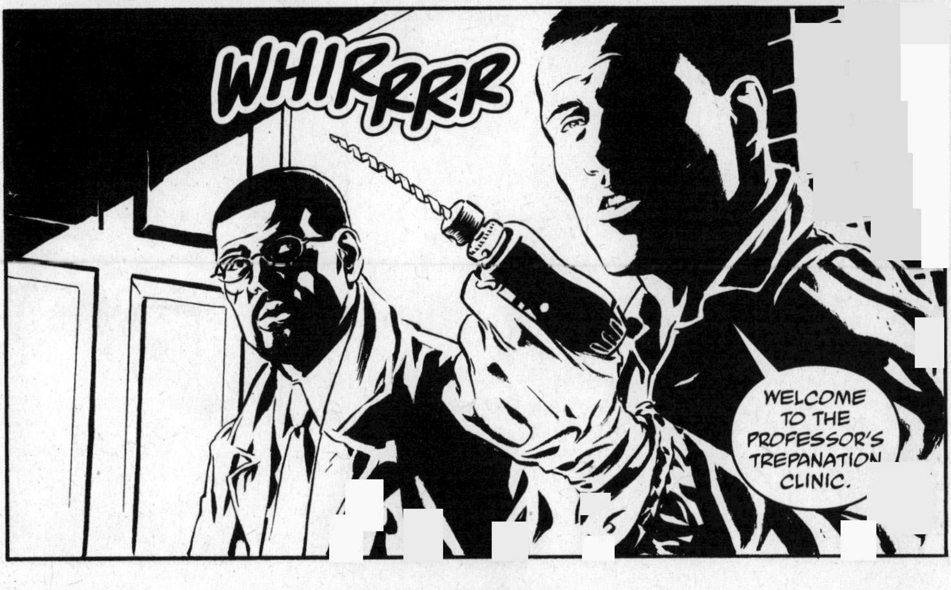
WHIRRRR
WELCOME TO THE PROFESSOR'S TREPANATION CLINIC.

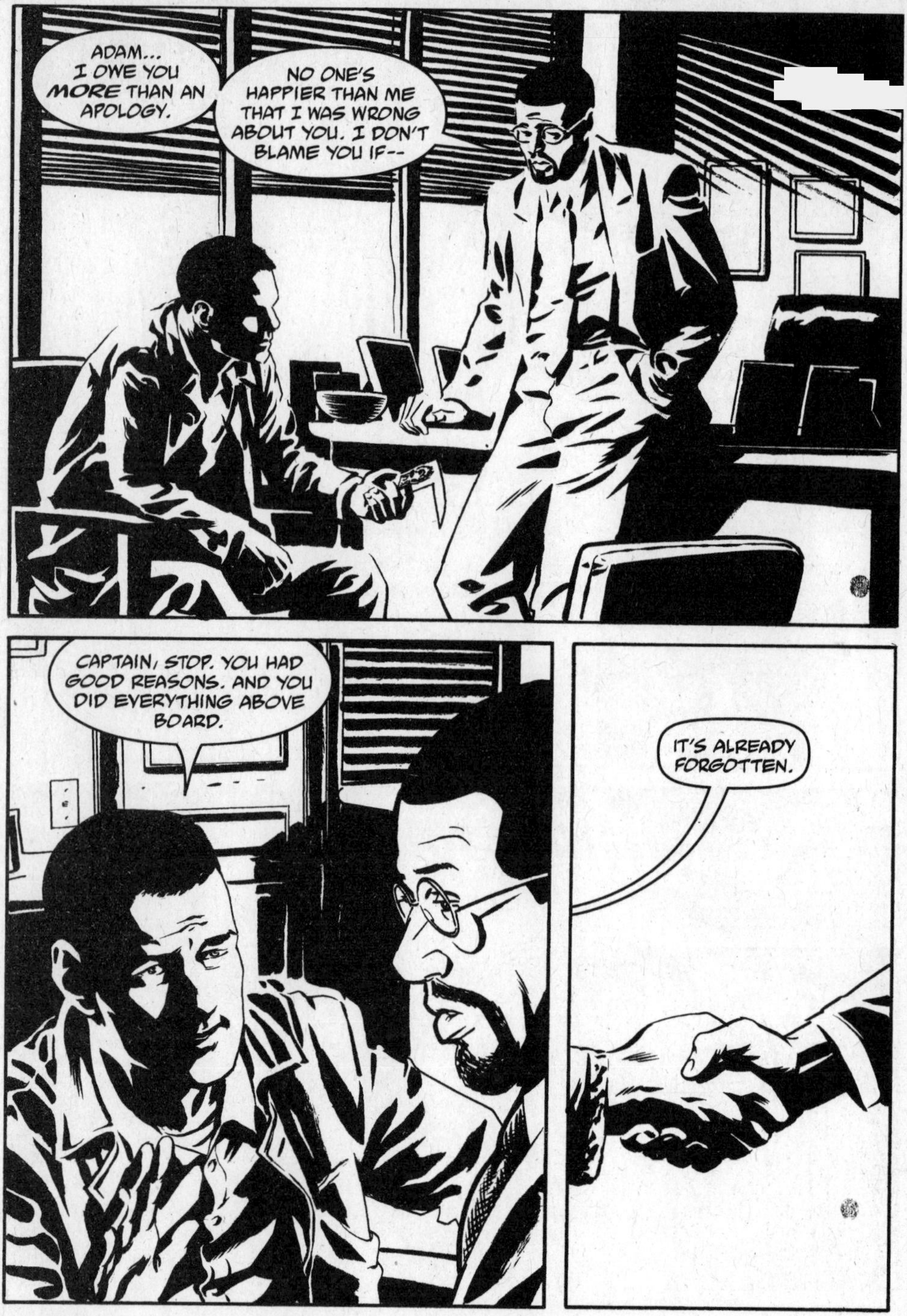
ADAM... I OWE YOU MORE THAN AN APOLOGY.
NO ONE'S HAPPIER THAN ME THAT I WAS WRONG ABOUT YOU. I DON'T BLAME YOU IF--
CAPTAIN, STOP. YOU HAD GOOD REASONS. AND YOU DID EVERYTHING ABOVE BOARD.
IT'S ALREADY FORGOTTEN.

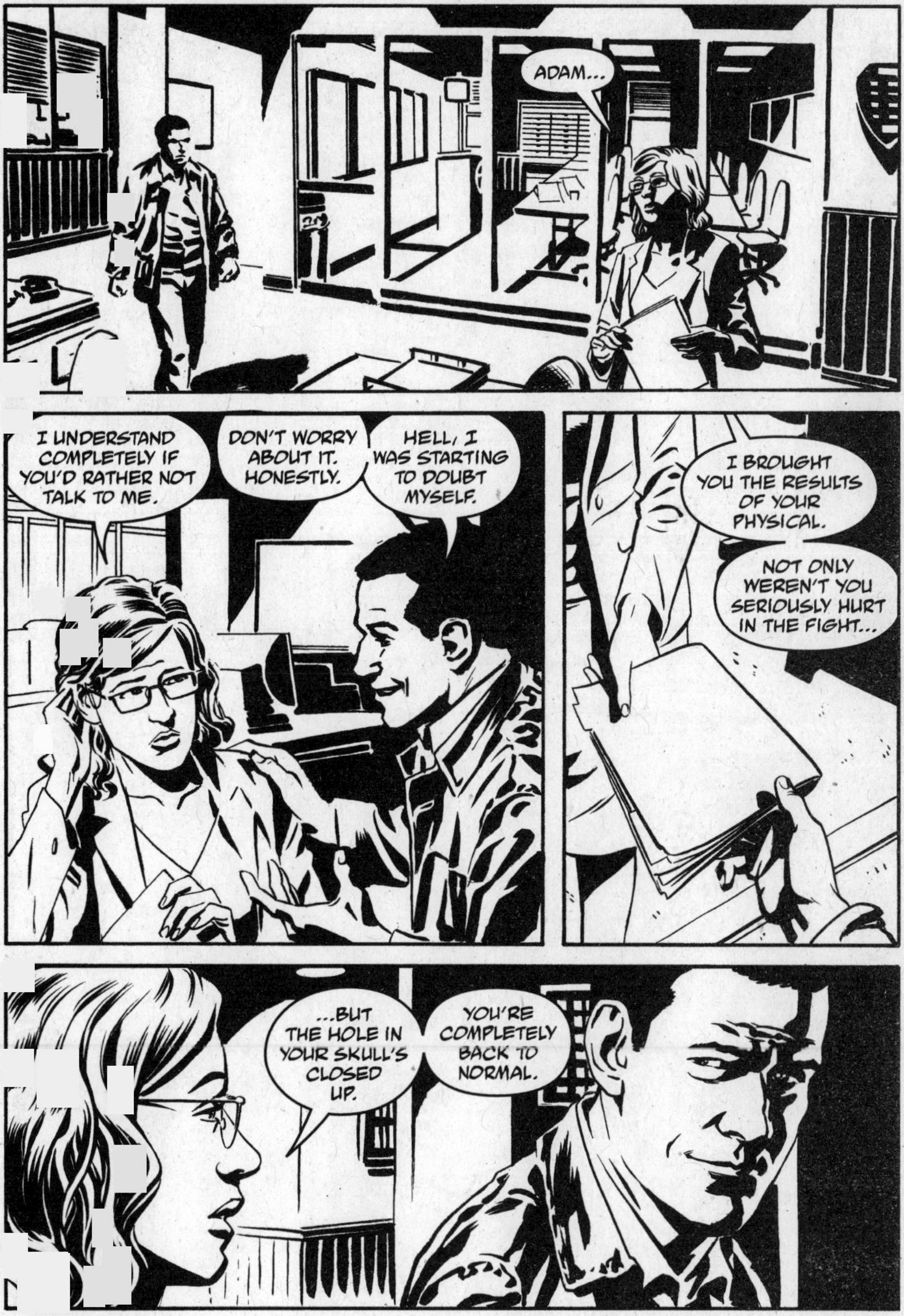
ADAM...
I UNDERSTAND COMPLETELY IF YOU'D RATHER NOT TALK TO ME.
DON'T WORRY ABOUT IT. HONESTLY.
HELL, I WAS STARTING TO DOUBT MYSELF.
I BROUGHT YOU THE RESULTS OF YOUR PHYSICAL.
NOT ONLY WEREN'T YOU SERIOUSLY HURT IN THE FIGHT...
...BUT THE HOLE IN YOUR SKULL'S CLOSED UP.
YOU'RE COMPLETELY BACK TO NORMAL.

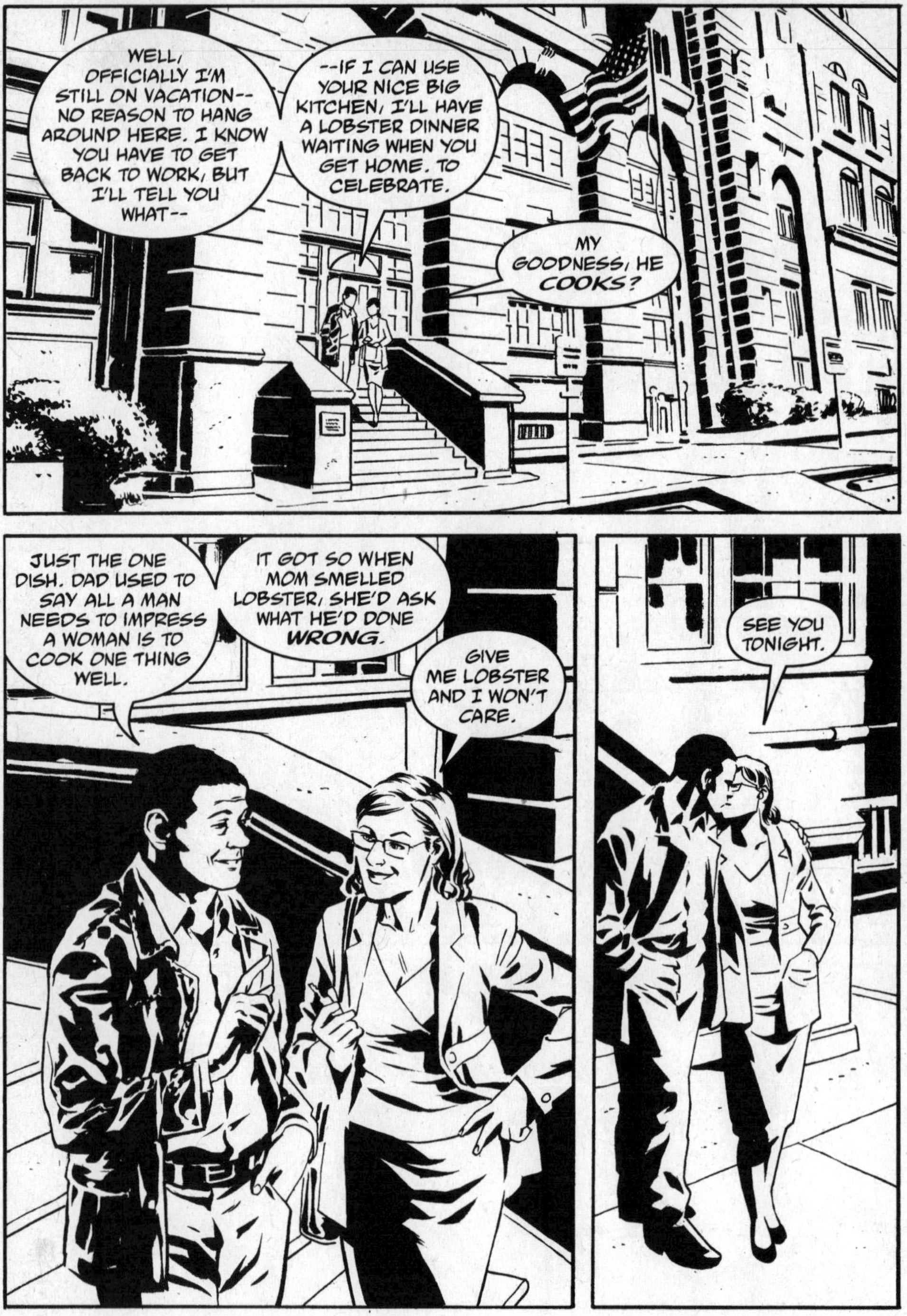
WELL, OFFICIALLY I'M STILL ON VACATION-- NO REASON TO HANG AROUND HERE. I KNOW YOU HAVE TO GET BACK TO WORK, BUT I'LL TELL YOU WHAT--
--IF I CAN USE YOUR NICE BIG KITCHEN, I'LL HAVE A LOBSTER DINNER WAITING WHEN YOU GET HOME. TO CELEBRATE.
MY GOODNESS, HE COOKS?
JUST THE ONE DISH. DAD USED TO SAY ALL A MAN NEEDS TO IMPRESS A WOMAN IS TO COOK ONE THING WELL.
IT GOT SO WHEN MOM SMELLED LOBSTER, SHE'D ASK WHAT HE'D DONE WRONG.
GIVE ME LOBSTER AND I WON'T CARE.
SEE YOU TONIGHT.

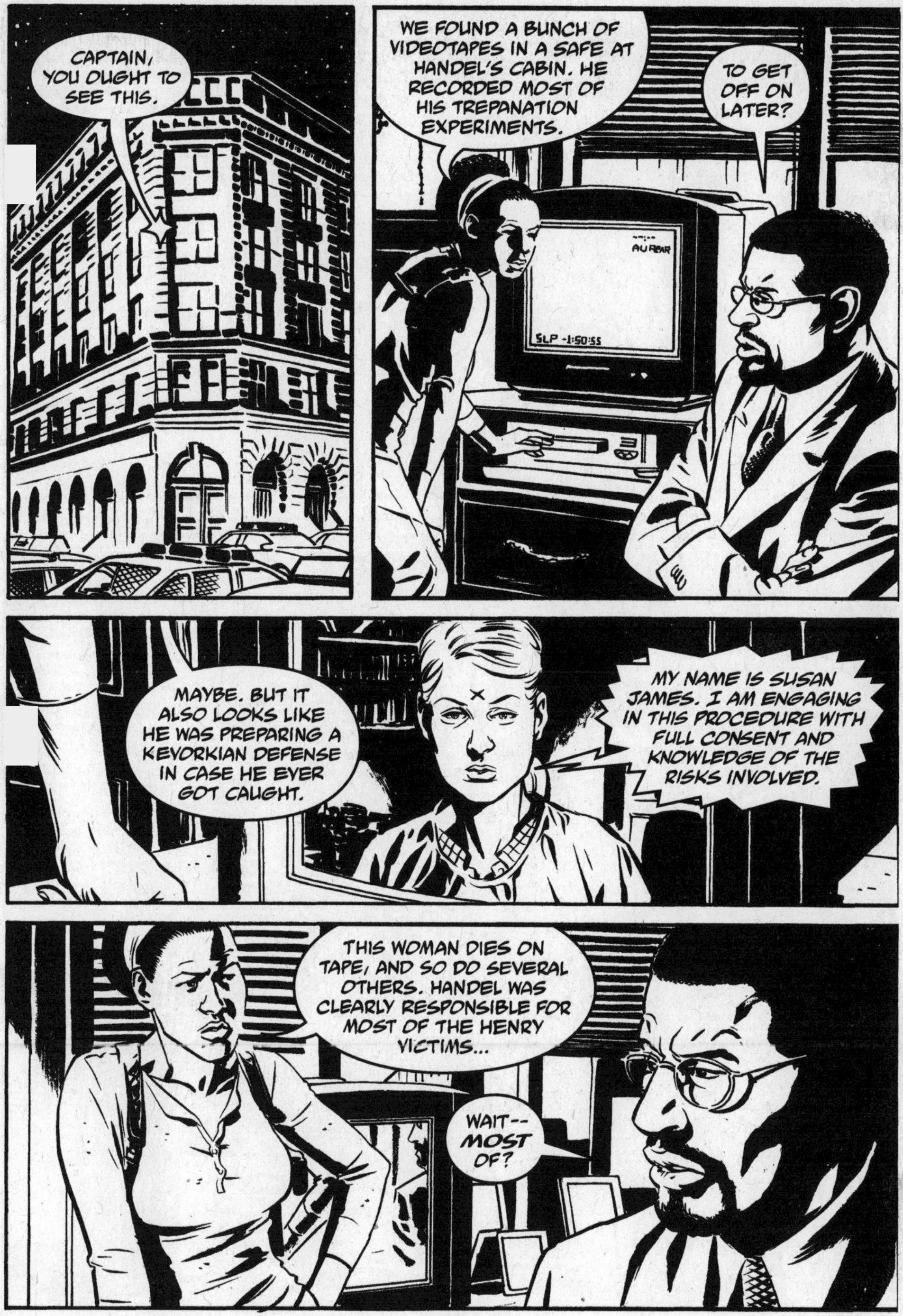
CAPTAIN, YOU OUGHT TO SEE THIS.
WE FOUND A BUNCH OF VIDEOTAPES IN A SAFE AT HANDEL'S CABIN. HE RECORDED MOST OF HIS TREPANATION EXPERIMENTS.
TO GET OFF ON LATER?
SLP -1:50:55
MAYBE. BUT IT ALSO LOOKS LIKE HE WAS PREPARING A KEVORKIAN DEFENSE IN CASE HE EVER GOT CAUGHT.
MY NAME IS SUSAN JAMES. I AM ENGAGING IN THIS PROCEDURE WITH FULL CONSENT AND KNOWLEDGE OF THE RISKS INVOLVED.
THIS WOMAN DIES ON TAPE, AND SO DO SEVERAL OTHERS. HANDEL WAS CLEARLY RESPONSIBLE FOR MOST OF THE HENRY VICTIMS...
WAIT-- *MOST* OF?

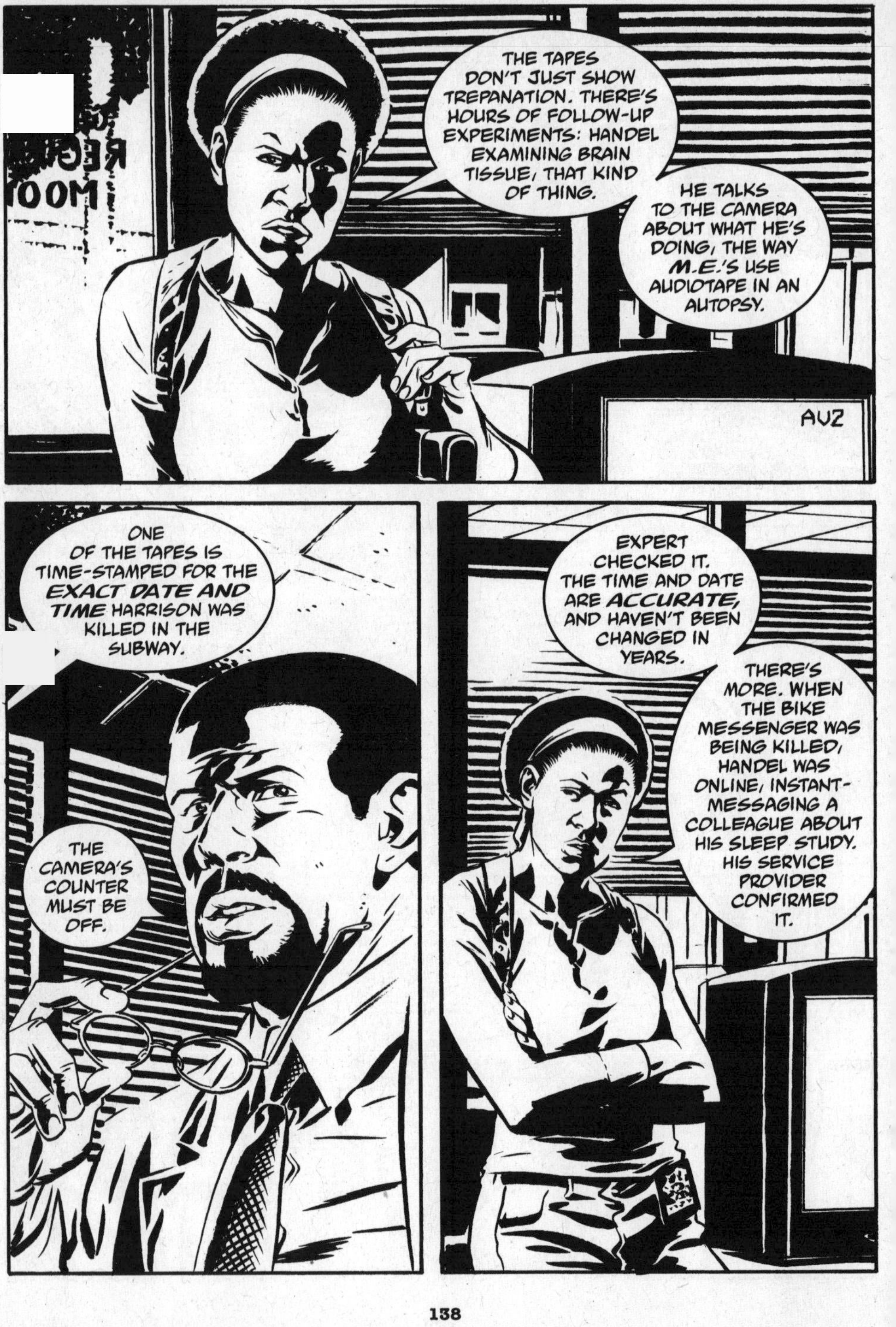
THE TAPES DON'T JUST SHOW TREPANATION. THERE'S HOURS OF FOLLOW-UP EXPERIMENTS: HANDEL EXAMINING BRAIN TISSUE, THAT KIND OF THING.
HE TALKS TO THE CAMERA ABOUT WHAT HE'S DOING, THE WAY M.E.'S USE AUDIOTAPE IN AN AUTOPSY.
AVZ
ONE OF THE TAPES IS TIME-STAMPED FOR THE EXACT DATE AND TIME HARRISON WAS KILLED IN THE SUBWAY.
THE CAMERA'S COUNTER MUST BE OFF.
EXPERT CHECKED IT. THE TIME AND DATE ARE ACCURATE, AND HAVEN'T BEEN CHANGED IN YEARS.
THERE'S MORE. WHEN THE BIKE MESSENGER WAS BEING KILLED, HANDEL WAS ONLINE, INSTANT-MESSAGING A COLLEAGUE ABOUT HIS SLEEP STUDY. HIS SERVICE PROVIDER CONFIRMED IT.

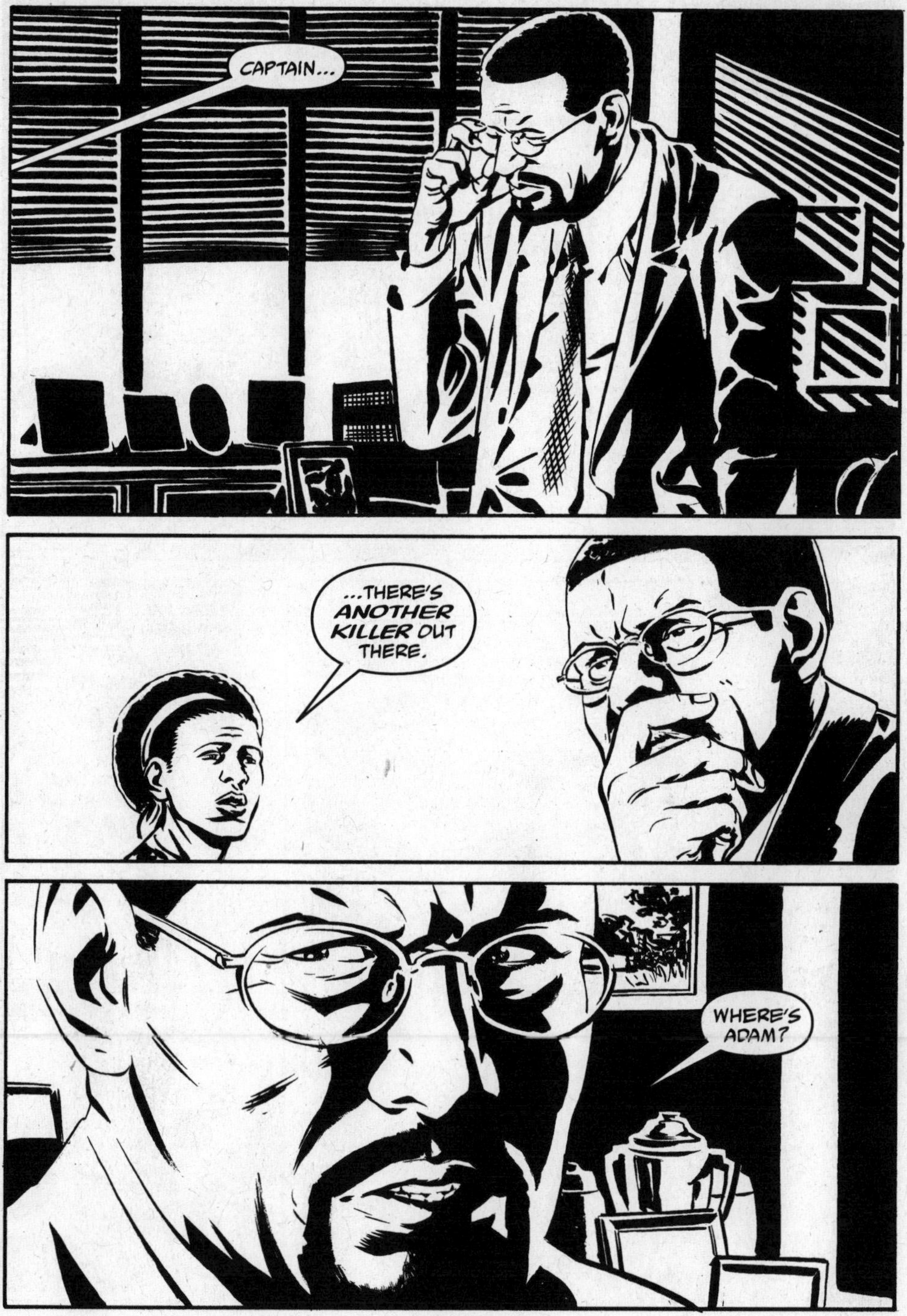
CAPTAIN...
...THERE'S ANOTHER KILLER OUT THERE.
WHERE'S ADAM?

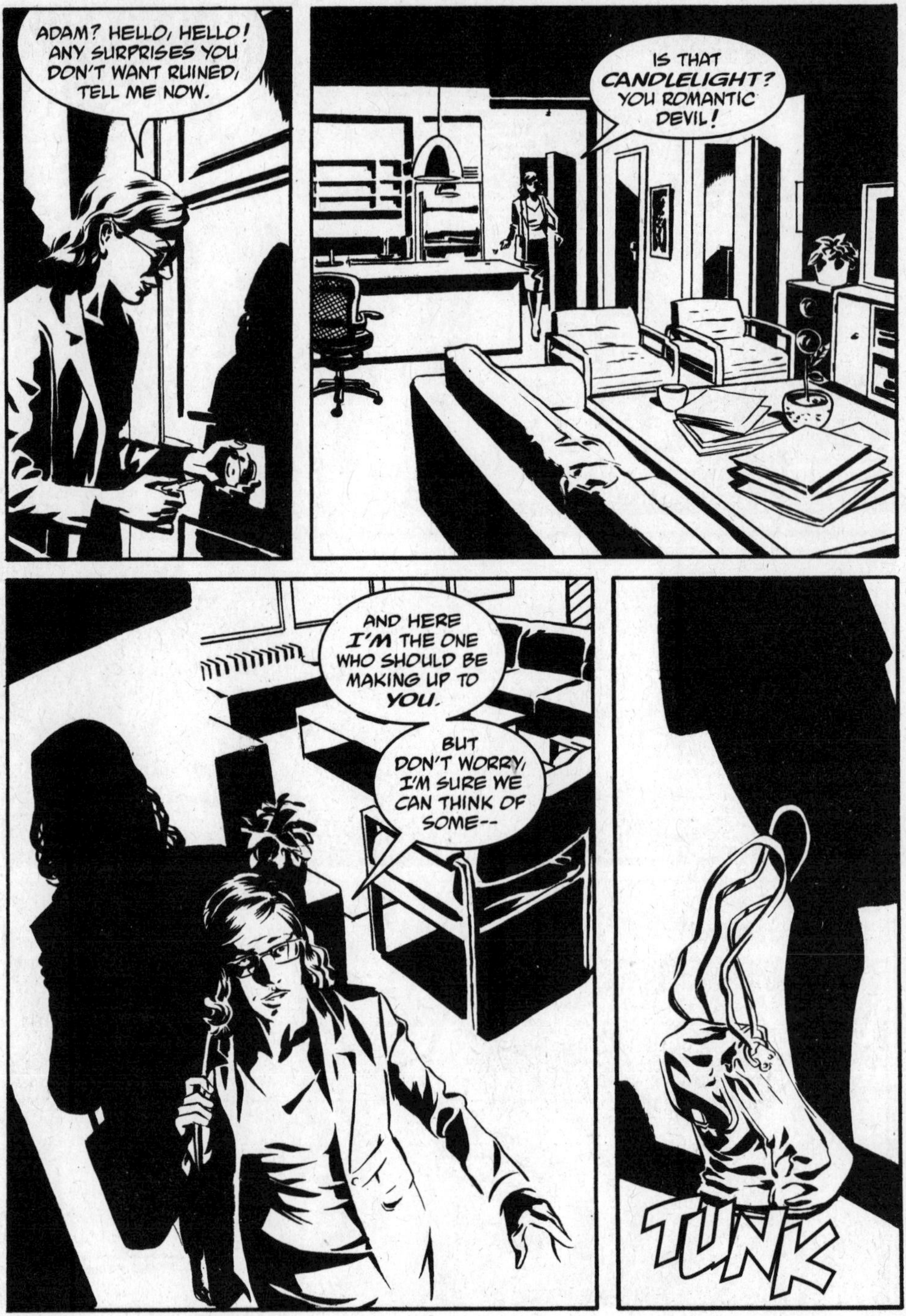
ADAM? HELLO, HELLO! ANY SURPRISES YOU DON'T WANT RUINED, TELL ME NOW.
IS THAT CANDLELIGHT? YOU ROMANTIC DEVIL!
AND HERE I'M THE ONE WHO SHOULD BE MAKING UP TO YOU.
BUT DON'T WORRY, I'M SURE WE CAN THINK OF SOME--
TUNK

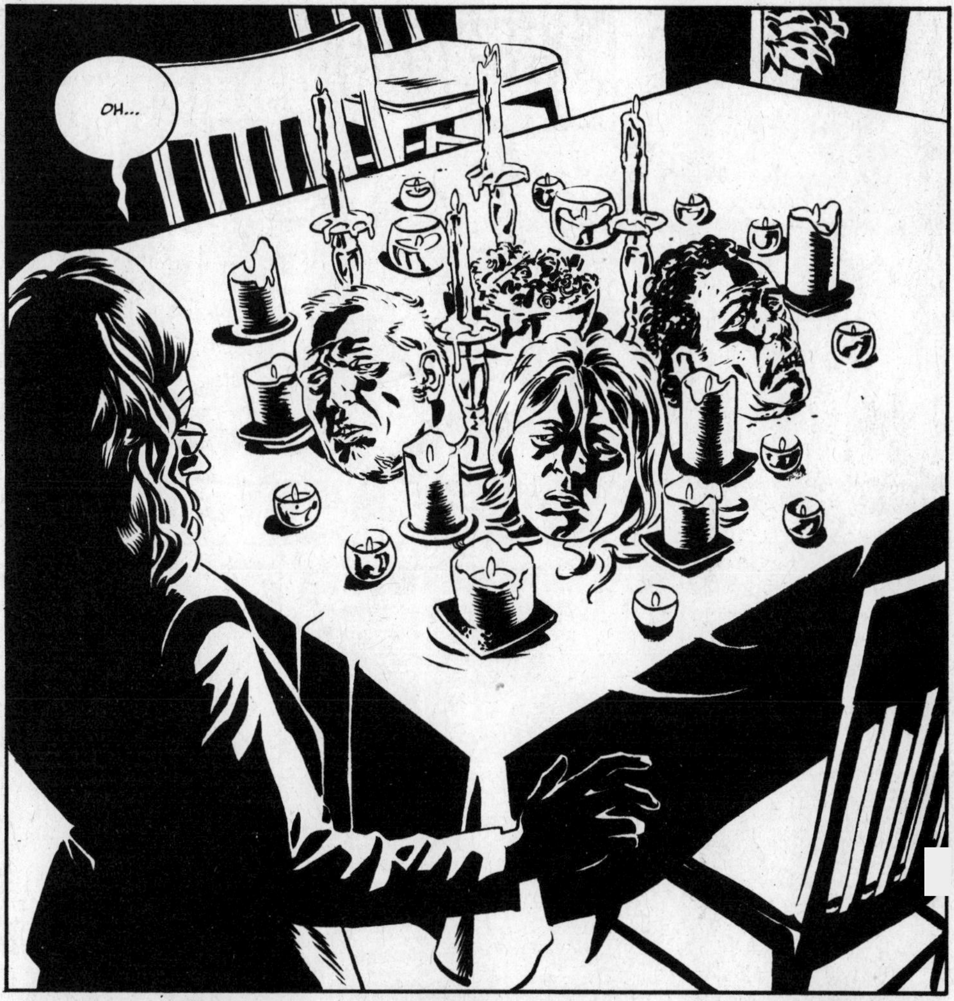
OH...

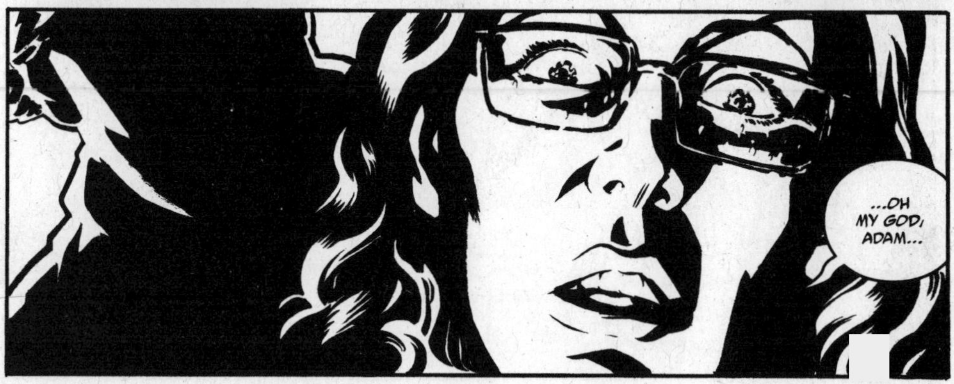
...OH
MY GOD,
ADAM...

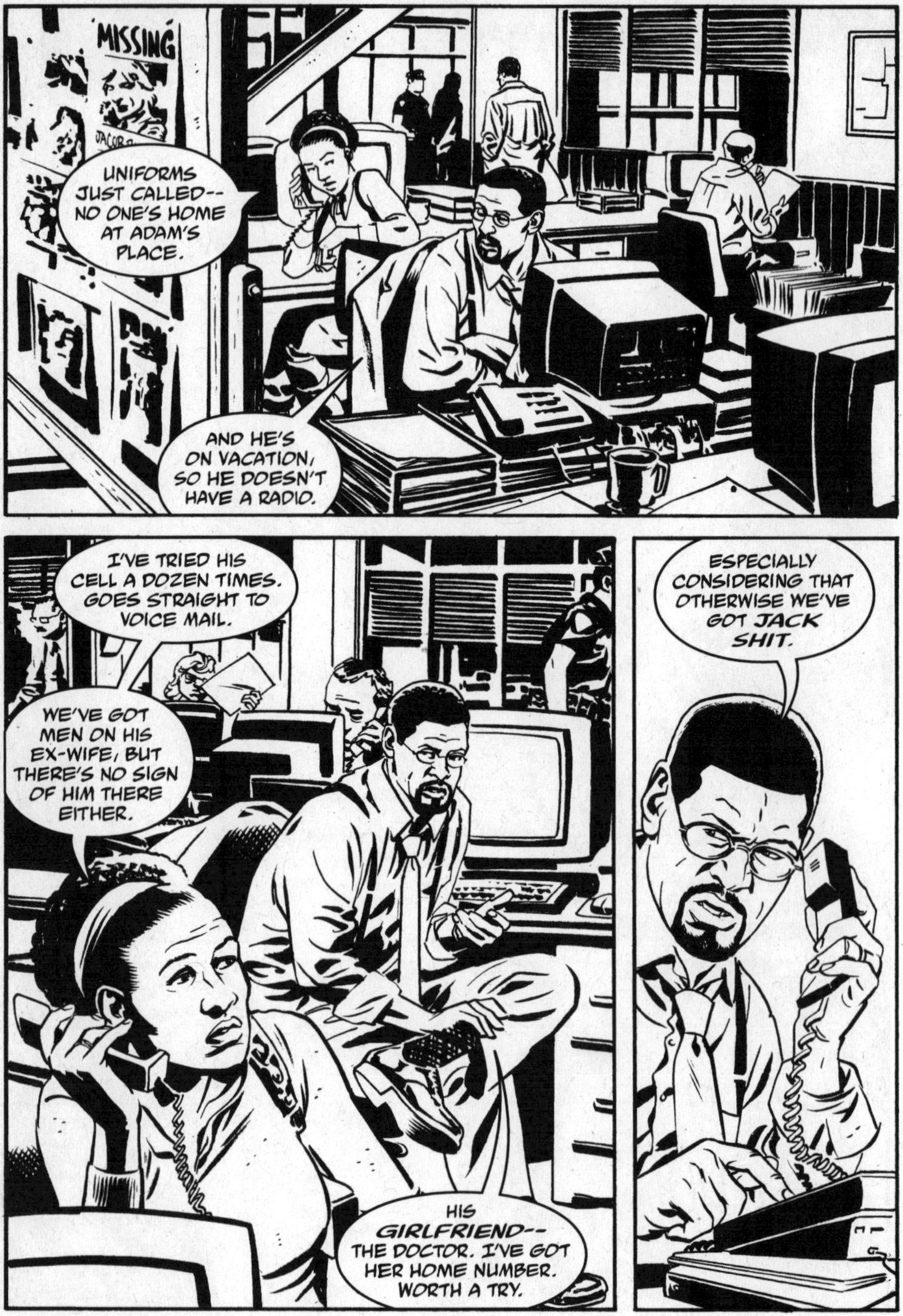
MISSING
UNIFORMS JUST CALLED-- NO ONE'S HOME AT ADAM'S PLACE.
AND HE'S ON VACATION, SO HE DOESN'T HAVE A RADIO.
I'VE TRIED HIS CELL A DOZEN TIMES. GOES STRAIGHT TO VOICE MAIL.
WE'VE GOT MEN ON HIS EX-WIFE, BUT THERE'S NO SIGN OF HIM THERE EITHER.
HIS *GIRLFRIEND*-- THE DOCTOR. I'VE GOT HER HOME NUMBER. WORTH A TRY.
ESPECIALLY CONSIDERING THAT OTHERWISE WE'VE GOT *JACK SHIT*.

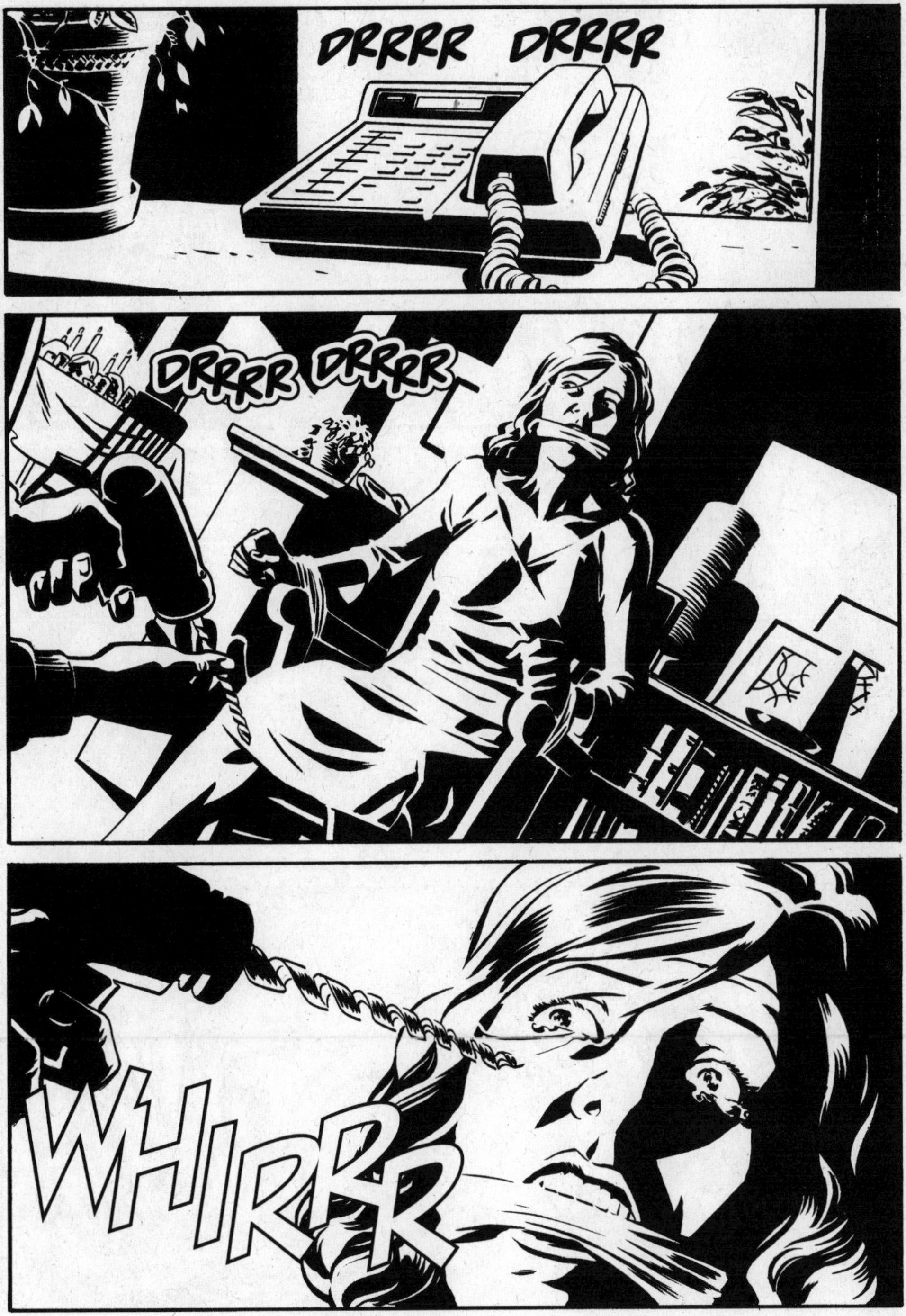
DRRRR DRRRR
DRRRR DRRRR
WHIRRR

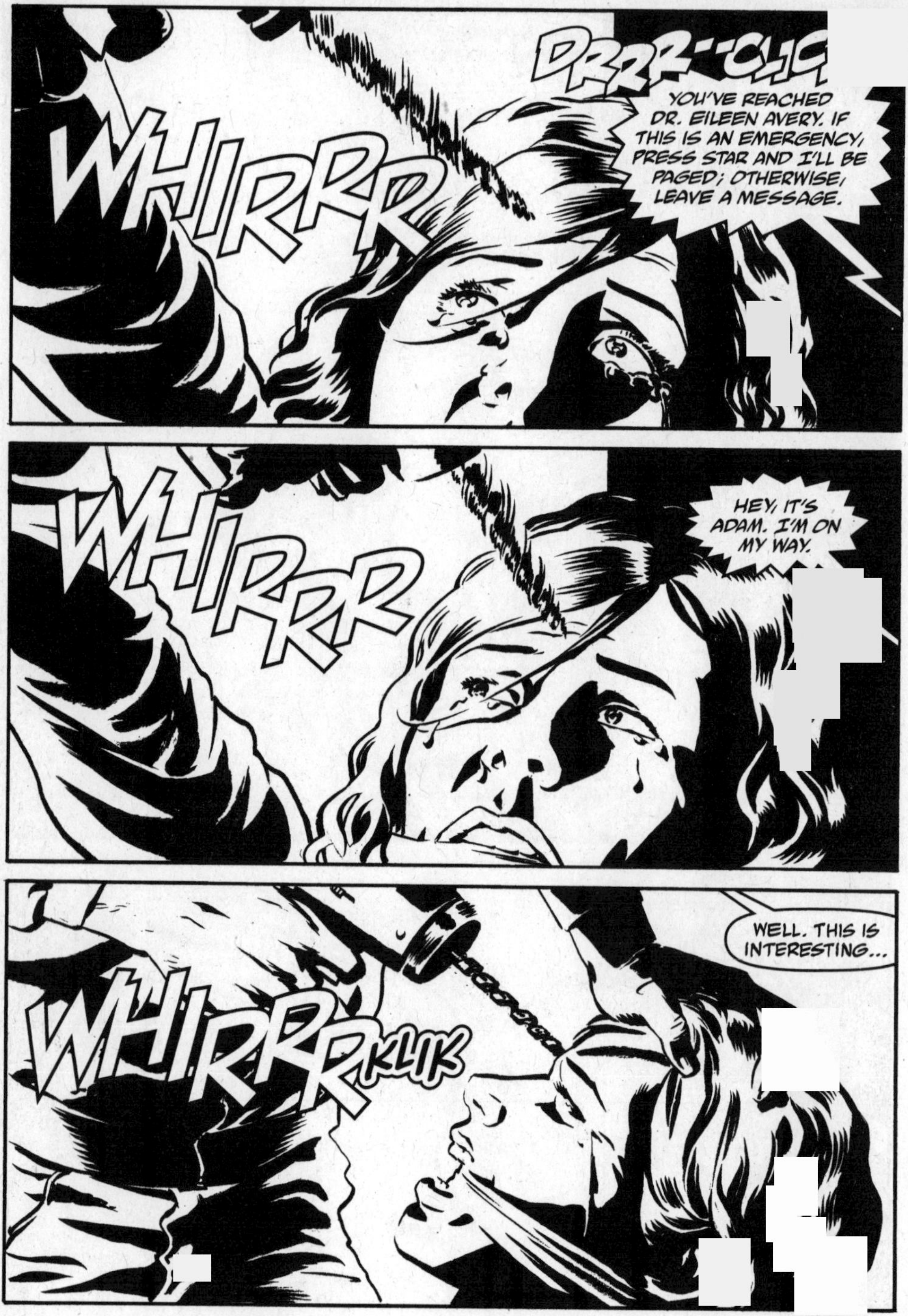
DRRR-CLIC
WHIRRR
YOU'VE REACHED DR. EILEEN AVERY. IF THIS IS AN EMERGENCY, PRESS STAR AND I'LL BE PAGED; OTHERWISE, LEAVE A MESSAGE.
WHIRRR
HEY, IT'S ADAM. I'M ON MY WAY.
WHIRRR
KLIK
WELL. THIS IS INTERESTING...

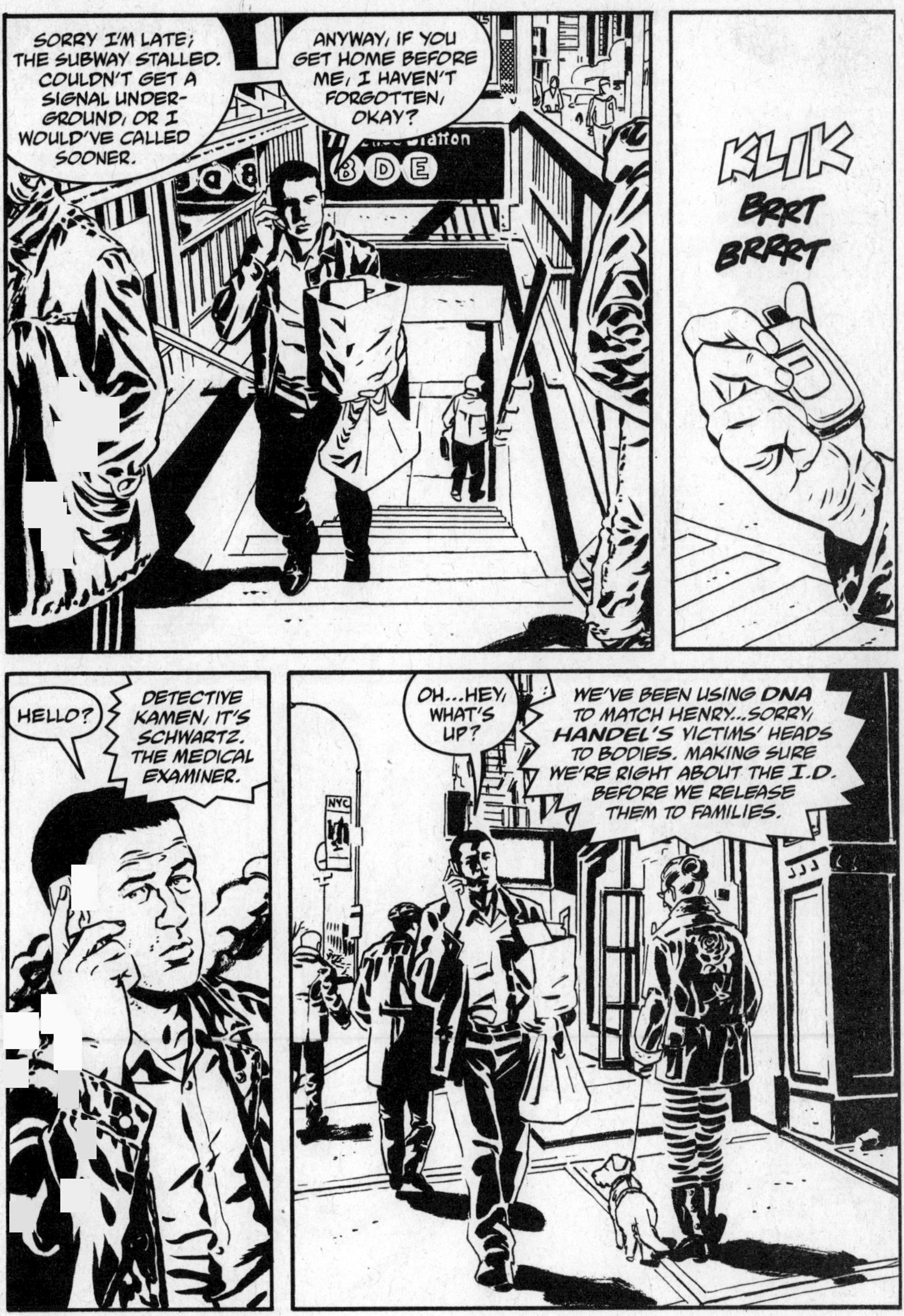
SORRY I'M LATE; THE SUBWAY STALLED. COULDN'T GET A SIGNAL UNDER-GROUND, OR I WOULD'VE CALLED SOONER.
ANYWAY, IF YOU GET HOME BEFORE ME, I HAVEN'T FORGOTTEN, OKAY?
BDE
KLIK
BRRT
BRRRT
HELLO?
DETECTIVE KAMEN, IT'S SCHWARTZ. THE MEDICAL EXAMINER.
OH...HEY, WHAT'S UP?
WE'VE BEEN USING DNA TO MATCH HENRY...SORRY, HANDEL'S VICTIMS' HEADS TO BODIES. MAKING SURE WE'RE RIGHT ABOUT THE I.D. BEFORE WE RELEASE THEM TO FAMILIES.
NYC

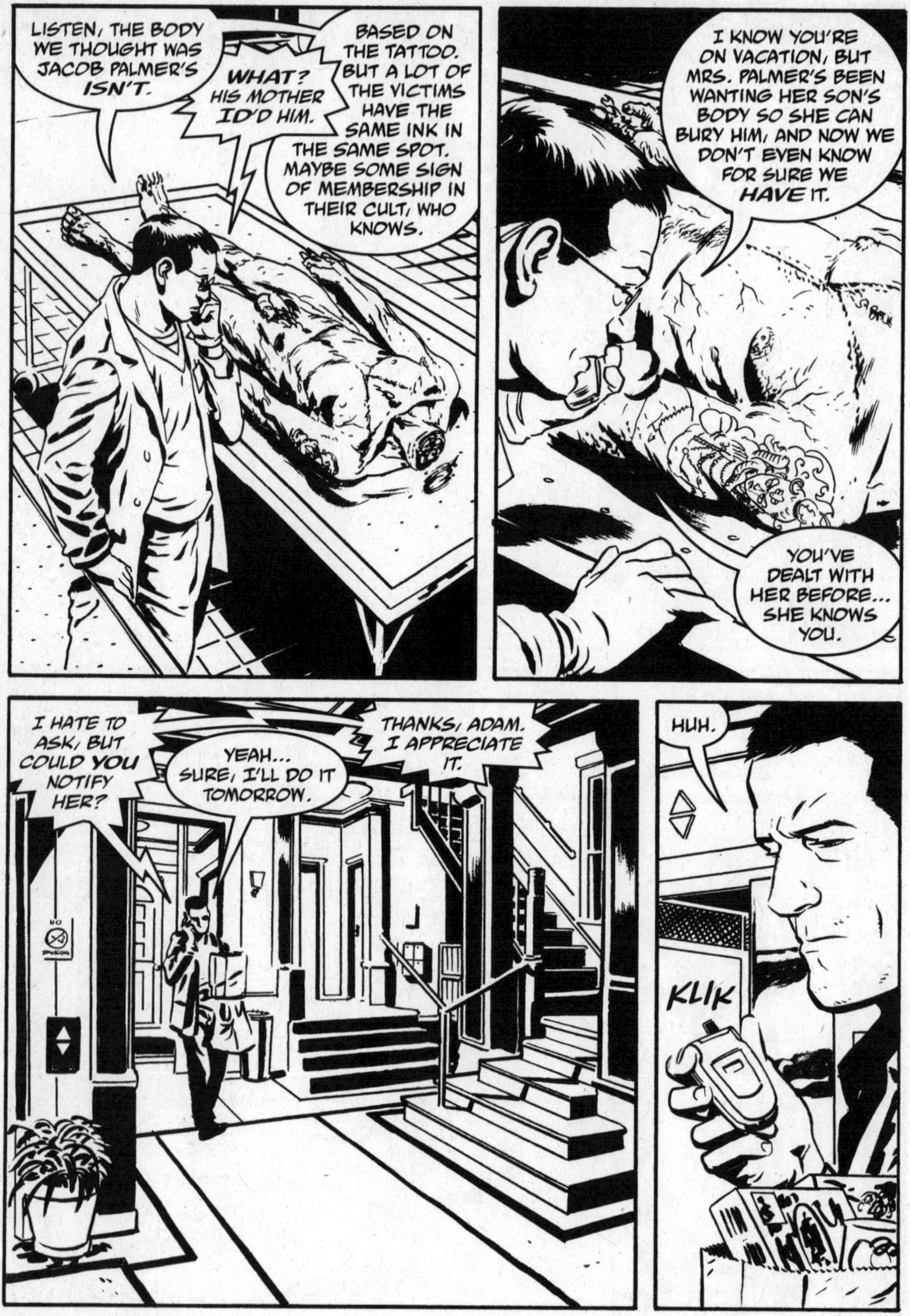
LISTEN, THE BODY WE THOUGHT WAS JACOB PALMER'S *ISN'T*.
WHAT? HIS MOTHER *ID'D* HIM.
BASED ON THE TATTOO. BUT A LOT OF THE VICTIMS HAVE THE SAME INK IN THE SAME SPOT. MAYBE SOME SIGN OF MEMBERSHIP IN THEIR CULT, WHO KNOWS.
I KNOW YOU'RE ON VACATION, BUT MRS. PALMER'S BEEN WANTING HER SON'S BODY SO SHE CAN BURY HIM, AND NOW WE DON'T EVEN KNOW FOR SURE WE *HAVE* IT.
YOU'VE DEALT WITH HER BEFORE... SHE KNOWS YOU.
I HATE TO ASK, BUT COULD *YOU* NOTIFY HER?
YEAH... SURE, I'LL DO IT TOMORROW.
THANKS, ADAM. I APPRECIATE IT.
HUH.
KLIK

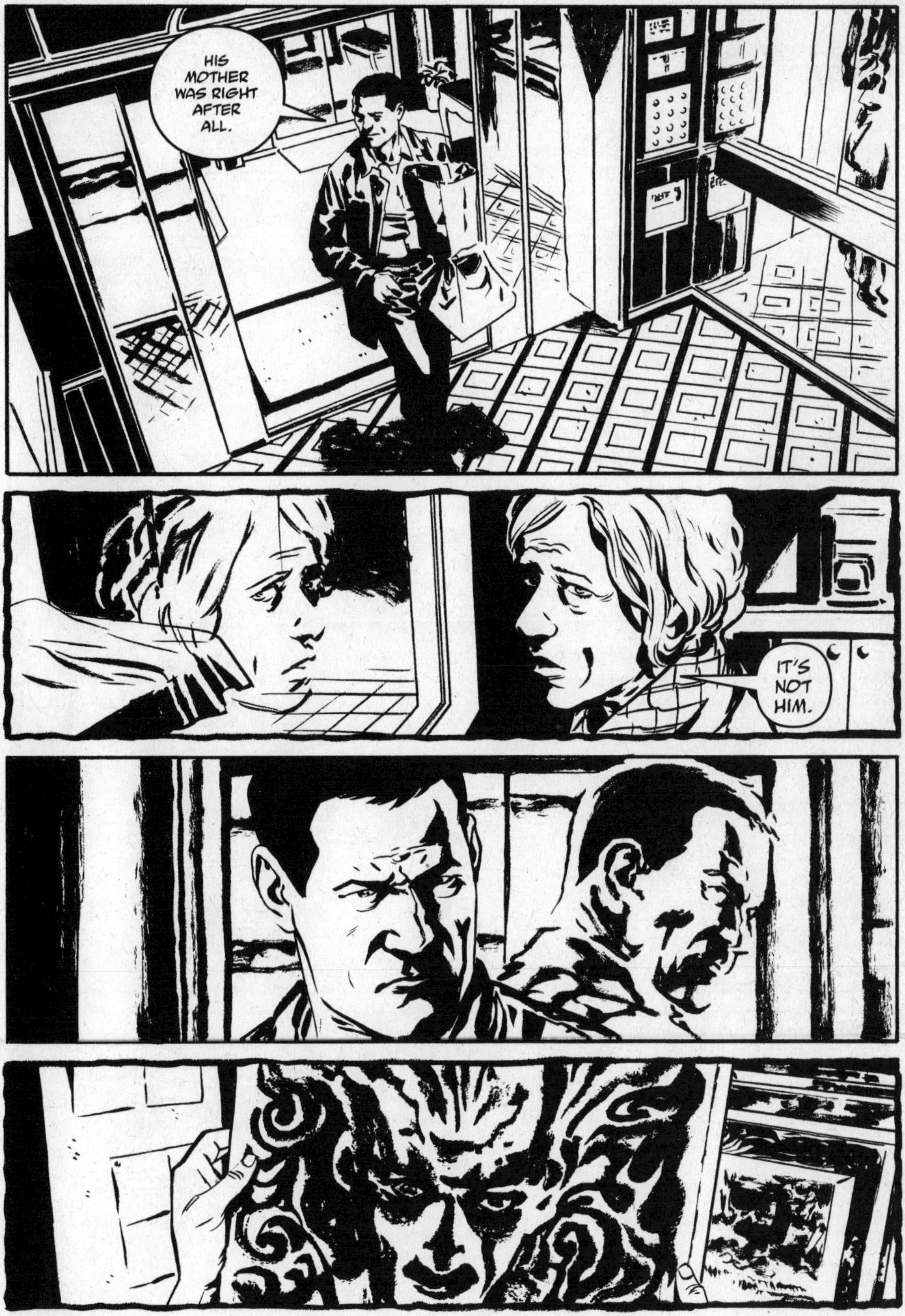
HIS MOTHER WAS RIGHT AFTER ALL.
IT'S NOT HIM.

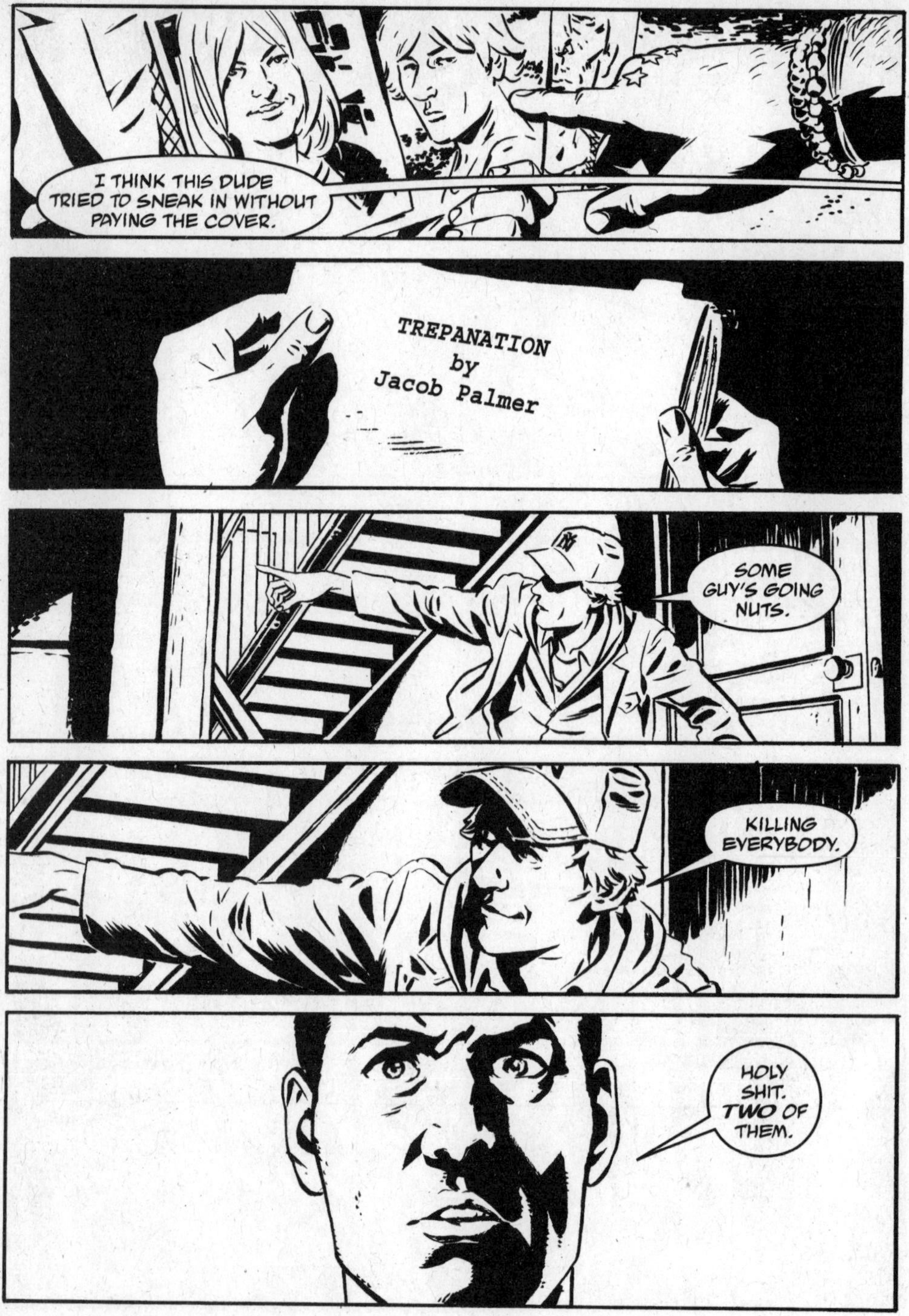
I THINK THIS DUDE TRIED TO SNEAK IN WITHOUT PAYING THE COVER.
TREPANATION by Jacob Palmer
SOME GUY'S GOING NUTS.
KILLING EVERYBODY.
HOLY SHIT. TWO OF THEM.

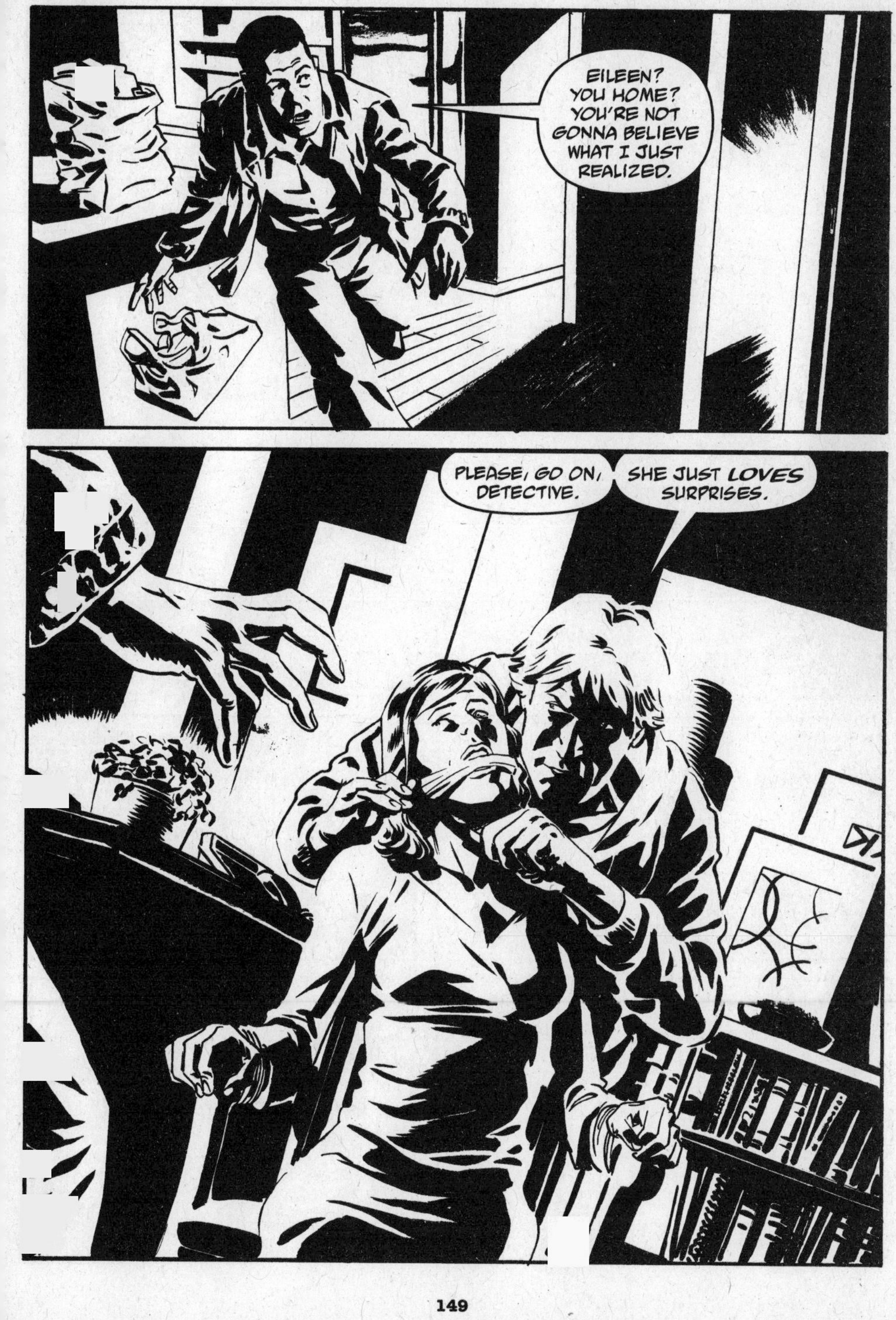
EILEEN? YOU HOME? YOU'RE NOT GONNA BELIEVE WHAT I JUST REALIZED.
PLEASE, GO ON, DETECTIVE.
SHE JUST LOVES SURPRISES.

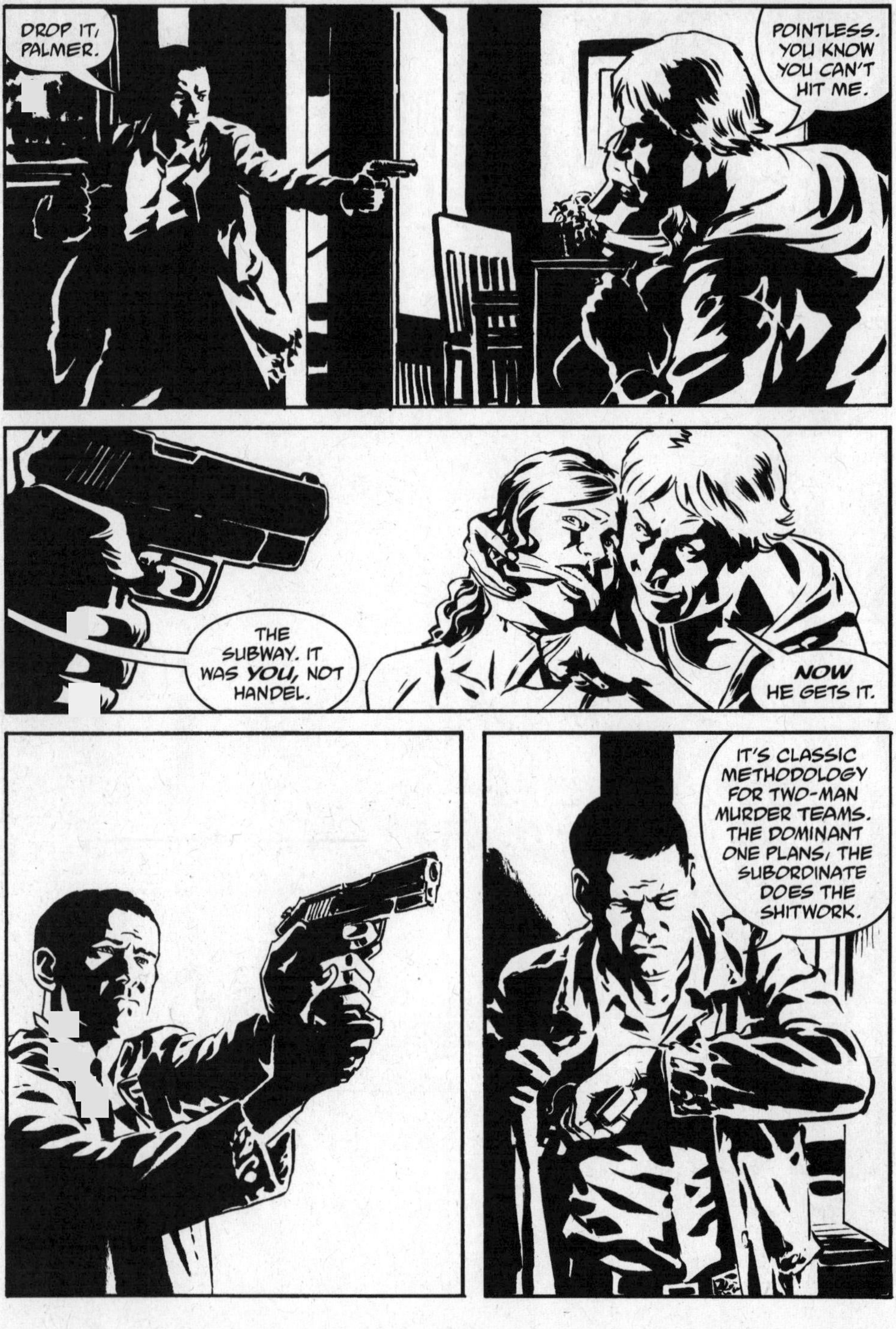
DROP IT, PALMER.
POINTLESS. YOU KNOW YOU CAN'T HIT ME.
THE SUBWAY. IT WAS YOU, NOT HANDEL.
NOW HE GETS IT.
IT'S CLASSIC METHODOLOGY FOR TWO-MAN MURDER TEAMS. THE DOMINANT ONE PLANS, THE SUBORDINATE DOES THE SHITWORK.

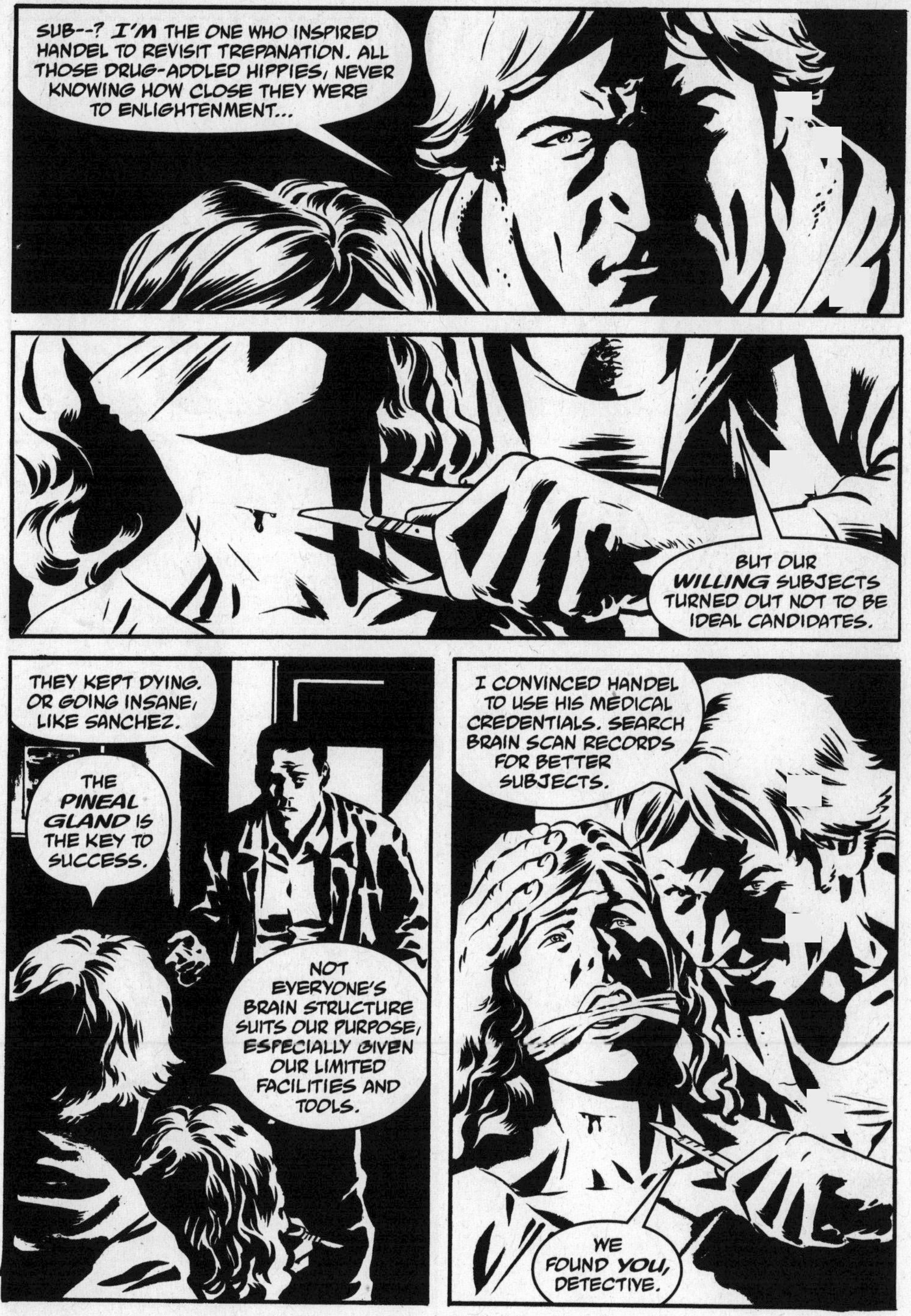
SUB--? I'M THE ONE WHO INSPIRED HANDEL TO REVISIT TREPANATION. ALL THOSE DRUG-ADDLED HIPPIES, NEVER KNOWING HOW CLOSE THEY WERE TO ENLIGHTENMENT...
BUT OUR WILLING SUBJECTS TURNED OUT NOT TO BE IDEAL CANDIDATES.
THEY KEPT DYING. OR GOING INSANE, LIKE SANCHEZ.
THE PINEAL GLAND IS THE KEY TO SUCCESS.
NOT EVERYONE'S BRAIN STRUCTURE SUITS OUR PURPOSE, ESPECIALLY GIVEN OUR LIMITED FACILITIES AND TOOLS.
I CONVINCED HANDEL TO USE HIS MEDICAL CREDENTIALS. SEARCH BRAIN SCAN RECORDS FOR BETTER SUBJECTS.
WE FOUND YOU, DETECTIVE.

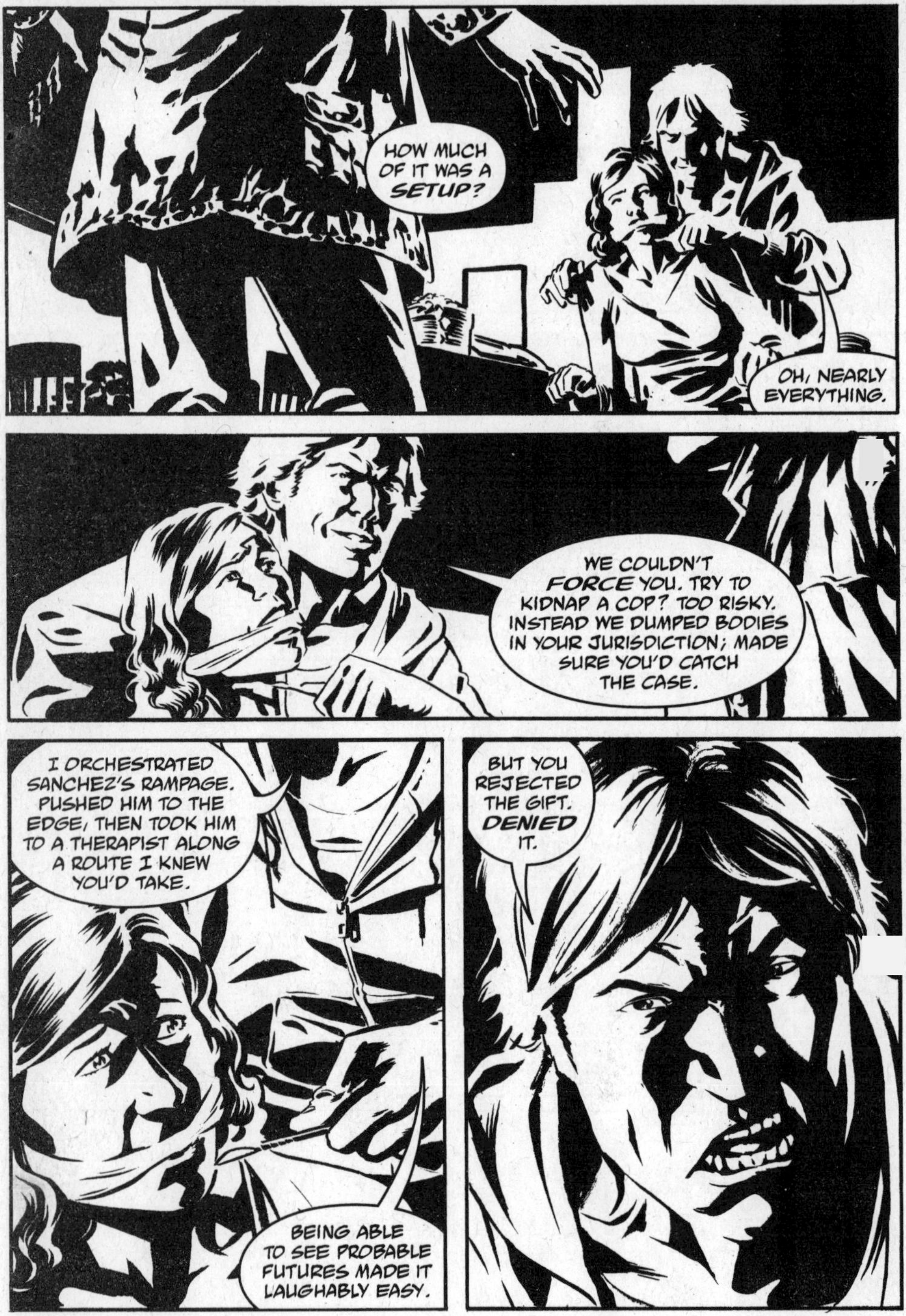

HOW MUCH OF IT WAS A SETUP?
OH, NEARLY EVERYTHING.
WE COULDN'T FORCE YOU. TRY TO KIDNAP A COP? TOO RISKY. INSTEAD WE DUMPED BODIES IN YOUR JURISDICTION; MADE SURE YOU'D CATCH THE CASE.
I ORCHESTRATED SANCHEZ'S RAMPAGE. PUSHED HIM TO THE EDGE, THEN TOOK HIM TO A THERAPIST ALONG A ROUTE I KNEW YOU'D TAKE.
BEING ABLE TO SEE PROBABLE FUTURES MADE IT LAUGHABLY EASY.
BUT YOU REJECTED THE GIFT. DENIED IT.

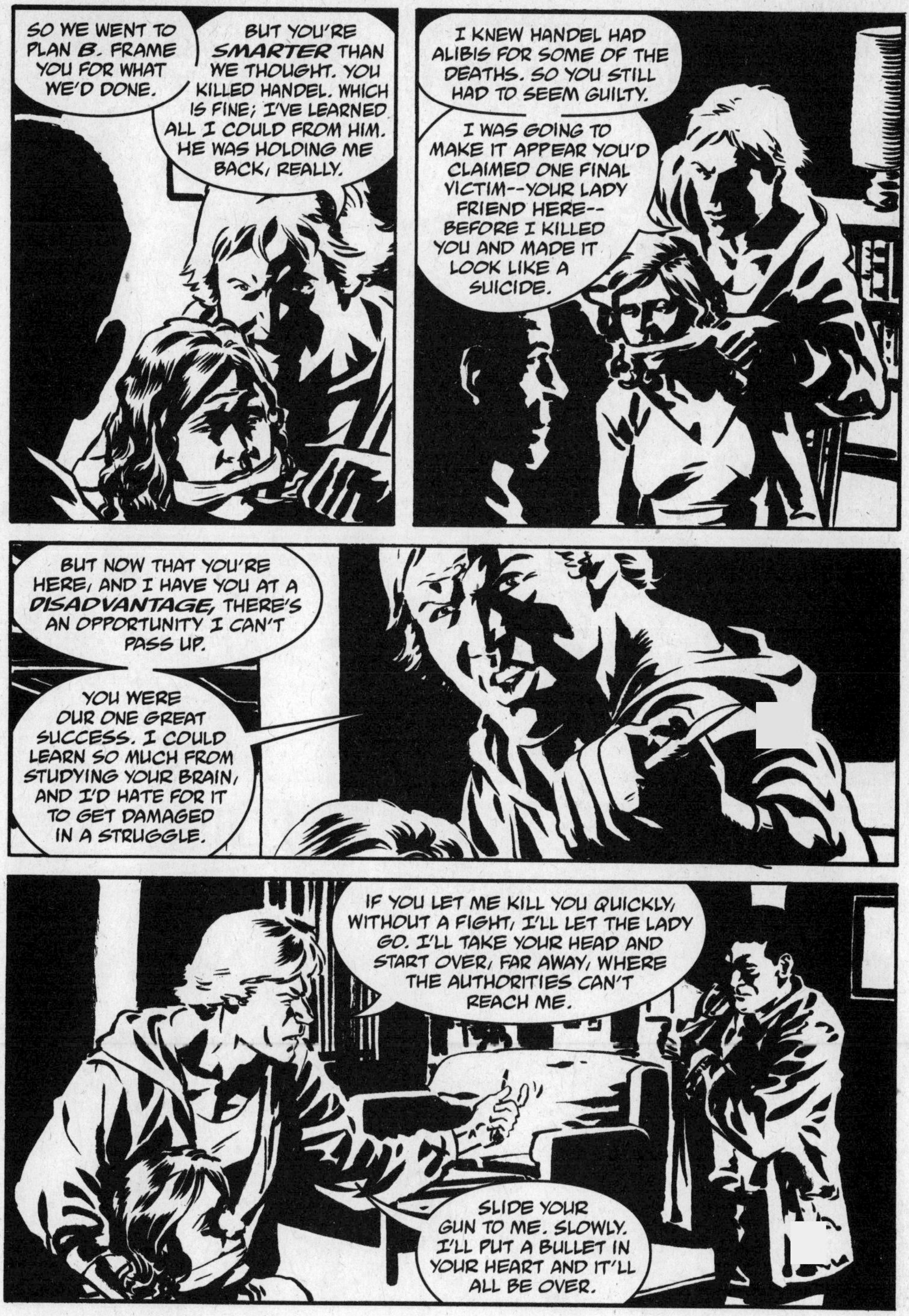
SO WE WENT TO PLAN B. FRAME YOU FOR WHAT WE'D DONE.
BUT YOU'RE SMARTER THAN WE THOUGHT. YOU KILLED HANDEL. WHICH IS FINE; I'VE LEARNED ALL I COULD FROM HIM. HE WAS HOLDING ME BACK, REALLY.
I KNEW HANDEL HAD ALIBIS FOR SOME OF THE DEATHS. SO YOU STILL HAD TO SEEM GUILTY.
I WAS GOING TO MAKE IT APPEAR YOU'D CLAIMED ONE FINAL VICTIM--YOUR LADY FRIEND HERE--BEFORE I KILLED YOU AND MADE IT LOOK LIKE A SUICIDE.
BUT NOW THAT YOU'RE HERE, AND I HAVE YOU AT A DISADVANTAGE, THERE'S AN OPPORTUNITY I CAN'T PASS UP.
YOU WERE OUR ONE GREAT SUCCESS. I COULD LEARN SO MUCH FROM STUDYING YOUR BRAIN, AND I'D HATE FOR IT TO GET DAMAGED IN A STRUGGLE.
IF YOU LET ME KILL YOU QUICKLY, WITHOUT A FIGHT, I'LL LET THE LADY GO. I'LL TAKE YOUR HEAD AND START OVER, FAR AWAY, WHERE THE AUTHORITIES CAN'T REACH ME.
SLIDE YOUR GUN TO ME. SLOWLY. I'LL PUT A BULLET IN YOUR HEART AND IT'LL ALL BE OVER.

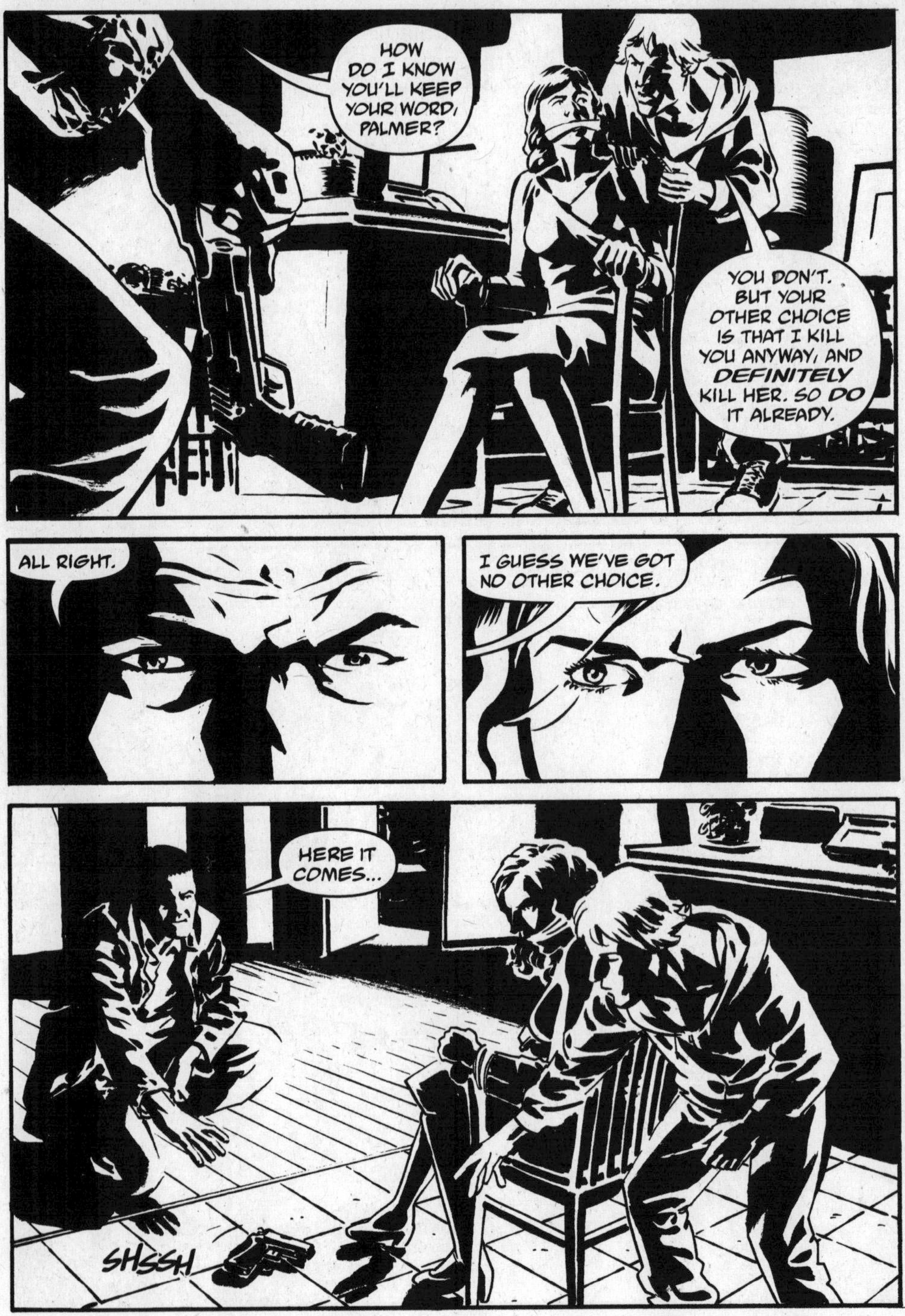
HOW DO I KNOW YOU'LL KEEP YOUR WORD, PALMER?
YOU DON'T. BUT YOUR OTHER CHOICE IS THAT I KILL YOU ANYWAY, AND DEFINITELY KILL HER. SO DO IT ALREADY.
ALL RIGHT.
I GUESS WE'VE GOT NO OTHER CHOICE.
HERE IT COMES...
SHSSH

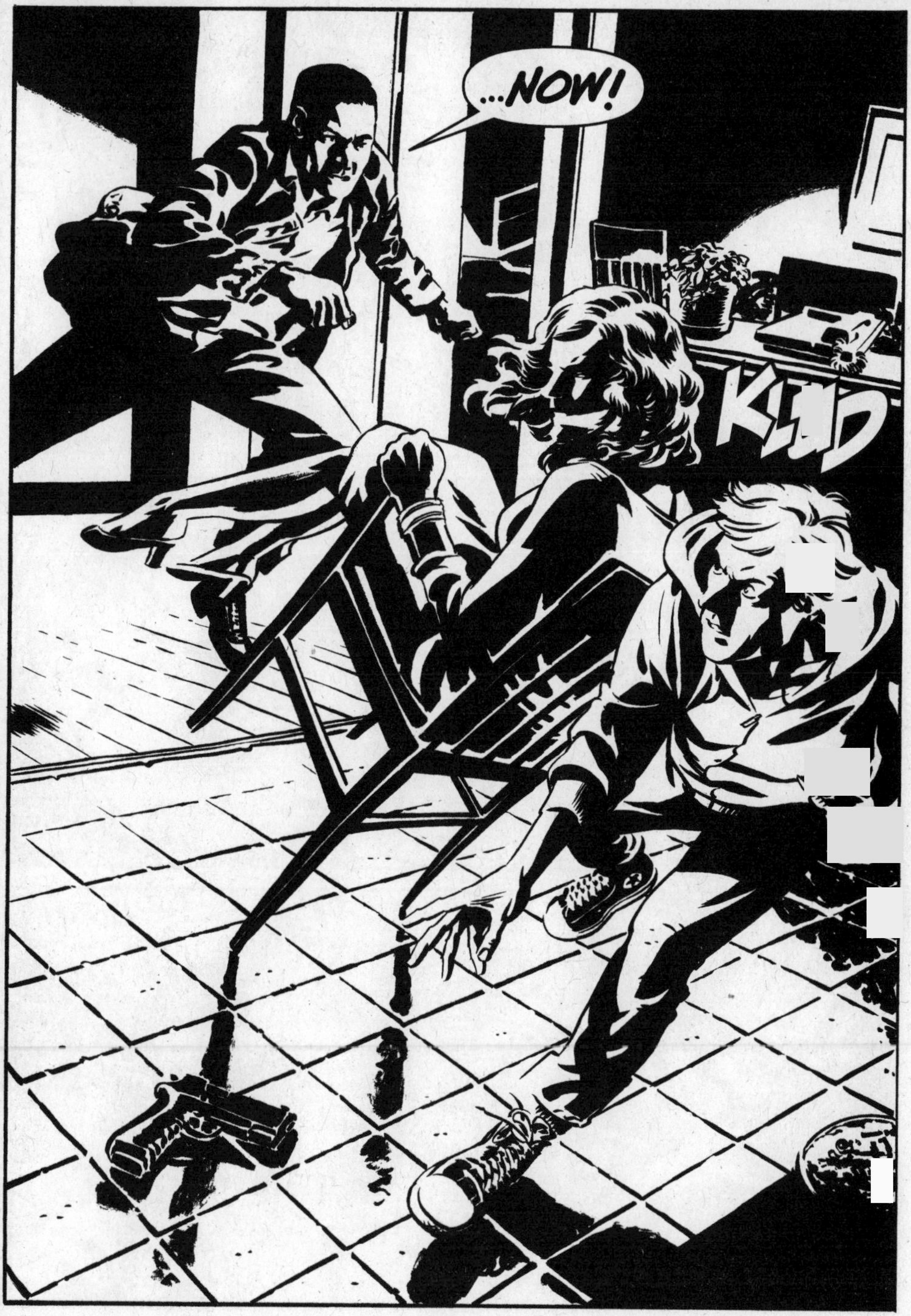
...NOW!
KLUD

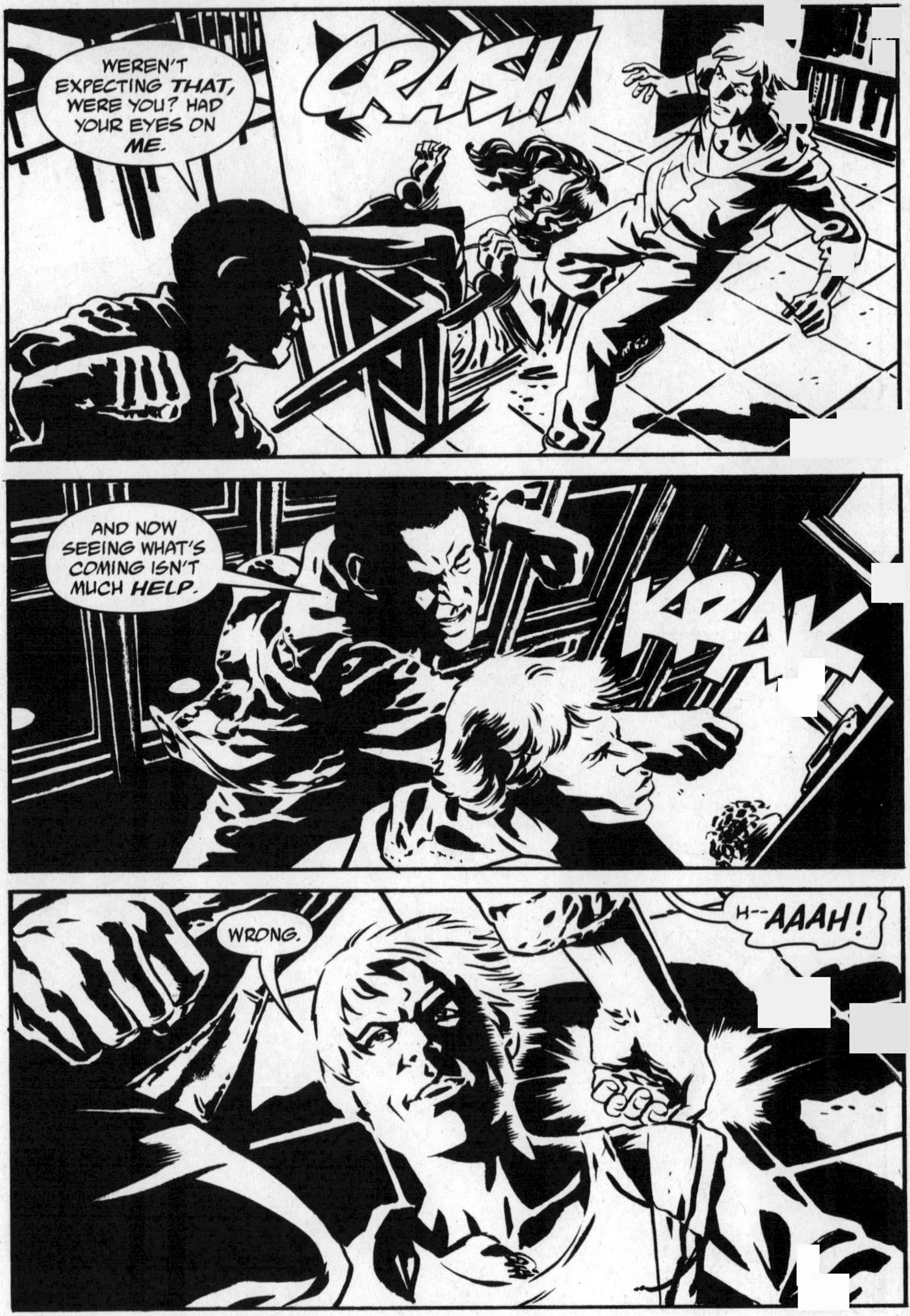
WEREN'T EXPECTING THAT, WERE YOU? HAD YOUR EYES ON ME.
CRASH
AND NOW SEEING WHAT'S COMING ISN'T MUCH HELP.
KRAK
WRONG.
H--AAAH!

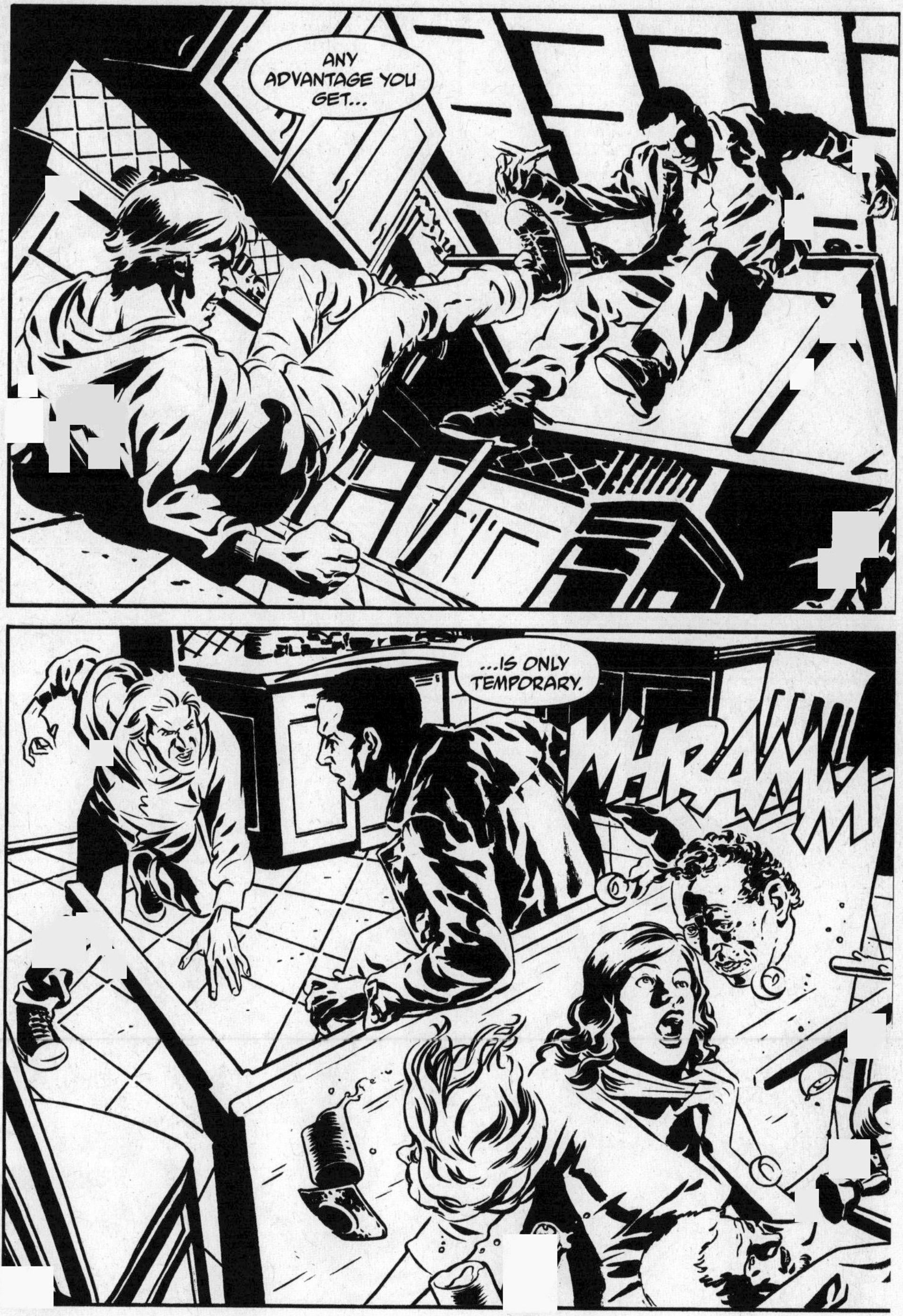
ANY ADVANTAGE YOU GET...
...IS ONLY TEMPORARY.
WHRAAM

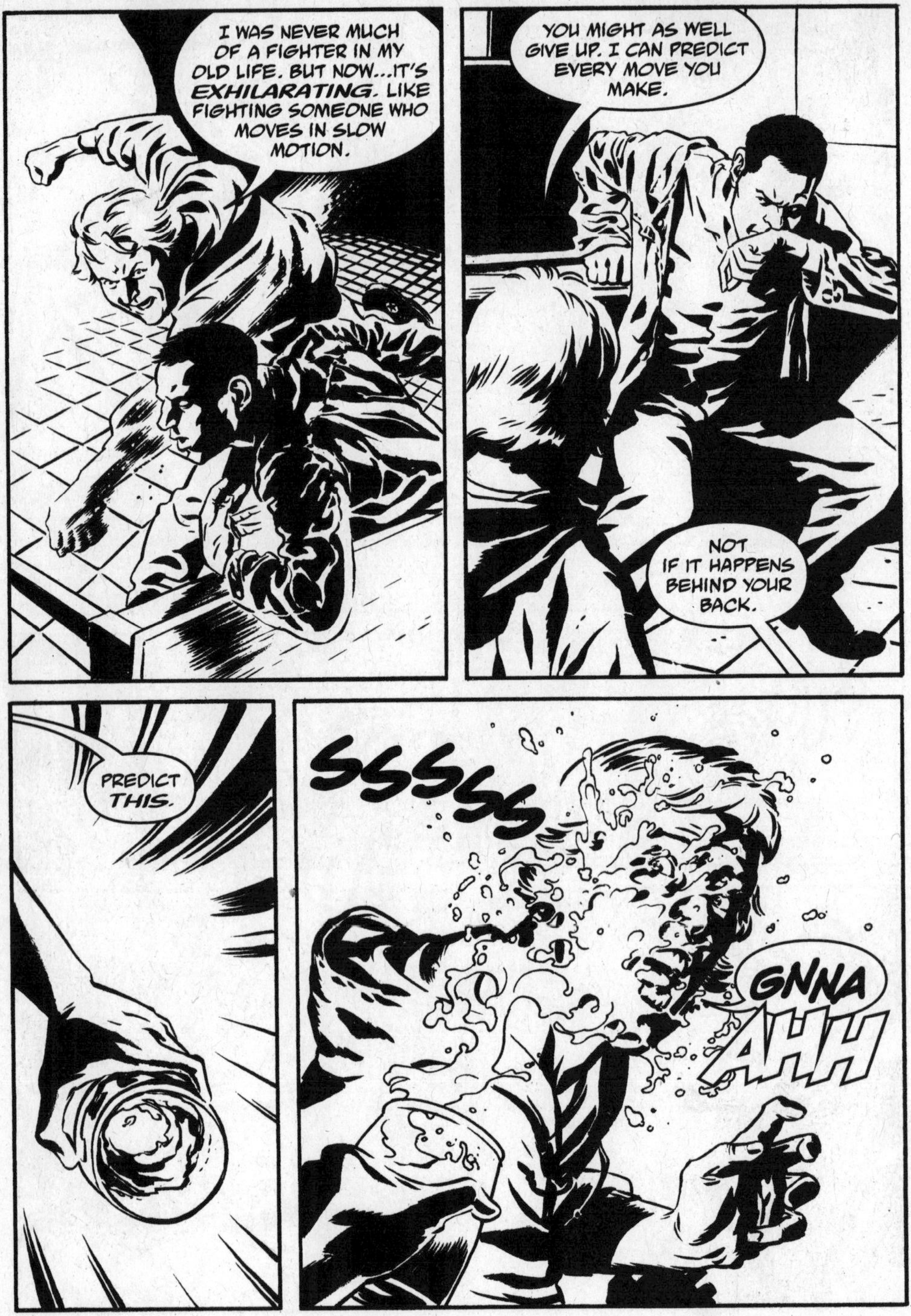
I WAS NEVER MUCH OF A FIGHTER IN MY OLD LIFE. BUT NOW...IT'S EXHILARATING. LIKE FIGHTING SOMEONE WHO MOVES IN SLOW MOTION.
YOU MIGHT AS WELL GIVE UP. I CAN PREDICT EVERY MOVE YOU MAKE.
NOT IF IT HAPPENS BEHIND YOUR BACK.
PREDICT THIS.
SSSSS
GNNA AHH

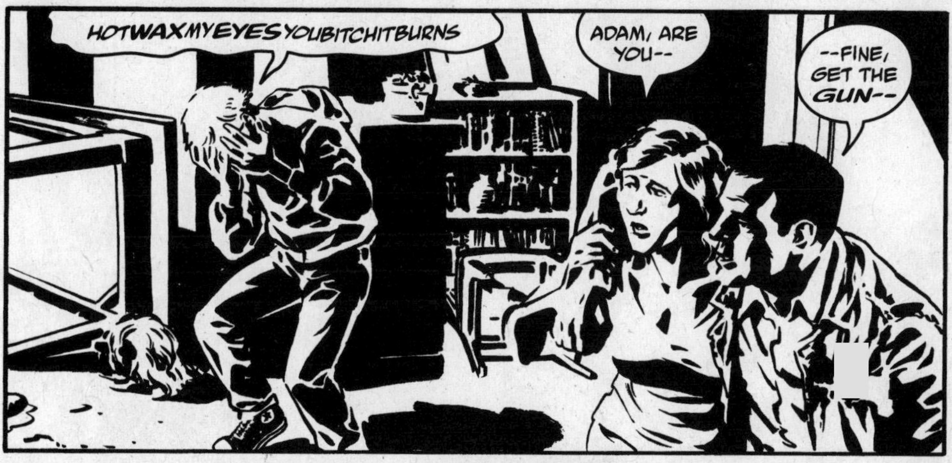
HOTWAXMYEYESYOUBITCHITBURNS
ADAM, ARE YOU--
--FINE, GET THE GUN--

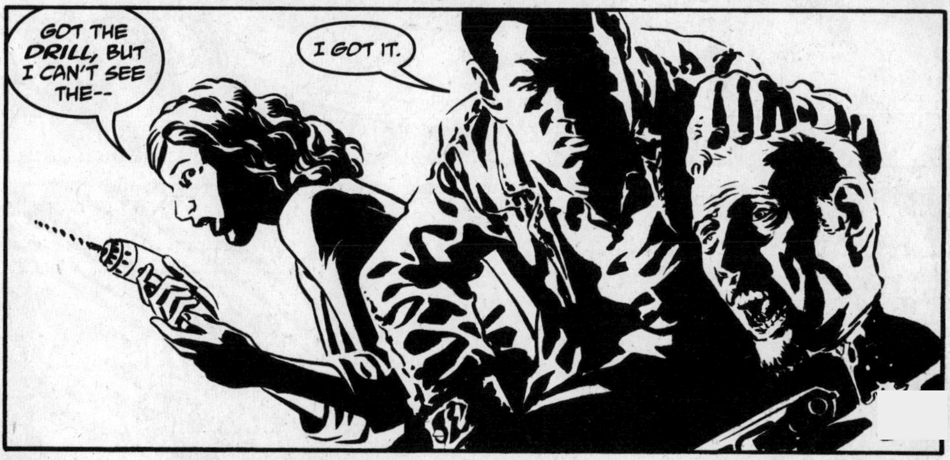
GOT THE DRILL, BUT I CAN'T SEE THE--
I GOT IT.

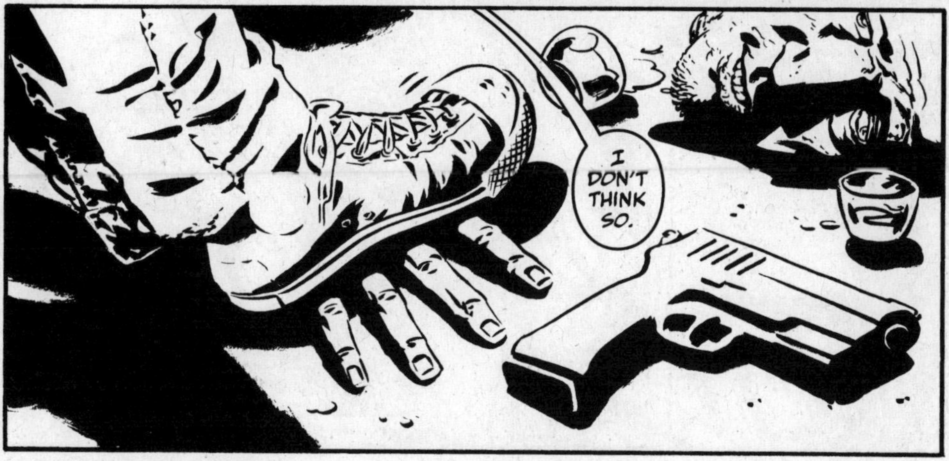
I DON'T THINK SO.

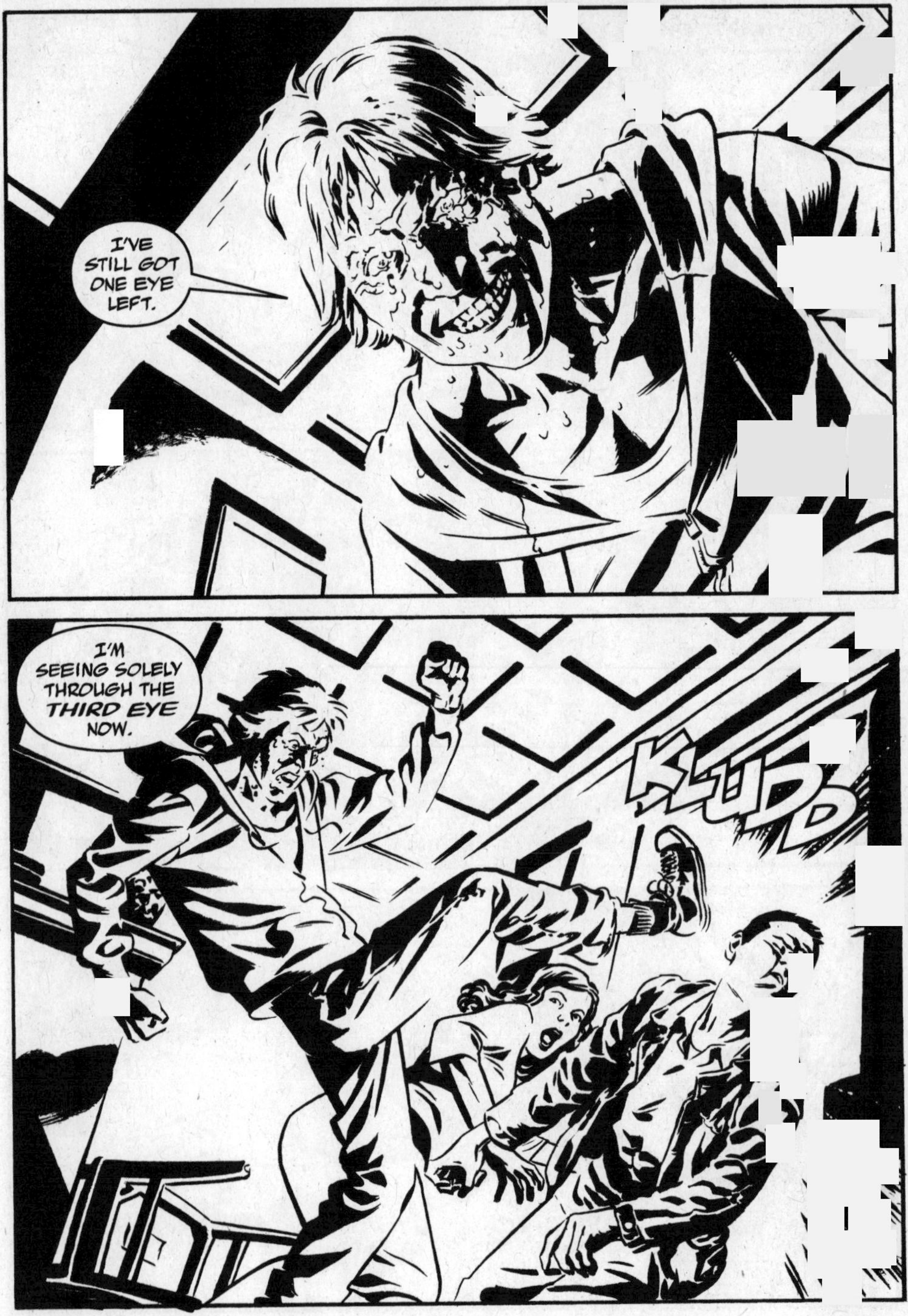
I'VE STILL GOT ONE EYE LEFT.
I'M SEEING SOLELY THROUGH THE THIRD EYE NOW.
KLUDD

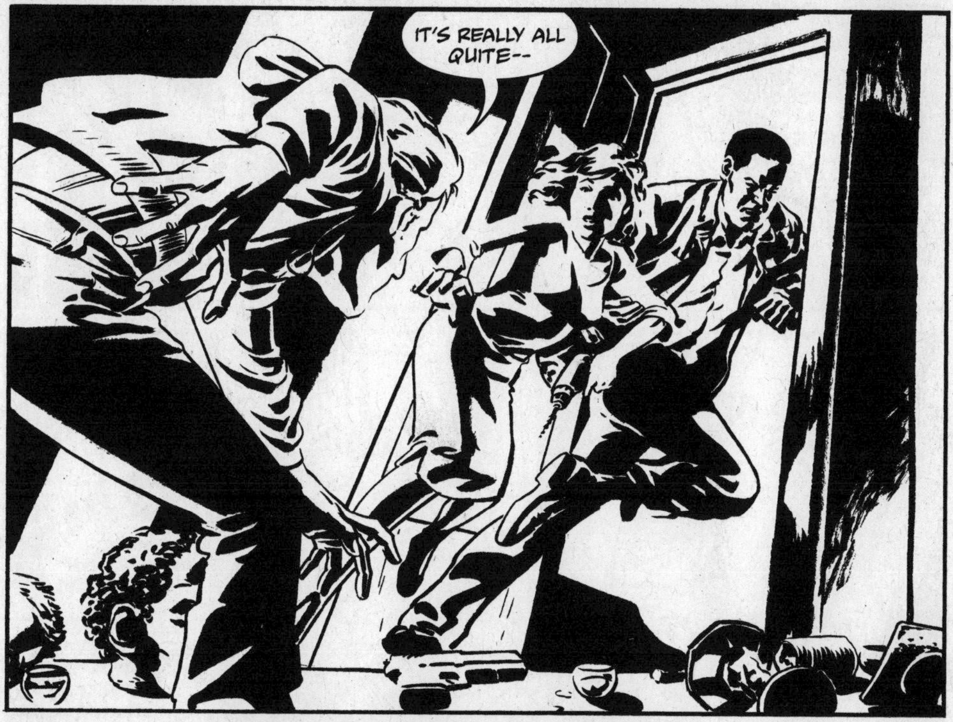
IT'S REALLY ALL QUITE--

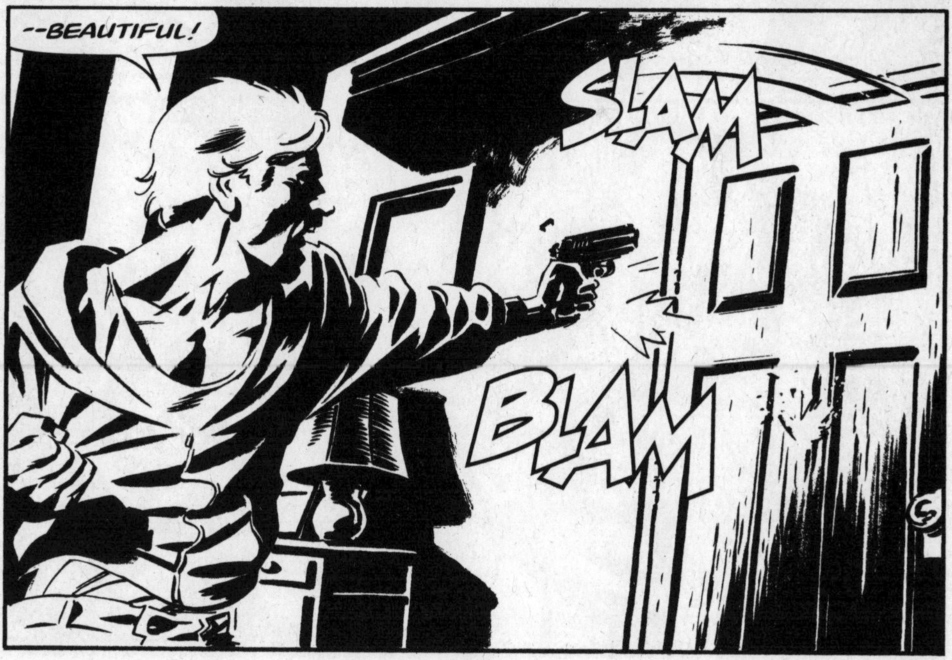
--BEAUTIFUL!
SLAM
BLAM

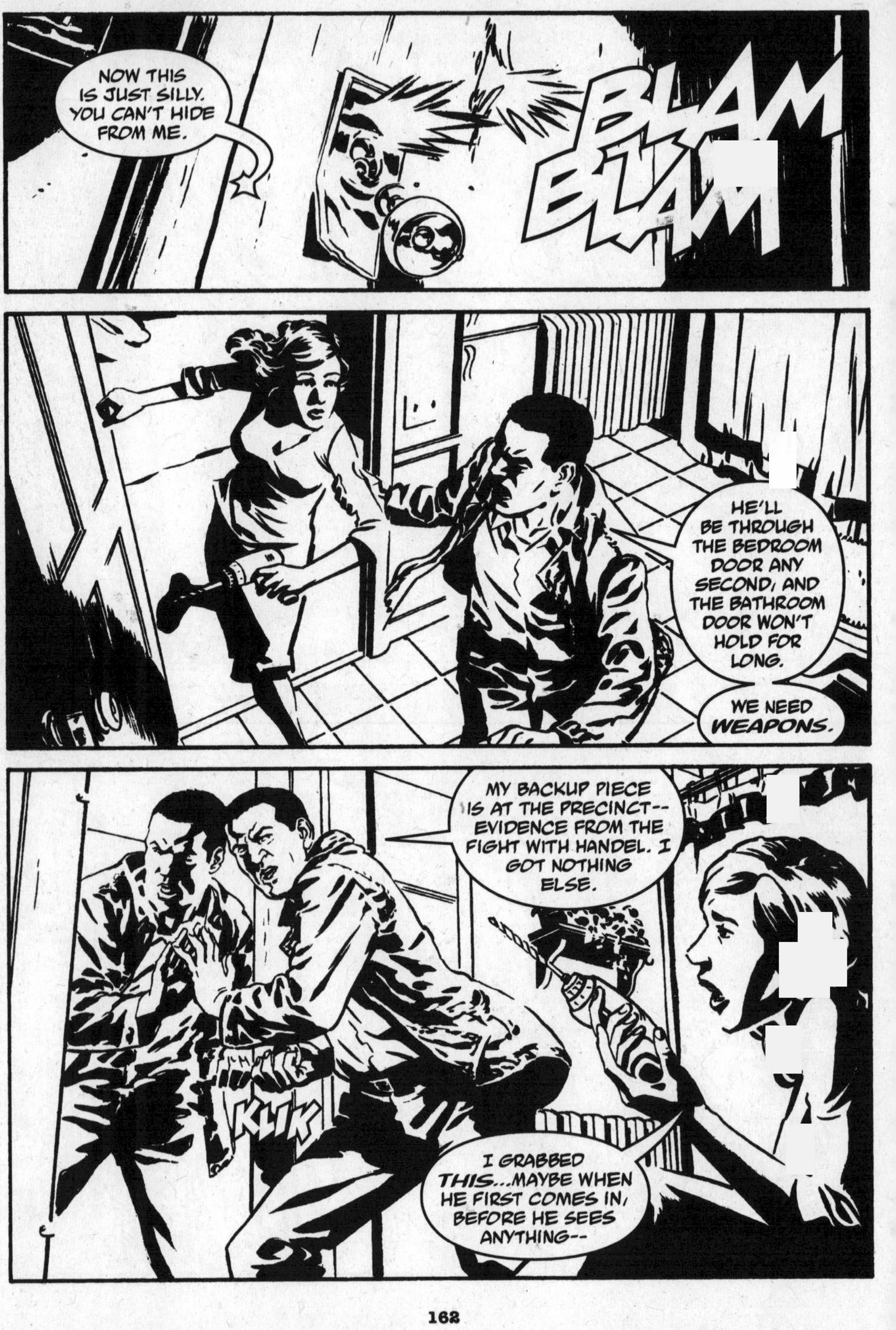
NOW THIS IS JUST SILLY. YOU CAN'T HIDE FROM ME.
BLAM BLAM
HE'LL BE THROUGH THE BEDROOM DOOR ANY SECOND, AND THE BATHROOM DOOR WON'T HOLD FOR LONG.
WE NEED *WEAPONS*.
MY BACKUP PIECE IS AT THE PRECINCT-- EVIDENCE FROM THE FIGHT WITH HANDEL. I GOT NOTHING ELSE.
KLIK
I GRABBED *THIS*...MAYBE WHEN HE FIRST COMES IN, BEFORE HE SEES ANYTHING--

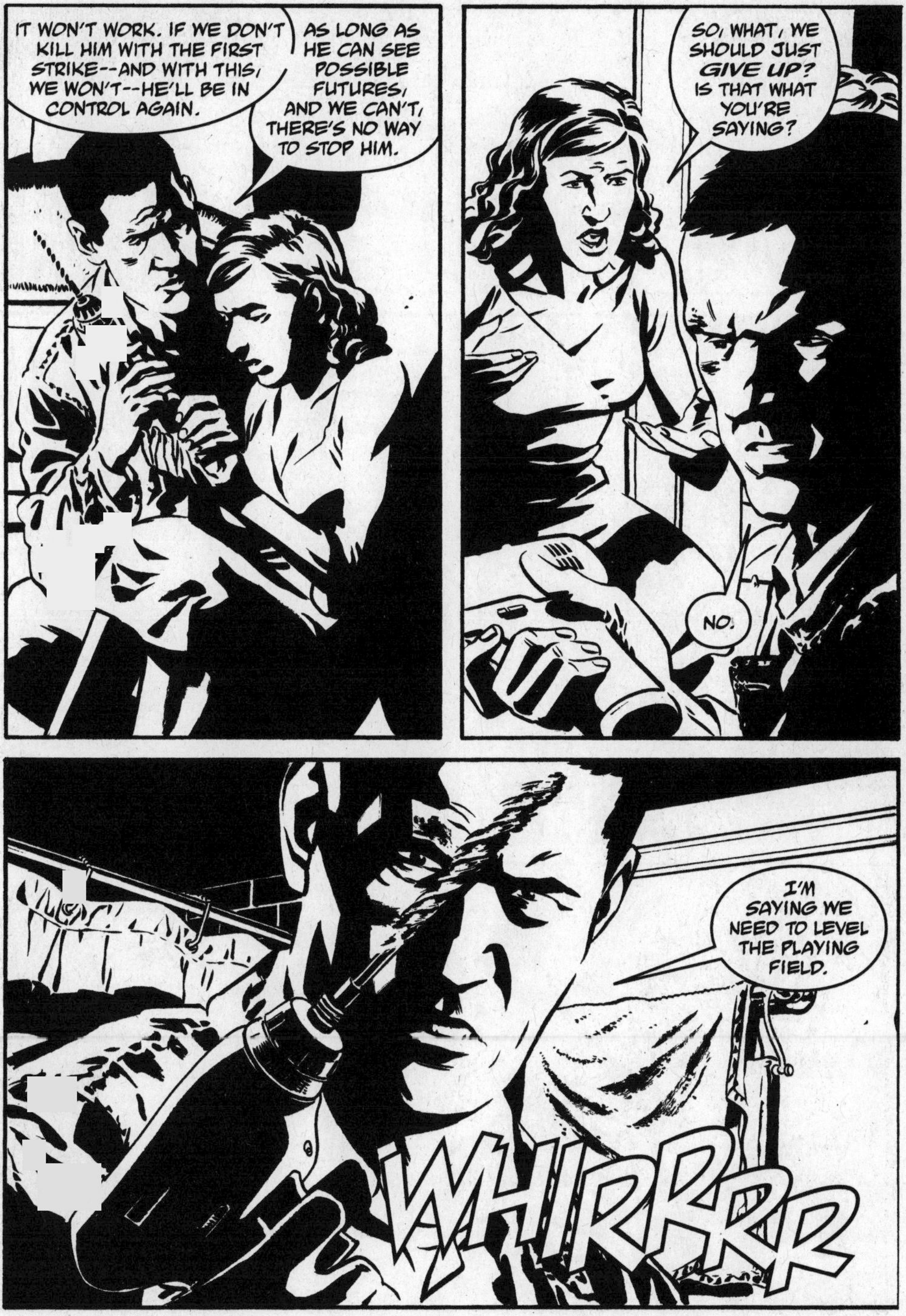

IT WON'T WORK. IF WE DON'T KILL HIM WITH THE FIRST STRIKE--AND WITH THIS, WE WON'T--HE'LL BE IN CONTROL AGAIN.
AS LONG AS HE CAN SEE POSSIBLE FUTURES, AND WE CAN'T, THERE'S NO WAY TO STOP HIM.
SO, WHAT, WE SHOULD JUST GIVE UP? IS THAT WHAT YOU'RE SAYING?
NO.
I'M SAYING WE NEED TO LEVEL THE PLAYING FIELD.
WHIRRRR

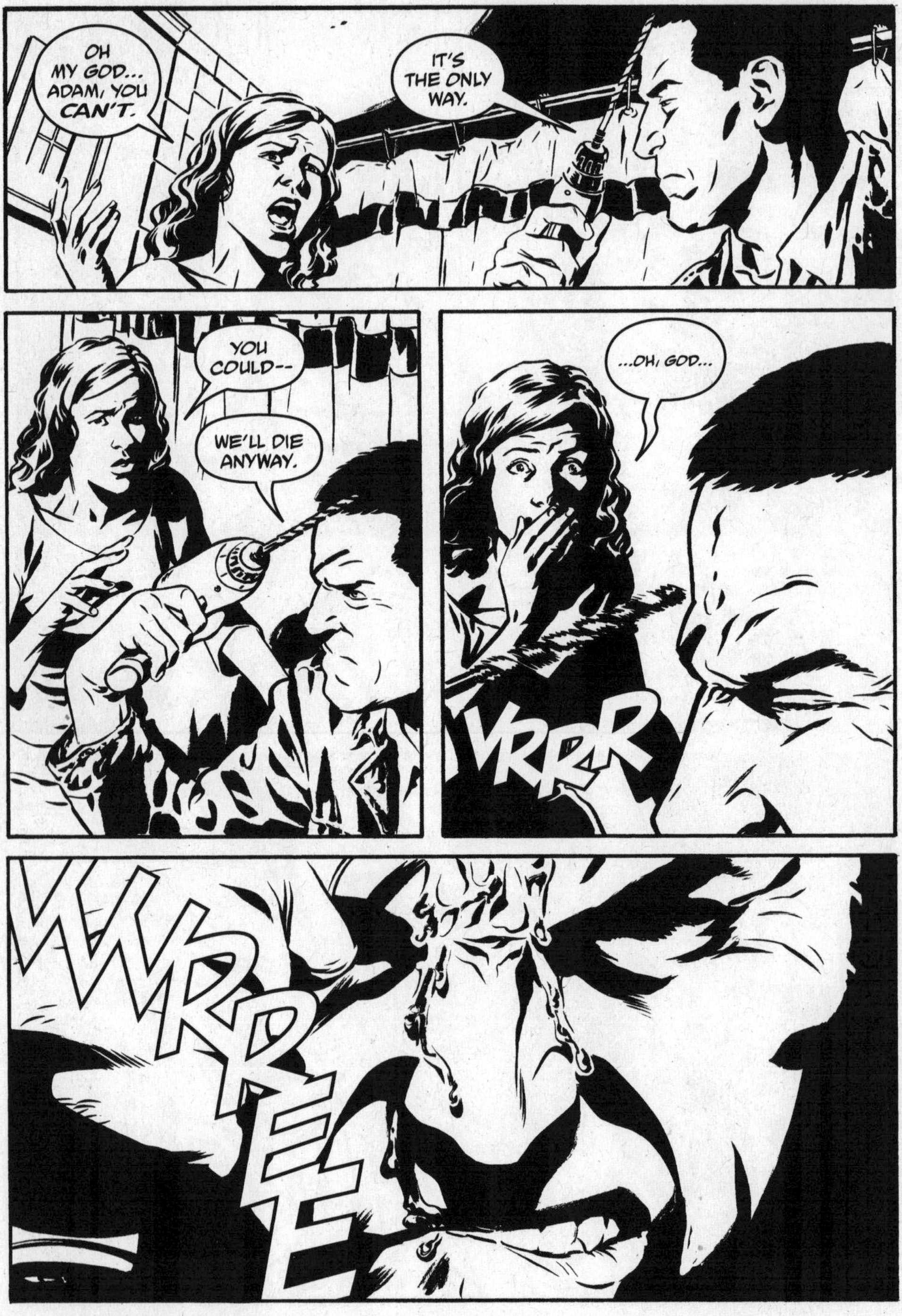
OH MY GOD... ADAM, YOU CAN'T.
IT'S THE ONLY WAY.
YOU COULD--
WE'LL DIE ANYWAY.
...OH, GOD...
VRRR
WWRREEE

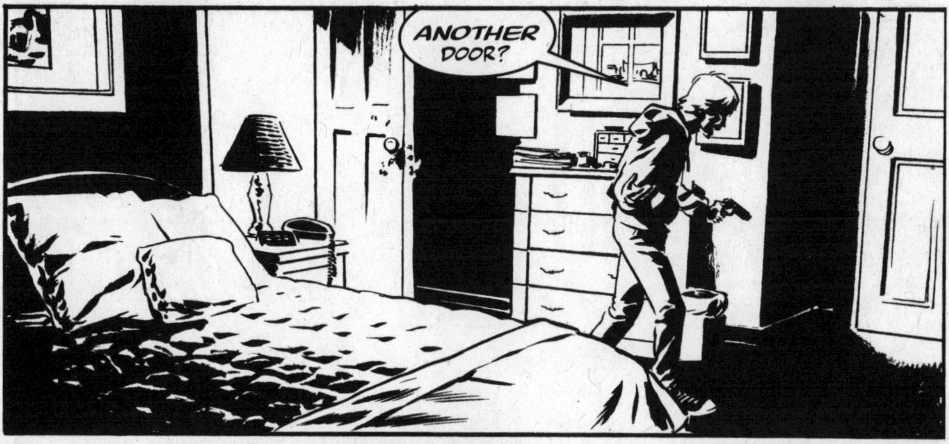
ANOTHER DOOR?

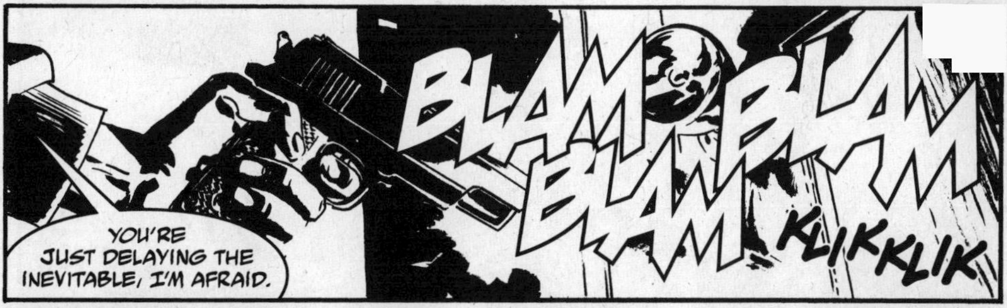
BLAM
BLAM
BLAM
KLIKKLIK
YOU'RE JUST DELAYING THE INEVITABLE, I'M AFRAID.

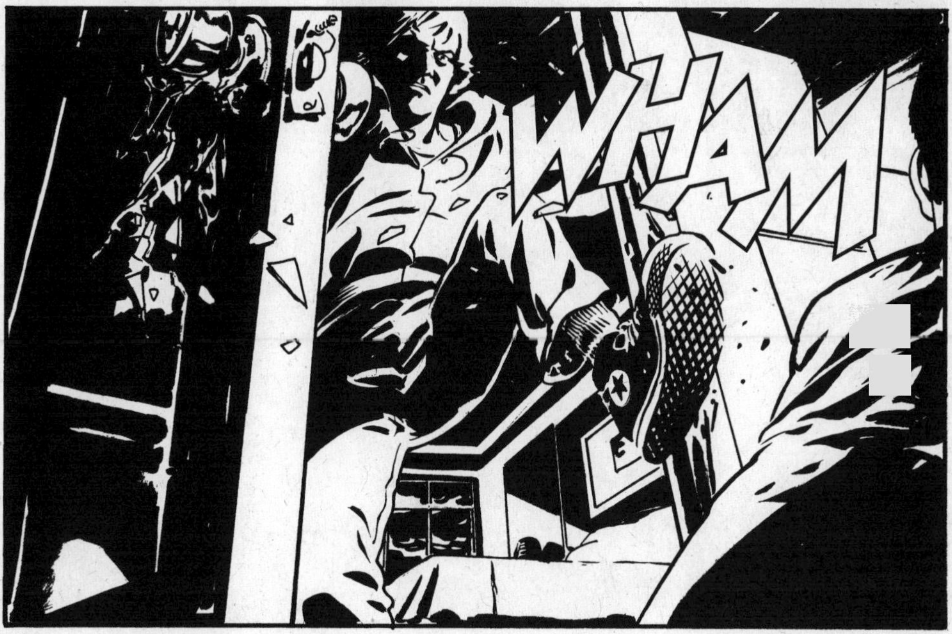
WHAM

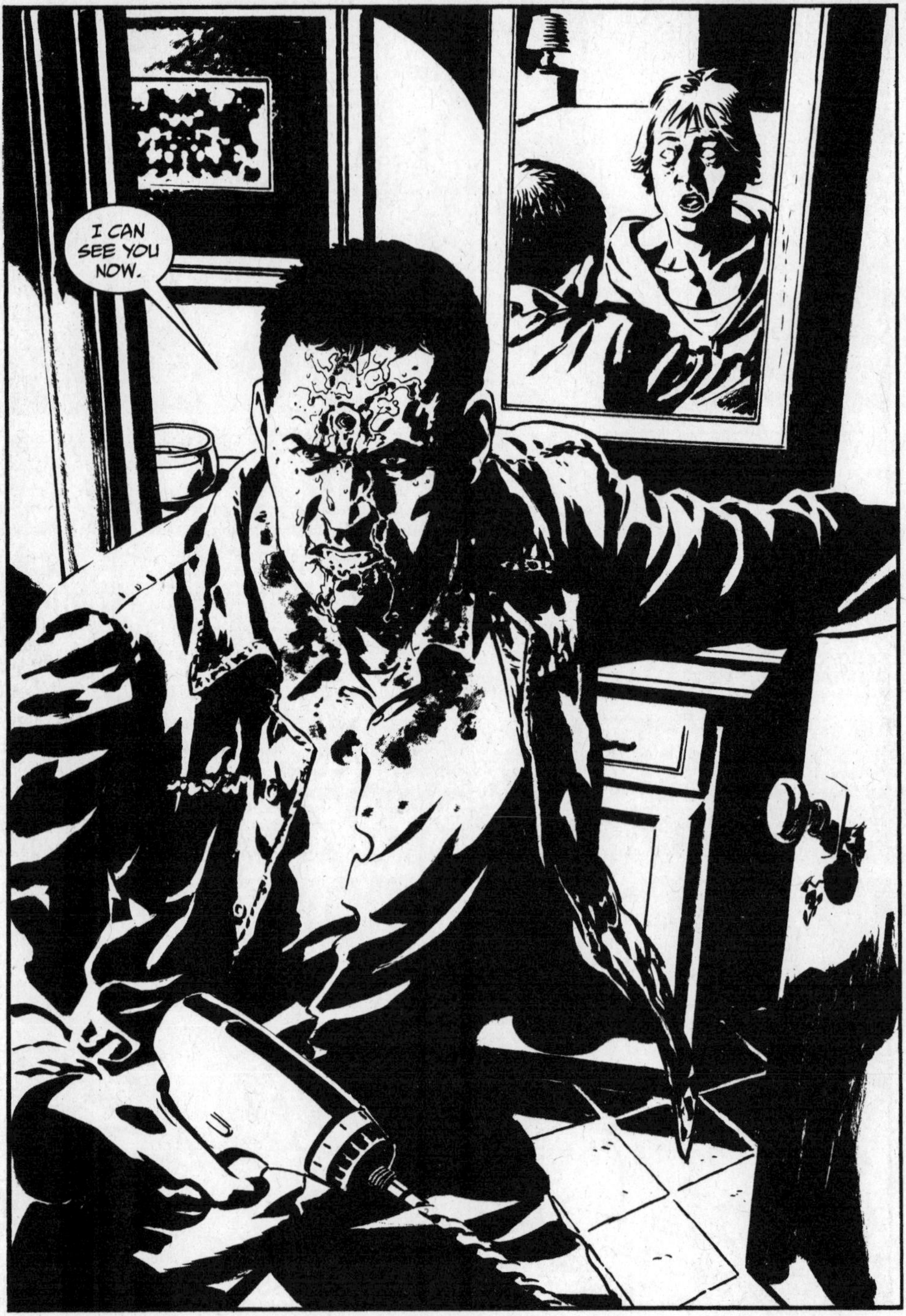
I CAN SEE YOU NOW.

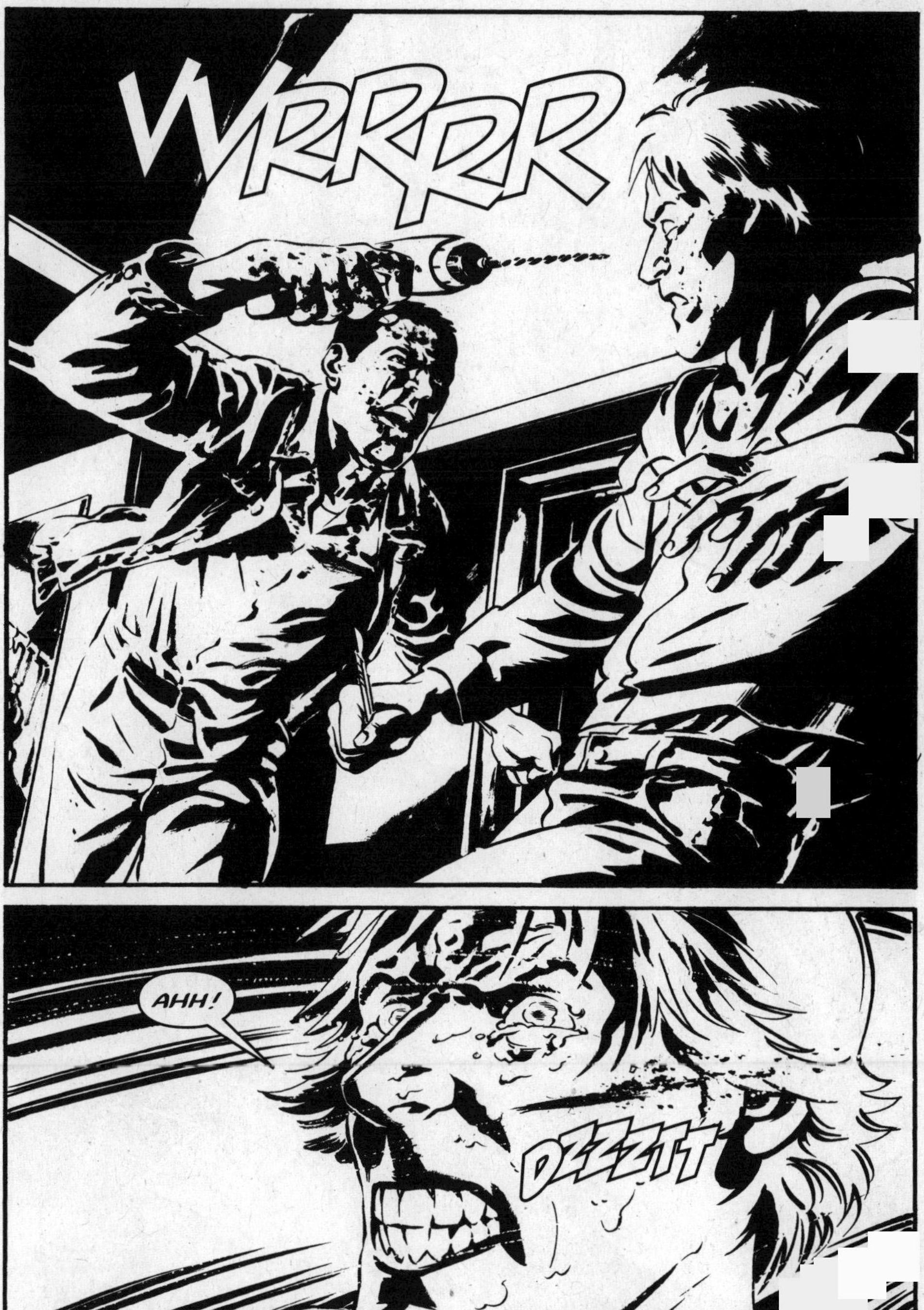
WRRRR
AHH!
DZZZTT

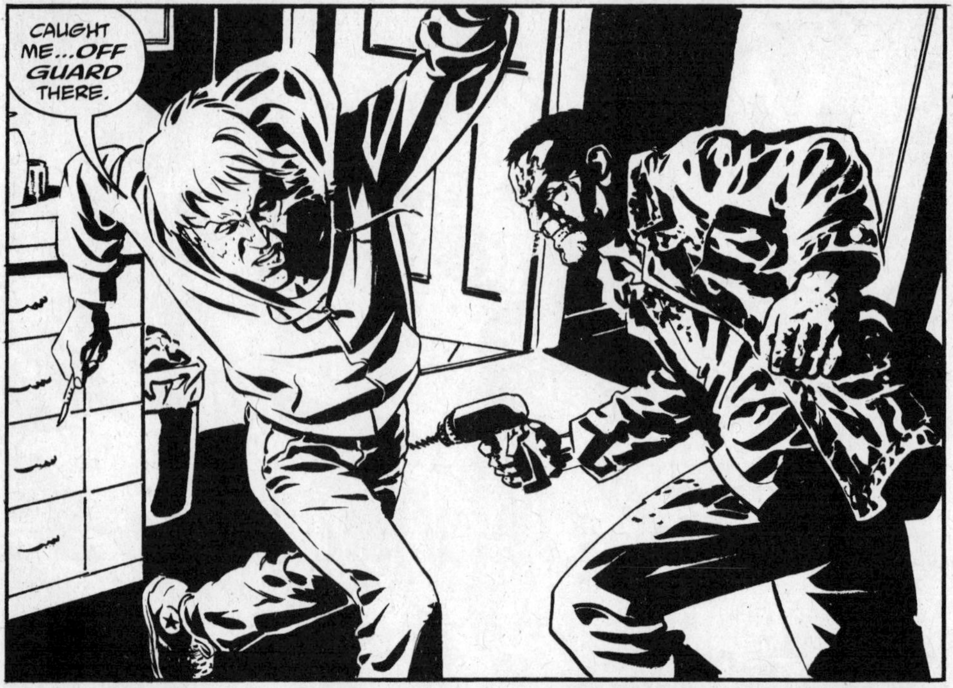
CAUGHT ME...OFF GUARD THERE.

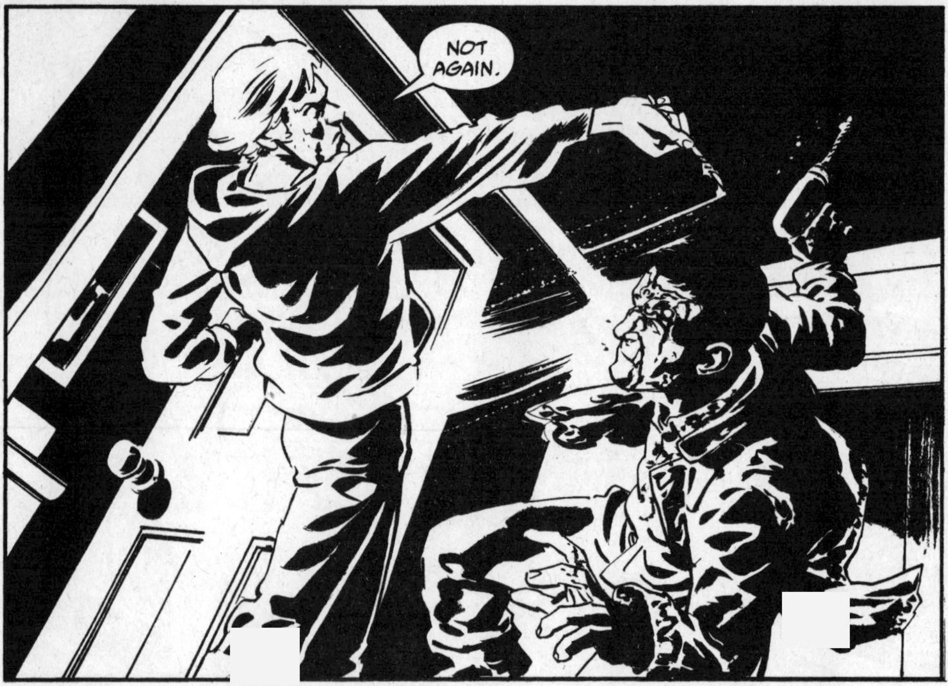
NOT AGAIN.

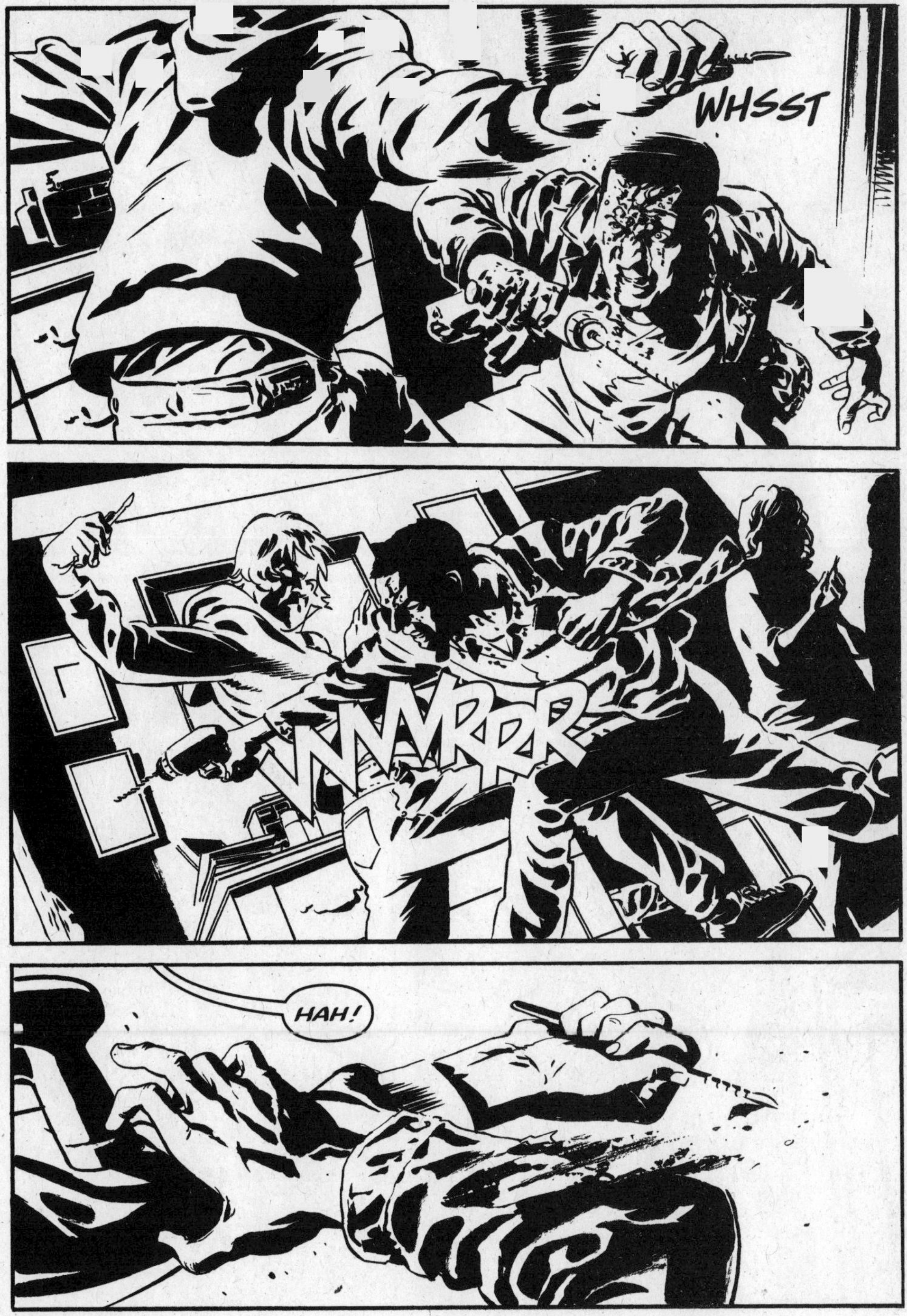
WHSST
WWWRRR
HAH!

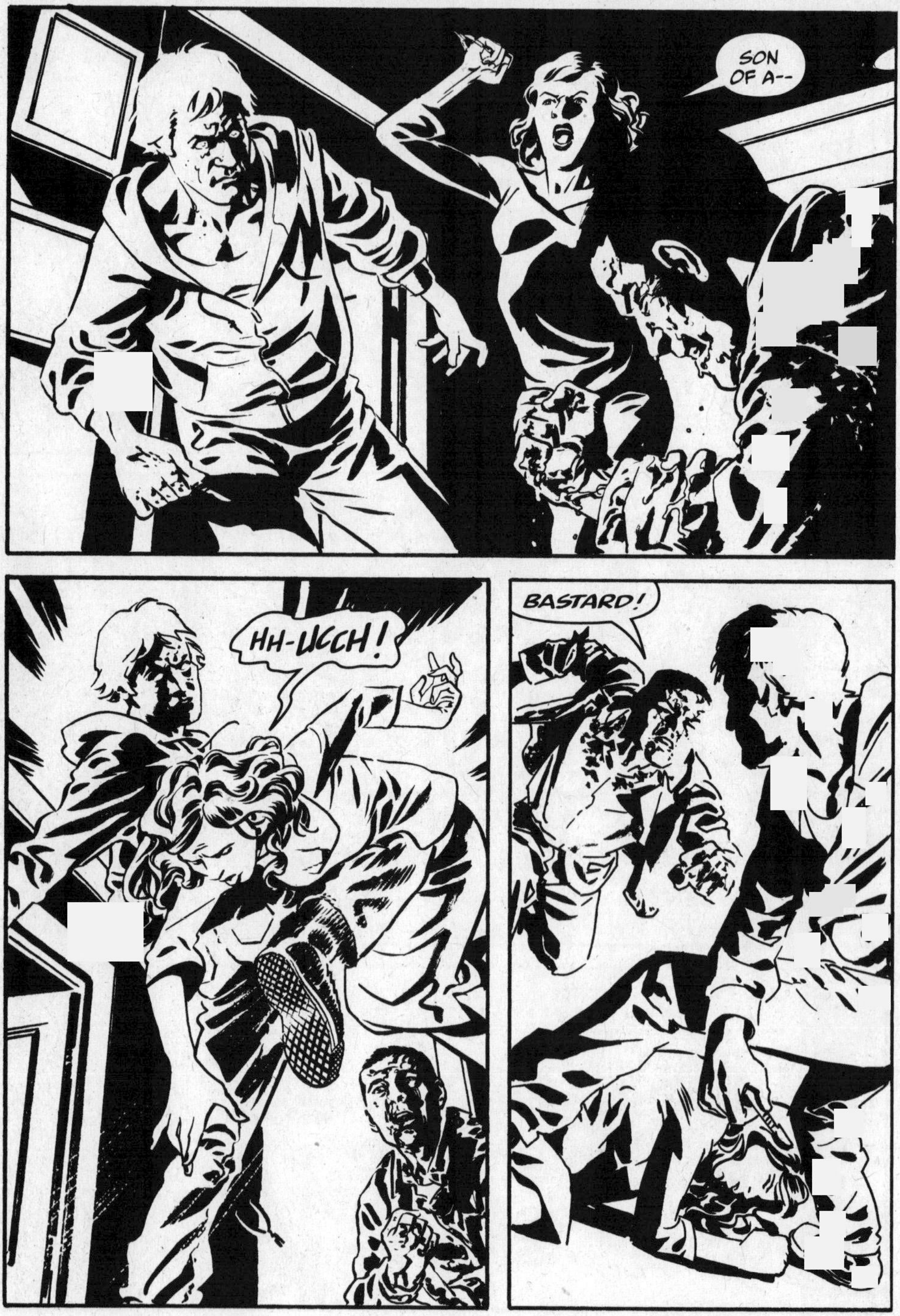
SON OF A--
HH-UCCH!
BASTARD!

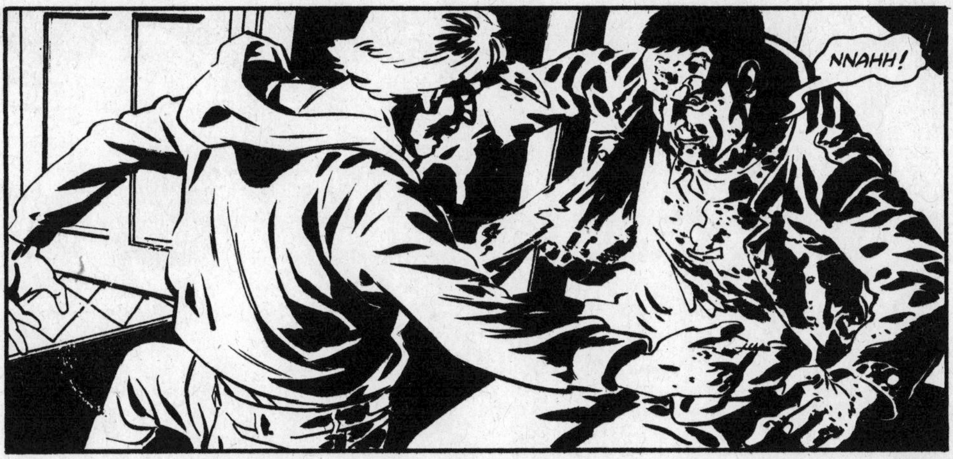
NNAHH!

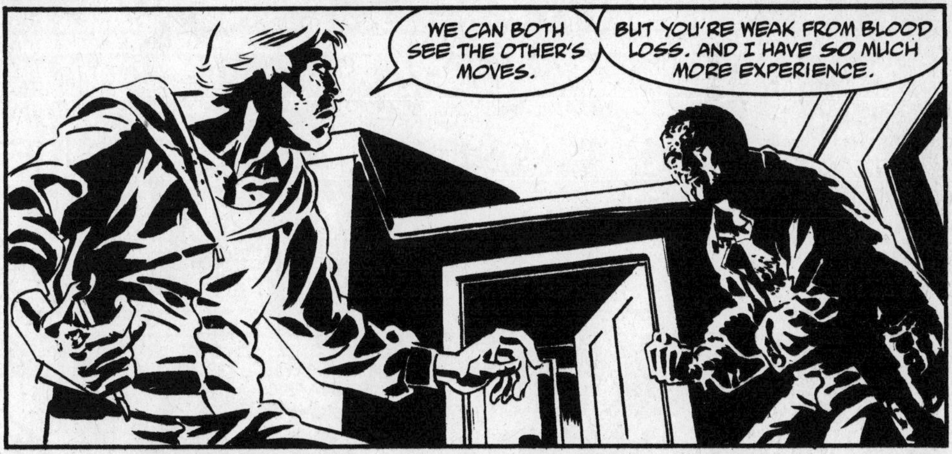
WE CAN BOTH SEE THE OTHER'S MOVES.
BUT YOU'RE WEAK FROM BLOOD LOSS. AND I HAVE SO MUCH MORE EXPERIENCE.

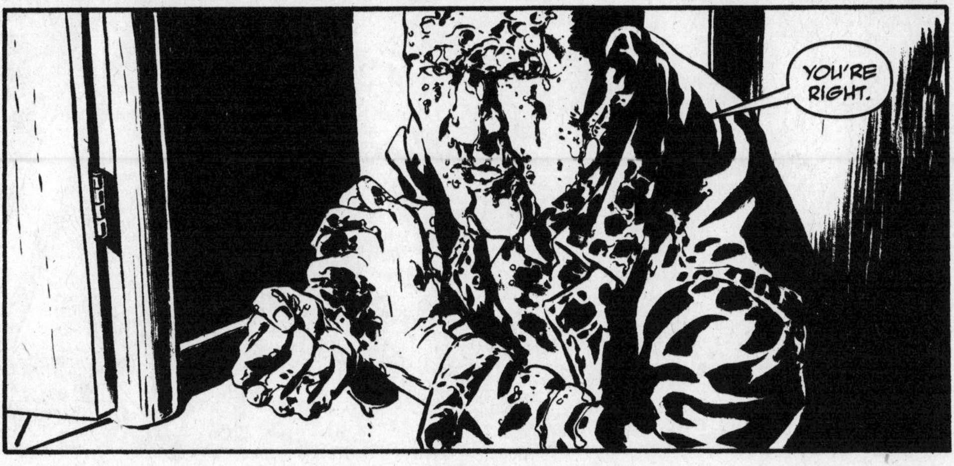
YOU'RE RIGHT.

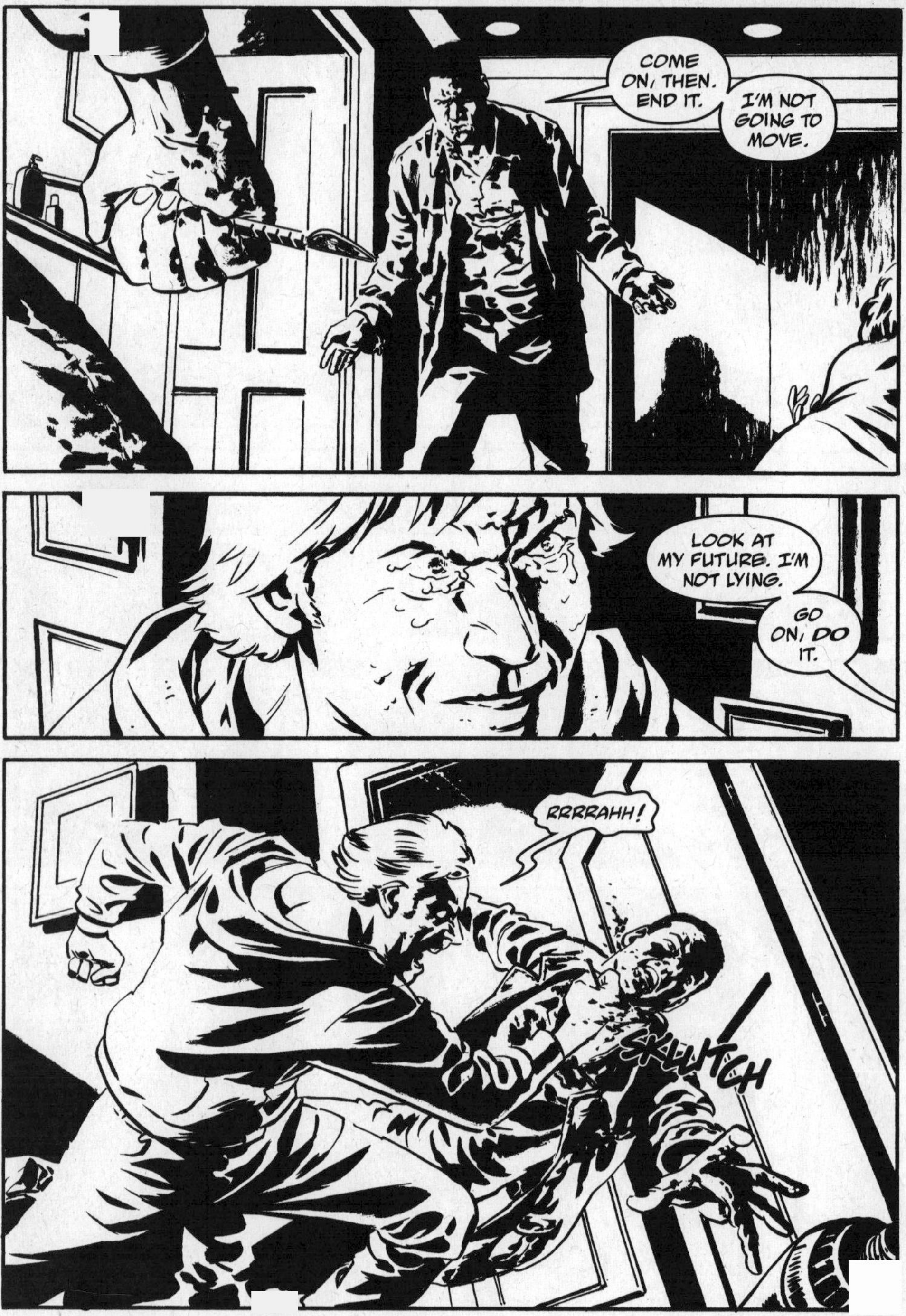
COME ON, THEN. END IT.
I'M NOT GOING TO MOVE.
LOOK AT MY FUTURE. I'M NOT LYING.
GO ON, DO IT.
RRRRAHH!
SKLLTCH

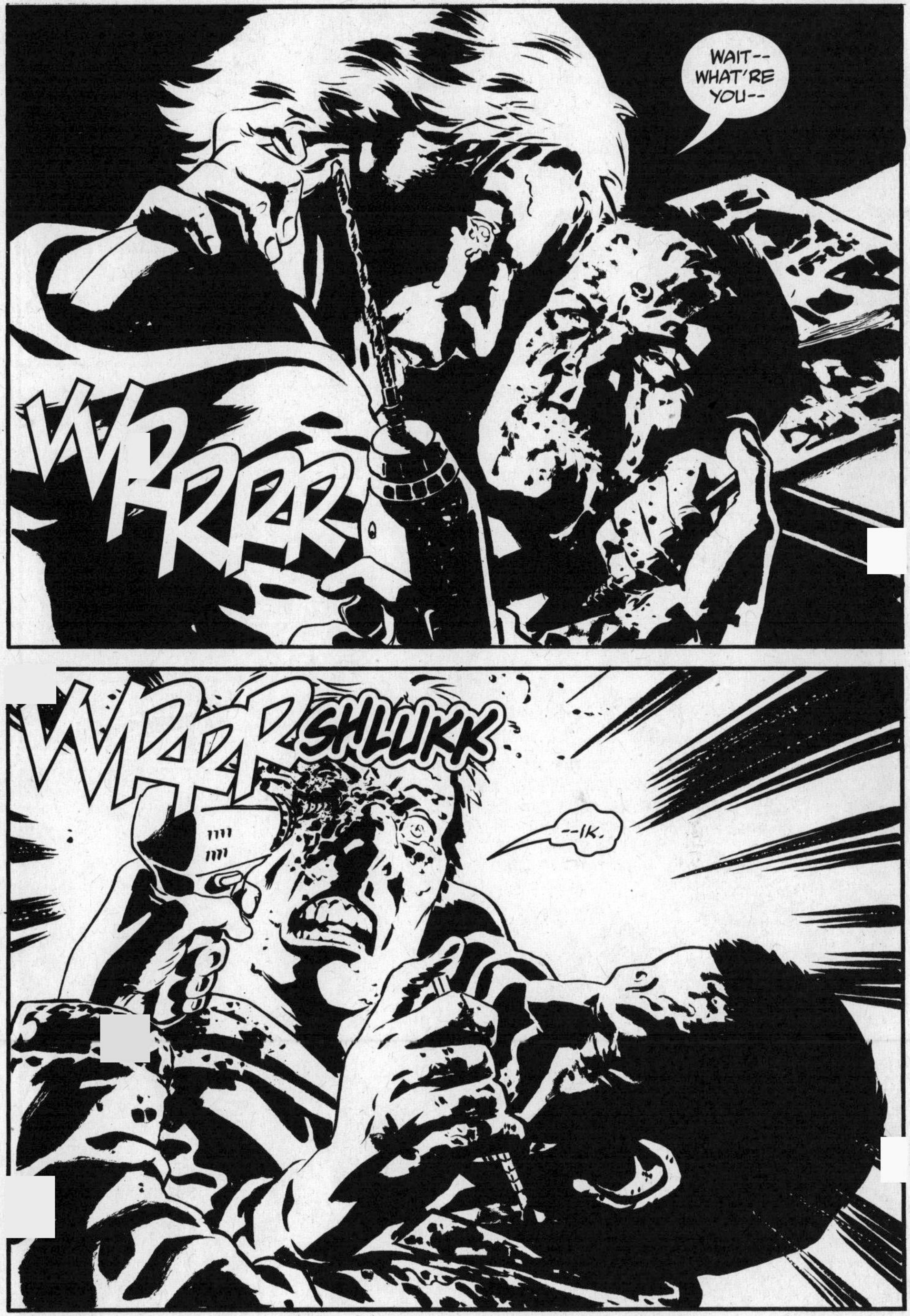
WAIT--
WHAT'RE
YOU--
WRRRR
WRRR
SHLUKK
--IK.

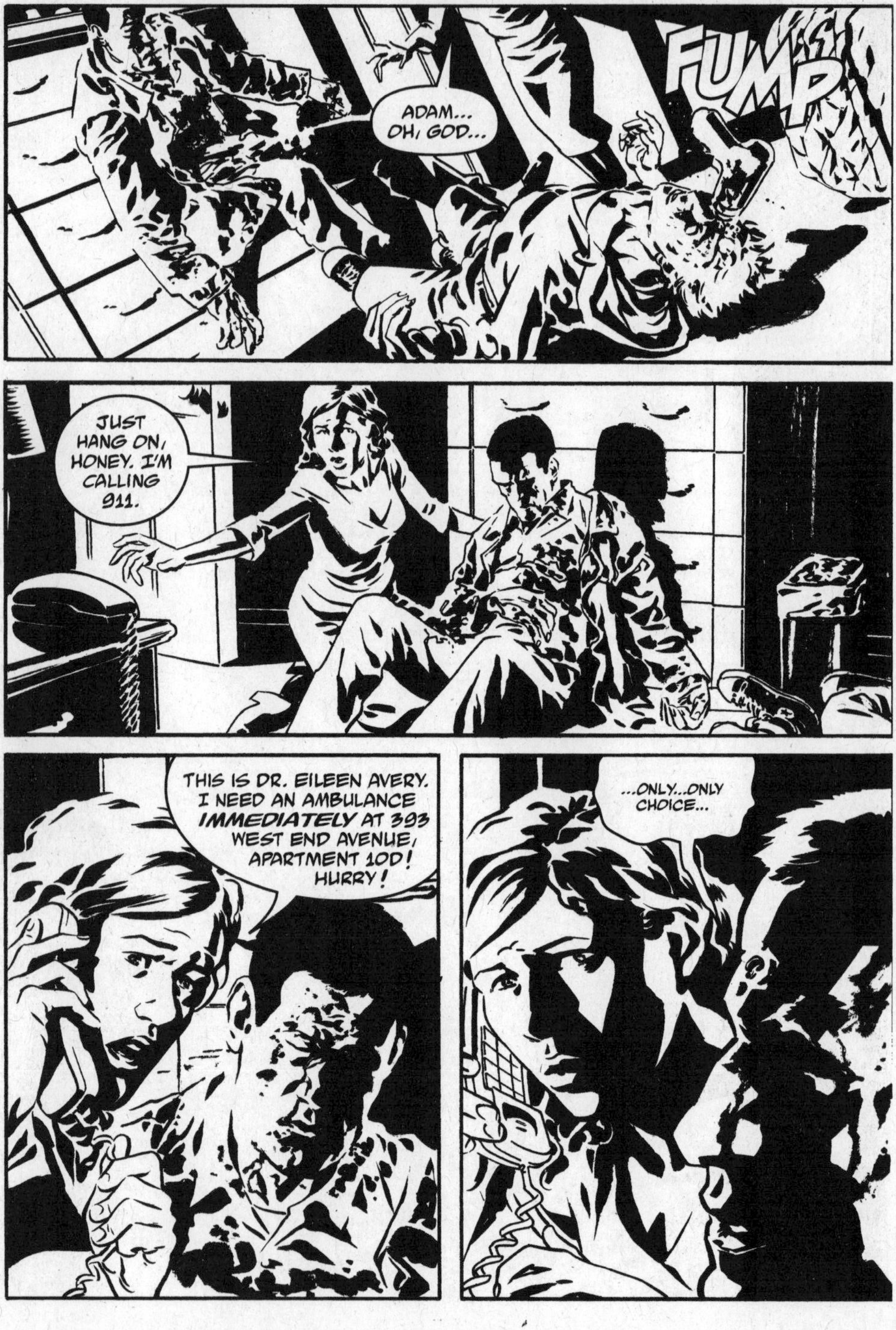

ADAM... OH, GOD...
FUMP
JUST HANG ON, HONEY. I'M CALLING 911.
THIS IS DR. EILEEN AVERY. I NEED AN AMBULANCE *IMMEDIATELY* AT 393 WEST END AVENUE, APARTMENT 10D! HURRY!
...ONLY...ONLY CHOICE...

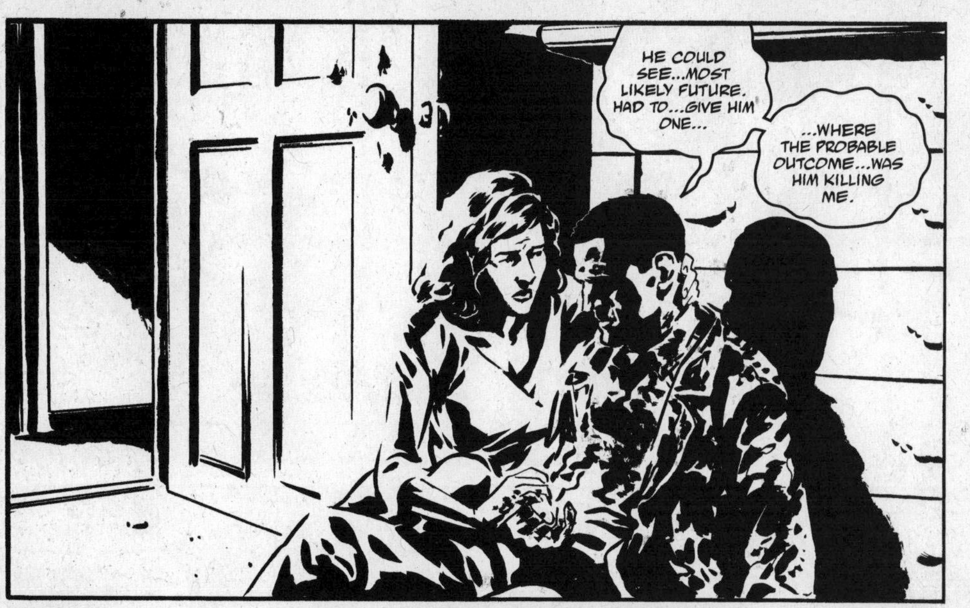
HE COULD SEE...MOST LIKELY FUTURE. HAD TO...GIVE HIM ONE...
...WHERE THE PROBABLE OUTCOME...WAS HIM KILLING ME.

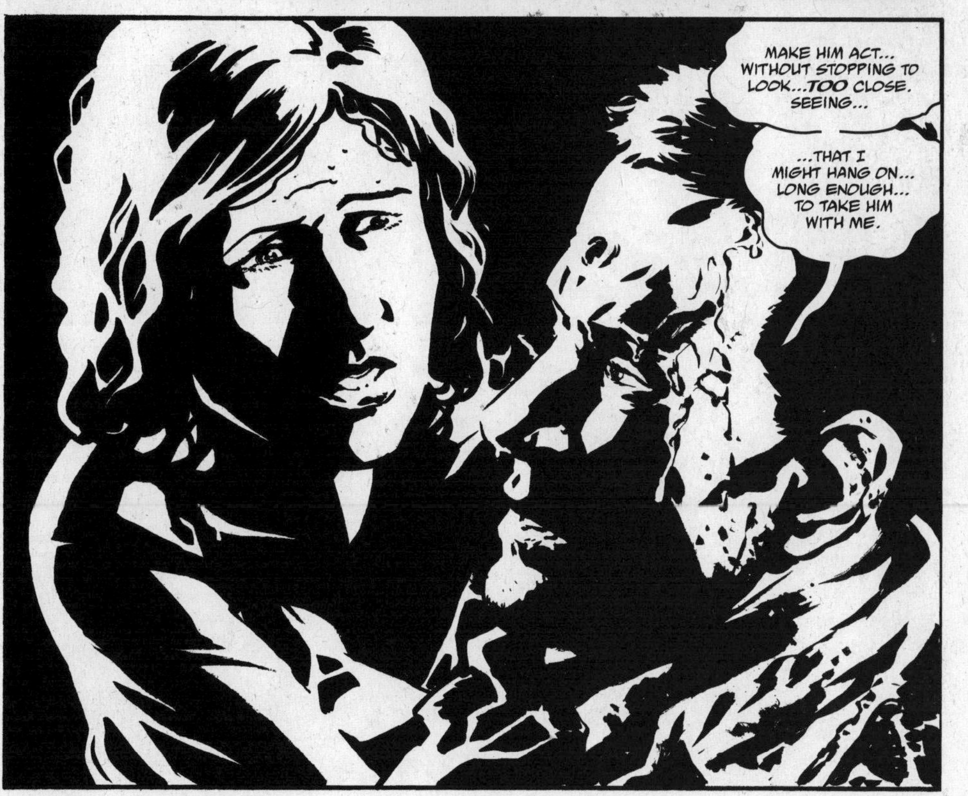
MAKE HIM ACT... WITHOUT STOPPING TO LOOK...*TOO* CLOSE. SEEING...
...THAT I MIGHT HANG ON... LONG ENOUGH... TO TAKE HIM WITH ME.

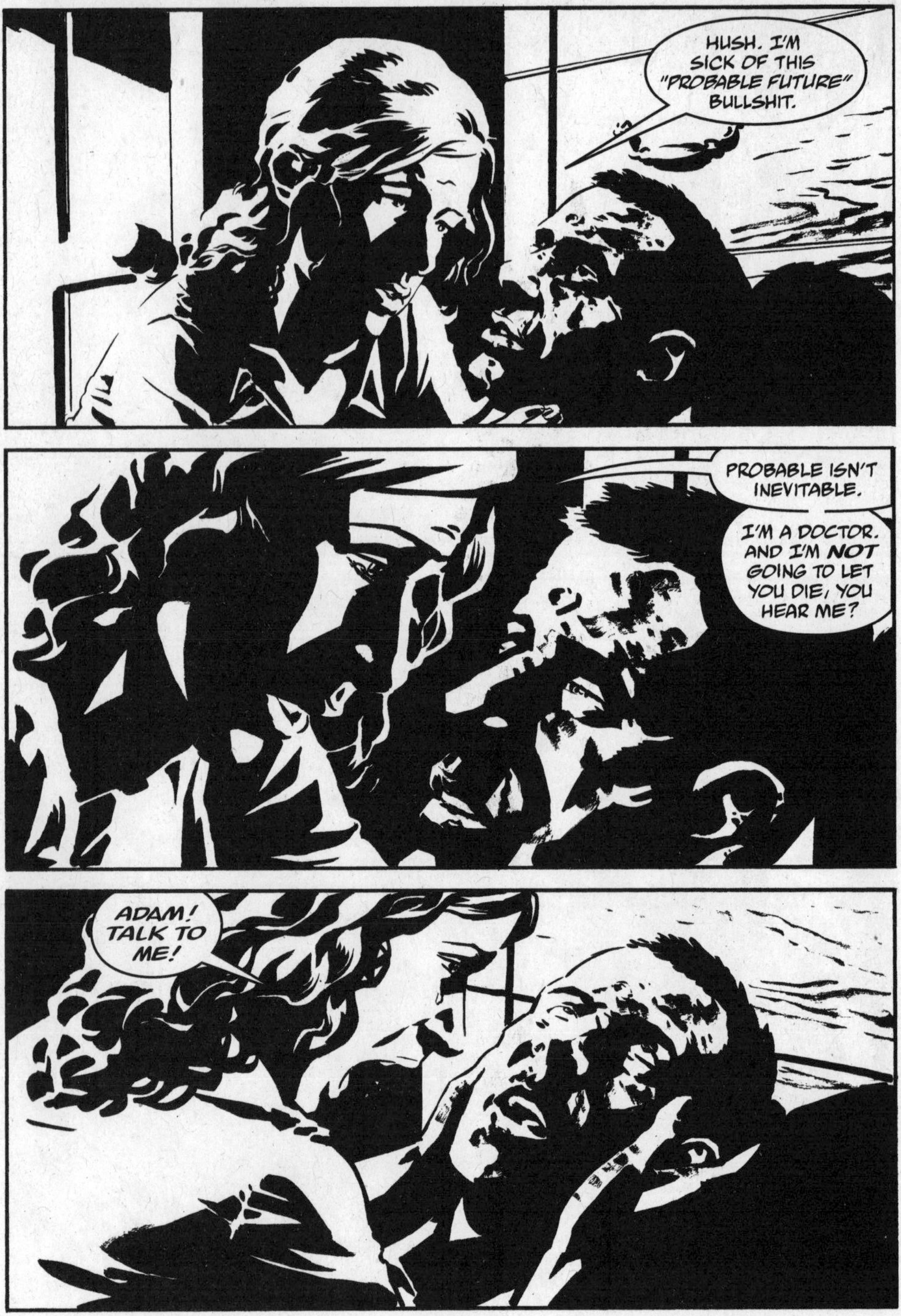
HUSH. I'M SICK OF THIS "PROBABLE FUTURE" BULLSHIT.
PROBABLE ISN'T INEVITABLE.
I'M A DOCTOR. AND I'M **NOT** GOING TO LET YOU DIE, YOU HEAR ME?
ADAM! TALK TO ME!

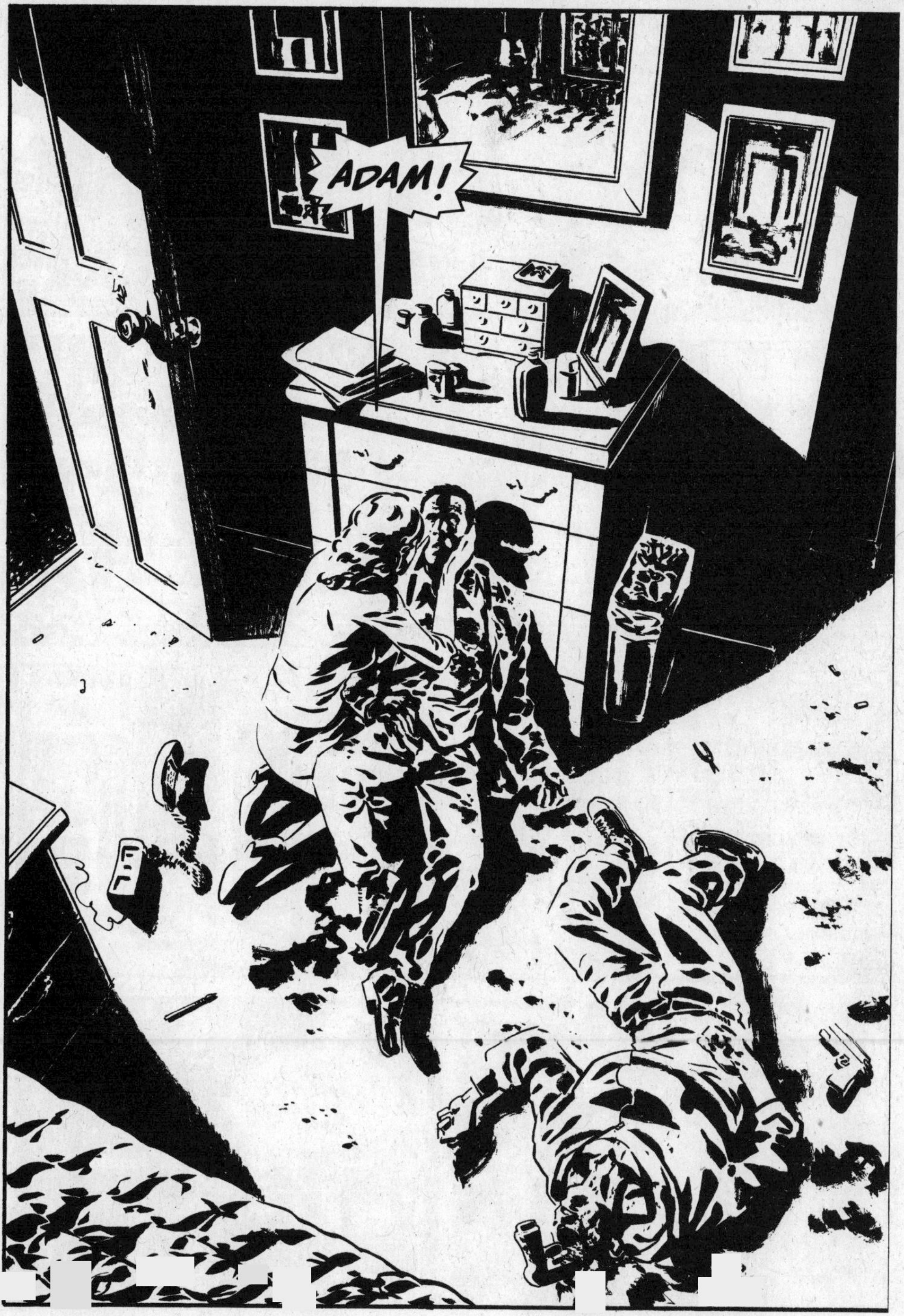
ADAM!

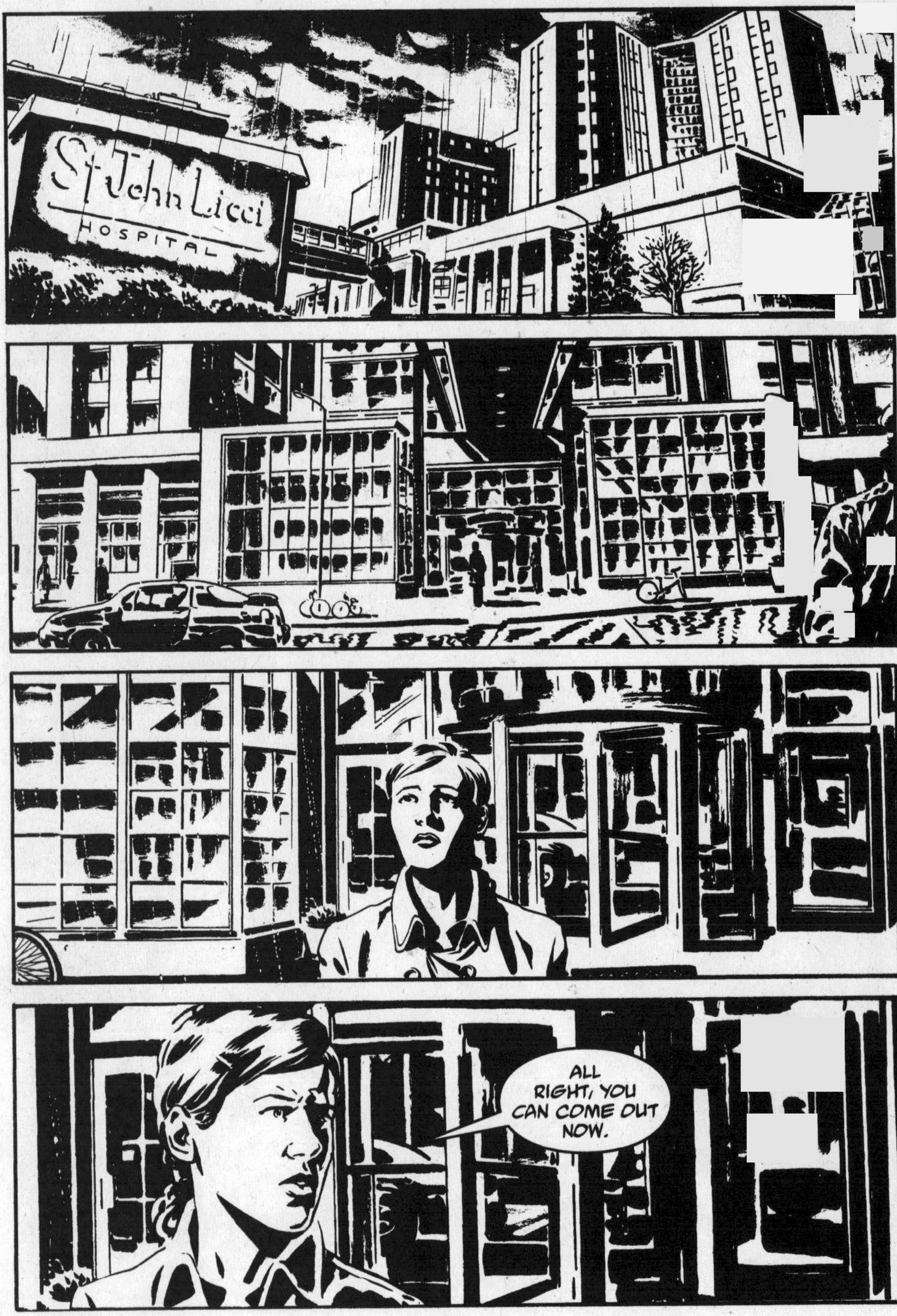
St John Licci
HOSPITAL
ALL RIGHT, YOU CAN COME OUT NOW.

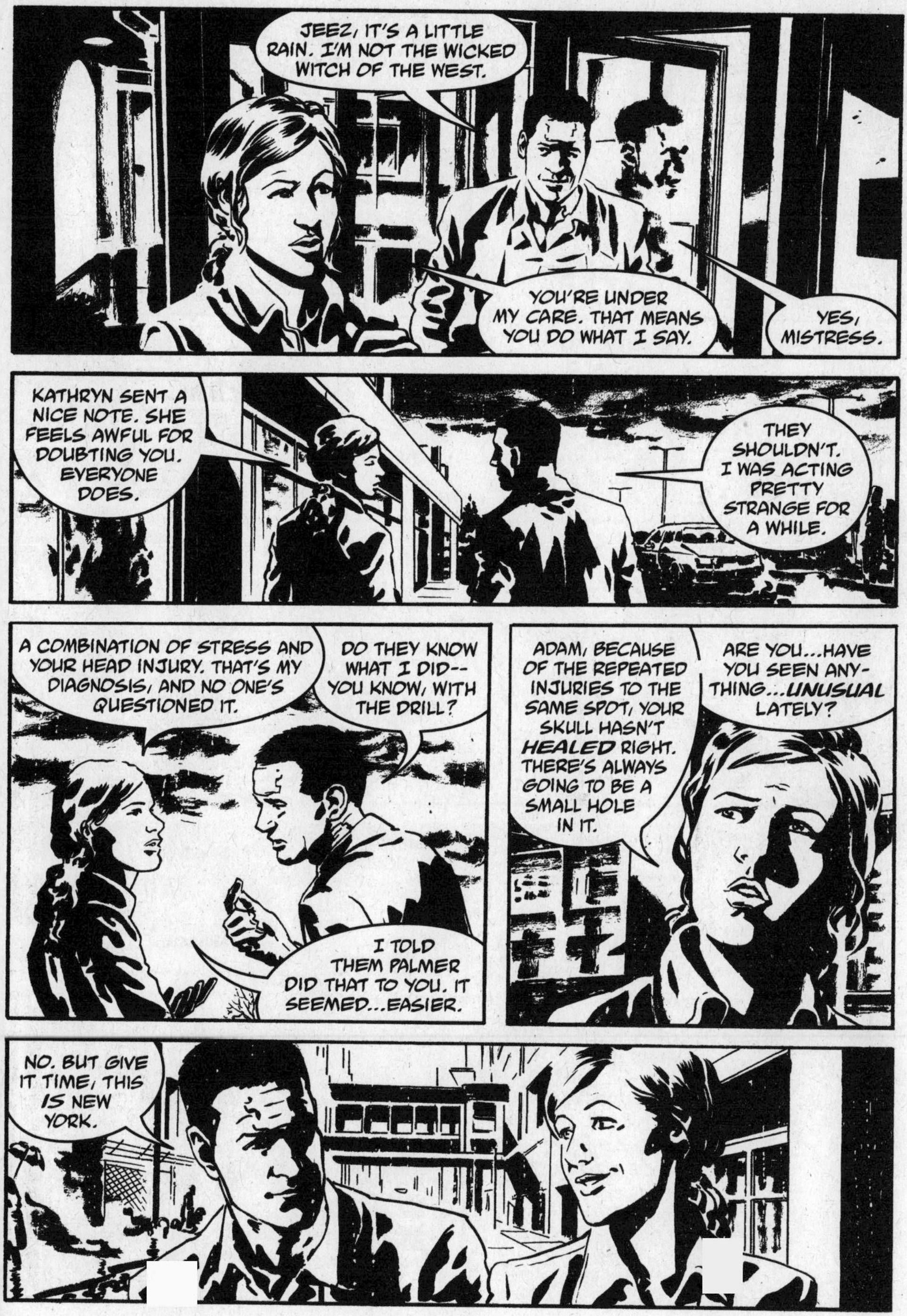
JEEZ, IT'S A LITTLE RAIN. I'M NOT THE WICKED WITCH OF THE WEST.
YOU'RE UNDER MY CARE. THAT MEANS YOU DO WHAT I SAY.
YES, MISTRESS.
KATHRYN SENT A NICE NOTE. SHE FEELS AWFUL FOR DOUBTING YOU. EVERYONE DOES.
THEY SHOULDN'T. I WAS ACTING PRETTY STRANGE FOR A WHILE.
A COMBINATION OF STRESS AND YOUR HEAD INJURY. THAT'S MY DIAGNOSIS, AND NO ONE'S QUESTIONED IT.
DO THEY KNOW WHAT I DID-- YOU KNOW, WITH THE DRILL?
I TOLD THEM PALMER DID THAT TO YOU. IT SEEMED...EASIER.
ADAM, BECAUSE OF THE REPEATED INJURIES TO THE SAME SPOT, YOUR SKULL HASN'T *HEALED* RIGHT. THERE'S ALWAYS GOING TO BE A SMALL HOLE IN IT.
ARE YOU...HAVE YOU SEEN ANYTHING...*UNUSUAL* LATELY?
NO. BUT GIVE IT TIME, THIS *IS* NEW YORK.

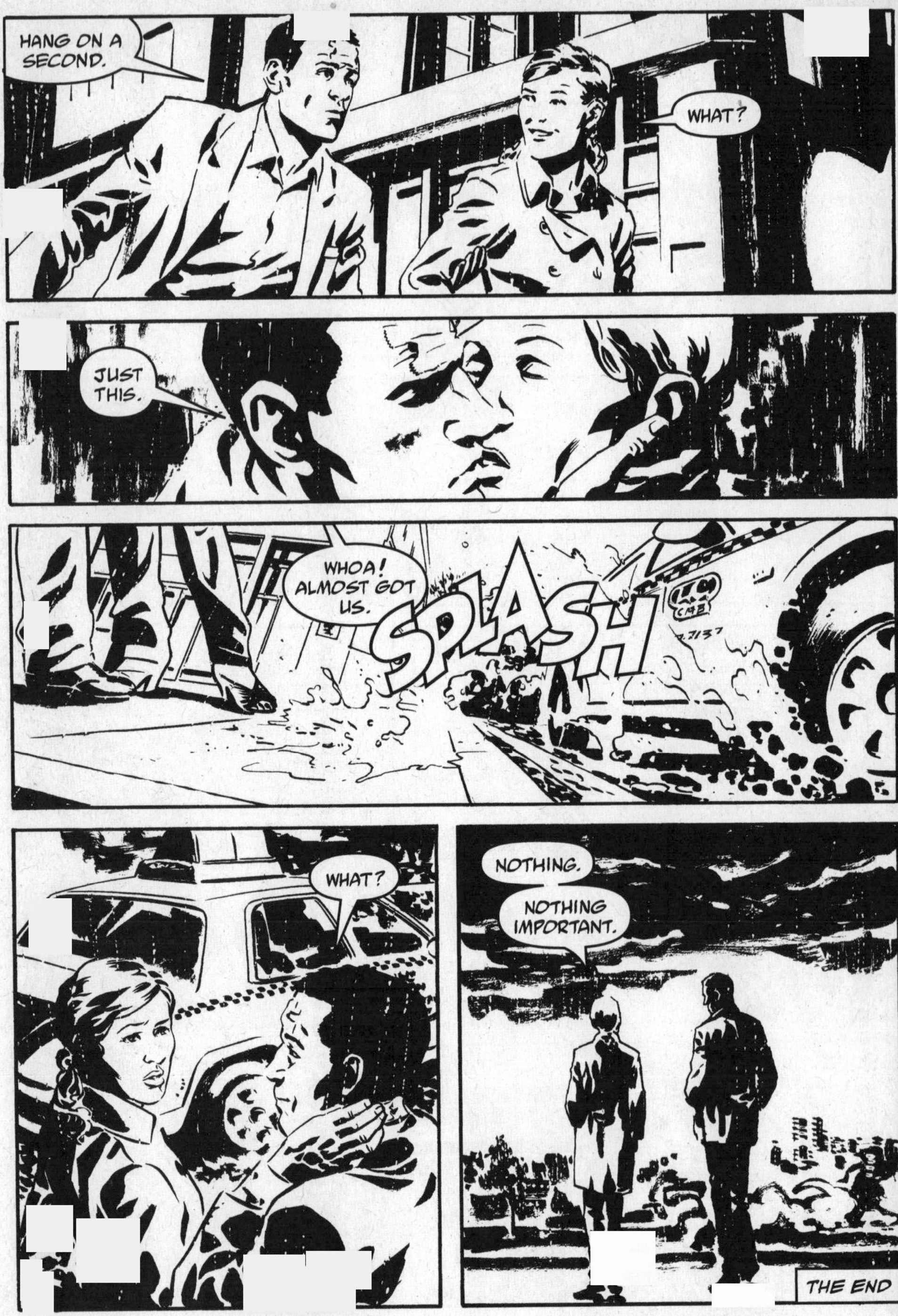
HANG ON A SECOND.
WHAT?
JUST THIS.
WHOA! ALMOST GOT US.
SPLASH
WHAT?
NOTHING.
NOTHING IMPORTANT.
THE END

DON'T MISS THESE OTHER VERTIGO CRIME BOOKS

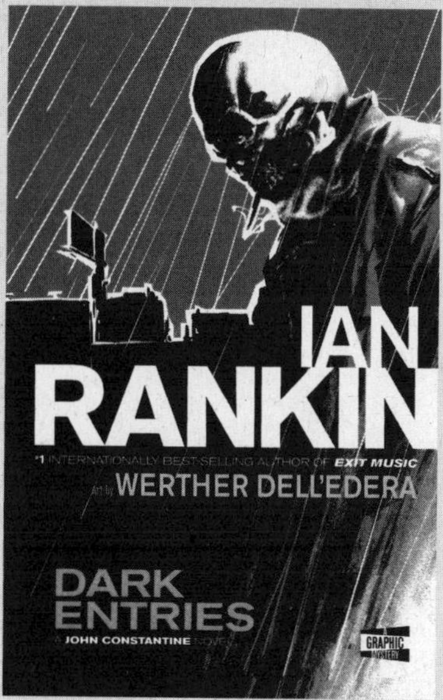
IAN
RANKIN
#1 INTERNATIONALLY BEST-SELLING AUTHOR OF EXIT MUSIC
Art by WERTHER DELL'EDERA
DARK
ENTRIES
A JOHN CONSTANTINE NOVEL

DARK ENTRIES

AVAILABLE NOW

Occult detective John Constantine has seen his share of strange things in his career, but nothing could prepare him for the horrors of... reality television. "Haunted Mansion" is currently the hottest show on TV, but when the macabre house actually starts attacking the contestants, Constantine is hired to be the ultimate mole. Locked inside with a cast of wannabe-celebrities, his every move being monitored by a deadly figure from his past, Constantine must figure out who (or what) is pulling the strings before he gets cancelled – *permanently*.

Written by **Ian Rankin**, the Edgar-winning author of the "Inspector Rebus" series and the #1 international-bestselling author of *Exit Music*. Art by **Werther Dell'Edera.**

FILTHY RICH

AVAILABLE NOW

Richard "Junk" Junkin has always lived on the wrong side of trouble... A former pro football star whose career was cut short by injury (and a nasty gambling problem), Junk now spends his time dreaming of what might have been, selling cars in Jersey and lusting after the boss's unbelievably spoiled, unbelievably sexy and unbelievably rich daughter, Victoria.

So when the boss asks him to be Victoria's personal bodyguard while she tears up the New York City club scene, Junk leaps at the chance. But before long, he finds that Victoria wants a lapdog and not a chaperone, someone who's going to do all of her dirty work – *all* of it – someone who wants to get filthy rich...

Written by **Brian Azzarello** – the multiple Eisner-Award-winning writer of Vertigo's long-running crime series 100 BULLETS and the New York Times bestseller JOKER. Art by **Victor Santos.**

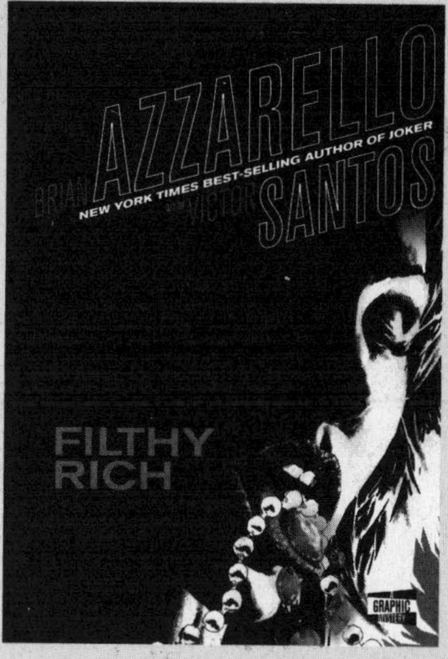
BRIAN AZZARELLO
NEW YORK TIMES BEST-SELLING AUTHOR OF JOKER
and VICTOR SANTOS
FILTHY
RICH

MORE VERTIGO CRIME

THE CHILL
AVAILABLE NOW

Written by **JASON STARR**
(Best-selling author of *Panic Attack* and *The Follower*)

Art by **MICK BERTILORENZI**

A modern thriller steeped in Celtic mythology –
a broken-down cop tracks a seductive killer who
possesses the supernatural power known as "the
chill." Can he stop her before her next victim
dies horribly... but with a smile on his face?

THE BRONX KILL
AVAILABLE NOW

Written by **PETER MILLIGAN**
(GREEK STREET)

Art by **JAMES ROMBERGER**

A struggling writer is investigating his Irish cop
roots for his next novel. When he returns home
from a research trip, his wife is missing and finding
her will lead him to a dark secret buried deep in his
family's past.

THE EXECUTOR
MAY 2010

Written by **JON EVANS**
(Author of *Dark Places* and *Invisible Armies*)

Art by **ANDREA MUTTI**

When a washed-up ex-hockey player is mysteriously
named executor of an old girlfriend's will, he must
return to the small town he left years earlier. There, he
finds a deadly secret from his past that could hold the
key to his girlfriend's murder... if it doesn't kill him first.

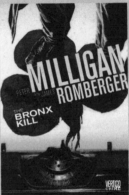